Lecture Notes in Computer Science 972

Edited by G. Goos, J. Hartmanis and J. van Leeuwen

Advisory Board: W. Brauer D. Gries J. Stoer

Springer

Berlin
Heidelberg
New York
Barcelona
Budapest
Hong Kong
London
Milan
Paris
Tokyo

Jean-Michel Hélary Michel Raynal (Eds.)

Distributed Algorithms

9th International Workshop, WDAG '95
Le Mont-Saint-Michel, France
September 13-15, 1995
Proceedings

 Springer

Series Editors

Gerhard Goos, Karlsruhe University, Germany

Juris Hartmanis, Cornell University, NY, USA

Jan van Leeuwen, Utrecht University, The Netherlands

Volume Editors

Jean-Michel Hélary
Michel Raynal
IRISA-IFSIC, Université de Rennes I
Campus de Beaulieu, F-35042 Rennes Cedex

Cataloging-in-Publication data applied for

Die Deutsche Bibliothek - CIP-Einheitsaufnahme

Distributed algorithms : 9th international workshop ;
proceedings / WDAG '95, Le Mont-Saint-Michel, France,
September 1995. Jean-Michel Hélary ; Michel Raynal (ed.). -
Berlin ; Heidelberg ; New York ; Barcelona ; Budapest ; Hong
Kong ; London ; Milan ; Paris ; Tokyo : Springer, 1995
 (Lecture notes in computer science ; Vol. 972)
 ISBN 3-540-60274-7
NE: Hélary, Jean-Michel [Hrsg.]; WDAG <9, 1995, Mont-Saint-
 Michel>; GT

CR Subject Classification (1991): F.1, D.1.3, F.2.2, C.2.2, C.2.4, D.4.4-5,
G.2.2

ISBN 3-540-60274-7 Springer-Verlag Berlin Heidelberg New York

© Springer-Verlag Berlin Heidelberg 1995
Printed in Germany

Typesetting: Camera-ready by author
SPIN 10485480   06/3142 – 5 4 3 2 1 0   Printed on acid-free paper

Preface

The Ninth International Workshop on Distributed Algorithms (WDAG'95) took place September 13-15, in Le Mont-Saint-Michel, France. It continued a tradition of successful workshops with a pleasant atmosphere. Earlier workshops in the series were held in:

Ottawa (1985),
Amsterdam (1987, proceedings published by Springer-Verlag, LNCS 312),
Nice (1989, LNCS 392),
Bari (1990, LNCS 484),
Delphi (1991, LNCS 579),
Haifa (1992, LNCS 647),
Lausanne (1993, LNCS 725), and
Terschelling (1994, LNCS 857).

Continuation of the event is supervised by the WDAG Steering Committee, consisting of: D. Dolev (IBM Almaden & Hebrew Univ.); F. Mattern (Univ. Saarlandes); N. Santoro (Carleton Univ.); A. Schiper (EPFL, Lausanne); P. Spirakis (CTI & Univ. Patras); R. Tan (Univ. Oklahoma); G. Tel (Univ. Utrecht); S. Toueg (Cornell Univ.); P. Vitányi (CWI & Univ. Amsterdam); S. Zaks (Technion).

The topics discussed in these meetings cover all aspects of distributed algorithms, including:

algorithms for control and communication,
fault-tolerant algorithms,
network protocols,
protocols for real-time distributed systems,
issues in asynchrony, synchrony and real-time,
algorithms for managing replicated data,
distributed detection of properties,
mechanisms for security in distributed systems,
self-stabilizing algorithms,
wait-free algorithms, and
techniques for the design and analysis of systems.

In response to the call for papers, 48 papers in these areas were submitted (22 from Europe, 15 from North America, 6 from Asia, 2 from Africa, 2 from Australia and 1 from South America). The program committee selected at its meeting on June 8 in Rennes 18 out of these for presentation at the workshop. The selection was based on perceived originality and quality. In addition, D. Dolev, M. Gouda, P. Jayanti and G. Le Lann were invited to gave a lecture. M. Gouda, P. Jayanti and G. Le Lann provided tutorial texts which are included in these proceedings.

The program committee for WDAG'95 consisted of:

M. Ahamad (Georgia Tech, Atlanta, USA)
J. Beauquier (U. of Paris-Sud, Orsay, France)
J. Brzezinski (Techn. U. of Poznan, Poznan, Poland)
I. Cidon (Sun Microsystems, Mt. View, CA, USA)
D. Dolev (Hebrew U., Jerusalem, Israel)
J.M. Helary (IRISA, Rennes, France, **co-chair**)
P. Jayanti (Dartmouth College, Dartmouth, USA)
G. Le Lann (INRIA, Rocquencourt, France)
K. Marzullo (U. of California at San Diego, USA)
T. Masuzawa (NAIST, Nara, Japan)
M. Raynal (IRISA, Rennes, France, **co-chair**)
A. Schiper (EPFL, Lausanne, Switzerland)
A. Singh (U. of California at Santa Barbara, USA)
G. Tel (Utrecht U., Utrecht, Netherlands)
S. Zaks (Technion, Haifa, Israel)

The workshop was sponsored by grants from:

France Télécom - CNET,
Le Conseil Régional de Bretagne, and
L'Université de Rennes 1

We want to thank everybody who helped to make this workshop possible: the authors for submitting papers, the program committee and referees for their effort in composing the program, the sponsors and Springer-Verlag. We particularly wish to thank INRIA for placing at our disposal the best professional assistance. E. Lebret and C. Guyot did an excellent job in organizing the workshop and we greatly appreciate the time and trouble M. Hurfin and R. Baldoni took to ensure the success of the workshop.

July 1995   Jean Michel HÉLARY, Michel RAYNAL

List of Referees

The Program Committee wishes to thank the following persons, who acted as referees for WDAG'95:

Mustaque Ahamad

Jean Arlat

Hagit Attiya

Roberto Baldoni

Amotz Bar-Noy

Joffroy Beauquier

Jerzy Brzezinski

Navin Budhiraja

Tushar Deepak Chandra

Bernadette Charron-Bost

Shun Yan Cheung

Francis Chin

Manhoi Choy

Israel Cidon

Robert Cori

Dany Dolev

Eddy Fromentin

Satoshi Fujita

Jean-Michel Hélary

Michel Hurfin

Michiko Inoue

Prasad Jayanti

Hirotsugu Kakugawa

Shmuel Katz

Gerard Le Lann

Yoshifumi Manabe

Keith Marzullo

Toshimitsu Masuzawa

Pascale Minet

Eliot Morison

Paul Muhlethaler

Abhay Parekh

Michel Raynal

Jakka Sairamesh

Andre Schiper

Assaf Schuster

Ambuj Singh

Gerard Tel

Sam Toueg

Dariusz Wawrzyniak

Pawel Wojciechowski

Shmuel Zaks

Table of Contents

Shared Memory

Byzantine Failures

Self-Stabilization

Detection of Properties

The Triumph and Tribulation
of System Stabilization

Mohamed G. Gouda

Department of Computer Sciences
University of Texas at Austin
Austin, Texas 78712-1188

Abstract. We give a concise outline of the theory of system stabilization. Our primary objective is to demonstrate the richness, depth, and
ultimately the utility of this beautiful theory. Our secondary objective is
to identify a number of problems that arise in the theory, and so highlight
several research directions that can be pursued in the future. The stabilization of a system is defined as the ability of the system to converge to
a closed (under execution) set of system states. We identify two forms
of convergence (strong and weak) and two forms of closed sets of states
(strong and weak), and so we end up with four forms of stabilization.
The outlined theory is based on these four forms of stabilization.

Dedication. This paper is dedicated to the memory of my grandparents Asma
(1897-1972) and Ahmed (1864-1967): on my mind and in my heart.

1 Introduction

The subject of this paper is the theory of system stabilization. This is a relatively
new theory, at least in the realm of computing science. Hence, only few results
have been attained in it. On the other hand, the evidence suggests that it is an
intriguing theory, intellectually satisfying and widely applicable, and what more
can a scientist ask for?

The theory of system stabilization deals with the ability of a system, starting from any state, to converge to a specific set of states that is closed under
system execution. This theory is built around three important concepts: closure
(under system execution), convergence, and stabilization. The main thrust of
the theory is to answer two questions: how to verify the stabilization properties
of a given system, and how to design a system such that it has a given set of
stabilization properties. This theory can be used in explaining and investigating
several important areas of computing systems: system initialization and reset,
fault recovery, fault containment, and system adaptivity.

In this paper, we give an outline of the theory of system stabilization. The
objective is to present the important subjects in the theory without addressing
any of them in great detail. The presentation in the paper is intentionally concise
so that the paper can fit in the available space. Our apologies are in order for
not including proofs and examples.

2 Closure, Convergence, and Stabilization

A system is a pair (U, T), where U is a set of states, and T is a set of transitions: each transition in T is an ordered pair of states in U. For a transition (p, q) in T, state p is called the pre-state of the transition and state q is called the post-state of the transition.

A computation of a system (U, T) is a non-empty sequence (p.0, p.1, ...) such that the following three conditions hold.

i. Every element p.i in the sequence is a state in U.

ii. Every pair (p.i, p.(i+1)) in the sequence is a transition in T.

iii. Either the sequence is infinite, or it is finite and its last state is not a pre-state of any transition in T.

This abstract definition of a system applies to sequential, parallel, as well as distributed systems. In the case of a parallel or distributed system, however, a state of the system is a concatenation of the states of the system processes and the states of the communication channels between them, if any.

In a system (U, T), a subset P of U is strongly closed iff for every transition in T, if the pre-state of the transition is in P, then the post-state of the transition is in P.

In a system (U, T), a subset P of U is weakly closed iff every computation of the system, whose initial state is in P, has a non-empty suffix where each state is in P.

It follows from these definitions that every strongly closed subset is also weakly closed, but the reverse is not necessarily true. As an example, consider a system (U, T) where U = {p.0, p.1, p.2, p.3} and T = {(p.0, p.1), (p.1, p.1), (p.1, p.2), (p.2, p.3), (p.3, p.3)}. Each of the following subsets is strongly closed: the empty subset, {p.3}, {p.2, p.3}, {p.1, p.2, p.3}, and U. Thus, each of these subsets is also weakly closed. On the other hand, the subset {p.1, p.3} is weakly closed but not strongly closed.

One is tempted to think that each weakly closed subset P contains a strongly closed subset Q such that each system computation, whose initial state is in P, has a state in Q. If this was the case, the concept of weak closures would be redundant, and only strong closures would be needed. However, this is not the case. Consider the weakly closed subset {p.1, p.3} in the above example. Indeed, this subset contains a strongly closed subset, namely {p.3}. However, not every system computation whose initial state is in {p.1, p.3} has a state in {p.3}. In particular, the system computation (p.1, p.1, ...) does not have the state p.3. Thus, the weakly closed subset {p.1, p.3} cannot be replaced by the strongly closed subset {p.3}.

Let (U, T) be a system, P be a strongly closed subset of U, and Q be a (strongly or weakly) closed subset of U. Subset P strongly converges to Q iff every system computation, whose initial state is in P, has a state in Q.

Let (U, T) be a system, P be a strongly closed subset of U, and Q be a (strongly or weakly) closed subset of U. Subset P weakly converges to Q iff for every state r that occurs in a system computation, whose initial state is in P, there is a system computation, whose initial state is r, and that computation has a state in Q.

Weak convergence is related to "probabilistic convergence" in the following sense. Consider a system (U, T), where the following three conditions hold.

  i. P weakly converges to Q.

 ii. The number of states in U is finite.

iii. For each state p in U, and each transition (p, q) in T, the probability, that transition (p, q) occurs in a computation whenever p occurs in that computation, is non-zero.

Then, with probability one, every computation of system (U, T), whose initial state is in P, has a state in Q.

This relationship between weak and probabilistic convergence can be proven as follows. Consider an arbitrary computation c of system (U, T). Because U is finite, at least one state r occurs infinitely many times in computation c. Because the probability that each transition, whose pre-state is r, occurs in c whenever r occurs in c is non-zero, then with probability one, each such transition occurs infinitely many times in c. Therefore, with probability one, each state that follows state r in system (U, T) occurs infinitely many times in c. This argument can be repeated a finite number of times to show that with probability one, each state that is reachable from state r in system (U, T) occurs infinitely many times in c. Because P weakly converges to Q, there is a state in Q that is reachable from r. With probability one, this state occurs (infinitely many times) in computation c.

It follows from this discussion that in systems with finite number of states, weak convergence can be easily converted to probabilistic convergence: Merely ensure that each transition has a non-zero probability of being executed, whenever the system reaches the pre-state of that transition. Henceforth, we ignore probabilistic convergence, and focus only on strong and weak convergence.

It is straightforward to show that if P strongly converges to Q then P weakly converges to Q, and that the reverse is not necessarily true. The definitions of strong and weak convergence yield four concepts.

  i. Strong convergence to strong closure.

 ii. Strong convergence to weak closure.

iii. Weak convergence to strong closure.

 iv. Weak convergence to weak closure.

These four concepts are related as follows: (i) implies both (ii) and (iii), and each of (ii) and (iii) implies (iv).

Let P be a (strongly or weakly) closed subset of U in a system (U, T). System (U, T) strongly stabilizes to P iff U strongly converges to P. System (U, T) weakly stabilizes to P iff U weakly converges to P.

Because strong convergence implies weak convergence, it follows that strong stabilization implies weak stabilization. The definitions of strong and weak stabilization yield four concepts.

   i. Strong stabilization to strong closure.

  ii. Strong stabilization to weak closure.

 iii. Weak stabilization to strong closure.

 iv. Weak stabilization to weak closure.

These four concepts are related as follows: (i) implies both (ii) and (iii), and each of (ii) and (iii) implies (iv).

Having different degrees of stabilization is advantageous for two reasons. First, it allows us to compare and rate the stabilization properties of different systems. Second, because strong stabilization is costly or impossible to achieve in some cases, a weaker degree of stabilization can be sought in these cases.

Examples of systems that strongly stabilize to strong closures are given in [8], [9], [12], [13], [17], [18] [23], [29], and [30]. Examples of systems that strongly stabilize to weak closures are given in [11]. Examples of systems that strongly stabilize, with probability one, to strong closures are given in [7] and [15].

3 Laws of Stabilization

In this section, we state some laws concerning the closure, convergence, and stabilization properties of systems. These laws can be derived from the definitions in Section 2, and they can be used in reasoning about system stabilization. In these laws, let (U, T) be an arbitrary system, and let P, Q, R, and S be subsets of U.

   i. Base:
    U is strongly closed,
    U strongly converges to U, and
    (U, T) strongly stabilizes to U.

  ii. Junctivity of Closure:
    If   both P and Q are strongly closed,
    then both P∪Q and P∩Q are strongly closed.

    If   both P and Q are weakly closed,
    then both P∪Q and P∩Q are weakly closed.

 iii. Junctivity of Convergence:
    If   P strongly converges to Q,
    and R strongly converges to S,
    then P∪R strongly converges to Q∪S,
    and P∩R strongly converges to Q∩S.

If   P strongly converges to Q,
and R weakly converges to S,
then PUR weakly converges to QUS,
and P∩R weakly converges to Q∩S.

If   P weakly converges to Q,
and R weakly converges to S,
then PUR weakly converges to QUS.

iv. Junctivity of Stabilization:
    If   (U, T) strongly stabilizes to P,
    and (U, T) strongly stabilizes to Q,
    then (U, T) strongly stabilizes to both PUQ and P∩Q.

    If   (U, T) strongly stabilizes to P,
    and (U, T) weakly stabilizes to Q,
    then (U, T) weakly stabilizes to both PUQ and P∩Q.

    If   (U, T) weakly stabilizes to P,
    and (U, T) weakly stabilizes to Q,
    then (U, T) weakly stabilizes to PUQ.

v. From Closure to Convergence:
   If   P is strongly closed,
   and Q is a weakly closed superset of P,
   then P strongly converges to Q.

vi. From Convergence to Convergence
    (Transitivity of Convergence):
    If   P strongly converges to Q,
    and Q strongly converges to R,
    then P strongly converges to R.

    If   P weakly converges to Q,
    and Q weakly converges to R,
    then P weakly converges to R.

vii. From Convergence to Stabilization:
     If   (U, T) strongly stabilizes to P,
     and P strongly converges to Q,
     then (U, T) strongly stabilizes to Q.

     If   (U, T) weakly stabilizes to P,
     and P weakly converges to Q,
     then (U, T) weakly stabilizes to Q.

The first law, base, demonstrates that the three properties of closure, convergence, and stabilization are meaningful. In particular, each of these properties applies to the set of all system states. The next three laws, junctivity, show how to use two instances of each of these properties to deduce two more instances of the same property. The last three laws, from-to, show how to use an instance of closure, convergence, and stabilization to deduce a new instance of convergence, convergence, and stabilization, respectively.

4 Proof Obligations of Stabilization

In this section, we discuss the proof obligations needed for establishing the stabilization properties of systems. In what follows, let (U, T) be an arbitrary system, and let P, Q, Q.0, Q.1, ... be subsets of U. Also, let (D, $\ll$) denote a well-founded domain, where each decreasing, with respect to the less-than relation $\ll$, sequence of the elements in D is finite.

4.1 Proving Strong Closure

In order to establish that subset P is strongly closed in system (U, T), prove that for every state p in P, and every transition (p, q) in T, state q is in P.

4.2 Proving Weak Closure

In order to establish that subset P is weakly closed in system (U, T), exhibit an infinite sequence (Q.0, Q.1, ...) of subsets of U such that the following three assertions hold.

i. P is a subset of ($\cup$i, $0 \leq i$, Q.i).

ii. For every k, ($\cup$i, $0 \leq i < k$, Q.i) is strongly closed.

iii. For every i, $0 \leq i$, every computation of system (U, T), whose states are all in Q.i, has a non-empty suffix where every state is in P.

Two comments concerning this infinite sequence (Q.0, Q.1, ...) are in order. First, if there is an integer n such that for every i, $i \geq n$, Q.i = Q.n, then the infinite sequence (Q.0, Q.1, ...) is in effect finite. Second, if for every i, $i \geq 0$, Q.i = P, then P is strongly closed.

Assertion (i) can be proven using predicate calculus. Assertion (ii) can be proven as discussed in Section 4.1. Assertion (iii) can be proven for every i, $0 \leq i$, as follows. Exhibit a well-founded domain (D, $\ll$) and a total function f : Q.i $\rightarrow$ D, such that for every transition (p, q) in T, where p and q are in Q.i,

(if q is not in P then f.q $\ll$ f.p) and
(if p is in P then q is in P)

4.3 Proving Strong Convergence

In order to establish that subset P strongly converges to Q in system (U, T), prove the following three assertions.

i. P is strongly closed.

ii. Q is (strongly or weakly) closed.

iii. Every computation of system (U, T), whose initial state is in P, has a state in Q.

Assertions (i) and (ii) can be proven as discussed in Sections 4.1 and 4.2. Assertion (iii) can be proven by exhibiting a well-founded domain $(D, \ll)$ and a total function $f : P \to D$, such that for every state p in P, and every transition (p, q) in T, if q is not in P then $f.q \ll f.p$.

A modular proof of the property (P strongly converges to Q) in system (U, T) can be achieved by resorting to the transitivity of strong convergence. In particular, one can identify a finite sequence $(Q.0, \ldots, Q.(n-1))$ of subsets of U such that the following three conditions hold.

i. $P = Q.0$.

ii. $Q = Q.(n-1)$.

iii. For every i, $0 \leq i < n-1$, Q.i strongly converges to Q.(i+1).

We refer to the sequence $(Q.0, \ldots, Q.(n-1))$ as a strong convergence stair.

4.4 Proving Weak Convergence

In order to establish that subset P weakly converges to Q in system (U, T) prove the following three assertions.

i. P is strongly closed.

ii. Q is (strongly or weakly) closed.

iii. For every state r that occurs in a system computation, whose initial state is in P, there is a system computation, whose initial state is r, and that computation has a state in Q.

Assertions (i) and (ii) can be proven as discussed in Sections 4.1 and 4.2. Assertion (iii) can be proven by exhibiting an infinite sequence $(Q.0, Q.1, \ldots)$ of subsets of U such that the following three conditions hold.

a. P is a subset of $(\cup i, 0 \leq i, Q.i)$.

b. Q.0 is a subset of Q.

c. For every Q.j, there is Q.i, $0 \leq i < j$, such that for every state p in Q.j, there is a transition (p, q) in T, where q is in Q.i.

A modular proof of the property (P weakly converges to Q) in system (U, T) can be achieved by resorting to the transitivity of weak convergence. In particular, one can identify a finite sequence $(Q.0, \ldots, Q.(n-1))$ of subsets of U such that the following three conditions hold.

i. P = Q.0.

ii. Q = Q.(n-1).

iii. For every i, $0 \leq i < n-1$, Q.i weakly converges to Q.(i+1).

We refer to the sequence (Q.0, ... , Q.(n-1)) as a weak convergence stair.

5 System Composition Made Easy

In this section, we show that multiple systems can be combined into a single composite system that has the same stabilization properties of the constituent systems. Toward this goal, we need to change our view of a system from being a pair (U, T) of states and transitions, to being a pair (V, C) of variables and actions. The two views (U, T) and (V, C) of a system are related as follows.

i. There is one-to-one correspondence between the states in U and the assignments of values to the variables in V. We adopt the notation p ↔ x to mean that state p in U corresponds to assigning value x to the V variables.

ii. There is one-to-one correspondence between the transitions in T and the executions of actions in C. In particular, a transition (p, q) in T corresponds to an execution of action c in C iff there are two values x and y of the V variables such that the following three conditions hold.

   a. p ↔ x.

   b. q ↔ y.

   c. Executing action c when the V variables have value x yields the V variables with value y.

Let (V, C) be a system, where V is a set of variables and C is a set of actions, and let P be a subset of the system states. Subset P can be represented by a first order predicate, also denoted P for convenience, over the V variables such that for every system state p and every value x of the V variables, where p ↔ x,

(state p is in subset P
iff
assigning value x to the V variables makes predicate P true)

A predicate that represents a subset of the states of a system is called a state predicate of the system.

A state predicate of a system is called strongly (or weakly) closed iff the corresponding subset of system states is strongly (or weakly, respectively) closed. Having extended the concept of closure to state predicates, we can also extend the concepts of convergence and stabilization to state predicates.

Let (V.0, C.0), ... , (V.(n-1), C.(n-1)) be n systems, where each V.i is a set of variables, and each C.i is a set of actions. These systems can be combined into a system (V, C) as follows.

$$V = V.0 \cup ... \cup V.(n-1)$$
$$C = C.0 \cup ... \cup C.(n-1)$$

In this case, the systems (V.0, C.0), ... , (V.(n-1), C.(n-1)) are called the constituent systems of the composite system (V, C). In the remainder of this section, we state sufficient conditions for ensuring that if the constituent systems are all strongly (or weakly) stabilizing, then the composite system is strongly (or weakly, respectively) stabilizing. To state these conditions, we need to introduce three concepts: input and output variables of a system and composition graph of a composite system. We discuss these three concepts in order.

Let (V, C) be a system. A variable u in V is called an input variable iff no action in C writes variable u. A variable in V, that is not an input variable, is called an output variable.

Let (V, C) be a composite system whose constituent systems are (V.0, C.0), ... , (V.(n-1), C.(n-1)). System (V, C) can be represented by a directed graph G, called the composition graph of (V, C), with two types of nodes. A node of the first type, called a v-node, represents a variable in the set V.0 $\cup$ ... $\cup$ V.(n-1). A node of the second type, called a c-node, represents one of the action sets C.0, ... , or C.(n-1). In G, there is a directed edge from a v-node representing a variable u to a c-node representing an action set C.i iff u is an input variable in system (V.i, C.i). Also in G, there is a directed edge from a c-node representing an action set C.i to a v-node representing a variable u iff u is an output variable in system (V.i, C.i).

Theorem of Hierarchical Composition:
Let (V, C) be a composite system whose constituent systems are (V.0, C.0), ... , (V.(n-1), C.(n-1)).
If   each constituent system (V.i, C.i) stabilizes to predicate P.i,
and   the composition graph G of (V, C) satisfies the two conditions:
        i. each v-node has at most one incoming edge in G, and
        ii. there are no directed cycles in G,
then system (V, C) stabilizes to the predicate P.0 $\wedge$ ... $\wedge$ P.(n-1).

Conditions (i) and (ii) in this theorem are somewhat severe. To relax condition (i), we introduce the concept of an isolation node.

Consider a v-node u with two incoming edges from two c-nodes C.i and C.j. Node u is called an isolation node iff for each value combination of the input variables of C.i and C.j, one of the following two conditions hold.

i. For each value of the output variables of C.i, executing each action in C.i keeps the variables of C.j unchanged.

ii. For each value of the output variables of C.j, executing each action in C.j keeps the variables of C.i unchanged.

In this definition, node u is called an isolation node because the stabilization of system (V.i, C.i) does not interfere with the stabilization of system (V.j, C.j), or vice versa. We leave it for the reader to extend the definition of an isolation node to a v-node with more than two incoming edges.

Theorem of Acyclic Composition:
Let (V, C) be a composite system whose constituent systems are (V.0, C.0), ... , (V.(n-1), C.(n-1)).

If	each constituent system (V.i, C.i) stabilizes to predicate P.i,
and	the composition graph G of (V, C) satisfies the two conditions:

      i. each v-node with two or more incoming edges in G is an
         isolation node, and
      ii. there are no directed cycles in G,

then   system (V, C) stabilizes to the predicate P.0 $\wedge$ ... $\wedge$ P.(n-1).

To relax condition (ii), we introduce the concept of a separation node. Consider a v-node u with one incoming edge from c-node C.i and one outgoing edge to c-node C.j. Node u is called a separation node iff for every value of variable u, one of the following two conditions hold.

   i. For each value of the variables of C.i, other than u, executing each action in C.i keeps variable u unchanged.

  ii. For each value of the variables of C.j, other than u, executing each action in C.j keeps the output variables of C.j unchanged.

In this definition, node u is called a separation node iff the value of variable u remains unchanged or system (V.j, C.j) has stabilized, in other words, the stabilization of system (V.i, C.i) does not affect the stabilization of system (V.j, C.j). We leave it for the reader to extend the definition of a separation node to a v-node with multiple incoming and outgoing edges.

Theorem of General Composition:
Let (V, C) be a composite system whose constituent systems are (V.0, C.0), ... , (V.(n-1), C.(n-1)).

If	each constituent system (V.i, C.i) stabilizes to predicate P.i,
and	the composition graph G of (V, C) satisfies the two conditions:

      i. each v-node with two or more incoming edges in G is an
         isolation node, and
      ii. each directed cycle in G has at least one separation node,

then   system (V, C) stabilizes to the predicate P.0 $\wedge$ ... $\wedge$ P.(n-1).

A preliminary version of this method of system composition is presented in [19]. Other methods for composing stabilizing systems are presented in [24] and [26].

6 Applications of System Stabilization

Stabilization properties can be used in studying several areas of computing systems: initialization and reset, fault recovery, fault containment, and system adaptivity. Next, we discuss each of these four areas in turn.

6.1 Initialization and Reset

The stabilization properties of a system can be used to simplify the initialization and reset procedures for that system. This is beneficial especially for parallel and distributed systems whose initialization and reset procedures are usually very complicated.

Consider a system (V, C) whose initial or reset state is required to satisfy some state predicate Q. If a state predicate P strongly converges to Q in this system, then an initialization or reset procedure for the system is as follows. First, the system is initialized or reset to any state that satisfies predicate P. Second, the system is left to execute for some time until its current state satisfies Q. Note that if the system strongly stabilizes to Q, then the first step in this procedure is not needed.

Stabilizing systems for distributed reset are presented in [3] and [6].

6.2 Fault Recovery

Let (V, C) be a system, and let P and Q be two state predicates of that system. System (V, C) recovers from P to Q iff the following three conditions hold.

   i. Each state of (V, C), that satisfies Q, satisfies P.

  ii. Both P and Q are strongly closed in (V, C).

 iii. P strongly converges to Q in (V, C).

In this definition of fault recovery, faults are not mentioned explicitly. Rather, the definition implies that each fault occurrence may change the state of the system from one that satisfies predicate Q to one that satisfies predicate P. Further occurrences of faults keep the system in states that satisfy predicate P. The ability of the system to recover from these fault occurrences is expressed by saying that P strongly converges to Q. In other words, when faults cease to occur for some time, the system returns to states that satisfy predicate Q during that period. Predicate P represents the system invariant when faults do occur, and predicate Q represents the system invariant when faults cease to occur.

One may feel uncomfortable about a definition of fault recovery that does not explicitly mention faults. If so, one can introduce faults to the above definition as follows. First, define a set F of faults, where each fault is an action that reads and writes the V variables in system (V, C). Second, add the requirement, that P is strongly closed in the fault system (V, F), to the above definition. Note that the fault system (V, F) is the same as the original system (V, C) except that set C of system actions is replaced by set F of fault actions. Third, the resulting definition is identified as system (V, C) recovers from F via P to Q.

This augmented definition of fault recovery is based on the assumption that the only effect of a fault on a system (V, C) is to change the current state of

(V, C). This assumption can always be realized by adding auxiliary variables to set V and augmenting some actions in set C. For example, to represent a fault that causes an action c in C to failstop and never be executed again, an auxiliary variable, named up, is added to set V and action c is augmented so that it cannot change the value of any variable when up = false. In this case, the failstop fault can be represented by the fault action up := false. Other types of faults such as Byzantine faults, stuck-at faults, and timing faults, can all be represented in the same way.

Consider a system (V, C) that recovers from P to Q. If P = true, then the fault recovery is called stabilizing, else it is called non-stabilizing. If P = S, then the fault recovery is called masking, otherwise it is called non-masking.

In choosing a state predicate P so that a system (V, C) recovers from P to Q, we are faced with two contradictory objectives. The first objective is to choose P as weak as possible (i. e. close to true) so that system (V, C) can recover from most faults. The second objective is to choose P as strong as possible (i. e. close to Q) so that during recovery the system is guaranteed to remain in states close to those satisfying Q. Fortunately, it is possible to achieve both these objectives. First, define two state predicates P.0 and P.1 of system (V, C), where P.0 is weak (i. e. close to true) and P.1 is strong (i. e. close to Q). Second, ensure that system (V, C) recovers from P.0 to Q and from P.1 to Q.

The above definition of fault recovery admits the following three laws.

i. Union of Fault Recovery:
   If   system (V, C) recovers from P to Q,
   and system (V, C) recovers from R to Q,
   then system (V, C) recovers from P ∨ R to Q.

ii. Intersection of Fault Recovery:
   If   system (V, C) recovers from P to Q,
   and system (V, C) recovers from P to R,
   then system (V, C) recovers from P to Q ∧ R.

iii. Transitivity of Fault Recovery:
   If   system (V, C) recovers from P to Q,
   and system (V, C) recovers from Q to R,
   then system (V, C) recovers from P to R,

For more details and many examples about this novel view of fault recovery, the reader is referred to [2], [4], and [14].

6.3   Fault Containment

Let (V, C) be a system and P and Q be two state predicates of (V, C). Also, let ef be a function that maps each state of (V, C) that satisfies predicate P, to a non-negative integer. System (V, C) contains P to Q for ef iff the following three conditions hold.

i. (V, C) recovers from P to Q.

ii. For every pair of states p and q that satisfy P, if there is an action in C whose execution at state p yields a state q, then ef.p $\geq$ ef.q.

iii. For every state p that satisfies S, ef.p $= 0$.

Function ef in this definition is called an effect of fault function. One example of an effect of fault function for a mutual exclusion system is as follows.

$$\text{ef.p} \quad = \quad \max(0, \text{x.p - 1})$$

where x.p is the number of processes in their critical sections at state p. Effect of fault functions satisfy the following law.

Effect of Fault Functions:
If   system (V, C) contains P to Q for ef,
and system (V, C) contains P to Q for eg,
and x, y, and z are non-negative integers,
then system (V, C) contains P to Q for x$*$ef $+$ y$*$eg $+$ z$*$ef$*$eg.

6.4 System Adaptivity

An adaptive system is one whose computation adapts to the current state of its environment. As shown below, system adaptivity can be explained formally as a form of strong convergence. Before we define system adaptivity, we need to introduce the concept of a fixed point.

Let (V, C) be a system and Q be a strongly closed predicate of (V, C). Also, let U be a subset of V. Predicate Q is a fixed point for U iff starting at any state that satisfies Q, executing any action in C does not change the values of the variables in U. Note that if U is empty, then any strongly closed predicate is a fixed point for U.

Let (V, C) be a system and P and Q be two strongly closed predicates of (V, C), and let U be a subset of V. System (V, C) is adaptive from P to Q for U iff the following three conditions hold.

i. P is a boolean expression that involves only input variables in V.

ii. P strongly converges to Q.

iii. Q is a fixed point for U.

Consider a system (V, C) that is adaptive from P to Q for U. Each change in the state of the environment of (V, C) causes a corresponding change in the values of the input variables of (V, C). If the new values of the input variables make predicate P true, then the system eventually reaches states that satisfy predicate Q. System (V, C) stays within those states that satisfy Q at least until a later change in the state of the environment causes P to become false. While system (V, C) is within states that satisfy Q, the variables in set U have fixed values.

This concept of system adaptivity can be generalized as follows. Let (V, C) be a system, and let (P.0, ... , P.(r-1)) and (Q.0, ... , Q(r-1)) be two r-tuples of strongly closed predicates of (V, C). Also, let (U.0, ... , U.(r-1)) be an r-tuple of subsets of V. System (V, C) is adaptive from (P.0, ... , P.(r-1)) to (Q.0, ... , Q.(r-1)) for (U.0, ... , U.(r-1)) iff the following three conditions hold.

i. Every P.i is a boolean expression that involves only input variables in V.

ii. Every P.i strongly converges to Q.i.

iii. Every Q.i is a fixed point for U.i.

An example of an adaptive system is an air-conditioner. When the measured temperature (of the environment) is more than the required temperature, the state of the air-conditioner becomes on and stays on until the measured temperature is less than or equal the required temperature. In this case, the state of the air-conditioner becomes off and stays off until the measured temperature is more than the required temperature, and the cycle repeats.

7 Tribulations of System Stabilization

The above theory of system stabilization comes with several problems. In this section, we briefly discuss three of these problems. The first problem of the theory of stabilization is that some well-known models of parallel and distributed systems cannot be used to represent stabilizing systems [20]. One example of such models is Petrinets.

An informal explanation of why effective Petrinets cannot be stabilizing is as follows. A stabilizing Petrinet N should be able to converge from an arbitrary state where there is a large number of tokens in each place to a state where the total number of tokens in the net is small. Thus, transition firings in N should consume more tokens than they produce. Unfortunately, this means that N can reach a state where there are not enough tokens to enable any transition in N. In other words, N can reach a deadlock state. (One way to avoid this deadlock state is to provide N with a special transition that can fire and produce tokens when it detects that N has no tokens.)

Other models that cannot be used to represent stabilizing systems are systems of CSP and finite state automata that communicate messages over unbounded channels. These are all well-known models of parallel, concurrent, and distributed systems, and the fact that they cannot represent stabilizing systems is disturbing at best.

The second problem of the theory of stabilization is that some stabilization properties of a system are fragile and can disappear if the system is transformed using some seemingly harmless system transformations [20]. It follows that if a system is designed to be stabilizing, then many natural implementations of that design may not be stabilizing. This observation suggests that implementation of stabilizing systems should proceed with care to ensure that the stabilization properties, achieved in the design, are preserved in the implementation.

The third problem of the theory of stabilization is the great difficulty that one encounters in verifying the stabilization properties of systems. It has been my experience that the ratio of the time to design a stabilizing system to the time to verify its stabilization properties is about one to ten. This is unacceptably low ratio considering that the ratio for verifying standard safety and progress properties is about one to three. Therefore, better proof systems are needed for verifying stabilization properties.

8   What to Do in the Next Ten Years

The theory of system stabilization is relatively new, and so the area has many issues and problems that merit further consideration and research. Some of these problems are mentioned in this section.

In Section 2, we introduced two forms of closure and two forms of convergence, and ended up with four forms of stabilization. Are there other meaningful forms of closure, convergence, and stabilization? To add some structure to this, otherwise open ended, problem, I propose that any new forms of closure, convergence, and stabilization should satisfy the laws in Section 3.

In Section 4, we discussed proof obligations for verifying the stabilization properties of systems. Then in Section 8, we complained that it is very hard to carry out such verifications. Is it possible to come up with stronger proof obligations that are easier to check? These stronger proof obligations would be useful even if they are only applicable to special classes of stabilization properties or special classes of systems. Also, what tools for automated verification of system stabilization?

In Section 5, we presented a method for combining systems while preserving their stabilization properties. This method is provably sound, but its effectiveness is yet to be investigated. In particular, the following questions needs to be addressed. What types of systems can be composed using this method? Are there other methods for composing other types of systems?

In Section 6, we discussed four applications of the theory of system stabilization. In all these applications, we used only strong closure and strong convergence. Can weak closure or weak convergence be used in these applications? Are there other applications of the theory of stabilization? Early efforts to answer this last question indicate that system diagnostics, system learning, network protocols [5], [21], [22], [28], and hardware design [1] can all be viewed as applications of the theory of stabilization.

Finally, we have ignored in the current paper the whole area of stabilization complexity. Early efforts in this area are reported in [10], [16], [25] and [27]. Nonetheless, this area remains largely uncharted, and is now ripe for thorough investigation.

Acknowledgments: I started to work on system stabilization in the spring of 1986. Since then, I was fortunate enough to have nineteen excellent coauthors who helped me a great deal in exploring this magnificent area. Those coauthors are M. Abadir, A. Arora, P. Attie, G. Brown, J. Burns, J. Cobb, J. Couvreur, S.

Dolev, M. Evangelist, N. Francez, F. Haddix, T. Herman, R. Howell, R. Miller, N. Multari, L. Rosier, M. Schneider, G. Varghese, and C. Wu. To each of these coauthors: Thank you for your help. I am also thankful to J. Cobb for reading earlier drafts of this paper and suggesting several improvements. My grandparents, who never had a formal education, were very excited when I told them I was planning to study engineering and science. At the time, I did not know what their excitement was all about. Ten years after they passed away, I started to understand. This paper is dedicated to their memory.

References

1. M. Abadir, M. G. Gouda, "The Stabilizing Computer," *Proceedings of the International Conference on Parallel and Distributed Systems,* Taiwan, pp. 90-96, 1992.

2. A. Arora, M. G. Gouda, "Closure and Convergence: A Foundation for Fault-Tolerant Computing," *IEEE Transactions on Software Engineering,* special issue on Software Reliability, Vol. 19, No. 3, pp. 1015-1027, November 1993.

3. A. Arora, M. G. Gouda, "Distributed Reset," *IEEE Transactions on Computers,* Vol. 43, No. 9, pp. 1026-1038, 1994.

4. A. Arora, M. G. Gouda, G. Varghese, "Constraint Satisfaction as a Basis for Designing Nonmasking Fault-Tolerance," in *Specification of Parallel Algorithms,* edited by G. E. Blelloch, K. M. Chandy, S. Jagannathan, DIMACS Series in Discrete Mathematics and Theoretical Computer Science, Vol. 18, 1994.

5. A. Arora, M. G. Gouda, T. Herman "Composite Routing Protocols," *Proceedings of the Second IEEE Symposium on Parallel and Distributed Processing,* December 1990.

6. B. Awerbuch, R. Ostrovsky, "Memory-efficient and Self-Stabilizing Network Reset," *Proceedings of the 13th Annual ACM Symposium on Principles of Distributed Computing,* 1994.

7. J. Beauquier, S. Cordier, S. Delaet, "Optimum Probabilistic Self-Stabilization on Uniform Rings," *Proceedings of the Second Workshop on Self-Stabilizing Systems,* Technical Report, Department of Computer Science, University of Las Vegas, Las Vegas, Nevada, May 1995.

8. B. Bourgon, A. K. Datta, "A Self-Stabilizing Distributed Heap Maintenance Protocol," *Proceedings of the Second Workshop on Self-Stabilizing Systems,* Technical Report, Department of Computer Science, University of Las Vegas, Las Vegas, Nevada, May 1995.

9. G. M. Brown, M. G. Gouda, C. L. Wu, "Token Systems that Self-Stabilize," *IEEE Transactions on Computers,* Vol. 38, No. 6, pp. 845–852, June 1989.

10. J. E. Burns, M. G. Gouda, R. E. Miller, "On Relaxing Interleaving Assumptions," *Proceedings of the MCC Workshop on Self-Stabilization,* Austin, Texas, 1989.

11. J. E. Burns, M. G. Gouda, R. E. Miller, "Stabilization and Pseudostabilization," *Distributed Computing,* special issue on Self-Stabilization, Vol. 7, No. 1, pp. 35-42, November 1993.

12. J. Couvreur, M. G. Gouda, N. Francez, "Asynchronous Unison," *Proceedings of the 12th International Conference on Distributed Computing Systems*, Tokyo, pp. 486-493, 1992.

13. E. W. Dijkstra, "Self-Stabilizing Systems in Spite of Distributed Control," *Communications of the ACM*, Vol. 17, No. 11, pp. 643-644, 1974.

14. S. Dolev, T. Herman, "SuperStabilizing Protocols for Dynamic Distributed Systems," *Proceedings of the Second Workshop on Self-Stabilizing Systems*, Technical Report, Department of Computer Science, University of Las Vegas, Las Vegas, Nevada, May 1995.

15. S. Dolev, J. Welch, "Self-Stabilizing Clock Synchronization in the Presence of Byzantine Faults," *Proceedings of the Second Workshop on Self-Stabilizing Systems*, Technical Report, Department of Computer Science, University of Las Vegas, Las Vegas, Nevada, May 1995.

16. M. Evangelist, M. G. Gouda, "Convergence/Response Tradeoffs in Concurrent Systems," *Proceedings of the Second IEEE Symposium on Parallel and Distributed Processing*, December 1990.

17. S. Ghosh, A. Gupta, M. H. Karaata, S. V. Pemmaraju "Self-Stabilizing Dynamic Programming Algorithms on Trees," *Proceedings of the Second Workshop on Self-Stabilizing Systems*, Technical Report, Department of Computer Science, University of Las Vegas, Las Vegas, Nevada, May 1995.

18. M. G. Gouda, "Stabilizing Observers", *Information Processing Letters*, Vol. 57, pp. 99-103, 1994.

19. M. G. Gouda, T. Herman, "Adaptive Programming," *IEEE Transactions on Software Engineering*, Vol. 17, No. 9, pp. 911–921, September 1991.

20. M. G. Gouda, R. R. Howell, L. E. Rosier, "The Instability of Self-Stabilization," *Acta Informatica*, Vol. 27, pp. 697–724, 1990.

21. M. G. Gouda, N. Multari, "Stabilizing Communication Protocols," *IEEE Transactions on Computing*, special issue on Protocol Engineering, Vol. 40, No. 4, pp. 448–458, April 1991.

22. M. G. Gouda, M. Schneider, "Maximum Flow Routing," *Proceedings of the Second Workshop on Self-Stabilizing Systems*, Technical Report, Department of Computer Science, University of Las Vegas, Las Vegas, Nevada, May 1995.

23. C. Johnen, J. Beauquier, "Space-Efficient Distributed Self-Stabilizing Depth-First Token Circulation," *Proceedings of the Second Workshop on Self-Stabilizing Systems*, Technical Report, Department of Computer Science, University of Las Vegas, Las Vegas, Nevada, May 1995.

24. S. Katz, K. J. Perry, "Self-Stabilizing Extensions for Message-Passing Systems," *Distributed Computing*, Vol. 7, pp. 17-26, 1993.

25. C. Lin, J. Simon, "Possibility and Impossibility Results for Self-Stabilizing Phase Clocks on Synchronous Rings," *Proceedings of the Second Workshop on Self-Stabilizing Systems*, Technical Report, Department of Computer Science, University of Las Vegas, Las Vegas, Nevada, May 1995.

26. M. Schneider, "Self-Stabilization," *ACM Computing Surveys*, Vol. 25, No. 1, March 1993.

27. S. K. Shukla, D. J. Rosenkrantz, S. S. Ravi, "Observations on Self-Stabilizing Graph Algorithms for Anonymous Networks," *Proceedings of the Second Workshop on Self-Stabilizing Systems*, Technical Report, Department of Computer Science, University of Las Vegas, Las Vegas, Nevada, May 1995.

28. J. Spinelli, R. G. Gallager, "Event Driven Topology Without Sequence Numbers," *IEEE Transactions on Communications*, Vol. 37, No. 5, pp. 468-474, 1989.

29. M. S. Tsai, S. T. Huang, "Self-Stabilizing Ring Orientation Protocols," *Proceedings of the Second Workshop on Self-Stabilizing Systems*, Technical Report, Department of Computer Science, University of Las Vegas, Las Vegas, Nevada, May 1995.

30. I. Yen, F. B. Bastani, "A Highly Safe Self-Stabilizing Mutual Exclusion Algorithm," *Proceedings of the Second Workshop on Self-Stabilizing Systems*, Technical Report, Department of Computer Science, University of Las Vegas, Las Vegas, Nevada, May 1995.

Wait-free Computing*

Prasad Jayanti

Dartmouth College
Hanover, NH 03755, USA
prasad@cs.dartmouth.edu

Abstract. This tutorial has two independent parts. The first part (Sections 1, 2, 3, and 4) is aimed at introducing beginning graduate students to the subject of wait-free synchronization. It explores some important questions that have been studied and the techniques to solve them. The second part (Section 5) is a tutorial on robust wait-free hierarchies. It explains the motivation for studying such hierarchies and presents known results on this subject in one unified framework.

1 Introduction

Our study concerns concurrent systems that consist of multiple processes communicating through shared objects. We assume that processes are *asynchronous*: the speed at which a process executes its program varies arbitrarily with time and is independent of the speeds of other processes. This assumption is justified since processes may experience variable delays because of page faults, interrupts, or quantum expiration etc. Each shared object supports a set of operations that have well defined meaning. A process accesses a shared object by invoking an operation on the object and waiting until a response is returned. There can be several types of shared objects in the system, each supporting a different set of operations. The most common type is a shared memory cell that supports *read* and *write* operations so that any process may read or update the value of the cell. Such an object is commonly known as a *register*.[2] Another possibility is a *queue* object supporting *enq* and *deq* operations so that processes can insert and remove items from the object.

Our interest lies in programming multiple processes in a way that they can cooperate with each other to solve problems. Such programming often requires processes to synchronize in complex ways. Here are two examples of synchronization commonly found in Operating Systems texts:

1. Producers-Consumers Synchronization: Processes are divided into *producers*, which repeatedly produces items, and *consumers* which repeatedly look for items to consume. The processes must synchronize so that each produced item is eventually consumed and is consumed exactly once.

---

* Work supported by NSF grant CCR-9410421 and Dartmouth College Startup grant.
[2] Thus, our use of the term *register* has no relation to its use in Computer Architecture as a storage cell in the CPU.

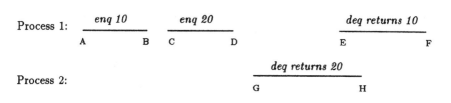

Fig. 1. A behavior of a queue

2. Readers-Writers Synchronization: Processes are divided into *readers* and *writers* and they all share a *buffer*. From time to time, a writer may wish to update the buffer while a reader may wish to read the buffer. The size of buffer is assumed to be much larger than the size of a register in the system (otherwise this problem becomes trivial). The processes must synchronize so that each read operation on the buffer returns a "sensible" value, one that is recent and that was actually written by some writer. (The exact meaning of "sensible" will be clear a little later when we describe linearizability.)

The above synchronization problems can be viewed in a different light. For instance, solving the producers-consumers synchronization amounts to implementing a queue object that processes can share. And solving the readers-writers synchronization amounts to implementing a register object of the size of buffer. In fact, this observation that synchronization can be viewed as implementing a particular type of shared object applies to most synchronization problems. Our interest in this article will therefore revolve around the "implementation problem": how a shared object of a particular type can be implemented from the types of shared objects available in a system. In the following, we will explain what it means to design an implementation and what correctness guarantee the implementation should extend.

The following elements constitute an implementation: (1) the type of the object $\mathcal{O}$ being implemented, (2) the shared objects $O_1, \ldots, O_n$ that $\mathcal{O}$ is implemented from, their types and initial values, (3) the processes $P_1, \ldots, P_N$ that may access $\mathcal{O}$, and (4) for each process P_i and each operation op supported by the type of $\mathcal{O}$, an *access procedure* $\mathcal{P}_{i,op}$ that P_i may execute in order to apply the operation op on $\mathcal{O}$. The value returned by the access procedure is deemed to be the response from $\mathcal{O}$. The procedure $\mathcal{P}_{i,op}$ specifies how P_i should simulate the operation op on $\mathcal{O}$ in terms of operations on $O_1, \ldots, O_n$.

If operations are applied on an object one after another, without overlap, the correctness of the object's behavior can be easily judged from its type. For example, if the object is a queue, its behavior is correct if and only if every dequeue operation returns the earliest enqueued item that was not already dequeued. However, in reality, operations applied by different processes on an implemented object may overlap. Judging whether an object's behavior, in the presence of such overlapping operations, is correct is no longer possible from simply knowing its type. For example, assuming that the queue was initially empty, is the behavior of the queue in Figure 1 correct? To resolve this, we adopt a correctness condition, known as *linearizability*, that was proposed by Herlihy and Wing [HW90]. This condition requires that each operation, although it spans over an interval time, must appear as though it took place instantaneously at some point in this interval. For example, the behavior of the queue in Figure 1 is linearizable because collapsing the three operations of P_1 to the instants A, C and E, and collapsing the operation of P_2 to the instant H gives the sequence of non-overlapping operations — enq 10, enq 20, deq 10, deq 20 — which agrees with the type specification of queue. Henceforth, unless stated otherwise, linearizability is our correctness condition for all shared objects, whether they are primitive objects supported in hardware or are implemented in software.

Implementing (linearizable) objects is by no means easy. To appreciate the difficulty, consider the previously mentioned problem of implementing a buffer $\mathcal{B}$, shared by readers and writers, from registers. Let us assume that the size of $\mathcal{B}$ is ten times the size of a register. Our first thought might be to implement $\mathcal{B}$ from ten registers $R_1, \ldots, R_{10}$ in the following manner. To read $\mathcal{B}$, a reader reads each of $R_1, \ldots, R_{10}$ and, if the values obtained in these ten reads are $v_1, \ldots, v_{10}$, returns $[v_1, \ldots, v_{10}]$ as the value of $\mathcal{B}$. To write a value $[v_1, \ldots, v_{10}]$ in $\mathcal{B}$, a writer writes v_1 in R_1, v_2 in R_2, and so on. Unfortunately, this implementation is not linearizable, as the following scenario demonstrates. Each R_i initially has 0. In an attempt to write $[1, 1, \ldots, 1]$ in $\mathcal{B}$, a writer writes 1's into each of $R_1 \ldots R_5$ and then slows down. A reader initiates a read operation on $\mathcal{B}$, reads 1 from each of $R_1 \ldots R_5$ and 0 from each of $R_6 \ldots R_{10}$, and returns $[1, \ldots, 1, 0, \ldots, 0]$. The writer then completes its operation by writing 1's into each of $R_6 \ldots R_{10}$.

This difficulty, caused by overlapping operations interfering with each other, has traditionally been solved by associating a "lock" with each shared object [CHP71]. A process must obtain the lock before manipulating the state of the object ($R_1, \ldots, R_{10}$ in the above example) and release the lock at the end of its operation. There has been extensive research on how to implement locks from registers and other objects [Ray86] and also on the subject of how well different implementations of locks perform [MS91]. Lock-based implementations are popular since they are simple and effective most of the times, but they have several drawbacks. If a slow process holds the lock on an object, it can delay faster and higher priority processes from accessing the object. Unless systems are carefully designed, deadlocks can occur: Process P holds the lock on A and waits for the lock on B, while process Q holds the lock on B and waits for the lock on A. Finally, if a process crashes while holding a lock, the entire system may come to a stand-still since all other processes may be potentially waiting for this lock to be released.

The above arguments make a case for implementations where no process can be arbitrarily delayed by other processes. Such implementations, known as *wait-free implementations*, were proposed by Lamport [Lam77]. Specifically, an implementation is *wait-free* if every access procedure completes and returns a response in a finite number of steps of the process executing that access procedure, regardless of whether other processes are slow or fast or have crashed. This article presents the research on the challenging problem of designing implementations that guarantee both linearizability and wait-freedom.

The rest of this article is organized as follows. Sections 2 and 3 introduce a beginner to some important problems, techniques and results in wait-free implementations. Section 4, where we hoped to survey the various topics of wait-free synchronization research, is omitted due to space constraints. Section 5 is a tutorial on robust wait-free hierarchies, a topic of current research. It includes motivation for studying hierarchies and presents all the results on this subject in one unified framework. This section is self-contained.

Since our study focuses only on implementations which are wait-free, we will use the terms "implementation" and "implement" as shorthands for "wait-free implementation" and "wait-free implement", respectively.

2   Register Implementations

A *K-writer, M-reader, N-valued register*, henceforth denoted as $[K, M, N]$ register, is an object that supports *read* and *write v* operations $(1 \leq v \leq N)$, and may be accessed by at most K readers, processes that may only apply the read operation, and at most M writers, processes that may only apply a write operation. Is a $[K, M, N]$ register stronger than a $[K', M', N']$ register if $[K, M, N] > [K', M', N']$?[3] In other words, are there objects which can be implemented from $[K, M, N]$ registers but not from $[K', M', N']$ registers? This was the question that sparked off research on wait-free implementations. Amazingly, the answer is no: for any K, M and N, one can implement a $[K, M, N]$ register from just $[1, 1, 2]$ registers.[4] This result is the consequence of a series of implementations demonstrating that $[1, 1, 2]$ registers can implement a $[1, 1, N]$ register [Lam86, Vid88], that $[1, 1, N]$ registers can implement a $[1, M, N]$ register [New87, SAG87], and that $[1, M, N]$ registers can implement a $[K, M, N]$ register [VA86, Blo87, PB87, Sch88, LTV89, IS92]. (The earliest wait-free implementation was by Lamport, implementing a $[1, M, N]$ register from $[1, M, 2]$ registers [Lam77]. In this implementation, the writer is wait-free, but the readers are not. Peterson was the first to exhibit a fully wait-free implementation [Pet83]. His work also implements a $[1, M, N]$ register from $[1, M, 2]$ registers.) These implementations are too complex to describe here. However, to get a feel for these implementations, let us consider the simple problem of implementing a $[1, M, N]$ register from $[1, 1, \infty]$ registers.

Let W denote the writer and $R_1, \ldots, R_M$ denote the readers of the $[1, M, N]$ register $\mathcal{R}$ that is being implemented. We will implement $\mathcal{R}$ from a total of M^2

---

[3] We define $[K, M, N] > [K', M', N']$ if at least once component in the first tuple is larger than the corresponding component in the second tuple and the remaining two components of the first tuple are at least as large as the corresponding components in the second tuple.

[4] 1-valued register makes no sense, so we don't consider $[1, 1, 1]$ registers.

	write 10	write 20	write 30	
Writer:	————————	————————	————————	

		read	read	read
Reader:		———————	———————	———————

Fig. 2. A behavior of a register

$[1, 1, \infty]$ registers: M of these are $w_1, \ldots, w_M$, where w_i is used for communication from W to R_i, and the remaining are $r_{i,j}$ ($1 \le i, j \le M$, $i \ne j$), used for communication from R_i to R_j. All M^2 implementing registers are initialized to $(0, init)$, where $init$ is the desired initial value of $\mathcal{R}$. The writer W maintains a local variable called $seq\text{-}num$, which is the number of write operations that it has so far applied on $\mathcal{R}$. This variable is of course initialized to 0. To write v in $\mathcal{R}$, the writer increments $seq\text{-}num$, and then writes $(seq\text{-}num, v)$ in each of $w_1, \ldots, w_M$. To read $\mathcal{R}$, a reader R_i reads all information that it can access, extracts the most recent value, informs other readers of this value, and then returns this value. More specifically, R_i performs the following sequence of actions. It reads w_i and each $r_{j,i}$. Let $(s_1, v_1), \ldots, (s_M, v_M)$ be the values obtained in these reads. Let k be such that $s_k \ge s_l$ for all $1 \le l \le M$. It writes (s_k, v_k) in each $r_{i,j}$ to inform other readers of the latest value it has seen. Finally, it returns v_k as the value of $\mathcal{R}$.

The reader of this paper is encouraged to verify that this implementation is linearizable. The simplicity of this implementation is due to the use of a monotonically increasing sequence number; this is acceptable because our implementing registers are ∞-valued. If the implementing registers were restricted to be bounded valued, say 2-valued, the implementation would be a lot harder.

2.1 Weaker Registers

Lamport investigated registers, known as *safe* and *regular* registers, that support a weaker notion of correction than linearizability [Lam86]. Specifically, a $[1, 1, N]$ safe register provides the following guarantee: if a read operation does not overlap with any write operation, it returns the most recently written value; otherwise it returns an arbitrary value. A $[1, 1, N]$ regular register offers a stronger guarantee: a read operation r returns either the value written by the latest write operation that precedes r or the value written by one of the write operations that overlap r. For an illustration of these definitions, see Figure 2. If the register is safe, the third read must return 30, but the first two reads, since they overlap with writes, may return any values. If the register is regular, the third must still return 30, the second must return either 20 or 30, and the first may return of 10, 20 or 30. In particular, the first read may return 30 and the second read may return 20. Notice that this behavior is not linearizable. Thus, a

$[1, 1, N]$ regular register offers weaker properties than a $[1, 1, N]$ linearizable register. However, Lamport proved the surprising result that a $[1, 1, N]$ linearizable register can be implemented from $[1, 1, 2]$ safe registers [Lam86].

Putting the above results together, we see that a $[K, M, N]$ (linearizable) register, the strongest conceivable register object, can be implemented from the seemingly weak $[1, 1, 2]$ safe registers. In addition to its intellectual appeal, this giant leap makes interesting inferences possible, as we will explain in the next section.

2.2 Some Applications of Register Implementations

Since no single model can capture the characteristics of all real systems, researchers in distributed computing have proposed and studied a variety of computation and communication models. Included among these are the *asynchronous message passing model* and the *asynchronous shared-registers model*. In both models, processes execute their programs at arbitrarily varying speeds, and may even crash.[5] The two models differ in how processes communicate. In the first model, processes communicate by passing messages to each other. Every message that is sent reaches its destination after an arbitrary (but finite) delay. In the second model, processes communicate by reading and writing (shared) registers. With these and other models, understanding the capabilities and the limitations of a model, namely, which problems can be solved in a given model and which cannot be, is a topic of fundamental interest. Clearly, if we can prove a theorem by which results obtained for one model automatically apply to a second model, that would be helpful. We will now prove such a theorem for the two models mentioned above. Specifically, we will show:

Theorem 1 ([ABD95]). *Let N be the number of processes in the system and t be the maximum number of processes that may crash. Assume $t < N/2$. Let $\mathcal{P}$ be any problem of interest. If $\mathcal{P}$ cannot be solved in the asynchronous message passing model, then it cannot be solved in the asynchronous shared-registers model.*

Proof. To prove the theorem, it suffices to show that a register can be implemented in the message passing model.[6] Since a register is known to be implementable from 1-writer, 1-reader, regular registers, it suffices to show that a 1-writer, 1-reader, regular register $\mathcal{R}$ can be implemented in the message passing model. This implementation is as follows.

Let $P_1, \ldots, P_N$ be the processes in the system. Without loss of generality, let P_1 and P_2 be the writer and the reader, respectively, of $\mathcal{R}$. Assume that each process P_i $(1 \leq i \leq N)$ has two private variables, $seq\text{-}num_i$ and val_i, where

---

[5] A process is said to crash if it stops executing its program and never subsequently resumes.

[6] When we write *register*, with no qualifiers such as $[K, M, N]$ in front, we mean a register that can take on any integer value and can be read and written by all processes in the system.

$seq\text{-}num_i$ is initialized to 0 and val_i is initialized to the desired initial value of $\mathcal{R}$. The reader (P_2) has an extra local variable called $rseq$, also initialized to 0. Processes behave as follows:

- To write a value v in $\mathcal{R}$, the writer (P_1) increments $seq\text{-}num_1$, and sends the message $(seq\text{-}num_1, v)$ to every process, including itself. It waits until it receives $(seq\text{-}num_1, ack)$ from $N-t$ processes. Once that happens, it considers the write operation to have completed.

- To read the value of $\mathcal{R}$, the reader (P_2) increments $rseq$ and then sends $(rseq, ?)$ to each of the N processes. It waits until it receives a response of the form $(rseq, *, *)$ from $N-t$ processes. Let $(rseq, s_1, v_1), \ldots, (rseq, s_{N-t}, v_{N-t})$ be the responses received. Let k be such that $s_k \geq s_l$ for all $1 \leq l \leq N-t$. The reader returns v_k as the value of $\mathcal{R}$.

- Each process P_i, when it receives a message of the form $(seq\text{-}num, v)$, checks if $seq\text{-}num > seq\text{-}num_i$; if so, it sets the local variable val_i to v and sends $(seq\text{-}num, ack)$ to the writer.

- Each process P_i, when it receives a message of the form $(rseq, ?)$, sends $(rseq, seq\text{-}num_i, val_i)$ to the reader.

The reader should verify that the above protocol indeed implements a regular register (assuming $t < N/2$). This completes the proof of the theorem. (Why does not this protocol implement a linearizable register? How should it be modified to implement one?)

The above theorem and the implementation presented in its proof are adapted from the work of Attiya, Bar-Noy, and Dolev in which more sophisticated versions of such implementations are presented [ABD95].

Fischer, Lynch, and Paterson proved that a problem known as consensus is unsolvable in an asynchronous message passing model even if $t = 1$ [FLP85]. (The consensus problem is defined in Section 3.1.) It follows from the above theorem that consensus is unsolvable in the shared-registers model even if $t = 1$.

As a second example of how the results on register implementations are useful, consider the following problem. Imagine that we have an unlimited supply of registers, but are told that up to t of these may be faulty. Let us consider the fault model in which faulty registers respond to all operations, but their responses may be arbitrary. Consider the following question: Can one implement a register from the above supply of registers so that the implemented register behaves correctly despite the fact that at most t implementing registers may be faulty? The answer is yes: it is easy to implement a correct 1-writer, 1-reader, safe register from $2t + 1$ registers in the pool; since a register is known to be implementable from 1-writer, 1-reader, safe registers, it follows that a correct register can be implemented from the given pool of registers.

3 The Bigger Picture

Although registers are useful for information sharing, they are certainly not the only objects of interest. For instance, producers-consumers synchronization requires processes to share a queue. Other applications may need other types of shared objects, such as stacks, heaps, sets etc. Since there are infinitely many types (see Section 5.1 for a formal definition of type), no system can support all types of objects in its hardware. Thus, it is often the case that the types of shared objects required by an application must be implemented in software from the available objects. This naturally raises two questions:

Q1. Given a type T and a set $\mathcal{S}$ of types, can one implement an object of type T from objects of types in $\mathcal{S}$?

Q2. Are there "universal types" with the property that an object of *any* type can be implemented from objects of a universal type?

If we can answer instances of question Q1, we can determine whether or not particular tasks are feasible on a given multiprocessor. For instance, if it is impossible to implement a queue from registers, we can conclude that a multiprocessor whose shared-memory consists only of registers is unsuitable for producers-consumers synchronization.

If the second question has a positive answer and simple universal types can be identified, then the shared-memory of future multiprocessors can be designed to support objects of such types. This makes it possible to solve arbitrary synchronization tasks on such machines.

Herlihy pioneered research on both these questions [Her91]. In the next two subsections, we will study the techniques used to answer these questions.

3.1 Determining the Feasibility of Implementations

Consider the question of implementing an object of one type from objects of other types. If it is known that the implemented object is accessed by only one process, it is not hard to see that an object of *any* type can be implemented from just registers. On the other hand, if the implementation may be accessed by two or more processes, it is not clear that registers suffice. Thus, when we ask if some object can be implemented from other objects, it seems important to also specify the number of processes that may access the implementation. We therefore refine the question Q1 posed above to:

Q1'. Given a type T, a set $\mathcal{S}$ of types, and a positive integer N, can one implement an object of type T, shared by N processes, from objects of types in $\mathcal{S}$?

If the answer to this question is yes, we might prove it by displaying an implementation. But what if the answer is no? How can we possibly prove that the answer is no? Herlihy suggested a simple approach: identify some coordination problem which can be solved among N processes using objects of type T, but cannot be solved among N processes using objects of types in $\mathcal{S}$. The coordination problem that he picked for this purpose is a problem known as consensus.

The *consensus problem for processes* $P_1, \ldots, P_N$ is stated as follows. Each process P_i is initially given an input v_i (no process knows the inputs of other processes). The processes may then communicate with each other so that the following properties are realized:

1. Each P_i *eventually* outputs some value. In other words, P_i cannot perform an infinite number of steps without outputting a value. If P_i outputs d_i, we say that P_i *has decided* d_i.
   (Notice that if a process crashes and therefore has performed only a finite number of steps, it is exempted from deciding.)
2. No two processes decide different values. Thus, if P_i decides d_i and P_j decides d_j, then $d_i = d_j$.
3. The decision value is the input of some process.

(Sometimes we refer to a version of this problem, known as *binary consensus*, in which inputs are taken from the set $\{0, 1\}$.)

It turns out that binary consensus for two processes cannot be solved using registers alone, but it can be solved using queues and registers, or stacks and registers, or test&set objects and registers, or fetch&add objects and registers [Her91]. However, consensus for three processes cannot be solved using (any combination of) registers, queues, stacks, test&set objects and fetch&add objects, but it can be solved using compare&swap objects [Her91]. From these results, it follows that queues, stacks, test&set objects, and fetch&add objects, shared by two or more processes, cannot be implemented from registers. Also, compare&swap objects, shared by three or more processes, cannot be implemented from any combination of registers, queues, stacks, test&set objects, and fetch&add objects.

Thus, in several instances, determining the solvability of consensus can help answer Question Q1$'$. But how does one determine the solvability of consensus? We introduce the basic ideas by showing two specific results: how consensus for two processes can be solved using only queues and registers, and why this problem cannot be solved using only registers.

Theorem 2 ([Her91]). *The consensus problem for two processes can be solved using queues and registers.*

Proof. The following is a protocol that solves consensus for processes P_0 and P_1 using two registers R_0 and R_1, and a queue Q. Initialize Q to contain two items, *winner* and *loser*, with winner as the front item in the queue. The registers R_0 and R_1 do not need to be initialized to any special values. Let v_0 and v_1 denote the inputs that P_0 and P_1 receive initially. Each process P_i performs the following actions. P_i writes v_i in R_i and then dequeues an item from Q. If the dequeued item is winner, P_i decides v_i; otherwise it reads and decides the value in the register $R_{\bar{i}}$. It is easy to verify that this protocol is correct.

Theorem 3 ([CIL87, DDS87, LA87, Her91]). *The binary consensus problem for two processes cannot solved using only registers.*

Proof. Suppose that there is a protocol $\mathcal{P}$ by which two processes, P_0 and P_1, can solve binary consensus, communicating only via registers $R_1, \ldots, R_n$. The protocol specifies the initial values of $R_1, \ldots, R_n$, the initial states of P_0 and P_1 with the exception of their initial inputs, and the programs that P_0 and P_1 must execute in order to solve consensus.

Consider the system constituted by processes P_0, P_1 and registers $R_1, \ldots, R_n$. A state of this system, known as a *configuration*, is comprised of the internal states of processes P_0 and P_1 and the values of registers $R_1, \ldots, R_n$. Since the protocol $\mathcal{P}$ specifies the initial values of $R_1, \ldots, R_n$ and the initial states of P_0 and P_1 (with the exception of their initial inputs), assigning binary inputs to P_0 and P_1 uniquely specifies an initial configuration. Let $\mathcal{I}_{u,v}$ denote the initial configuration corresponding to P_0's input being u and P_1's input being v.

The configuration changes when a process executes a step of its program. In such a program step, a process P can perform any one of the following two types of actions: read a register and, based on the value obtained, change (P's) state, or write a value in a register and change (P's) state.

A *schedule* is a sequence of process names and denotes the order in which processes have performed steps. (For example, the schedule P_0, P_0, P_1, P_0 denotes that four steps have been performed, the third step is by P_1, and the remaining are by P_0.) Recall from the introduction that processes are asynchronous: they execute their programs at arbitrarily varying rates. Consequently, the order in which processes take turns and perform steps is unpredictable. In other words, any schedule is possible once the system is turned on.

Given a finite schedule σ and a configuration C, let $\sigma(C)$ denote the configuration that results when the system is started in configuration C and processes take steps in the order specified by σ. (Since the protocol $\mathcal{P}$ is fixed, $\sigma(C)$ is unique.) We say $\sigma(C)$ is *reachable* from C through schedule σ.

We will now define what it means for a configuration to be 0-valent or 1-valent. Informally, a configuration is u-valent if, beginning from that configuration, no matter how processes are interleaved, no decision other than u is possible. More specifically, a configuration C is *u-valent* ($u \in \{0, 1\}$) if, for all finite schedules σ, no process has decided $\bar{u}$ in $\sigma(C)$. We make two observations: (1) no configuration, reachable from an initial configuration, can be both 0-valent and 1-valent (otherwise, processes can be made to take infinitely many steps without deciding, implying that the protocol is not correct), and (2) if a configuration C is u-valent ($u \in \{0, 1\}$), every configuration reachable from C is also u-valent. We will call a configuration *monovalent* if it is either 0-valent or 1-valent. A configuration is *bivalent* if it is neither 0-valent nor 1-valent. Thus, if a system's configuration is bivalent, it means that either decision is still possible and the exact value of the decision will depend on the order in which process steps are interleaved.

We now prove two statements: (S1) the initial configuration $\mathcal{I}_{0,1}$ is bivalent, and (S2) given any bivalent configuration C that is reachable from an initial configuration, there is an infinite schedule σ such that, for all finite prefixes σ' of σ, $\sigma'(C)$ is bivalent. It follows from S1 and S2 that, if the initial configuration is $\mathcal{I}_{0,1}$, it is possible to interleave the steps of P_0 and P_1 in such a way that some process takes infinitely many steps without deciding. This implies that $\mathcal{P}$ is not a correct protocol, a contradiction.

To prove S1, consider the initial configuration $\mathcal{I}_{0,0}$. Suppose that process P_0 is executing steps by itself, with P_1 not taking any steps. Since P_0 must eventually decide and the decision value must be some process' input, it follows that P_0 decides 0. Furthermore, since $\mathcal{I}_{0,0}$ and $\mathcal{I}_{0,1}$ differ only in the input of P_1, if P_1 is not taking any steps, P_0 cannot distinguish between the initial configurations $\mathcal{I}_{0,0}$ and $\mathcal{I}_{0,1}$. It follows that, if the initial configuration is $\mathcal{I}_{0,1}$ and P_0 is executing steps by itself, then P_0 eventually decides 0. By a symmetric argument, if the initial configuration is $\mathcal{I}_{0,1}$ and P_1 is executing steps by itself, then P_1 eventually decides 1. Thus, the initial configuration $\mathcal{I}_{0,1}$ is bivalent.

To prove S2, let C be any bivalent configuration reachable from an initial configuration. Suppose that there is no infinite schedule σ with the properties stated in S2. Let η be a schedule of maximal length such that $D = \eta(C)$ is bivalent. By the maximality of η, $D_0 = P_0(D)$ and $D_1 = P_1(D)$ are both monovalent. (Here D_i is the configuration that results when process P_i takes a step from configuration D.) Furthermore, since D is bivalent, it follows that one of D_0 and D_1 is 0-valent and the other is 1-valent. Without loss of generality, assume that D_0 is 0-valent and D_1 is 1-valent. Let s_0 denote the step that P_0 performs to change the configuration from D to D_0, and R be the register that P_0 accesses in this step. Similarly, let s_1 denote the step that P_1 performs to change the configuration from D to D_1, and R' be the register that P_1 accesses in this step.

We claim that R and R' must be the same register. If not, it is easy to verify that the configuration reached when P_1 takes a step from D_0 is the same as the configuration reached when P_0 takes a step from D_1. That is, $P_1(D_0) = P_0(D_1)$. Yet, the former should be 0-valent and the latter should be 1-valent, a contradiction.

We claim that P_0 is not reading R in step s_0. Suppose that this claim is false. Then the registers have the same value in D_0 as they do in D. It follows that they have the same values in $D_1' = P_1(D_0)$ as they do in D_1. Furthermore, it is easy to see that the state of process P_1 is the same in D_1' and in D_1. Therefore, if P_1 executes steps by itself from D_1', it decides the same value as when it executes steps by itself from D_1. Yet D_1' is 0-valent and D_1 is 1-valent, a contradiction. By a similar argument, P_1 is also not reading R in step s_0.

We conclude from above that P_0 is writing some value u_0 in R in step s_0 and P_1 is writing some value u_1 in R in step s_1. Clearly, the configurations D_0 and D differ only in the states of P_0 and R. Allowing P_1 to take a step from either D or D_0 causes it to write u_1 in R. Thus, the registers have the same values in configuration $D_1' = P_1(D_0)$ as they do in D_1, and P_1 is in the same state in D_1' and in D_1. Therefore, if P_1 executes steps by itself from D_1', it decides the same value as when it executes steps by itself from D_1. Yet D_1' is 0-valent and D_1 is 1-valent, a contradiction. This completes the proof of statement S2. As already explained, S1 and S2 imply that the protocol $\mathcal{P}$ is incorrect. Hence the theorem.

The valency proof technique was first proposed and used by Fischer, Lynch and Paterson to prove that consensus is unsolvable in an asynchronous message passing system even if at most one process in the system may crash [FLP85]. This technique has subsequently been adapted to other communication models to obtain many more impossibility results [CIL87, DDS87, LA87, Her91].

3.2 Universal Types

Are there "universal" types with the property that an object of *any* type can be implemented from objects of a universal type? The answer is yes. Consider the type for which states are integers and the operations are tuples (f, g), where f and g are any computable functions from integers to integers, with the following behavior: when in state s, applying the operation (f, g) changes the state to $f(s)$ and returns the response $g(s)$. It is easy to see that an object of any type can be implemented from just a single object of this type. This demonstration of the existence of universal types is however not satisfactory. After all, we seek universal types because we hope to support objects of such types in the shared-memory of multiprocessors, but the universal type described above is clearly too impractical to be suitable for such a purpose.

We may therefore ask if there are universal types which are simple enough that they can be supported in hardware. Surprisingly, the answer is yes: if the consensus problem can be solved for N processes using objects of type T, then an object of *any* type, which is shared by at most N processes, can be implemented from only type T objects and registers. In other words, if type T objects are powerful enough to solve consensus for N processes, then they are (together with registers) powerful enough to solve *any* synchronization problem that involves N or fewer processes. Herlihy, who gave this characterization of universal types, proved it by exhibiting a *universal construction* that transforms the sequential specification of any type into a concurrent implementation using only registers and consensus objects [Her91]. He also identified several common and simple universal types [Her91]. For instance, if the shared-memory supports a *move*$(a1, a2)$ operation, which copies the contents at location $a1$ into location $a2$ of shared-memory, or a *swap*$(a1, a2)$ operation, which swaps the contents at the locations $a1$ and $a2$ of shared-memory, or a *compare&swap*(a, u, v) operation, it turns out that we can solve consensus among arbitrarily many processes. (The operation *compare&swap*(a, u, v) behaves as follows: if the value at location a is u, the value is changed to v and *true* is returned as the response; otherwise the value of location a is left unchanged and *false* is returned as the response.) Thus, objects of all types, shared by any number of processes, can be implemented in systems whose shared-memory supports any one of the above operations in addition to the usual read and write operations.

To understand the general ideas involved in universal constructions, let us consider how an object of any type can be implemented in a system whose shared-memory supports only *read*, *write* and *compare&swap* operations. For illustration, let us implement a queue, shared by processes $P_1, \ldots, P_N$, which never contains more than 511 items, with each item fitting into a single word of memory. In a single processor system, such a queue can be represented as an array of 512 words, with the first word storing the length of the queue. We now describe the concurrent queue implementation. In the following, a block refers to a chunk of 512 contiguous shared-memory words.

We divide the shared-memory among processes so that each process "owns" a pool of blocks (assume that each pool has an unbounded number of blocks). One of these blocks, say, block B of process P_1, is initialized so that it represents the initial state of the queue. A shared-variable, let us call it PTR, is initialized to point to block B. (The shared-variable PTR is distinct from all of the blocks owned by processes.) To enqueue an item v, a process P_i performs the following sequence of steps. P_i reads PTR into a local variable *old-ptr*. It then identifies a free block F in its pool that has never been used before and copies the contents of the block pointed by *old-ptr* into block F. (This copying is done one word at a time, using *read* and *write* operations.) P_i makes whatever changes are appropriate to add item v to the representation of the queue in F. Let *new-ptr* be a local variable of P_i that holds a pointer to F. P_i performs the operation *compare&swap*(PTR, *old-ptr*, *new-ptr*) in an attempt to install the state in block F as the new state of the queue. If compare&swap returns *true*, F is indeed the new state of the queue and P_i considers its enqueue operation to have completed. If compare&swap returns *false*, it means that some process has updated PTR since the time P_i read it; thus, the present state of the queue is not the same as what P_i read in the block pointed by *old-ptr*. In this case, P_i repeats the above sequence of steps. The dequeue operation is performed similarly.

The above implementation is linearizable, but is not wait-free. In particular, the compare&swap operations from a process P_i may repeatedly fail, returning *false*. However, if a compare&swap from P_i fails, it is only because some process has successfully swapped a value into PTR between P_i's reading of PTR and P_i's subsequent application of compare&swap. Thus, for each failed iteration of one process, there is a distinct successful operation from another process. As a result, individual processes may starve, but the system as a whole is guaranteed to make progress. Implementations with this property are known as *non-blocking implementations*. Unlike lock-based implementations, non-blocking implementations are immune to process crashes: the crash of some processes cannot prevent the rest of the system from making progress.

It is possible to transform a non-blocking implementation into a wait-free implementation. The standard approach is to require that each process, instead of being interested in only completing its own operation, must also check if there are other processes with outstanding operations and help them complete those operations. The details of how such help is implemented are fairly involved and are therefore not described here. The reader is referred to [Her93].

Another drawback of the above implementation is the unrealistic requirement that each process must own an unbounded number of blocks. This can be overcome by employing clever memory management algorithms [Her91, Her90].

4 A Survey of Other Works

I hoped to convey in this section the scope of research on wait-free synchronization by describing the various problems that have been studied, and providing references to appropriate works. The topics include atomic snapshots and time stamps, fault-tolerant wait-free implementations, randomized wait-free implementations, attempts towards more practical universal constructions, the (productive) application of topology to wait-free computing etc. This material, omitted here because of space constraints, will be incorporated into future revisions of this article, which will be available as technical reports from Dartmouth.

5 Robust Wait-free Hierarchies

Recently there has been considerable interest in attempting to classify types, based on their ability to support wait-free implementations. In this section, we review the motivation for such classification, examine the properties desirable in a classification, and explain the status of research on the question of whether a useful classification of types exists.

Researchers in this area have used different models and, even when the models are the same, have tended to use different terminology, making it hard to interpret and compare results. Here we state the existing results in a unified model that we describe below.

5.1 Model and Definitions

Type: A *type* is a tuple (n, OP, RES, Q, δ), where n is a positive integer denoting the number of ports, OP is a set of operations, RES is a set of responses, Q is a set of states, and $\delta \subseteq Q \times OP \times N_n \times Q \times RES$ is a transition relation, known as the *sequential specification* of the type (here N_n denotes the set $\{1, 2, \ldots, n\}$). Intuitively, if $(\sigma, op, i, \sigma', res) \in \delta$ it means the following: applying the operation op at port i of an object in state σ can cause the object to move to state σ' and return the response res. The relation δ is required to satisfy two properties:

Totality: For all $\sigma \in Q$, $op \in OP$, and $i \in N_n$, there is at least one pair $\overline{(\sigma', res)}$ such that $(\sigma, op, i, \sigma', res) \in \delta$. (This condition ensures that it is legitimate to apply any operation at any port from any state.)
Computability: There is a Turing machine M such that (i) M halts on all inputs, and (ii) on input (σ, op, i) ($\sigma \in Q$, $op \in OP$, and $i \in N_n$), M computes at least one pair (σ', res) such that $(\sigma, op, i, \sigma', res) \in \delta$. (This condition ensures that it is possible to implement an object of this type at least in the case when operations are applied sequentially, without overlap.)

A type is *n-ported* if the number of ports associated with the type is n. A type is *deterministic* if, for all $\sigma \in Q$, $op \in OP$ and $i \in N_n$, there is at most one pair (σ', res) such that $(\sigma, op, i, \sigma', res) \in \delta$. Thus, for deterministic types, δ can be regarded as a function $\delta : Q \times OP \times N_n \rightarrow Q \times RES$. A type is *non-deterministic* if it is not deterministic.

A type is *oblivious* if the effect of an operation does not depend on the port at which it is applied; more precisely, if for all $\sigma \in Q$, $op \in OP$ and $i, j \in N_n$, $\delta(\sigma, op, i) = \delta(\sigma, op, j)$. Thus, for oblivious types, the sequential specification can be given without reference to ports. A type is *non-oblivious* if it is not oblivious. Next we will see some examples of oblivious and non-oblivious types considered in the literature.

The type **1-reader 1-writer** N**-valued register** is a deterministic non-oblivious 2-ported type for which $OP = \{read\} \cup \{write\, v \mid 0 \le v \le N - 1\}$, $RES = \{ack\} \cup \{0, 1, \ldots, N - 1\}$, $Q = \{0, 1, \ldots, N - 1\}$, and sequential specification δ is as follows: $\delta(\sigma, read, 1) = (\sigma, \sigma)$ (*read* at port 1 returns the state without modifying it), $\delta(\sigma, write\, v, 1) = (\sigma, ack)$ (*write* at port 1 has no effect), $\delta(\sigma, read, 2) = (\sigma, ack)$ (*read* at port 2 has no effect on state and returns no useful information), and $\delta(\sigma, write\, v, 2) = (v, ack)$ (*write* v at port 2 changes the state to v).

The following are some examples of deterministic oblivious types that will appear in different contexts in this section. The type **fetch&increment** supports a single operation *fetch&increment*, and its states are integers. The *fetch&increment* operation increments the state by one and returns its previous value. The type **test&set** supports two operations, *test&set* and *reset*, and has two states, 0 and 1. The *test&set* operation changes state to 1 and returns the previous state, while the *reset* operation changes state to 0 and returns *ack* as response. The type (binary) **compare&swap** supports operations of the form *compare&swap(old, new)*, where *old* and *new* are binary values, and has two states, 0 and 1. If the state equals *old*, the operation changes the state to *new* and returns *true*; otherwise it leaves the state unchanged and returns *false*. The type **register** supports *read* and *write* v operations and its states are integers. *read* returns the state without modifying it, and *write* v changes the state to v and returns *ack*. The last type we will describe is **consensus**. For this type, $OP = \{propose\ 0,\ propose\ 1\}$, $RES = \{0, 1\}$, and $Q = \{S, S_0, S_1\}$. Its sequential specification is given in Figure 3 (each edge in the figure is labeled by an operation and its response). For oblivious types, we will write a number before a type's name to denote the number of ports associated with that type. For example, N**-consensus** denotes the N-ported **consensus** type.

The notion of type (in the sense presented above) was first described by Herlihy and Wing [HW90]. Their definition encompasses only oblivious types. The distinction between oblivious and non-oblivious types was made explicit by Kleinberg and Mullainathan [KM93]. The definitions given above are adapted from Bazzi, Neiger and Peterson [BNP94], Borowski, Gafni and Afek [BGA94], and Jayanti [Jay95].

Processes and Objects: A *concurrent system* consists of *processes* and *objects*. Processes, objects, and the concurrent system can all be formally modeled using I/O automata [LT88] as was described by Herlihy [Her91]. However, our approach below is informal.

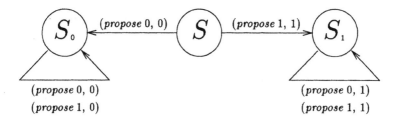

Fig. 3. Sequential specification of consensus

Each object has two attributes, a type and an initial value, where the initial value is a state of the type. An object has as many ports as are associated with its type. A process accesses an object by invoking an operation at a port of that object and waiting until a response is returned at that port by the object. But how does a process determine the port at which to access the object? Let us call this the *binding problem*. Different rules for binding processes to ports give rise to different models. Here we will examine three (of the several) possibilities:

(M1). Initially, before the system execution begins, processes are bound to ports. Each port may be bound to at most one process and each process may be bound to at most one port of any given object. A process can apply an operation only at a port to which it is bound. This binding of processes to ports cannot change during an execution and is the same over all executions.. This model of binding has sometimes been referred to as *hardwired binding* [BGA94].

(M2). Same as M1 with one difference: we allow a process to be bound to more than one port of an object.

If an object is of an oblivious type, it serves no purpose to bind a process to more than one port of the object. Thus, for oblivious types, the distinction between models M1 and M2 is irrelevant.

(M3). Each time a process wants to access an object, it determines dynamically, during the execution, the port at which to access the object. Thus, to apply an operation op on an object O, a process first determines the port number i of O at which to access, binds itself to port i, invokes the operation op at port i, waits until a response is returned at port i, and then releases port i. (The binding and the releasing steps in the above description are only conceptual.) For a subsequent operation on O, the process may choose to bind to a different port. We require that no more than one process be simultaneously bound to any given port. (In other words, any protocol which permits an execution in which two or more processes are bound simultaneously to a port is an incorrect protocol.) Borowski, Gafni and Afek, who proposed this model of binding, called it *softwired binding* [BGA94].

Several variations of these models are possible: for instance, a process may decide (during the execution) the port of an object it wants to bind to, but once a choice is made, it cannot later change its mind and bind to a different port of the same object.

While the plethora of binding models can make interpretation of results difficult, it is comforting that for a large class of results the exact model of binding is irrelevant. For a result that concerns only oblivious types, if the number of ports associated with each type is at least as large as the number of processes in the system, then the model of binding is a non-issue. This is because each process can be bound to a port of each object initially; and more complex binding schemes serve no useful purpose.

In this article, unless otherwise stated, the binding model M1 is assumed.

Linearizability: An object's type specifies its legal behavior only in the case when operations are applied on the object one after the other, without overlap. However, in a concurrent system, operations from different processes may overlap. So we resort to an additional correctness condition called *linearizability*: each operation on an object, spanning over an interval of time from the invocation of the operation to its response, must appear to occur at some instant in this interval. This is made more precise below. For a detailed exposition of linearizability, refer to the work of Herlihy and Wing in which this concept was first defined [HW90].

Consider a history H of an object, which is a sequence of invocation and response events of the object. An operation *precedes* another in H if the response of the former occurs before the invocation of the latter. Two operations are *concurrent* if neither precedes the other. H is *sequential* if it has no concurrent operations. H is *complete* if every invocation has a corresponding response. A complete sequential history is *consistent with type T and initial value σ* if, beginning from state σ of T, the sequential history is consistent with the sequential specification of T.

Let O be an object of type T and initial value σ. Let H be a complete (but not necessarily sequential) history of object O. H is *linearizable with respect to type T and initial value σ* if it is possible to permute events in H to obtain a sequential history S such that (i) if an operation precedes another in H, then it does so also in S, and (ii) S is consistent with type T and initial value σ.

Implementation: In the following, we explain the notion of an implementation and define what it means to implement a type from a set of types. The discussion assumes the binding model M1.

An implementation of object $\mathcal{O}$ of type $T = (n, OP, RES, Q, \delta)$ and initial value σ from (a possibly infinite set of) objects $O_1, O_2, \ldots$ of types $T_1, T_2, \ldots$ and initial values $\sigma_1, \sigma_2, \ldots$, respectively, specifies two elements:

1. Let $P_1, \ldots, P_n$ be the processes bound to ports $1, \ldots, n$ of $\mathcal{O}$, the implemented object. For each process P_i and each implementing object O_j, the implementation specifies if P_i should be bound to a port of O_j; if so, which one.

2. For each operation $op \in OP$ and $i \in N_n$, the implementation specifies a deterministic procedure $\mathcal{P}_{op,i}$. A process bound to port i of $\mathcal{O}$ executes the procedure $\mathcal{P}_{op,i}$ in order to apply the operation op on $\mathcal{O}$. The value returned by this procedure is deemed to be the response from $\mathcal{O}$. The procedure specifies how the operation op at port i of $\mathcal{O}$ should be simulated in terms of operations on the implementing objects $O_1, O_2, \ldots$

The following is the correctness condition for such an implementation: in an execution, if the history of each implementing object O_j is linearizable with respect to its type T_j and initial value σ_j, then the history of $\mathcal{O}$ is linearizable with respect to type T and initial value σ.

The implementation above is *wait-free* if each process P_i, bound to port i of $\mathcal{O}$, can complete each procedure $\mathcal{P}_{op,i}$ in a finite number of steps, regardless of the rate of progress of other processes. Since our study focuses only on implementations which are wait-free, we will use the terms "implementation" and "implement" as shorthands for "wait-free implementation" and "wait-free implement", respectively.

Let T be a type and S be a set of types. T *has an implementation from S* or, equivalently, S *implements T*, if, for all states σ of T, there is an implementation of an object of type T with initial value σ from objects whose types are in S.

Universal Types: Herlihy proved a fundamental result that there are "universal types" which can implement every other type. This result, which is the basis of all hierarchies that have been proposed, is explained below.

A type T is N-*universal* if $\{T, \texttt{register}\}$ implements every N-ported type.[7] Extending this definition to a set S of types, S is N-universal if $S \cup \{\texttt{register}\}$ implements every N-ported type. Since most synchronization tasks can be cast as types,[8] the above definition can be interpreted in informal terms as follows: if a concurrent system has at most N processes, then every synchronization task, no matter how complex, can be solved using just registers and objects of a N-universal type.

Theorem 4 (Herlihy's universality result). *The type N-consensus is N-universal.*

As a simple consequence of this theorem and the above definitions, a type T is N-universal if and only if $\{T, \texttt{register}\}$ implements N-consensus.

---

[7] It is well known that 2-register implements N-register (for any N). Thus, it is not necessary to explicitly state the number of ports of register.

[8] For example, the classical *producer-consumer* synchronization task is exactly captured by the type queue that supports *enq* and *deq* operations.

5.2 Motivation for Hierarchies

Clearly, for any type, the maximum N such that it is N-universal is a measure of its ability to support implementations. By this measure, types do differ in their abilities. For example, for all N, **register** is 1-universal but not 2-universal [CIL87, DDS87, LA87, Her91], N-**test&set** is 2-universal but not for 3-universal [LA87, Her91], and N-**compare&swap** is N-universal [Her91]. In fact, for each positive integer k, there is a type which is k-universal but not $(k + 1)$-universal [JT92]. The study of classifying types is motivated by these differences in the abilities of types. The objective is to classify types into a hierarchy so that types at higher levels are stronger, *i.e.*, have a greater ability to support implementations, than types at lower levels.

5.3 Desirable Properties of Hierarchies

A *hierarchy of types* (henceforth abbreviated as hierarchy) is a function that maps types to levels in $\{1, 2, 3, \cdots\}$. We say that a type T is at level l in hierarchy h if $h(T) = l$. Since hierarchies are just functions, any specific hierarchy is interesting only if it has "useful" properties. Such properties have been identified in [Jay93] and are stated below:

P1. If a type is not N-universal, then that type is at level $N - 1$ or lower.
P2. If a type is N-universal, then that type is at level N or higher.
P3. If T is a type and $\mathcal{S}$ is a set of types such that each type in $\mathcal{S}$ is at a lower level than T, then T has no implementation from $\mathcal{S}$.

The first property ensures that a type is not mapped to a higher level than its ability suggests, and the second property ensures that it is not mapped to a lower level than its ability suggests. The third property captures our expectation that, in a hierarchy of types, each type should be stronger than any combination of lower level types. A hierarchy with property P1 is a *wait-free hierarchy*, and a hierarchy that has properties P1 and P2 is a *tight hierarchy*. A hierarchy that has property P3 is a *robust hierarchy*.[9]

It is clear that a tight hierarchy exists and is unique: it maps each type T to the maximum N such that T is N-universal. Is there a hierarchy with properties P1 and P3? Yes, the trivial hierarchy which maps every type to level 1 satisfies P1 and P3. There is no obvious answer if our search is for a non-trivial hierarchy, *i.e.*, one that maps types to at least two different levels, that has properties

---

[9] This definition of robustness is a little different from the original definition in [Jay93] which required that no type T, which is at level N, has an implementation from lower level types *for N processes*. Since the number of ports is now a part of a type's definition, the reference to number of processes in the definition of robustness is no longer necessary. For the specific hierarchy h_m^r (to be defined later in this article), which received most attention, the two definitions are equivalent: h_m^r is robust according to the previous definition if and only if it is robust according to the present definition. However, a previous result [Jay93] that every robust wait-free hierarchy is a coarsening of h_m^r does not hold any more.

P1 and P3. The most interesting question, of course, would be to determine whether there is a hierarchy which has all three properties, that is, whether the tight hierarchy is robust.

5.4 Specific Hierarchies

We will now consider some specific hierarchies that have been studied.

Hierarchy h_1^r: Herlihy was the first to propose a hierarchy of types [Her91]. His hierarchy, which will be denoted as h_1^r, is defined as follows:

> *Definition*: For each type T, $h_1^r(T)$ is the maximum N such that N-consensus has an implementation from $\{T, \text{register}\}$, where the implementation is restricted to use only one object of type T. (There is no limit on the number of registers that may be used in the implementation.)

From Herlihy's universality result (Theorem 4) it follows that if $h_1^r(T) = N$, then T is N-universal. Thus, h_1^r is a wait-free hierarchy (*i.e.*, it has property P1). Is h_1^r tight and/or robust? Our work proves that the answer is no [Jay93]. Specifically, for all N, we exhibit an N-ported deterministic oblivious type called weak-sticky with the following property: To implement N-consensus from $\{\text{weak-sticky}, \text{register}\}$, $N - 1$ weak-sticky objects are both necessary and sufficient. This property implies that (i) $h_1^r(\text{weak-sticky}) = 2$, and (ii) weak-sticky is N-universal. From (i) and (ii) it is immediate that h_1^r is not tight. The hierarchy h_1^r is not robust because $\{\text{weak-sticky}, \text{register}\}$ implements N-consensus despite the fact that N-consensus is at level N while weak-sticky and register are only at levels 2 and 1, respectively.

Hierarchy h_m^r: Clearly, the proof of non-robustness of h_1^r has exploited the fact that, in determining the level of a type in h_1^r, we are restricted to use at most one object of that type. In fact, relaxing this restriction and allowing the use of at most k objects (for any fixed integer k), rather than one object, does not help: the resulting hierarchy would still not be tight or robust. (The proof again makes use of the above mentioned property of weak-sticky and is identical to the proof of non-robustness of h_1^r.) This motivates the following hierarchy, which will be denoted as h_m^r, in which no such resource limit is imposed.

> *Definition*: For each type T, $h_m^r(T)$ is the maximum N such that $\{T, \text{register}\}$ implements N-consensus.

(This definition is naturally extended to a set $\mathcal{S}$ of types as follows: $h_m^r(\mathcal{S})$ is the maximum N such that $\mathcal{S} \cup \{\text{register}\}$ implements N-consensus. In the names of these hierarchies, the subscript indicates whether the implementation may use only 1 or many objects of the argument type. The superscript r indicates that the implementation may use registers.)

The h_m^r hierarchy was proposed and studied in [Jay93]. Here are some of its properties:

A1. $h_m^r(T) = N$ if and only if T is N-universal but not $(N+1)$-universal. (This is a simple consequence of Herlihy's universality result.) Thus, h_m^r is (the unique) tight hierarchy.

A2. For all N, N-**consensus** is at level N. Thus, there are no empty levels in h_m^r.

A3. No N-ported type can be at a level greater than N. (This follows from a simple application of the bivalency argument [FLP85].) However, some N-ported types may be at levels less than N. For example, N-**test&set** is at level 2, no matter what N is.

Characterizing the Robustness of h_m^r: We present a proposition that states what it takes to prove that h_m^r is (or is not) robust. The following observations will be helpful in proving the proposition.

O1. Given any m-ported type T and n-ported type T', one can (easily) define a type Ω, which is $\max(m,n)$-ported, such that Ω implements each of T and T', and $\{T, T'\}$ implements Ω. The type Ω is the *composition* of T and T' [BGA94]. We can extend this to define the composition Ω of any finite set S of types such that S implements Ω, and Ω implements each type in S.

O2. Suppose that S is a finite set of two or more types such that (i) $S \cup \{\texttt{register}\}$ implements N-**consensus**, and (ii) for all $S \in S$, $\{S, \texttt{register}\}$ does not implement N-**consensus**. Then there are two types T and T' (not necessarily from S) such that neither $\{T, \texttt{register}\}$ nor $\{T', \texttt{register}\}$ implements N-**consensus**, but $\{T, T', \texttt{register}\}$ implements N-**consensus**. The proof is by the following procedure. If S has exactly two types, let these be T and T' and we are done. Otherwise, let S' be any set such that $S = S' \cup \{T'\}$ and $S' = S - \{T'\}$. If $S' \cup \{\texttt{register}\}$ does not implement N-**consensus**, let T be the composition of S'; clearly T and T' satisfy the required properties. If, on the other hand, $S' \cup \{\texttt{register}\}$ implements N-**consensus**, then repeat the above procedure with S'.

O3. If an infinite set S of types implements N-**consensus**, then a finite subset of S implements N-**consensus**. Furthermore, each object used in the implementation of an N-consensus object is accessed only a finite number of times by each process.

First note that a process accesses an implementation of a consensus object only once (subsequent accesses can blindly return the same response as the first one). Furthermore, since the implementation is wait-free, the access by a process must complete in a finite number of steps of that process. From this and König's lemma, together with the assumption that any non-determinism of the types in S is bounded,[10] it is easy to show that the implementation must use only a finite number of objects and that each such object is accessed only a finite number of times by any process.

---

[10] This means that, for each type $T = (n, OP, RES, Q, \delta)$, for all $\sigma \in Q$, $op \in OP$ and $i \in N_n$, $\delta(\sigma, op, i)$ is a finite set.

Proposition 5. *The hierarchy* h_m^r *is robust if and only if, for all types T and T', the following statement holds: If $\{T, \texttt{register}\}$ does not implement N-consensus and $\{T', \texttt{register}\}$ does not implement N-consensus, then $\{T, T', \texttt{register}\}$ does not implement N-consensus; equivalently,* $h_m^r(\{T, T'\}) = \max(h_m^r(T), h_m^r(T'))$.

Proof Suppose that neither $\{T, \texttt{register}\}$ nor $\{T', \texttt{register}\}$ implements N-consensus. Then, each of T and T' is at a lower level than N. We also know that N-consensus is at level N and $\texttt{register}$ is at level 1. Therefore, if $\{T, T', \texttt{register}\}$ implements N-consensus, it follows from the definition of robustness that h_m^r is not robust.

For the other direction, suppose that h_m^r is not robust. Then there is a set S of types and a type Ω such that Ω is at level N, each type in S is at a lower level than N, and S implements Ω. Since $h_m^r(\Omega) = N$, $\{\Omega, \texttt{register}\}$ implements N-consensus. Since S implements Ω, it follows that $S \cup \{\texttt{register}\}$ implements N-consensus. By Observation O3, for some finite subset S' of S, $S' \cup \{\texttt{register}\}$ implements N-consensus. By Observation O2, there are T and T' such that neither $\{T, \texttt{register}\}$ nor $\{T', \texttt{register}\}$ implements N-consensus, but $\{T, T', \texttt{register}\}$ implements N-consensus. □

The robustness of h_m^r was not resolved in [Jay93]. However, a property similar to the one stated in the above proposition was shown not to hold. Specifically, two types T and T' were exhibited such that neither type implements even 2-consensus, but $\{T, T'\}$ implements N-consensus [Jay93]. (One of these types is $\texttt{register}$ while the other is a novel non-deterministic oblivious type.)

Importance of Resolving the Robustness of h_m^r: We will now argue that resolving the question of whether h_m^r is robust is useful, regardless of whether the answer is yes or no. The following proposition will be helpful in this discussion.

Proposition 6. *The hierarchy h_m^r is robust if and only if, for all types T and T', the following statement holds: If neither T nor T' is N-universal, then $\{T, T'\}$ is also not N-universal.*

Proof Follows trivially from Proposition 5 and Herlihy's universality result. □

To understand the importance of robustness, consider the types N-$\texttt{test\&set}$ and N-$\texttt{fetch\&add}$. Each of these is known to be 2-universal but not 3-universal [Her91]. Based *solely* on this knowledge, can we conclude that the set $\{N\text{-}\texttt{test\&set}, N\text{-}\texttt{fetch\&add}\}$ is also not 3-universal? As the above proposition points out, if h_m^r is robust, we can indeed draw such a conclusion; otherwise we cannot. More generally, if h_m^r is robust, a set of types is N-universal if and only if the set contains a type which is N-universal. Thus, the difficult problem of computing the combined power of a set of types reduces to the simpler problem of computing the power of the individual types in the set. On the other hand, if h_m^r is not robust, a set of types could be N-universal even if no type in the set is. Thus, it opens up the possibility of implementing a strong universal type (*e.g.*, N-$\texttt{compare\&swap}$) from a set of weak types (*e.g.*, $\{N\text{-}\texttt{test\&set}, N\text{-}\texttt{fetch\&add}, \ldots\}$).

What notion of "strength" does h_m^r capture? Our motivation for studying hierarchies has been to classify types so that types at higher levels are stronger than those at lower levels. As we will now explain, the phrase "Type T is stronger than type T'" can have several interpretations, some stronger than others. We will take a close look at the interpretation that h_m^r supports and argue why this interpretation is useful.

One interpretation of "T is stronger than T'" is that we can solve a strictly larger class of problems using objects of type T than using objects of type T'. Let us call this the *strong interpretation*. For this interpretation, our expectation that each type should be stronger than every lower-level type does not hold for h_m^r. This follows from the following results:

- Herlihy and Shavit [HS93b] and Rachman [Rac94] exhibit, for all N, a $(2N+1)$-ported (non-deterministic, oblivious) type T with two properties: (i) it is at level 1 in h_m^r, and (ii) using an object of this type, a problem known as *2-set agreement* [Cha90] can be solved among $2N + 1$ processes.[11]
- The 2-set agreement problem cannot be solved among $2N+1$ processes using (any number of) N-consensus objects and registers. This was proved by Borowski and Gafni [BG93b], Herlihy and Rajsbaum [HR94] and Rachman [Rac94].

Thus, despite the fact that N-**consensus** is at level N in h_m^r, $\{N$-**consensus**, **register**$\}$ cannot solve a problem that a type at level 1 can.

A second interpretation of "T is stronger than T'" is that T is universal for a larger number of processes than T'; that is, $M > N$, where M and N are the largest integers such that T is M-universal and T' is N-universal. We call this the *weak interpretation*. Here the strength of a type is associated with the maximum number of processes for which arbitrary synchronization tasks are feasible using only objects of that type and registers. For this interpretation, from the definition of h_m^r and Herlihy's universality result, it is immediate that each type is stronger than every lower level type. Furthermore, if h_m^r is robust, then each type is stronger than any set of types from lower levels. We explain below how a comparison based on this interpretation is useful.

Imagine the designer of a multiprocessor system who must decide the type of shared objects that should be supported in hardware. For specificity, suppose that he has to choose between the types T and T'. Which should he pick? Since the purpose of shared objects is to allow multiple processes to synchronize, the more desirable type is the one which lets greater number of processes to synchronize. Unfortunately, the designer is not likely to have any knowledge of the kinds of synchronization tasks that potential applications would require processes to engage in. That being the case, the best that the designer can do is to pick the type which maximizes the number of processes among which arbitrary synchronization tasks are feasible. In other words, the preferred type is the one

---

[11] Chaudhuri defined the *k-set agreement task*: each process is initially given an input and is required to eventually decide an output such that there are no more than k distinct outputs among all processes, and each output is the input of some process.

that is universal for a larger number of processes. Thus, between types T and T', the designer will choose the one that is stronger by the weak interpretation.

5.5 Recent Results

In this section, we review some recent results and how they relate to robustness. Some of these results refer to *tasks*: a task for N processes is any problem in which each process starts with a private input value and is required to eventually decide an output value. In any run, the vector $[v_1, v_2, \ldots, v_N]$, where v_i is the input of process P_i, constitutes the *input configuration* and the vector $[d_1, d_2, \ldots, d_N]$, where d_i is the output of P_i, constitutes the *output configuration*. A task specifies a set of legal input configurations, and for each such input configuration, one or more legal output configurations [BMZ90]. For example, the (binary) *consensus task* specifies that, in any run, the input of each process must be either 0 or 1, the outputs of all processes must be the same and that the output must be the input of some process. It is easy to show that the formulation of consensus as a task and as a type are equivalent: a set S of types implements N-**consensus** if and only if there is a wait-free solution to the consensus task for N processes where processes communicate using only objects of types in S.

Work of Chandra et al. Three results from Chandra, Hadzilacos, Jayanti and Toueg [CHJT94] are described here. The first two results concern only oblivious types and hold for any of the three binding models (M1, M2 or M3) explained in Section 5.1.[12] The third result concerns non-oblivious types and it holds only for model M1.

The first result states that $(N-1)$-ported consensus objects cannot be helpful in implementing an N-ported consensus object, regardless of what other types of objects they are used with. Specifically,

Theorem 7. *Let S be any set of oblivious types (the types in S may be non-deterministic). If $S \cup \{\text{register}\}$ does not implement N-consensus then $S \cup \{N\text{-consensus}, \text{register}\}$ does not implement N-consensus. (This theorem holds for all three binding models, M1, M2 or M3.)*

For example, from our knowledge that a 10-consensus object cannot be implemented from 10-ported test&set objects and registers, we can conclude, using the above theorem, that such an implementation remains impossible even if we may additionally use 9-consensus objects. The above theorem can be easily rephrased as follows: for all oblivious types T, $\mathbf{h_m^r}(\{T, N\text{-consensus}\}) = \max(\mathbf{h_m^r}(T), N)$. In light of Proposition 5, this property is similar to the one required to establish the robustness of $\mathbf{h_m^r}$.

---

[12] The model described in [CHJT94] uses a different terminology. The results from that paper are therefore restated here using the present terminology.

Theorem 7 was used to prove the following close relationship between wait-free and t-resilient solutions to the consensus task.[13]

Theorem 8. *Let $t \geq 2$ and S be any set of oblivious types such that S includes* register *and each type in S is at least $(t + 1)$-ported (the types may be non-deterministic). Assume that processes may communicate using only objects of types in S. Consider the following two problems: (i) t-resilient consensus among N processes, and (ii) wait-free consensus among $t + 1$ processes. Each problem is solvable if and only if the other is. (This theorem holds for all three binding models, M1, M2 or M3.)*

(Lo proved that this theorem cannot be extended to hold for $t = 1$ [Lo95].)

Finally, Chandra et al. exhibit a non-oblivious non-deterministic 3-ported type called booster with the following two properties (these properties are proved for the binding model M1):

1. {booster, register} does not implement 2-consensus.
   Thus, $h_m^r(\text{booster}) = 1$.
2. {booster, register, 2-consensus} implements 3-consensus.
   Thus, $h_m^r(\{\text{booster}, 2\text{-consensus}\}) \geq 3$.

Thus, $h_m^r(\{\text{booster}, 2\text{-consensus}\}) > \max(h_m^r(\text{booster}), h_m^r(2\text{-consensus}))$. By Proposition 5, h_m^r is not robust. The following theorem summarizes this result.

Theorem 9. *If types may be non-deterministic and non-oblivious and the model of binding is M1, the hierarchy h_m^r is not robust.*

Recall that the model M1 requires that each process be bound to at most one port of any given object. Thus, in a protocol that attempts to solve consensus between two processes using booster objects, although each booster object has three ports, only two of these are bound to processes; the remaining port is unused. This feature is exploited in proving the above-mentioned impossibility of implementing 2-consensus from {booster, register}. It is interesting to know if Theorem 9 can be proved for the binding models M2 or M3.

Work of Peterson et al. To describe the results of Peterson, Bazzi and Neiger [PBN94], we need the notion of an implementation that supports no more than a fixed number of accesses by each process. An implementation is *k-limited-access* if the correctness of the implementation is guaranteed only in those executions in which no process applies more than k operations on the implemented object. (Thus, a regular implementation is ∞-limited-access.) Informally, the main result states that if a deterministic N-ported type is not strong enough to implement N-consensus, then it is weak enough to be implementable from $(N - 1)$-consensus.

---

[13] A solution for a task is t-resilient if, despite the crash of at most t processes at arbitrary points in time, the remaining processes eventually decide output values that respect the task specification.

Theorem 10. *Let T be any deterministic type with N or fewer ports (T may be oblivious or non-oblivious). Then, exactly one of the following must hold:*

1. *T implements N-consensus.*
2. *For all k, there is a k-limited-access implementation of T from $\{(N-1)\text{-consensus}, \text{register}\}$.*

(This theorem holds for the binding model M2.)

Corollary 11. *If types must be deterministic (but may be oblivious or non-oblivious) and the binding model is M2, then h_m^r is robust.*

Proof Suppose that h_m^r is not robust. By Proposition 5, there are types T and T' and a positive integer N such that neither $\{T, \text{register}\}$ nor $\{T', \text{register}\}$ implements N-consensus, and $\{T, T', \text{register}\}$ implements N-consensus.

Let $\mathcal{O}$ be an N-consensus object implemented from objects $A_1, A_2, \ldots, A_a$ of type T, objects $B_1, B_2, \ldots, B_b$ of type T', and objects $R_1, R_2, \ldots, R_r$ of type register. (That the number of implementing objects is finite follows from Observation O3 of Section 5.4.) In the following, we will refer to this implementation as $\mathcal{I}$. Let $P_1, \ldots, P_N$ be the processes bound to ports $1, \ldots, N$, respectively, of $\mathcal{O}$.

Since types T and T' may have more than N ports, each of $A_1 \ldots A_a$ and $B_1 \ldots B_b$ may have more than N ports to which processes are bound (although there are only N processes, this is possible since model M2 permits a process to bind to more than one port of an object). However, if more than N ports of A_i are bound to processes, we will show how to replace A_i, in the implementation $\mathcal{I}$, with another object A_i' of some N-ported type T_i so that the implementation remains correct and, like T, $\{T_i, \text{register}\}$ does not implement N-consensus. We define T_i by coalescing multiple ports of T into a single port, as explained below.

For clarity, we will illustrate this transformation with a specific example (generalizing this is straightforward). Suppose that A_1 has $N+1$ ports and the implementation $\mathcal{I}$ binds processes $P_1, \ldots, P_{N-1}$ to ports $1, \ldots, N-1$, respectively, of A_1, and binds P_N to ports N and $N+1$. Let T, the type of A_1, be $(N+1, OP, RES, Q, \delta)$. Define a new N-ported type $T_1 = (N, OP', RES, Q, \delta')$ as follows:

- $OP' = OP \times \{1, 2\}$.
  Intuitively, the operation $[op, 1]$ at any port i, $1 \leq i \leq N$, will have the same effect as op at port i of T. The operation $[op, 2]$ will have no effect at any of the first $N-1$ ports, but when applied at port N, it will have the same effect as op at port $N+1$ of T. This is formalized by the transition relation specified below.
- $\delta'(q, [op, 1], i) = \delta(q, op, i)$, for $1 \leq i \leq N$
  $\delta'(q, [op, 2], i) = \{(q, ack)\}$, for $1 \leq i \leq N-1$
  $\delta'(q, [op, 2], N) = \delta(q, op, N+1)$

In the implementation $\mathcal{I}$, replace A_1 with A_1' of the above defined type and bind processes $P_1, \ldots, P_N$ to ports $1, \ldots, N$, respectively, of A_1'. Each step of implementation $\mathcal{I}$ in which a process P_i $(1 \leq i \leq N-1)$ applies operation op to A_1 is simulated by letting P_i apply $[op, 1]$ to A_1'. Process P_N simulates op at port N of A_1 by applying $[op, 1]$ to A_1', and simulates op at port $N+1$ of A_1 by applying $[op, 2]$ to A_1'. It should be clear that this transformation preserves correctness. Furthermore, since $\{T, \mathtt{register}\}$ does not implement N-**consensus**, it follows that $\{T_1, \mathtt{register}\}$ does not implement N-**consensus**. The remaining objects $A_2 \ldots A_a, B_1 \ldots B_b$ are similarly replaced with objects $A_2' \ldots A_a', B_1' \ldots B_b'$ of N-ported types $T_2 \ldots T_a, T_1' \ldots T_b'$, respectively.

By Observation O3 of Section 5.4, each implementing object A_i' or B_j' is accessed by a process only a finite number of times. Let k be most number of times that any implementing object is accessed by a process. Since $\{T_i, \mathtt{register}\}$ does not implement N-**consensus**, by Theorem 10, we can obtain a k-limited-access implementation of A_i' from $(N-1)$-consensus objects and registers. Similarly, we can obtain a k-limited-access implementation of B_j' from $(N-1)$-consensus objects and registers. Since an N-consensus object was implementable using objects $A_1', A_2', \ldots, A_a'$, objects $B_1', B_2', \ldots, B_b'$, and registers $R_1, R_2, \ldots, R_r$, it follows that that an N-consensus object is implementable from $(N-1)$-consensus objects and registers. But a simple bivalency argument shows that this is impossible [JT92]. □

Work of Borowski et al. The main result of Borowski, Gafni and Afek states that any task which can be solved using objects of types at level N or less, can be solved instead using only N-consensus objects, provided that at most $2N$ processes are involved [BGA94].

Theorem 12. *Let $\mathcal{S}$ be any set of deterministic types such that each type in $\mathcal{S}$ is at level N or less in $\mathrm{h}_\mathrm{m}^\mathrm{r}$ (the types may be oblivious or non-oblivious). Let τ be any task that can be solved among $M \leq 2N$ processes using only objects whose types are in $\mathcal{S}$. Then τ can be solved among M processes using only N-consensus objects and registers. (This theorem holds for the binding model M3.)*

Corollary 13. *If types must be deterministic (but may be oblivious or non-oblivious) and the binding model is M3, then $\mathrm{h}_\mathrm{m}^\mathrm{r}$ is robust.*

Proof Suppose that $\mathrm{h}_\mathrm{m}^\mathrm{r}$ is not robust. By Proposition 5, there are types T and T' and a positive integer N such that $\mathrm{h}_\mathrm{m}^\mathrm{r}(T) \leq N$, $\mathrm{h}_\mathrm{m}^\mathrm{r}(T') \leq N$, and the consensus task among $N+1$ processes can be solved using objects of types T, T' and $\mathtt{register}$. Since N is at least 1 (no type is at a lower level than 1), $N+1 \leq 2N$. Thus, by Theorem 12, the consensus task among $N+1$ processes can be solved using only N-consensus objects. But a simple bivalency argument shows that this is impossible [JT92]. □

Interestingly, as we will now explain, Theorem 12 cannot be strengthened to hold for $M \geq 2N+1$. Herlihy and Shavit [HS93b] and Rachman [Rac94] exhibited a (non-deterministic and oblivious) type at level 1 such that, using just a single object of this type, the 2-set agreement task can be solved among three processes. Thus, if Theorem 12 holds for $M = 2N+1$, it should be possible to solve 2-set agreement among three processes using only 1-consensus objects and registers. Notice that 1-consensus objects are of no use in models M1 or M2, and, in model M3, they can be easily simulated using registers. Thus, it should be possible to solve to 2-set agreement among three processes using only registers. But this is impossible, as was proved by Borowski and Gafni [BG93a], Herlihy and Shavit [HS93a], and Saks and Zaharoglou [SZ93].

Work of Bazzi et al. Bazzi, Neiger and Peterson showed that in most protocols that implement a consensus object, the use of registers may add to the convenience of designing and comprehending the protocol, but is not essential [BNP94].

Theorem 14. *Let T be any type (oblivious or non-oblivious) such that either T is deterministic or T implements* 2-consensus. *If $\{T, \texttt{register}\}$ implements N-consensus, then T implements N-consensus. (This theorem holds for all three binding models M1, M2, or M3.)*

Thus, there is one case that this theorem does not cover, namely, when a type is non-deterministic and it does not implement 2-consensus. An earlier result by Jayanti proves that the theorem cannot be extended to that case: (for all N) there is an N-ported non-deterministic oblivious type $\texttt{DAD}(N)$ such that $\texttt{DAD}(N)$ does not implement 2-consensus, but $\{\texttt{DAD}(N), \texttt{register}\}$ implements N-consensus [Jay93].

Combining Theorem 14 with Corollaries 11 and 13, we have the following result, which applies for binding models M2 and M3: for all deterministic types T and T', if neither type implements N-consensus then $\{T, T'\}$ does not implement N-consensus. Jayanti's result, explained above, proves that this result cannot be extended to non-deterministic types, even if we restrict our attention to oblivious types [Jay93, Jay95].

Other Works: Kleinberg and Mullainathan exhibited a type with the property that, using a single object of this type, consensus can be solved among two processes but not among three processes, but using multiple objects, consensus can be solved among arbitrarily many processes [KM93]. The type **weak-sticky** exhibited by Jayanti to prove the non-robustness of h_m^r has a similar property [Jay93]. Cori and Moran prove a similar result [CM94]: they exhibit two types T and T' such that using a single object of any one type, consensus cannot be solved among more than two processes, but using two objects — one of each type — consensus can be solved among arbitrarily many processes.

5.6 Discussion and Open Problems

If we consider only deterministic types, Corollaries 11 and 13 state that h_m^r is robust for binding models M2 and M3. The robustness of h_m^r for binding model

M1 is open. Any proof that h_m^r is not robust for model M1 must involve the use of non-oblivious types. This is because, for oblivious types, the models M1 and M2 are equivalent, and therefore, by Corollary 11, h_m^r is robust for model M1.

If non-deterministic types are also included into consideration, there are no results other than Theorem 9. In particular, the robustness of h_m^r in models M2 and M3 is open. Clearly, any future proof that h_m^r is not robust will be more interesting if it only uses oblivious types. Similarly any proof of robustness will be more interesting if it applies to all types, including non-oblivious ones.

Another basic question is about the models themselves. Are all the binding models described here interesting? Are there others that we should consider? Are non-oblivious types interesting?

The hierarchy h_m^r, which is based on a type's ability to implement consensus, is interesting only because consensus is universal: any object, no matter what its type, can be implemented using only consensus objects and registers. However, a consensus object is a "one-shot" object: once processes access it and drive it to state S_0 or S_1 (see Figure 3), it cannot be of any further use. Hence, implementing a "long-lived" object, one that is repeatedly accessed by processes, typically requires an infinite number of consensus objects. This is clearly not desirable. But is there a type which is not only universal, but also has the property that bounded number of objects of this type suffice to implement an object of any type? The answer is yes: Herlihy proved that consensus-with-reset is such a type:[14] every N-ported type has an implementation from $\{N\text{-consensus-with-reset}, \text{register}\}$, where the implementation requires only a bounded number of N-consensus-with-reset objects and a bounded number of registers [Her91]. Thus, if types are to be classified according to their ability to implement arbitrary types with only bounded resources, it is appropriate to define the following new hierarchy H_m^r: for a type T, $H_m^r(T)$ is the maximum N such that $\{T, \text{register}\}$ implements N-consensus-with-reset. Robustness should be redefined to capture the requirement that an implementation must require only a bounded number of objects: a hierarchy is robust if, for all types T, it is not possible to implement an object of type T from a bounded number of objects of lower level types. Robustness and other non-trivial properties of H_m^r are interesting open questions.

Acknowledgement

I thank Vassos Hadzilacos and Sam Toueg for valuable advice on how to approach this tutorial, and Gil Neiger for his comments on Section 5.

References

[ABD95] H. Attiya, A. Bar-Noy, and D. Dolev. Sharing memory robustly in message-passing systems. *Journal of the ACM*, 42(1):124–142, January 1995.

---

[14] This type is similar to consensus, but supports an additional operation called *reset*. Applying reset puts the object in state S and returns the response *ack*. See Figure 3.

[BG93a] E. Borowsky and E. Gafni. Generalized FLP result for *t*-resilient asynchronous computations. In *Proceedings of the 25th ACM Symposium on Theory of Computing*, pages 91–100, 1993.

[BG93b] E. Borowsky and E. Gafni. The implication of the Borowski-Gafni simulation on the set consensus hierarchy. Technical Report Technical Report 930021, UCLA Computer Science Department, 1993.

[BGA94] E. Borowsky, E. Gafni, and Y. Afek. Consensus power makes (some) sense. In *Proceedings of the 13th Annual Symposium on Principles of Distributed Computing*, pages 363–372, August 1994.

[Blo87] B. Bloom. Constructing two writer atomic registers. In *Proceedings of the 6th Annual Symposium on Principles of Distributed Computing*, pages 249–259, 1987.

[BMZ90] O. Biran, S. Moran, and S. Zaks. A combinatorial characterization of the distributed 1-solvable tasks. *Journal of Algorithms*, 11:420–440, 1990.

[BNP94] R. Bazzi, G. Neiger, and G. Peterson. On the use of registers in achieving wait-free consensus. In *Proceedings of the 13th Annual Symposium on Principles of Distributed Computing*, pages 354–363, 1994.

[Cha90] S. Chaudhuri. Agreement is harder than consensus: Set consensus problems in totally asynchronous systems. In *Proceedings of the 9th Annual Symposium on Principles of Distributed Computing*, pages 311–324, 1990.

[CHJT94] T. Chandra, V. Hadzilacos, P. Jayanti, and S. Toueg. Wait-freedom vs. *t*-resiliency and and the robustness of wait-free hierarchies. In *Proceedings of the 13th Annual Symposium on Principles of Distributed Computing*, pages 334–343, 1994.

[CHP71] P.J. Courtois, F. Heymans, and D.L. Parnas. Concurrent control with readers and writers. *Communications of the ACM*, 14(10):667–668, 1971.

[CIL87] B. Chor, A. Israeli, and M. Li. On processor coordination using asynchronous hardware. In *Proceedings of the 6th ACM Symposium on Principles of Distributed Computing*, pages 86–97, August 1987.

[CM94] R. Cori and S. Moran. Exotic behavior of consensus numbers. In *Proceedings of the 8th Workshop on Distributed Algorithms, Terschelling, The Netherlands*, pages 101–115, September-October 1994. Appeared in Lecture Notes in Computer Science, Number 857, Springer-Verlag.

[DDS87] D. Dolev, C. Dwork, and L. Stockmeyer. On the minimal synchronism needed for distributed consensus. *Journal of the ACM*, 34(1):77–97, January 1987.

[FLP85] M. Fischer, N. Lynch, and M. Paterson. Impossibility of distributed consensus with one faulty process. *JACM*, 32(2):374–382, 1985.

[Her90] M. P. Herlihy. A methodology for implementing highly concurrent data structures. In *Proceedings of the 2th ACM SIGPLAN Symposium on Principles and Practice of Parallel Programming*, pages 197–206, 1990.

[Her91] M.P. Herlihy. Wait-free synchronization. *ACM TOPLAS*, 13(1):124–149, 1991.

[Her93] M. P. Herlihy. A methodology for implementing highly concurrent data objects. *ACM Transactions on Programming Languages and Systems*, 15(5):745–770, November 1993.

[HR94] M. P. Herlihy and S. Rajsbaum. Set consensus using arbitrary objects. In *Proceedings of the 13th Annual Symposium on Principles of Distributed Computing*, pages 324–333, August 1994.

[HS93a] M. P. Herlihy and N. Shavit. The asynchronous computability theorem for *t*-resilient tasks. In *Proceedings of the 25th ACM Symposium on Theory of Computing*, pages 111–120, 1993.

[HS93b] M. P. Herlihy and N. Shavit. The topological structure of asynchronous computability. Draft, October 1993.

[HW90] M.P. Herlihy and J.M. Wing. Linearizability: A correctness condition for concurrent objects. *ACM TOPLAS*, 12(3):463–492, 1990.

[IS92] A. Israeli and A. Shaham. Optimal multi-writer multi-reader atomic register. In *Proceedings of the 11th Annual Symposium on Principles of Distributed Computing*, pages 71–82, 1992.

[Jay93] P. Jayanti. On the robustness of Herlihy's hierarchy. In *Proceedings of the 12th Annual Symposium on Principles of Distributed Computing*, August 1993.

[Jay95] P. Jayanti. Solvability of consensus: composition breaks down for non-deterministic types. *SIAM Journal of Computing*, 1995. Accepted for publication.

[JT92] P. Jayanti and S. Toueg. Some results on the impossibility, universality, and decidability of consensus. In *Proceedings of the 6th Workshop on Distributed Algorithms, Haifa, Israel*, November 1992. Appeared in Lecture Notes in Computer Science, Springer-Verlag, No: 647.

[KM93] J. Kleinberg and S. Mullainathan. Resource bounds and combinations of consensus objects. In *Proceedings of the 12th Annual Symposium on Principles of Distributed Computing*, August 1993.

[LA87] M.C. Loui and H.H. Abu-Amara. Memory requirements for agreement among unreliable asynchronous processes. *Advances in computing research*, 4:163–183, 1987.

[Lam77] L. Lamport. Concurrent reading and writing. *Communications of the ACM*, 20(11):806–811, 1977.

[Lam86] L. Lamport. On interprocess communication, parts i and ii. *Distributed Computing*, 1:77–101, 1986.

[Lo95] W. Lo. More on *t*-resilience vs. wait-freedom. In *Proceedings of the 14th Annual Symposium on Principles of Distributed Computing*, August 1995.

[LT88] N. A. Lynch and M. Tuttle. An introduction to input/output automata. Technical Report MIT/LCS/TM-373, MIT, MIT Laboratory for Computer Science, 1988.

[LTV89] M. Li, J. Tromp, and P. Vitanyi. How to construct wait-free variables. In *Proceedings of the International Colloquium on Automata, Languages and Programming. Lecture Notes in Computer Science, Volume 372*, 1989.

[MS91] J.M. Mellor-Crummey and M.L. Scott. Algorithms for scalable synchronization on shared-memory multiprocessors. *ACM Transactions on Computer Systems*, 9(1):21–65, February 1991.

[New87] R. Newman-Wolfe. A protocol for wait-free, atomic, multi-reader shared variables. In *Proceedings of the 6th Annual Symposium on Principles of Distributed Computing*, pages 232–248, 1987.

[PB87] G.L. Peterson and J. Burns. Concurrent reading while writing ii: the multi-writer case. In *Proceedings of the 28th Annual Symposium on Foundations of Computer Science*, 1987.

[PBN94] G. Peterson, R. Bazzi, and G. Neiger. A gap theorem for consensus types. In *Proceedings of the 13th Annual Symposium on Principles of Distributed Computing*, pages 344–353, August 1994.

[Pet83] G. L. Peterson. Concurrent reading while writing. *ACM TOPLAS*, 5(1):56–65, 1983.

[Rac94] O. Rachman. Anomalies in the wait-free hierarchy. In *Proceedings of the 8th Workshop on Distributed Algorithms, Terschelling, The Netherlands*, pages 156–163, September-October 1994. Appeared in Lecture Notes in Computer Science, Number 857, Springer-Verlag.

[Ray86] M. Raynal. *Algorithms for mutual exclusion*. MIT Press Series in Scientific Computation, 1986. Translated from French by D. Beeson.

[SAG87] A. Singh, J. Anderson, and M. Gouda. The elusive atomic register, revisited. In *Proceedings of the 6th Annual Symposium on Principles of Distributed Computing*, pages 206–221, 1987.

[Sch88] R. Schaffer. On the correctness of atomic multi-writer registers. Technical report, TR No: MIT/LCS/TM-364, MIT Laboratory for Computer Science, 1988.

[SZ93] M. Saks and F. Zaharoglou. Wait-free k-set agreement is impossible: The topology of public knowledge. In *Proceedings of the 25th ACM Symposium on Theory of Computing*, pages 101–110, 1993.

[VA86] P. Vitanyi and B. Awerbuch. Atomic shared register access by asynchronous hardware. In *Proceedings of the 27th Annual Symposium on Foundations of Computer Science*, 1986.

[Vid88] K. Vidyasankar. Converting lamport's regular register to atomic register. *IPL*, 28:287–290, 1988.

On Real-Time and Non Real-Time Distributed Computing

G. Le Lann

INRIA - BP 105
78153 Le Chesnay Cedex, France
E-mail : Gerard.Le_Lann@inria.fr

Abstract. In this paper, taking an algorithmic viewpoint, we explore the differences existing between the class of non real-time computing problems ($\aleph\Re$) versus the class of real-time computing problems ($\Re$). We show how a problem in class $\aleph\Re$ can be transformed into its counterpart in class $\Re$. Claims of real-time behavior made for solutions to problems in class $\aleph\Re$ are examined. An example of a distributed computing problem arising in class is studied, along with its solution. It is shown why off-line strategies or scheduling algorithms that are not driven by real-time/timeliness requirements $\Re$ are incorrect for class $\Re$. Finally, a unified approach to conceiving and measuring the efficiency of solutions to problems in classes $\aleph\Re$ and $\Re$ is proposed and illustrated with a few examples.

1 INTRODUCTION

Over the last 20 years, the distributed algorithms community has spent considerable effort solving problems in the areas of serializable or linearizable concurrent computing. These problems belong to a class denoted $\aleph\Re$, the class of non real-time computing problems.

Separately, over the last 30 years, the real-time algorithms community has spent considerable effort solving scheduling problems in the area of centralized computing, considering preemptable and non-preemptable resources. Only recently has distributed computing received some attention. These problems belong to a class denoted $\Re$, the class of real-time computing problems.

In this paper, taking an algorithmic viewpoint, we embark on exploring the differences between both classes. The scope of this paper is restricted to that of deterministic algorithms. Besides intellectual interest, investigation of these issues is expected to bring the two communities closer, via the clarification of a few essential concepts. In particular, we have observed that the qualifiers "real-time" and "distributed" may not carry the same meaning in both communities. Broadly speaking, with few exceptions, the distributed algorithms community does not consider problem specifications that include real-time requirements. Conversely, the real-time algorithms community often fails to understand what is implied with considering a distributed computing problem.

The remainder of this paper is organized as follows. In section 2, we introduce the distinctive attributes of class $\Re$. In section 3, we examine claims of real-time behavior made for solutions to problems in class $\aleph\Re$. In section 4, we introduce a problem of distributed computing that belongs to class $\Re$, along with its solution. A unified approach to conceiving and measuring the efficiency of solutions to problems in both classes is proposed in section 5.

In this paper, we have purposedly put more emphasis on problems and solutions in class $\Re$, given the intended audience.

2 CLASS $\Re$ VERSUS CLASS $\aleph\Re$ PROBLEMS

Quite often, it is believed that "real-time" means "fast". For example, the distinction between "meeting specific time bounds that are specified a priori" (which is a metric-free problem) on the one hand, and "observable response times are small" (which is an implementation dependent consideration) on the other hand, does not seem to be well understood. For example, it has been recently stated that "... protocols like Isis, Horus, Transis and Totem are real-time protocols if one is concerned with real-time deadlines of minutes or tens of seconds...".

As these protocols – and the related Asynchronous Consensus problem – are reasonably well understood, it seems appropriate to use them to carry out an analysis in order to explain why statements such as the one reported above are meaningless.

We will first introduce some notations, and then present the distinctive attributes of problems in class $\Re$, before proceeding with the analysis in section 3.

2.1 Notations

Correctness Recall that, in the context of this paper, a solution is an algorithm and its associated models and proofs. The specification of any problem P comprises the following subsets :

- the specification of some assumptions, denoted λ
- the specification of the properties sought, denoted Λ.

Assumptions are equivalent to axioms in Mathematics. Essentially, assumptions cover the models considered, namely the computational models, the failure models, the models of event releases. Examples of properties of interest are safety, liveness, timeliness. Similarly, the specification of any solution A comprises the following subsets, in addition to the specification of A :

- the specification of some assumptions, denoted γ,
- the presentation of the proofs that some properties Γ hold, given γ.

Whenever a model or a set of properties x_1 dominates another model or another set of properties x_2, i.e. x_1 is more general than x_2, this will be denoted by $x_1 \supseteq x_2$, $\supseteq$ being the inclusion symbol. It is said that A solves problem P if the following correctness conditions hold :

$[cc_1]$: $\Gamma(A) \supseteq \Lambda(P)$ and $[cc_2]$: $\gamma(A) \supseteq \lambda(P)$.

For most problems, establishing correctness conditions entails the expression of feasibility conditions, denoted [fc].

A useful interpretation of these correctness conditions is as follows : with A, a system is proved to be endowed with properties that are at least equal to (as strong as) those required, assuming advance knowledge that is at most equal to (not "richer" than) that given in the exposition of P.

These conditions may seem trivial. Nevertheless, quite surprisingly, many published papers describe results that violate $[cc_1]$ or $[cc_2]$ or both. Typically, some papers explore "tradeoffs" between various solutions, and conclude with some particular decision such as A_1 is "better" than A_2, because A_1 is less "costly" than A_2, totally ignoring the fact that A_1 is less "costly" for the sole reason that A_1 is based on postulating g1, which violates $[cc_2]$ whereas A_2, assumed for A_2, does not. Such meaningless analyses are commonplace when off-line solutions are compared with on-line solutions for problems in class $\Re$.

Very often, it is useful to view the models included in λ as defining an adversary that is endowed with some bounded power. For example, the adversary contemplated with non-public concurrent data structures is more restricted than the one embodied in problems involved with public concurrent data structures [5]. Similarly, periodic or sporadic releases models characterize adversaries that are more constrained that those embodied in arbitrary event releases models.

Optimality Informally, an algorithm A is optimal for a given problem if, (i) whenever the desired properties L can hold, they do hold via A, and if, (ii) A not being able to enforce these properties, there cannot exist an algorithm that would enforce them, given λ. More precisely, a correct algorithm A is optimal for a given problem if the following optimality condition holds :

[oc]: the [fc] under which $[cc_1]$ and $[cc_2]$ hold true are necessary and sufficient.

Let us give a few examples of necessary and sufficient feasibility conditions, denoted NS[fc]. In class $\Re$, examples of NS[fc]s are, (i) those given with the proof that the centralized non-preemptive earliest-deadline-first algorithm is optimal for periodic and sporadic arrival laws, when relative deadlines are equal to periods [15], (ii) those given with the proof that the centralized D-Over algorithm is optimal for aperiodic arrival laws in the presence of overload [3].

In class $\aleph\Re$, examples of NS[fc]s are, (i) the $3t + 1$ lower bound for sustaining up to t arbitrary failures in synchronous computational models [20], (ii) the $\Diamond W$ unreliable failure detector semantics for solving the consensus problem in the presence of crash failures in asynchronous computational models [6].

2.2 The distinctive attributes of class $\Re$

What makes a problem belong to class $\Re$ rather than to class $\aleph\Re$? There is no general agreement on the answer. What follows in an attempt to clarify the issue. Two attributes seem to be necessary and sufficient.

(i) A first distinctive attribute of a real-time computing problem is the presence, in its specification, of arbitrary and individual time bounds to be met by every operation that can be performed by every process.

In the real-time computing community parlance, such time bounds are often referred to as timeliness constraints (earliest/latest deadlines for termination, relative to release times, bounded jitters, linear or non-linear functions of system's parameters, etc.). They are the expression of a property that is essential and specific to this class of problems, that of timeliness. Timeliness is a composition of a safety property (it should never be the case that specified time bounds are not met) and a liveness property (progress is mandatory). Operations performed by processes are triggered by the occurrence, also called the release, of events. Timeliness properties cannot be achieved for unbounded densities of event releases. Hence :

(ii) A second distinctive attribute of a real-time computing problem is the presence, in its specification, of an event releases model.

In the distributed algorithms community, "real-time" is sometimes equated with considering synchronous or timed transitions computational models (in contrast with considering partially synchronous or asynchronous or fair transitions computational models). We believe it is essential to understand that, whatever computational models are considered in λ, it is the presence or the absence of timeliness constraints in Λ that determines whether a problem belongs to class $\Re$ or to class $\aleph\Re$ (respectively).

According to the above, we argue that some papers, such as e.g. [2], do not address real-time algorithmic issues. The problems considered in these types of papers consist in demonstrating that some time independent safety property – such as, e.g. mutual exclusion – is achieved for some [fc] to be met by the synchronous computational model assumed. These problems are not equivalent to those where it is asked to demonstrate that specific and arbitrarily chosen timeliness constraints – such as, e.g., strict relative deadlines to be met by the competing processes – are satisfied for some [fc] to be met by the models considered in λ, namely the event releases model and the – possibly synchronous – computational model.

To summarize, the distinctive attributes of any problem in class $\Re$ are as follows :

- specification set Λ includes a subset, denoted $\Lambda_\Re$, that specifies timeliness constraints
- specification set λ includes a subset, denoted $\lambda_\Re$, that specifies an event releases model.

Real-time computing problems either are decision problems or are optimization problems. Decision problems arise whenever it required to meet $\Lambda_\Re$ while $\lambda_\Re$ is not violated. The [fc]s serve the purpose of telling whether or not a real-time computing problem is feasible. Such problems are often referred to as "hard real-time" problems. Optimization problems arise whenever it is accepted or anticipated that $\lambda_\Re$ may be violated (e.g., "overloads"). In such cases, some of the timeliness constraints specified in $\Lambda_{\aleph}$ cannot be met. Value functions are then defined for every computation. Such functions can be constants or functions of times of (computation) termination. Optimization consists in maximizing the accumulated value for every possible run – to be derived from $\lambda_{\aleph}$ – or, equivalently, to minimize a value loss (e.g., minimum regret). Such problems are often referred to as "soft real-time" problems.

3 CLASS ℵℜ AND REAL-TIME COMPUTING

3.1 The Asynchronous Consensus problem

The Asynchronous Consensus problem, denoted [AC], is in class ℵℜ. [AC] is the following problem : $\lambda \equiv$ a group of n processors, asynchronous computational model, up to f processor crashes, reliable message broadcast, processors have arbitrary initial values $\Lambda \equiv$ all correct processors eventually decide (termination); they decide on the same final value (agreement) ; that final value must be the initial value of some correct processor (non triviality).

Over the last 10 years, a great deal of research has been devoted to circumventing a famous impossibility result [11]. A significant number of papers contain descriptions of algorithms and extensions to λ aimed at showing how [AC] can become tractable. Let $\delta(\lambda)$ be the assumptions that need be made, in addition to λ, in order to solve [AC].

3.2 How not to solve [AC]

With few exceptions, published solutions exploit the idea of augmenting the original asynchronous model with physical or logical timers. For example, this is the approach followed to implement Atomic Broadcast in such systems as Isis, Horus, Transis or Totem. Atomic Broadcast is equivalent to [AC] in asynchronous models.

It is reasonably obvious that timers are of no help. Timers that would be arbitrary timers are not ruled out by the original asynchronous model. Even if $\delta(\lambda)$ = perfect timers, it has been shown that [AC] cannot be solved [9]. Therefore, approaches based on $\delta(\lambda)$ = arbitrary timers cannot solve [AC] either. The reason why such approaches fail simply is that the $\delta(\lambda)$ considered does not bring in more common knowledge than what is provided by the original l. Consequently, the impossibility result still applies fully.

The analysis of existing "solutions" reveals that two categories are considered, namely the primary-partition category and the multi-partition category. Simple adversary arguments can be developed to show that any of these "solutions" either violates the termination requirement of Λ (e.g., because of unjustified exclusions) or violates the agreement requirements of Λ (e.g., because any two partitions reach different decisions). Some "solutions" assume that some group membership service GMS is available. Thanks to GMS, [AC] is solved with no extra $\delta(\lambda)$. But this is a violation of correctness condition $[cc_2]$. In many instances, assuming GMS is tantamount to assuming that [AC] is solved, which yields circular "solutions". Furthermore, it has been demonstrated that primary-partition GMS cannot be solved in asynchronous models [7].

To summarize, [AC], or any problem equivalent to [AC], has no deterministic solution that would be based on $\delta(\lambda) =$ timers. It follows trivially that claims of "real-time behavior", even in the order of centuries, are totally unfounded.

The evidence that timer-based approaches can only solve [AC] probabilistically is being acknowledged more openly than was the case previously. Having admitted this, some scientists develop the following "argument". The behavior of any real system can only be predicted with some probability – including real-time behavior. Therefore, everything being only probabilistically true, those deterministic algorithms that solve [AC] only approximately can be considered as yielding "sufficiently good" real-time behavior. Unfortunately, this superficial argument is flawed (this is discussed further in section 4.2.6). At best, this argument is void. Indeed, the real-time problem that we are told is solved is not even defined, as specifications $\Lambda_\Re$ and λ_{Re} are not given.

3.3 How to solve [AC]

Conversely, very few papers describe provably correct solutions to [AC]. The concept of unreliable failure detectors was first introduced in [8]. It was subsequently demonstrated that the completeness and the accuracy properties that define $\Diamond W$ are the NS $\delta(\lambda)$ under which [AC] can be solved [6]. Hence, correct and optimal solutions are available.

An interesting question to ask is whether a real-time extension of [AC] could be solved with some real-time extension of $\Diamond W$. This also raises the question as whether asynchronous computational models can be considered in class $\Re$. This discussion is deferred to section 5.

Let us now examine a problem in class $\Re$ and its solution. Before doing so, we will first re-state the well-known principles of partial advance knowledge and partial common knowledge that characterize problems in distributed computing. This is felt useful mainly for the reason that we keep seeing papers aimed at solving "distributed real-time computing" problems that violate these basic principles.

4 CLASS $\Re$ AND DISTRIBUTED COMPUTING

4.1 Partial knowledge

A distinctive attribute of any problem in distributed computing is incomplete information, or partial knowledge. If we look at the classes of problems considered by the distributed algorithms community over the last 20 years, we find such computational models as synchronous, partially synchronous and asynchronous models and such failure models as crash, timing and arbitrary failures, which induce a significant amount of uncertainty w.r.t. future system runs. Hence, a first principle is that of partial advance knowledge (of future system runs). Furthermore, distributed computations have to cope with an additional source of uncertainty, that is lack of knowledge of the current system state (even if the most conservative models are assumed). Hence a second principle is that of partial common knowledge (shared by the processors).

Consider a set of processors involved in some distributed computation. At best, via some algorithm, some processors may end up sharing some common knowledge about some partial past system state. Therefore, a distributed algorithm may be viewed as the union of two algorithms, one in charge of building/maintaining some common knowledge, referred to as the dissemination algorithm, the other one in charge of acting on the system state, referred to as the decision algorithm. Let κ be a measure of the common knowledge accessible to processors, as achieved by the dissemination algorithm. Of course, κ is a (possibly complex) function of the number of the different shared partial states as well as of the number of processors sharing each partial state. Let $C(\kappa)$ be the cost of obtaining κ. Cost may be measured in various ways, e.g. a number of steps (of the dissemination algorithm). In general, C is a monotonically increasing positive function of κ. Theoretically, κ ranges between 0 (0-common knowledge) and K, the best achievable approximation of full-common knowledge.

If we look at the classes of problems considered by the real-time algorithms community over the last 30 years, we mainly find event releases models such as periodic and sporadic releases and timeliness constraints that are expressed as simple linear functions of periods (equality, very often). Furthermore, most systems considered are centralized (typically, single-processor systems or centralized multiprocessors). These models do not fit well with those considered for distributed computations. Hence the growing recognition that more general releases models should be investigated, such as aperiodic or arbitrary event releases models, as well as more general properties such as arbitrary timeliness constraints. Clearly, such models induce a significant amount of uncertainty w.r.t. future system runs. However, given the principles of partial advance knowledge and partial common knowledge, it is not at all clear that these more general releases models yield increased uncertainty compared to that resulting from considering a distributed computational model.

In the recent past, we have noticed that these more general models and objectives are sometimes perceived as being "unnecessarily complicated". It is quite surprising that such views can be taken by scientists who address real-time distributed computing issues. Indeed, these more general models and objectives reflect reality more accurately than the good old models (periodic/sporadic releases, time bounds related to periods). Note that the event releases models in $\aleph\Re$ and the timeliness constraints in $\Lambda_\Re$ are specified by the "clients" (e.g., the end users of the systems to be designed). As these systems can only start operating in the future, specifying these models and constraints is tantamount to predicting the future behavior of the system's environment. Which client would be foolish enough to pretend that every possible external event can only be released periodically or sporadically for the next 10 years of operation and that the appropriate relative deadlines must always be equal to the periods ? Such assumptions are clearly unacceptable in the case of critical applications or whenever the environment is, by nature, non-cooperative. Condition $[cc_2]$ makes it mandatory for designers to consider assumptions g that do not artificially weaken the problem under consideration. Hence, any solution to a real-time distributed computing problem that would be based on clairvoyance assumptions or, more generally, on a violation of condition $[cc_2]$, is a non-solution. Let us refine this condition.

When considering a given problem P, the related λ yields the following two bounds on κ :

- $\kappa(\lambda)$, the upper bound on κ that is accessible at cost $C(\kappa(\lambda)) = 0$;$\kappa(\lambda)$ is a measure of partial advance knowledge as embodied in λ,
- $\kappa(\lambda)$, the upper bound on κ that is achievable at some non-zero cost by a dissemination algorithm (given the models considered in λ).

For example, for problem [HRTDM] considered in section 4.2, we would have $\kappa(\lambda)$ = atomic channel state transitions ; ternary channel.

For any optimal dissemination algorithm and for any given κ, this κ is reachable at a cost that matches some lower bound, denoted $C^*(\kappa)$ Depending on the types of problems considered, it may or may not be the case that $[oc]$ is met with any algorithm A that needs $K(\lambda)$, obtained at cost $C^*(K(\lambda))$ only. This is particularly true with problems in class $\Re$. More generally, this is true with any problem where Λ embeds some "performance" objectives. On-line job assignment, with minimization of makespan, would be an example ([B et al. 92], [DP92]). Optimality is further discussed in section 5.

4.2 The Hard Real-Time Distributed Multiaccess channel problem

This problem has been selected for the purpose of demonstrating that distributed real-time computing problems cannot be solved with solutions based on off-line computations, such as precomputed schedules or scheduling algorithms based on fixed priorities. More to the point, tc standing for the timeliness constraints specified by $\Lambda_\Re$, distributed real-time computing problems can only be solved with on-line tc-driven scheduling algorithms [18].

The problem The Hard Real-Time Distributed Multiaccess channel problem, denoted [HRTDM], arises when considering a broadcast communication channel that is shared by stations for transmitting messages. A station comprises a source and a sender. Messages released by a source are queued up for transmission by the local sender. Channels considered are equivalent to multi-writer/multi-reader concurrent atomic ternary objects. More precisely, [HRTDM] is as follows :

Set $\lambda - \lambda_\Re \equiv$ Computational model :
Synchronous. In the absence of access control, a channel can enter three states, namely "idle", "busy", "jammed". A channel is "idle" when no message transmission is attempted or under way. State "busy" corresponds to exactly one

message being transmitted. State "jammed" is an undesired state, which corresponds to many messages being transmitted concurrently (garbled transmission). Over such ternary channels, stations can only observe global channel states and global channel state transitions that result from their collective behavior. The number of stations that are active at any time is unknown. The number of stations has a finite upper bound, denoted n. The channel end-to-end propagation delay is small compared to message durations.

Failure models : Crash failures and send-omission failures allowed for stations. (Receive-omission failures can be considered, although this is not done here, for the sake of conciseness). Channel state transitions are assumed to be reliably propagated along the channel. We do not require that a message being transmitted by a correct sender (channel state = "busy") be correctly delivered to every station. However, we require that an erroneous message reception be distinguished from channel state "jammed".

Set $\lambda\Re$

Message releases model : Messages released by source i, $i \in [1, n]$, belong to a set denoted $M_i = m_{i,1}, m_{i,2}, ..., m_{i,p(i)}$. Every message has a finite transmission duration. Release times of messages follow arbitrary laws. Arbitrary laws are characterized via a sliding window model, as follows. W being the size of the sliding window considered, for every i, $p(i)$ integers $x_{i,k}$ are specified, $k \in [1, p(i)]$. Integer $x_{i,k}$ is the highest number of releases of message $m_{i,k}$ that can be found in any window of size W. Indirectly, this defines, $\varphi_i = X_i/W$, the upper bound on the density of message releases from source i, with $X_i = \sum_{k=1}^{p}(i)x_{i,k}$.

Set $\Lambda - \Lambda_\Re$

Message transmissions must be mutually exclusive (a safety property). Every message must be transmitted in bounded time (a liveness property).

Set $\Lambda_\Re$

Timeliness constraints : A relative latest deadline is assigned to each message. Relative deadline of message $m_{i,k}$ is denoted $d(m_{i,k})$. Deadline values are arbitrary. Let W be $maxd(m_{i,k})$, $k \in [1, p(i)]$, over all sets M_i.

- (T) every message released by a source must be transmitted before its deadline (a timeliness property)
- (D) the distributed algorithm selected belongs to a class that dominates every other class (a dominance property).

Note that (D) is equivalent to requiring that the feasibility conditions are "close enough" to NS[fc]s.

Preliminaries First, consider sets M_i' that are derived from sets M_i, by creating $x_{i,k}$ releases of every message $m_{i,k}$, $k \in [1, p(i)]$. A scenario is any collection comprising the n sets M_i', the set of $p(i)$ relative deadlines assigned to the X_i messages in every set M_i', as well as every possible pattern of release times that satisfies bounds φ_i. Feasibility conditions can be viewed as an (algorithm dependent) oracle that answers "yes" or "no" to any such question as "is (T) satisfied with this scenario ?".

In order to prove that [HRTDM] is solved, one must prove first that (T) holds whenever the set of senders considered is presented feasible scenarios. A feasible scenario is a scenario such that there exists a schedule that achieves property (T). At this point, it is useful to consider that the feasible scenarios embodied within the exposition of [HRTDM] are those that can be generated by an all-knowing adversary – referred to as Z in the sequel – which is free to decide on when sources will release messages over the set of stations, provided that the definition of sets M'_i and the φ_i boundaries are not violated. Hence, we have no other choice left than to consider releases referred to as non-concrete releases in the real-time scheduling algorithms community. In particular, note that the sliding window-based arbitrary releases model is more general than the sporadic releases model, in that multiple messages may be released simultaneously. With this type of model, the distinction between time-triggered versus event-triggered computations [KV93] is meaningless.

Proving that (T) holds consists in devising some distributed multiaccess algorithm A which, when being used to play against Z, guarantees that every deadline is satisfied. Hence, [cc_1] translates into having to meet the following double requirement, given A, in the presence of Z, $\forall i \in [1, n]$, $\forall j \in [1, X_i]$:

- (R_1) establish the expression of a function $B(m_{i,j})$ that gives a guaranteed upper bound on response times for message $m_{i,j}$
- (R_2) verify that $B(m_{i,j}) \preceq d(m_{i,j})$ holds true.

Proving that (D) holds consists in proving that A belongs to a class of algorithms that yield bounds $B(m_{i,j})$ that are always smaller than those obtained when considering other classes.

Adversary arguments can be developed considering Z as a global adversary or considering that Z is the union of several distinct adversaries. The former approach has been used in [HLLR95] to demonstrate that [HRTDM] cannot be solved with algorithms based on decisions made (fully, partially) off-line. The latter approach consists in proceeding as follows :

- pick up a distributed algorithm A, that defines the rule of the game played (i.e. imposed to the adversary/adversaries)
- extract one station, say i, from the set of stations considered
- consider that all other stations coalesce to "defeat" i, i.e. they are an adversary Z_i against which i is playing
- [cc_2] : prove that Z_i is not "weaker" than (i.e. as unrestricted as) Z
- [cc_1] : establish $B_A(m_{i,j}, Z_i)$ and prove that the double requirement $\{R_1, R_2\}$ is met for i (in the presence of Z_i, given A).

Doing the above for every possible value of i results into establishing conditions under which (T) holds true with A in the presence of Z (which is at most as strong as $\cup_i Z_i$).

Given the communication channels considered, a very basic issue that need be solved is how to enforce mutual exclusion among senders, i.e. how to handle contention.

How to handle contention Many existing network standards or off-the-shelf products or proposals from the research community are based on contention avoidance or on contention detection-and-resolution. Representatives of the contention avoidance category are decentralized polling/round-robin or token-passing algorithms. Representatives of the contention detection-and-resolution category are carrier-sense algorithms. It is reasonably obvious that probabilistic algorithms, such as that used in Ethernet, cannot solve [HRTDM].

Other off-the-shelf products or proposals from the research community are based on Synchronous Time Division (STDMA). It is also reasonably obvious that STDMA algorithms cannot solve [HRTDM]. Such algorithms can only work with a time slotted channel. How such slots can be instantiated is a crucial issue. If a unique (central) clock is used, then the solution is not distributed, hence it is unacceptable. If multiple clocks are used (e.g., one per station), then the question arises as how do they exchange messages so as to reach and maintain mutual synchrony. Inevitably, such message exchanges are conducted via either a contention avoidance or a contention detection-and-resolution algorithm. Hence, distributed STDMA does not solve [HRTDM]. Distributed STDMA can only be a "synchronous" extension of some underlying algorithm that solves [HRTDM].

It looks like the only correct solutions belong to the class of contention avoidance algorithms. This is a well accepted view, as demonstrated by recent survey publications such as [MZ95]. It is easy to demonstrate that such a view is mistaken. Note also that ternary channels are needed for a correct functioning of contention avoidance algorithms. Whenever structural changes occur (voluntarily or because of station failures), contention is unavoidable. State "jammed" is needed.

How not to solve [HRTDM] Deterministic contention avoidance algorithms cannot solve [HRTDM]. It is easy to show that Z can defeat any algorithm belonging to this class. This is essentially due to the fact that every such algorithm is based on static decisions, i.e. scheduling decisions made off-line. Such static decisions being known to Z, Z is able to generate feasible scenarios that will never match those assumptions made for the sake of computing scheduling decisions off-line. Let us briefly review three well known examples of contention avoidance algorithms. A detailed examination of this issue can be found in [HLLR95].

(i) Decentralized polling/round-robin
Senders are served in some predetermined order, which reflects the polling sequence. Consider that Z is given n messages exactly, 1 message per station, and assume that the corresponding scenario is feasible. For example, a valid schedule would be any schedule whereby $m_{i,1}$ and $m_{r,1}$ are transmitted first (in any order). Knowing the fixed polling sequence, Z can pick up release times that will lead senders to schedule some message(s) belonging to some station(s) $k(k_i, k_r)$ between $m_{i,1}$ and $m_{r,1}$ or ahead of $m_{i,1}$ and $m_{r,1}$. Either $d(m_{i,1})$ or $d(m_{r,1})$ or both deadlines are missed.

(ii) Token-Passing with timers
The addition of individual timers to polling algorithms does not help either to

solve [HRTDM]. A timer (THT's with the Token Bus or FDDI) is an upper bound θ on the service time granted to a sender. Let be θ_q the value of the timer associated with sender h, $h \in [1, n]$, by the virtue of some off-line computation. The same adversary argument used with polling can be invoked. In fact, decentralized polling defines individual timers implicitly. Considering the same feasible scenario as above, the only valid off-line computation of timer values should be $\theta_q = 0$, $k \neq i$, $k \neq r$. This would be, of course, a ridiculous decision. More generally, being aware of the fixed qk's, Z can easily pick up release times such that deadlines are missed with feasible scenarios.

(iii) Token-Passing with fixed priorities

With this type of algorithms, some method must be applied off-line to transform deadlines into fixed priorities. Given that we must solve [HRTDM], a "good" method would consist in defining a mapping function such that "short deadlines" are translated into "high priorities" (e.g., ranging between 0 and 7, 7 the highest, in the case of ISO-OSI 8802/5). The problem is, whatever the method, unbounded starvation can be experienced by any message assigned a fixed priority that is not the highest one. For such messages, deadlines are inevitably missed. If we now concentrate on the set of messages that, at any given time, are assigned the highest priority, it is obvious that such algorithms (e.g., the Token Ring protocol) boil down to (decentralized) polling. Conclusions drawn above fully apply.

In the real-time algorithms community, significant effort has been devoted to identifying good methods for transforming deadlines into fixed priorities off-line. It might be worth mentioning that Rate-Monotonic (Deadline Monotonic as well), which is a well publicized method in certain circles, does not help either in solving [HRTDM]. The correctness and the optimality of Rate-Monotonic have been established for a preemptable processor, considering a periodic releases model and assuming that a known relation holds between message periods and message deadlines [17]. The corresponding type of adversary is much weaker than the one embodied within [HRTDM], where releases and deadlines are arbitrary. Furthermore, a channel is a distributed resource (unlike a processor) that is not preemptable (unlike the assumptions that underlly the optimality of the Monotonic methods). So called Generalized Rate Monotonic (GRM) is a method that is claimed to overcome these limitations. In particular, GRM is claimed to be applicable to distributed systems. As (unvoluntarily) demonstrated in [22], such claims are unfounded. The unsolvable problem faced with GRM is that there cannot exist a method that could be used off-line to transform the deadlines into fixed priorities, while demonstrating that the transformed problem is equivalent to [HRTDM] or without violating [cc2]. It is in fact easy to demonstrate that GRM cannot solve general distributed scheduling problems, contrary to the claims made in [22]. GRM is a typical example of an approach based on an artificially restrictive view of reality (see section 4.1).

(iv) Conclusions

Simple adversary arguments have been used to demonstrate that [HRTDM] cannot be solved with contention avoidance algorithms. Such arguments help in avoiding the conventional byzantine debates on the hypothetized "real-time properties" of polling/round-robin or token-passing algorithms. A much often used argument developed in favor of such algorithms is the following one : ¡upper bounds $B(m_{i,j})$ – see section 4.2.2 – can be computed with such deterministic algorithms ; the double requirement $\{R_1, R_2\}$, i.e. $[cc_1]$, can be met ; hence, these algorithms are "good" for solving "real-time" computing problems¿.

The fundamental flaw of this argument is that such bounds are of no value, for the reason that they may never hold true (property (T) is not enforced) or they hold true under assumptions that violate $[cc_2]$ or they are too pessimistic (property (D) is not achieved). Distributed polling/round-robin or token-passing algorithms inevitably incorporate some off-line decisions. Such decisions match only a subset of the possible scenarios. Hence, the problem is not that the double requirement $\{R_1, R_2\}$ cannot be expressed. The problem is that the corresponding oracle may respond "yes" when it should respond "no" or it will respond "no" arbitrarily often when it should respond "yes". Adversary Z as embodied within [HRTDM] is too powerful to be mastered by a contention avoidance algorithm.

Another way of explaining why contention avoidance/off-line decision algorithms cannot solve [HRTDM] is as follows : such algorithms enforce sequential scheduling decisions, each spanning a set of multiple messages pending for transmission. Once such a decision is made, it cannot be altered. It is then easy for Z to defeat such decisions. The larger the set, the easier for Z. It then becomes obvious that the ideal way of playing (and winning) against Z is by providing oneself with the possibility of making or changing scheduling decisions on a per transmitted message basis (leaving aside the question of how fast such decisions can be made).

The fact that such decisions should be deadline-driven should not come as a surprise to readers familiar with the demonstrated optimality properties of the Earliest-Deadline-First algorithm. It should then be obvious that the only algorithms that make sense are those that make scheduling decisions based on the deadline data provided on-line.

How to solve [HRTDM] The solution builds upon the demonstrated optimality of centralized non-preemptive earliest-deadline-first (NP-EDF), in the class of non-idling algorithms, in the absence of overload, for the following models :

- non-concrete periodic and sporadic message releases, relative deadlines being equal to periods [15],
- aperiodic message releases, arbitrary deadlines [12].

The detailed solution can be found in [14]. A summary is provided below.

a) Timeliness property (T) Let us first have sets M_i' sorted by increasing relative deadlines. Let $m_{i,j}$ refer to the message ranked jth in set M_i', $j \in [1, X_i]$. Let us write $X = \sum_{x=1}^{n} X_i$. Consider set $M*$, the ordered union of sets M_i'. Any message ranked g in $M*$ is some unique message ranked jth in some specific set

M_i'. Let Ψ be the bijection $g \longleftrightarrow i,j$ and let message durations be denoted by e.

A NS[fc] for centralized NP-EDF is as follows :
(G) $\forall g, 1 \preceq g \prec X : d(m_g) \succeq B(m_g)$,
with $B(m_g = \max_{h \in [g+1,X]} \{e(m_h)\} + \sum_{u=1}^{g} e(m_u)$.

Hence, conditions $[cc_1]$, $[cc_2]$ and $[oc]$ are met in the case of an ideal distributed NP-EDF scheduling algorithm, denoted I, which would always be provided with instantaneous perfect global knowledge (of the senders waiting queues) at zero cost. Trivially, we have $B_I(m_{i,j}) = B_I(m_g)$, with $i,j = \Psi(g)$. Centralized NP-EDF or I being optimal, any valid schedule that would not be EDF-ordered can be transformed into an EDF-ordered (valid) schedule [12]. Hence, for any given feasible scenario, the lower bound of the rank for any message is obtained with I. Therefore, bounds BI are the lower bounds of any real bounds that can be enforced by any real distributed scheduling algorithm. For any such algorithm, denoted A, let us write $B_A(m_{i,j}) = B_I(m_{i,j}) + b_A(m_{i,j})$, where $b_A(m_{i,j})$ is an upper bound on the additional latency due to lack of perfect global knowledge.

Hence, for any algorithm A in class $D-NP-EDF$, (G) yields the following sufficient condition under which property (T) holds : $\forall i \in [1,n]$, $\forall j \in [1, X_i]$: $B_{D-NP-EDF}(m_{i,j}) \leq d(m_{i,j})$, with

$$B_{D-NP-EDF}(m_{i,j}) = \max_{h \in [j+1, X_i]} \{e(m_h)\} + \sum_{u=1}^{j} e_u + b_{D-NP-EDF}(m_{i,j})$$

b) Dominance property (D) What follows is a sketch of the proof. Consider the class of $D-NP-EDF$ algorithms based on contention detection-and-resolution and the class of contention avoidance algorithms, denoted CA. Pick up an algorithm in each class and consider a feasible scenario for which both algorithms generate a valid schedule (property (T) holds). Let us demonstrate that, for any message m in this scenario, we have :

$$b_{D-NP-EDF}(m) \prec b_{CA}(m)$$

Any distributed algorithm is bound to create deadline inversions (which occur also in our case because a channel is a non-preemptable resource). EDF ordering being optimal, it follows that $b(m)$ is an increasing function of the number of deadline inversions. Recall that $b(m)$ is a worst-case bound and that we are assuming that (T) holds. What is the magnitude of the number of deadline inversions ? Let us introduce the notion of a deadline equivalence class, which is a time window of some duration denoted v. Any two messages whose absolute deadlines differ at most by v belong either to the same equivalence class or to two time adjacent equivalence classes. Therefore, deadline inversions can only occur among messages that have absolute deadlines within v of each other.

With $D-NP-EDF$ algorithms, which are deadline-driven, parameter v is tunable. In particular, v does not depend on n, the highest number of senders. Conversely, with CA algorithms, v is not freely tunable. The token rotation time or the polling sequence/round-robin latency, which depend on n, are lower bounds of v. Hence, except maybe for ridiculously small values of n, $v(D - NP - EDF)$ can always be chosen to be smaller than $v(CA)$. Therefore, the number of deadline inversions being smaller with D-NP-EDF algorithms, it follows that corresponding schedules are closer to ideal EDF-ordered schedules. Consequently, message ranks are closer to lower bounds (than ranks obtained with CA algorithms). This completes the demonstration.

Note that property (D) has been established without making any assumption w.r.t. the algorithm used to schedule messages in senders waiting queues when class CA is considered. This establishes that $D - NP - EDF$ algorithms always outperform CA algorithms, even if individual senders waiting queues are scheduled according to EDF.

Having demonstrated that class $D - NP - EDF$ dominates class CA when considering [HRTDM], we have demonstrated that optimal solutions cannot belong to class CA. Given that possible solutions to the (basic) contention problem belong either to the contention avoidance class or to the contention detection-and-resolution class (that of $D - NP - EDF$), we have therefore demonstrated that optimal solutions to [HRTDM] can only belong to class $D - NP - EDF$, when considering non-idling algorithms.

Ideally, beyond proving (D), condition [oc] should be proved to hold. However, proving that a distributed on-line scheduling algorithm is optimal still raises a few fundamental issues (see section 5).

c) An example DOD/CSMA-CD (Deadline Oriented Deterministic/Carrier Sense Multiple Access-Collision Detection) is an algorithm that belongs to class $D - NP - EDF$. It is a deterministic deadline driven variation of the ISO/OSI 8802/3-Ethernet standard (see [LLR93] for a more complete presentation). Deterministic deadline-driven binary tree search (called time trees) is used by DOD/CSMA-CD to implement $D - NP - EDF$. We have considered an arbitrarily devilish global adversary – referred to as Z_0 – which is allowed to release messages in a fully unrestricted manner. In other words, with Z_0, we have considered n adversaries , every such adversary being characterized as follows : $\forall i \in [1, n]$, $\forall k \neq i$, $\varphi_k = \infty$. Obviously, Z_0 dominates every possible adversary defined as per [HRTDM]. Using adversary techniques, we have established the expression of the BDOD function and given the [fc] under which (T) holds.

/subsubsectionWhere are the probabilities ? Let Z be the adversary embodied in some λ_{Re}. There are obvious differences between the following three approaches :

a) Probabilistic or randomized algorithms Worst-case behavior of adversary Z is non-deterministic. Timeliness properties are established via the expression of bounds $B_A(Z)$ that hold true with some computable probability. This probability is a function of the probability that the real future adversary matches postulated Z – the assumption coverage – as well as of the accuracy of the modelling of algorithm A. This probability depends on λ_{Re} and on the proof used to demonstrate that [cc_1] holds.

b) Deterministic algorithms Worst-case behavior of (non-deterministic) adversary Z is deterministic. As shown with [HRTDM], timeliness properties are established via the expression of bounds $B_A(Z)$ that always hold true in the presence of Z. Hence, the computable probability that such bounds hold true in the future is the assumption coverage of postulated Z. Probabilities are not involved in the modelling of A or in the proof that $[cc_1]$ holds.

c) Approximately correct algorithms With such algorithms, most often, adversary Z is not defined. Furthermore, such bounds as $B(Z)$ are not given. Hence, probabilities that $[cc_1]$ holds cannot be computed, as there is no attempt made at establishing $[cc_1]$.

5   A UNIFIED ALGORITHMIC VIEW OF BOTH CLASSES

Recall that tc stands for the timeliness constraints that appear in Λ_{Re}. It should be clear by now that only those (distributed) on-line scheduling algorithms that are tc-driven can be contemplated for solving distributed real-time computing problems. Non real-time concurrency also implies that some decision algorithm is used to break ties in the case of actual simultaneity. Therefore, such algorithms enforce particular schedules whenever necessary. However, such algorithms are not tc-driven. Nevertheless, there is no reason why one could not take a problem in class $\aleph\Re$ and augment it with specification sets Λ_{Re} and λ_{Re}, so as to transform it into a problem in class $\Re$. In fact, recent work suggests that convergence of both classes is feasible. Let us illustrate this observation with a comparison of wait-freedom and timeliness.

5.1   Wait-freedom and timeliness

In asynchronous shared-memory computational models, unbounded wait-freedom is a liveness property. Bounded wait-freedom implies that there is an upper bound $U_i(op)$ on the number of (its own) steps that some process i takes in order to complete the execution of a given operation (op). Prima faciae, the fact that $U_i(op)$ holds regardless of the behavior of other processes is disturbing in light of elementary results in queueing theory, where it is held that $U_i(op)$ depends on the amount of service that process i receives, this amount being "what is left" by the other processes. (For example, other processes being released infinitely often, $U_i(op)$ could be infinite in the absence of a fair scheduling policy).

A first observation is that waiting queues are not part of the models considered when addressing problems of wait-free linearizability. Nevertheless, the fact that processes can release one operation at a time only is a constraint on their behavior. Futhermore, even under this constraint, there must be a rule that serves to break ties whenever real concurrency occurs on an elementary object. Such a rule is a scheduling policy, which explains why such bounds as $U_i(op)$ hold. Another explanation derives from the algorithms used to enforce wait-freedom. For example, in [H88], a general construction algorithm is described whereby a general wait-free concurrent object can be built out of multiple elementary wait-free objects. One feature of the algorithm could be characterized as "limited altruism", for the reason that "fast" processes help "slow" processes to proceed, to a certain extent. For example, "fast" process i performs the operation that "slow" process j intends to perform, before process i proceeds with its own operation. This type of rule clearly is a scheduling policy. Bounds $U_i(op)$ depend on the scheduling policy considered. Therefore, scheduling policies or algorithms being implicitly or explicitly considered, the apparent contradiction vanishes.

Furthermore, this opens the way to the concept of real-time wait-free concurrent objects. The specification of such an object is the specification of a concurrent object augmented with :

- Λ_{Re}, the specification of the (arbitrary) timeliness constraints to be met by every operation (denoted d)
- λ_{Re}, the specification of the event releases model.

As with every problem in class $\Re$, one has to find a scheduling algorithm such that, under λ_{Re}, for some [fc] to be established, the following timeliness property holds :

for every process i, for every operation $(op_{i,.})$, $\exists U_i(op_{i,.}) : U_i(op_{i,.}) \preceq d_i(opi,.)$.

The "plugging" of Λ_{Re} and λ_{Re} yields the "unplugging" of the implicit/explicit (tc-independent) scheduling algorithm yielding bounded wait-freedom, to be superseded by a tc-driven on-line scheduling algorithm.

5.2 Which computational models for class $\Re$

At first sight, asynchronous computational models do not make sense when considering a problem in class R. Unbounded delays for completing elementary operations seem to be antagonistic with the goal of enforcing timeliness properties for global operations. However, if we clearly distinguish the design phase of an algorithm from its implementation phase, there is no reason to reject asynchronous models. Consider for example the (deterministic) algorithms and constructs used to build wait-free concurrent objects or to solve [AC]. Imagine that such algorithms or constructs are "immersed" in a real system that is endowed with timeliness properties, via some other algorithm(s). For example, upper bounds are proved to hold for elementary computation/communication steps. It is then possible to establish which are the timeliness properties achieved by those algorithms or constructs that were proved correct in some asynchronous model. For example, the "immersion" of $\Diamond W$ [6] in a communication system that solves [HRTDM] yields a perfect failure detector, which can be used to solve any real-time extension of problem [AC].

Of course, a similar observation applies a fortiori in the case of solutions developed for partially synchronous models. Quite systematically until now, the real-time algorithms community has considered synchronous computational models for the design phase. This a sound approach whenever assumption set λ and related [fc] cannot be violated (or whenever such violations can be ignored). However, the danger with such models is that they lead to algorithms that cannot provably keep enforcing some minimal property whenever the postulated computation/communication bounds are violated, in contrast with algorithms designed for asynchronous or partially synchronous models which, in many cases, maintain some safety property (e.g. silence rather than disagreement in the case of [AC]), would the assumption set λ be invalidated at run-time. Such concerns typically arise with critical systems.

5.3 Optimality

Not much is known yet about optimal distributed real-time scheduling. It is not even clear that we have a satisfactory definition at hand (see further). It may then be more appropriate to begin with the identification of which is the class of algorithms that necessarily contains the optimal one(s), for any given problem. This is precisely what we have accomplished with [HRTDM], in establishing the dominance property of class $D - NP - EDF$ over any other known class. Optimality within class $D - NP - EDF$ is an open issue. Idling algorithms may dominate non-idling ones. Dissemination may yield feasibility conditions closer to NS[fc]s. For example, every message transmitted (i.e. ranked first in its waiting queue) could carry the deadlines of some of the pending messages. Such a dissemination scheme may greatly reduce the likelihood of collision occurrence, which would bring bounds B closer to optimal bounds. More generally, using the notations introduced in section 4.1, one could be tempted to equate optimality with a necessary and sufficient condition for κ, denoted $\kappa*$. Any algorithm that needs $\kappa*$ only, obtained at cost $C*(\kappa*)$ would be optimal. However, the decision algorithm embedded within A must also be taken into account. The "quality" of the decisions may improve significantly with "small" increments of common knowledge (in addition to $\kappa*$).

The general issue of optimality of distributed algorithms is being addressed through various concepts and definitions that have emerged recently. Many of them resemble concepts and definitions explored in game theory. Examples are competitive analysis of on-line algorithms s explored in game theory. Examples are competitive analysis of on-line algorithms [23], competitive analysis of distributed (on-line) algorithms (e.g., [10], [1]). An early application of competitive analysis to demonstrating optimality in the case of centralized preemptive on-line scheduling, in the presence of overload, can be found in [3].

Competitive ratios are a measure of "how well" an on-line player can perform against some adversary, in worst-case conditions. Competitive ratios depend on the ratio of advance knowledge given to the player, who selects the on-line algorithm, over the knowledge given to the adversary who, knowing the algorithm selected, is able to generate those scenarios that maximize some regret function.

In the context of [HRTDM], s being the scenarios that can be generated by Z, the competitive ratio of any algorithm A with respect to timeliness is defined to be $sup_(\alpha$ bound $B(A, \sigma)/$inf bound $B(Z, \sigma)$.

Of course, Z also is a distributed player. In departure from the original definitions, we consider that Z also incurs some cost due to distribution. Z wins over A because Z can generate schedules that minimize its deadline inversions while maximizing deadline inversions experienced by A.

Another departure from the original definitions is explored in [1], where any algorithm A is evaluated against other algorithms called champions (denoted H), that are optimal for specific schedules in s and correct for every possible schedule in s. The competitive ratio of an algorithm A with respect to latency, using the notations proper to this paper, is defined to be sup_σ bound $B(A, \sigma)/inf_H$ bound $B(H, \sigma)$. Competitive latency is examined only for schedules and algorithms that are said compatible. This restriction is equivalent to considering event releases models such that no queueing phenomenon ever develops, or, stated differently, to ignoring sojourn times in waiting queues. This is reminiscent of the observation made relative to wait-free concurrent objects.

Equating optimality with best achievable competitive ratios is not entirely satisfactory, for the reason that competitive ratios are not an homogeneous measure. By this, we mean that an algorithm whose competitive ratio would match the optimal ratio could still be dominated by some other algorithm, when being presented scenarios other than worst-case.

Nevertheless, competitive analysis of distributed algorithms seems to be a promising analytical vehicle, powerful enough to explore problems in both classes $\aleph\Re$ and $\Re$ homogeneously. This view is backed by the recent explosion of papers in this area.

Acknowledgments

I would like to thank Vassos Hadzilacos and Sam Toueg for fruitful discussions on Asynchronous Consensus and on bounded wait-freedom.

References

1. M. Ajtai, J. Aspnes, C. Dwork, O. Waarts, "A theory of competitive analysis for distributed algorithms", 35th Symposium on Foundations of Computer Science, Nov. 1994, 401-411.
2. M. Abadi, L. Lamport, "An old-fashioned recipe for real-time", ACM Trans. on Programming Languages and Systems, vol. 16, 5, Sept. 1994, 1543-1571.
3. S. Baruah et al., "On the competitiveness of on-line real-time task scheduling", IEEE Real-Time Systems Symposium, Dec. 1991, 106-115.
4. Y. Bartal et al., "New algorithms for an ancient scheduling problem", 24th ACM STOC, May 1992, 51-58.
5. H. Brit, S. Moran, "Wait-freedom vs. bounded wait-freedom in public data structures", Proc. of the 13th ACM Symp. on Principles of Distributed Computing, Aug. 1994, 52-60.

6. T. Chandra, V. Hadzilacos, S. Toueg, "The weakest failure detector for solving consensus", Proc. of the 11th ACM Symp. on Principles of Distributed Computing, Aug. 1992, 147-158.

7. T. Chandra, V. Hadzilacos, S. Toueg, "Impossibility of group membership in asynchronous systems", in preparation.

8. T. Chandra, S. Toueg, "Unreliable failure detectors for asynchronous systems", Proc. of the 10th ACM Symp. on Principles of Distributed Computing, Aug. 1991, 325-340.

9. D. Dolev, C. Dwork, L. Stockmeyer, "On the minimal synchronism needed for distributed consensus", Journal of the ACM, vol. 34, 1, Jan. 1987, 77-97.

10. X. Deng, C.H. Papadimitriou, "Competitive distributed decision-making", 12th IFIP Congress (Elsevier North-Holland Pub.), vol. 1, 1992, 350-355.

11. M. Fischer, N. Lynch, M. Paterson, "Impossibility of distributed consensus with one faulty process", Journal of the ACM, vol. 32, 2, April 1985, 374-382.

12. L. George, P. Mühlethaler, N. Rivierre, "Optimality and non-preemptive real-time scheduling revisited", INRIA Research Rep. n 2516, March 1995.

13. M.P. Herlihy, "Impossibility and universality results for wait-free synchronization", Proc. of the 7th ACM Symp. on Principles of Distributed Computing, Aug. 1988, 276-290.

14. J.F. Hermant, G. Le Lann, N. Rivierre, "A general approach to real-time message scheduling over distributed broadcast channels, to appear in Proc. of the IEEE/INRIA Conf. on Emerging Technologies and Factory Automation, Oct. 1995.

15. K. Jeffay, D.F. Stanat, C.U., Martel, "On non-preemptive scheduling of periodic and sporadic tasks", IEEE Real-Time Systems Symposium, San-Antonio, Dec. 1991, 129-139.

16. H. Kopetz, P. Verissimo, "Real-time and dependability concepts", in Distributed Systems, chapter 16, S.J. Mullender Ed. (Addison-Wesley Pub.), 1993.

17. C.L. Liu, J.W. Layland, "Scheduling algorithms for multiprogramming in a hard real-time environment", Journal of the ACM, vol. 20, 1, Jan. 1973, 46-61.

18. G. Le Lann, "Scheduling in critical real-time systems : a manifesto", Third Intl. Symp. on Formal Techniques in Real-Time and Fault-Tolerant systems, Lübeck (D), Sept. 1994, Lecture Notes in Computer Science n 863 (Springer-Verlag pub.), 511-528.

19. G. Le Lann, N. Rivierre, "Real-time communication over broadcast networks : the CSMA-DCR and the DOD/CSMA-CD protocols", INRIA Research Rep. n 1863, March 1993, 35 p.

20. L. Lamport, R. Shostak, M. Pease, "The Byzantine generals problem", ACM Trans. on Programming Lang. and Syst., vol. 4, 3, July 1982, 382-401.

21. N. Malcolm, W. Zhao, "Hard real-time communication in multiple-access networks", Journal of Real-Time Systems (Klüwer Academic Pub.), vol. 8, 1, Jan. 1995, 35-77.

22. L. Sha, S.S. Sathaye, "A systematic approach to designing distributed real-time systems", IEEE Computer, Sept. 1993, 68-78.

23. D.D. Sleator, R.E. Tarjan, "Amortized efficiency of list update and paging rules", Com. of the ACM, vol. 28, 2, Feb. 1985, 202-208.

Theory and Practice in Distributed Systems

Danny Dolev[1]

Institute of Computer Science,
Hebrew University,
Givat Ram, Jerusalem
ISRAEL 91904

Abstract. Various protocols used in practical distributed systems that circumvent theoretical impossibility results have been presented. We have described similar issues that arise when one compares practical solutions to real distributed systems. Topics of interest for future research have been discussed.

The Inherent Cost of Strong-Partial View-Synchronous Communication*

Özalp Babaoğlu, Renzo Davoli, Luigi Giachini, Paolo Sabattini

Department of Computer Science, University of Bologna, 40127 Bologna (Italy)

Abstract. We examine algorithmic issues associated with view-synchronous communication (VSC) group membership in large-scale distributed systems where network partitions may result in multiple views to be active concurrently. We first derive necessary conditions on the partial order of installed views such that VSC is meaningful and solvable in the presence of partitions. We then prove that *strong-partial VSC*, which guarantees concurrent views to be disjoint, is not easier than atomic commitment. As such, all know lower bound results for atomic commitment are also lower bounds for this problem, including the impossibility of non-blocking solutions in the presence of communication failures. We discuss the practical implications of our results in constructing group communication facilities for large-scale distributed systems.

1 Introduction

An increasing number of applications with reliability and global consistency requirements are being deployed over distributed systems with extremely large geographic extent. Scientific computing, data sharing, collaborative work, finance and commerce are typical application domains with such requirements. For the application builder, large-scale distributed systems, exemplified by the Internet, present new technical challenges beyond those that are faced in local-area network environments. Most notably, the abundance of long-haul links and the sparse connectivity of the communication fabric may result in failures to provoke network partitions that are frequent and long lasting. Even in the absence of failures, asynchrony that prevents communication delays to be bounded, may lead to the formation of "virtual partitions" that are indistinguishable from real ones [28].

Process groups and group-based communication, initially conceived simply as structuring and naming mechanisms [13], have later proven to be appropriate support technologies for reliable computing in distributed systems [11]. Aspects of the paradigm that make it particularly suitable for building reliable applications include a membership service that transforms failures into view changes and a reliable multicast facility with delivery guarantees for communicating within

* This work has been supported in part by the Commission of European Communities under ESPRIT Programme Basic Research Project 6360 (BROADCAST), the Italian National Research Council and the Italian Ministry of University, Research and Technology.

the group. The abstraction is typically realized through a *view-synchronous communication (VSC) service* [9, 11, 29], which defines global ordering guarantees with respect to the set of messages delivered in response to multicasts and view changes installed in response to failures and repairs. A large number of systems have been built that incorporate various flavors of the basic ideas in a local-area network setting [9, 25, 23, 26, 24].

Recently, there have been numerous proposals advocating group-based communication as a suitable infrastructure for developing reliable applications also in large-scale distributed systems [3, 6, 16, 2, 15]. The principal issue to be addressed in refining VSC semantics to this environment has to do with group membership management. Unlike local-area network based systems, VSC in large-scale distributed systems may result in multiple views of the group to exist concurrently as a result of virtual or real partitions. One possibility is to avoid the issue of concurrent views by defining the notion of a *primary partition* such that at most one view exists at any given time [27, 31]. The resulting service is called *linear group membership* since it defines a total order among all installed views and is appropriate for applications with strict consistency requirements such as replicated data management with one-copy semantics [4].

For certain classes of applications such as collaborative work, scientific computing or weak-consistency data sharing, progress may be possible and desirable in multiple partitions. To minimize latency in such system, it is appropriate for the membership service to deliver views (even concurrent ones) to all functional components and let the application decide if progress is possible. The resulting service is called *partial group membership* in that the set of installed views defines a partial order [1, 22, 29, 6]. The final issue has to do with the composition of concurrent views. If two concurrent views are allowed to overlap arbitrarily in their composition, the service is called *weak-partial group membership* [22, 29]. If, on the other hand, concurrent views are guaranteed to be disjoint in their composition, the service is called *strong-partial group membership*. Weak-partial semantics is not of practical interest since it is impossible to guarantee VSC message delivery semantics on top of it [5]. Strong-partial semantics, on the other hand, not only may be useful in its own right, but it can also be the basis of a linear membership service.

In this paper we consider the problem of implementing a view-synchronous communication service with strong-partial semantics in large-scale distributed systems. Our contribution is severalfold. We first derive a set of conditions that are necessary for the feasibility and well-foundedness of VSC when concurrent views are possible. We then give a formal specification for the service in terms of an abstract problem, called SP-VSC, and characterize the inherent costs of solving SP-VSC. We do so by proving that the well-known atomic commitment problem (ACP) [21, 8] of distributed transactions reduces to SP-VSC in an asynchronous system. As such, all lower bound results that have been obtained for ACP are also applicable to SP-VSC. Of particular interest are results related to nonblocking solutions — in the best case, nonblocking algorithms for SP-VSC require roughly twice as much time (as measured in end-to-end message delays) than their blocking counterparts [14]; if communication failures are admitted, there exists no nonblocking algorithm for solving SP-VSC [19, 10]. Practical implications of our results for large-scale distributed systems are significant: the cost of achieving strong-partial VSC may be prohibitive given that message delays can be extremely large; nonblocking solutions are impossible since communication failures are an intrinsic characteristic of these systems.

2 System Model

The system is a collection of processes executing at potentially remote sites. Processes communicate through a message exchange service provided by the network. The network need not be fully connected and is typically quite sparse. Both processes and communication links may fail by crashing. The system is asynchronous in the sense that neither communication delays nor relative process speeds can be bounded. Processes are associated unique names drawn from a potentially-infinite domain. A process maintains the same name throughout its life as long as it does not crash. Recovery of a process after a crash is modeled by renaming it. Note, however, that other events such as view changes due to network partitions or mergers do not rename processes.

Execution of process p is modeled through a sequence of events called its *history* and denoted h_p. Histories may be infinite sequences modeling infinite executions or they may be finite in which case the last event is either *leave* or *crash* representing, respectively, termination (by leaving the group) or failure of the process. Other relevant events that may appear in process histories are $mcast(m)$, $dlvr(m)$ and $vchg(v)$ denoting multicast of message m, delivery of a multicast message m and view change installing new view v, respectively. When necessary, we add subscripts to events to denote the process at which they occur. The prefix of history h_p containing the first k events executed by process p is denoted $h_p(k)$. Without loss of generality, we assume that the first event of any history is a view change that installs the initial view for the group.

Asynchronous systems place fundamental limits on what can be achieved by distributed computations in the presence of failures [17]. The principal difficulty stems from the inability to distinguish slow processes or communication links from those that have actually failed. In order to guarantee progress despite this limitation, one possibility is to employ unreliable *failure suspectors* in asynchronous systems [12]. Such "oracles" are allowed to make mistakes but have to satisfy a set of weak requirements for them to be useful nevertheless [12, 29]. In this paper we are not interested in the technical issues regarding the specification and implementation of failure suspectors. It suffices to note that false suspicions are sufficient for the formation of virtual partitions [28], which the view-synchronous communication service has to cope with. In the next Section we define this service.

3 View-Synchronous Communication Service

A *view-synchronous communication service*, denoted as VSC, provides reliable multicast as a basic primitive for communication among a group of processes.

For the multicast primitive to be terminating in an asynchronous system with failures, VSC includes a membership service that provides consistent information in the form of *views* regarding the components of the group that are currently believed to be up and reachable. At each process, VSC delivers multicast messages and view changes (through the *dlvr(m)* and *vchg(v)* events). View changes are triggered by process crashes and recoveries, communication failures and repairs, network partitions and mergers, explicit requests to join or leave the group, and in general, through failure suspicions. For sake of simplicity, we consider VSC as applied to a single group that has already been formed and from which there are no explicit leaves.

In an asynchronous system, correctness and reachability of group members as perceived by individual processes (through their failure suspectors) may be inconsistent. It is the task of VSC to guarantee that such information is turned into consistent views through the membership service. The real utility of VSC is not in its individual components — reliable multicasts and membership service — but in their integration. Informally, VSC guarantees that sets of delivered messages are totally ordered with respect to view changes. We now give a formal definition for VSC in terms of properties that view changes and message deliveries have to satisfy.

3.1 View Changes

Views are identified through unique identifiers drawn from a potentially-infinite domain. Given a view v, the function *comp(v)* returns the composition of v as a set of process names. Note that view identifiers are sufficient to distinguish views even if they have the same composition.

At each process p, the sequence of *vchg$_p$(v)* events defines a total order among the installed views. Events at a process are said to be executed *in the view* that was most recently installed. More formally,

Definition 3.1 (Current View) *Let e_p^k denote the kth event in the history of process p. We say that event e_p^k is executed in view v, denoted view$(e_p^k) = v$, if*

$$(\exists i < k : e_p^i = vchg_p(v)) \wedge (\nexists w : vchg_p(w) \in h_p(k) - h_p(i)).$$

We next define an ordering relation among views. With respect to a single process, this order is defined by the sequence of view installation events. Globally, views are related if *some* process installs them in a particular order.

Definition 3.2 (Successor View) *Given two views v and w, view w is called the immediate successor of view v at process p, denoted $v \prec_p w$, if view$(vchg_p(w)) = v$. If there exists some process p such that $v \prec_p w$ holds, w is called the immediate successor of v and we write $v \prec w$. The relation $\prec^*$ denotes the transitive closure of $\prec$.*

It is possible for two views to be incomparable with respect to $\prec^*$, in which case they are called *concurrent*. The possibility of concurrent views is precisely the aspect of VSC that makes it suitable for large-scale systems where partitions may occur. For VSC to be useful as an application development abstraction, there have to be some global guarantees regarding the order in which views are installed by different processes, even in the presence of partitions. In particular, those processes that install two given views should order them consistently in their histories.

Property 3.1 (Partial Order) *The successor relation* $\prec^*$ *induces a partial order on the set of installed views. In other words,* $\forall v, w : (v \prec^* w) \Rightarrow (w \not\prec^* v)$.

It is typical to represent the partial order relation among views as a labeled directed acyclic graph of immediate successors as shown in Figure 1.

The composition of views that are installed by VSC should have some bearing to the state of processes and communication links. Properties on view composition for VSC can be formally defined in terms of *reachability suspectors* [5], but for our purposes, it suffices to require that no process installs a view to which it does not belong.

Property 3.2 (Self Inclusion) *Every view installed by a process includes itself. In other words,* $\forall p, v : (vchg_p(v) \in h_p) \Rightarrow (p \in comp(v))$.

3.2 Message Delivery

Processes of the group communicate with each other through the reliable multicast primitive *mcast(m)*. Ideally, VSC should guarantee that each multicast message is delivered either by all or none of the group members. To render this idea feasible in an asynchronous system, VSC integrates message delivery guarantees with view installations. To guarantee liveness, message delivery semantics can be defined only with respect to successive view installations.

Property 3.3 (Intersection) *Given a process* p *and view* v, *let* M_p^v *denote the set of messages delivered by* p *in view* v. *In other words,* $M_p^v = \{m : dlvr_p(m) \in h_p \wedge view(dlvr_p(m)) = v\}$. *All processes that survive from one view* v *to the same next view* w *must have delivered the same set of messages in view* v:

$$\forall v, w : (v \prec w) \Rightarrow (\forall p, q \in comp(v) \cap comp(w) : \quad M_p^v = M_q^v).$$

Note that for a given view v, there may be several successor views. The condition must hold for each such pair of views. Next, we require that a given multicast message be delivered (by those processes that deliver it) in a single view.

Property 3.4 (Uniqueness) *No message is delivered in more than one view:*

$$\forall m : (dlvr_p(m) \in h_p) \wedge (dlvr_q(m) \in h_q) \Rightarrow (view(dlvr_p(m)) = view(dlvr_q(m))).$$

Finally, to avoid certain degenerate solutions, we require that each message m be delivered by any given process at most once, and only if some process actually multicast m. Furthermore, correct processes always deliver their own multicasts.

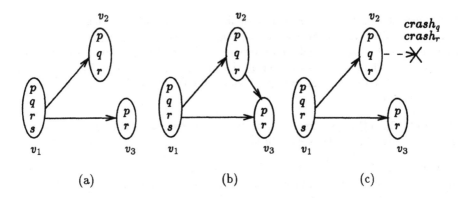

Fig. 1. (a) Process p does not install view v_2 to which it belongs. (b) A possible extension of the execution restoring the Disjoint Concurrent Views property. (c) A possible extension of the execution for which the Disjoint Concurrent Views property cannot be restored.

Property 3.5 (Integrity)

$$\forall p, (\exists e_p^k \in h_p : e_p^k = dlvr_p(m)) \Rightarrow \not\exists e_p^i \in h_p, i \neq k : e_p^i = dlvr_p(m),$$
$$\forall p, (\exists m : dlvr_p(m) \in h_p) \Rightarrow \exists q : mcast_q(m) \in h_q,$$
$$\forall p, (\exists e_p^k \in h_p : e_p^k = mcast_p(m)) \Rightarrow \exists e_p^i \in h_p, i > k : (e_p^i = dlvr_p(m) \vee e_p^i = crash_p).$$

A VSC service can now be defined in terms of the above properties for view installations and message deliveries.

Definition 3.3 (View-Synchronous Communication (VSC)) *A communication infrastructure is said to be* view synchronous *if it satisfies the Partial Order, Self Inclusion, Intersection, Uniqueness and Integrity properties for view installation and message delivery.*

4 Necessary Conditions for Strong-Partial VSC

View-synchronous communication with strong-partial semantics can be seen as a refinement of VSC that adds the following requirement to those of Definition 3.3:

Property 4.1 (Disjoint Concurrent Views) *Concurrent views have no common members in their composition. In other words, given any two views v and w,*

$$(v \not\prec^* w) \wedge (w \not\prec^* v) \Rightarrow (comp(v) \cap comp(w) = \emptyset).$$

Inclusion of this property to the definition has some subtle implications on the feasibility of VSC. We illustrate them through the following examples. First, consider the partial execution depicted in Figure 1(a). Let the prefixes of the histories for processes p, q and r be as follows:

$$h_p = vchg(v_1) \; vchg(v_3)$$
$$h_q = vchg(v_1) \; vchg(v_2)$$
$$h_r = vchg(v_1) \; vchg(v_2)$$

Note that up to this point, process p has not installed view v_2 even though $p \in comp(v_2)$. Process p has instead installed view v_3 which contains itself and process r. The question is if this execution satisfies Property 4.1 or not, but cannot be answered without knowing the future. For example, if process r extends its history to be $h_r = vchg(v_1) \; vchg(v_2) \; vchg(v_3)$ by installing view v_3 as shown in Figure 1(b), then the execution satisfies Property 4.1 since none of the three views are concurrent. If, however, the execution is extended by processes q and r crashing as shown in Figure 1(c), then views v_2 and v_3 will forever remain concurrent and no possible extension of the histories can restore Property 4.1. Since process p, at the time of installing view v_3, cannot know which of the two futures will occur, its only safe action is *not* to install any view and to terminate. This is clearly unreasonable since it leads to a system that does nothing to guarantee that a safety property is not violated.

It is easy to see that the above problem arises whenever the execution is such that there exists some installed view that is not installed by all of the correct processes in its composition. Thus, we obtain the first necessary condition for the solvability of strong-partial VSC.

Condition 4.1 (Closure of View Installation) *Any service that is live and implements strong-partial VSC must guarantee that each view is installed by all processes in its composition:*

$$\forall p, v : (vchg_p(v) \in h_p) \Rightarrow \forall q \in comp(v) : (vchg_q(v) \in h_q) \vee (crash_q \in h_q).$$

While Condition 4.1 is necessary for strong-partial VSC, it is not sufficient. Consider the example depicted in Figure 2(a). The prefixes of the process histories are as follows:

$$h_p = vchg(v_1) \; vchg(v_2) \; ? \; vchg(v_3)$$
$$h_q = vchg(v_1) \; mcast(m) \; dlvr(m) \; vchg(v_3)$$
$$h_r = vchg(v_1) \; vchg(v_2)$$

A simple verification shows that Condition 4.1 is satisfied in that each view is installed by all of the processes in its composition and the execution satisfies Property 4.1 for strong-partial. The problem, however, is that execution cannot satisfy VSC with respect to message delivery semantics.

Consider the prefix of process p's history up to the question mark. Before p installs view v_3, we are faced with the question of which messages to deliver, if any. Note that with respect to successor views v_1 and v_2, processes p and r are the only ones to survive between them. Both p and r deliver no messages in view v_1, thus Properties 3.3 and 3.4 are both satisfied. For view v_3, there are two different

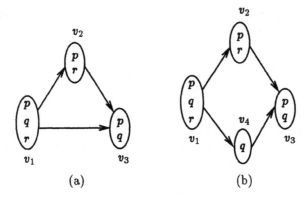

Fig. 2. (a) Execution that satisfies Closure of View Installation but not the message delivery semantics for VSC. (b) Modified execution that satisfies strong-partial VSC.

immediate predecessor views: v_1 and v_2. Process q has delivered message m in view v_1, obliging p to deliver it as well since $comp(v_1) \cap comp(v_3) = \{p, q\}$. Thus, to satisfy Property 3.3, p must deliver m before installing v_3. Doing so, however, violates Property 3.4 since m is delivered by q in view v_1 and by p in view v_2. It is easy to see that no matter how the question is resolved, it is impossible to satisfy both Properties 3.3 and 3.4.

The scenario of the above example can be easily generalized to executions where the resulting partial order on views contains multiple paths with a common process that merge to a final single view. Thus, we obtain the following result as a second necessary condition for the solvability of strong-partial VSC.

Condition 4.2 (Merge Rule) *Any service that implements strong-partial VSC must guarantee that two views with a common immediate successor do not overlap:*

$$\forall u, v, w : (u \prec w) \wedge (v \prec w) \Rightarrow comp(u) \cap comp(v) = \emptyset.$$

Figure 2(b) indicates one possible modification of the execution depicted in (a) such that Condition 4.2 is satisfied. For this execution, history of process q is

$$h_q = vchg(v_1) \; mcast(m) \; dlvr(m) \; vchg(v_4) \; vchg(v_3)$$

where it installs view v_4 before installing v_3. It is easy to show that Conditions 4.1 and 4.2 together are sufficient to guarantee Property 4.1 of strong-partial semantics.

5 The SP-VSC Problem

In light of the results from the previous Section, we define an abstract problem, called SP-VSC, that characterizes the complexity of the desired service. Conceptually, an instance of SP-VSC has to be solved every time a new view has to be installed. This action is typically triggered by a notification from the underlying failure suspector signaling a change in the group membership.

Our definition of SP-VSC as an abstract problem follows closely the formulation for the *primary-partition VSC problem* (PP-VSC) by Schiper and Sandoz [31]. Let v be the current view along the cut of system execution on which SP-VSC is defined. From each process p in the composition of v, SP-VSC takes as input the set of messages p has already delivered in view v. With this input, the goal of SP-VSC is then to output, at each process that has not crashed, the composition of the next view w and the set of additional messages that have to be delivered in view v before installing w. Formally,

SP-VSC Input: Given a cut c with current view v, for each process $p \in comp(v)$, input to SP-VSC is denoted $I\text{--}Msg_p$ and consists of the set of messages already delivered by p in view v on or before c. In other words, $I\text{--}Msg_p = \{m : (dlvr_p(m) \in h_p(c)) \land (view(dlvr_p(m)) = v)\}$ where $h_p(c)$ denotes the prefix of process p's history at cut c.

SP-VSC Output: At each process $p \in comp(v)$ that has not crashed, SP-VSC outputs $O\text{--}Msg_p$ and $O\text{--}Proc_p$ denoting the set of messages to be delivered in view v and the composition of the next view w such that $v \prec_p w$ and $comp(w) = O\text{--}Proc_p$.

The contents of the message set $O\text{--}Msg_p$ may be constructed incrementally. The outputting of $O\text{--}Msg_p$ at each process p, however, occurs as a single action. Let $POUT_p(c)$ be a predicate that is true on cut c if and only if process p has been output the set $O\text{--}Proc_p$ by cut c. Similarly, predicate $MOUT_p(c)$ is true on cut c if and only if process p has been output the set $O\text{--}Msg_p$ by cut c.

The following seven properties formally define a solution to the SP-VSC problem. The first property states that the algorithm eventually terminates at each process that has not crashed by outputting the new view composition. The second property requires that the set of messages to be delivered in view v is output before the composition of the new view. The third property enforces the new view composition to include a process at which it is output and states that view composition should not change during failure-free executions. Recall that our formulation attempts to formalize group membership with respect to failures and does not include explicit joins or leaves. In all of the following properties, free variables are assumed to be universally quantified.

SP-VSC1. Termination: $\exists c : POUT_p(c) \lor (crash_p \in h_p(c))$.

SP-VSC2. Order: $POUT_p(c) \Rightarrow MOUT_p(c)$.

SP-VSC3. Proc-Validity: $POUT_p(c) \Rightarrow (p \in O\text{--}Proc_p)$. Furthermore, in the absence of failures, $O\text{--}Proc_p = comp(v)$.

The next two properties relate the messages output by SP-VSC to the input. In particular, each message that is output must have been input by some process. Furthermore, a process cannot "undeliver" a message that it had already delivered when the problem was defined.

SP-VSC4. Msg-Validity 1: $MOUT_p(c) \Rightarrow O\text{--}Msg_p \subseteq \bigcup\limits_{q \in comp(v)} I\text{--}Msg_q$.

SP-VSC5. Msg-Validity 2: $MOUT_p(c) \Rightarrow I\text{--}Msg_p \subseteq O\text{--}Msg_p$.

The final two properties are agreement requirements on the set of messages to be delivered and the composition of the next view. At all processes that survive from the initial view into the same next view, SP-VSC must output the same message set. Any pair of processes in the initial view install next views that are either identical or disjoint in their composition.

SP-VSC6. Msg-Agreement:

$$POUT_p(c) \Rightarrow \forall q \in O\text{--}Proc_p : (POUT_q(c) \Rightarrow (O\text{--}Msg_q = O\text{--}Msg_p)).$$

SP-VSC7. Proc-Agreement:

$$(POUT_p(c) \wedge POUT_q(c)) \Rightarrow (O\text{--}Proc_p = O\text{--}Proc_q) \vee (O\text{--}Proc_p \cap O\text{--}Proc_q = \emptyset).$$

Since our lower-bound results will be based on SP-VSC, it is essential that the above formulation for the problem correctly characterizes the inherent complexity of implementing a view-synchronous communication service with strong-partial semantics. This is indeed the case as shown in the following result.

Lemma 5.1 (SP-VSC and VSC Service Equivalence) *SP-VSC and view-synchronous communication service with strong-partial semantics are equivalent problems in that given a solution for one, we can obtain a solution for the other.*

PROOF SKETCH: View-synchronous communication service with strong-partial semantics can be implemented using a solution for SP-VSC through the following construction. The multicast of a message through $mcast_p(m)$ is handled by any "best-effort" algorithm as long as the delivery of m is ensured at p. Notifications from an underlying failure suspector mechanism (for example based on periodic "pinging" and timeouts) cause an invocation of the SP-VSC algorithm in order to terminate the current view. When the algorithm terminates at process p, for each message $m \in O\text{--}Msg_p$, process p executes a $dlvr_p(m)$ event, unless it has already done so, and then it executes a view change event $vchg_p(v)$ installing view v where $comp(v) = O\text{--}Proc_p$.

Implementing SP-VSC given a view-synchronous communication service with strong-partial semantics can be achieved only after the service has been augmented with a reachability suspector that adds accuracy conditions on view composition and liveness conditions on view installation. The reader is referred to [7] for details. □

6 Reduction of Atomic Commitment to SP-VSC

We now show that the Atomic Commitment Problem (ACP) reduces to SP-VSC. In other words, any algorithm that solves SP-VSC as defined in the previous Section can be transformed to solve also ACP.

ACP arises in a distributed database context where the actions of subtransactions need to be coordinated to preserve the consistency of the data despite failures. An instance of ACP needs to be solved whenever a transaction completes. Informally, a solution to ACP must guarantee that either all or none of the processes that participated in the transaction make their changes to the data permanent.

Let T denote the set of processes that executed actions on behalf of the transaction. The input to ACP for each process $p \in T$ is a *vote$_p$* $\in \{YES, NO\}$ indicating the willing and ableness of p in making its changes permanent. A process that supplies an input value to ACP is said to *vote*. The output of ACP at each process p that has not crashed is a *decision$_p$* $\in \{COMMIT, ABORT\}$ that conveys the action to be taken. A process at which ACP outputs a value is said to *decide*. Formally, ACP can be specified through the following properties [8]:

ACP1: All processes that decide reach the same decision.

ACP2: If any process decides *COMMIT*, then all participants must have voted *YES*.

ACP3: If all processes vote *YES* and no failures occur, then all processes decide *COMMIT*.

ACP4: Each process decides at most once (that is, a decision is irreversible).

The transformation of an algorithm that solves SP-VSC into one that solves ACP consists of establishing mappings inputs and outputs of the two problems. In particular, we need to show how the input for SP-VSC can be obtained from the input for ACP and how the output of ACP can be obtained from the outputs of SP-VSC. One such transformation is shown in Figure 3.

Input: At each $p \in T$:
$$I\text{--}Msg_p = (p, vote_p)$$

Invoke SP-VSC Algorithm

Output: At process p, when SP-VSC outputs $O\text{--}Proc_p$ and $O\text{--}Msg_p$:
    if $((O\text{--}Proc_p = T) \wedge (\forall p \in T : (p, YES) \in O\text{--}Msg_p))$ then
        $decision_p = COMMIT$
    else
        $decision_p = ABORT$

Fig. 3. Transforming a solution for the SP-VSC problem into one for ACP.

Theorem 6.1 (ACP to SP-VSC Reduction) *The Atomic Commitment Problem reduces to SP-VSC.*

PROOF: We show that given an algorithm guaranteeing Properties SP-VSC1 through SP-VSC7 of Section 5, the transformation outlined in Figure 3 indeed achieves Properties ACP1–ACP4 of the atomic commitment problem. We proceed by cases.

ACP1. For contradiction, assume that for two correct processes $p \neq q$, the transformation results in $decide_p = COMMIT$ and $decide_q = ABORT$. For p to decide $COMMIT$ it must be that $O\text{-}Proc_p = T$ and $O\text{-}Msg_p$ contains YES votes from all processes in T. For q to decide $ABORT$, either $O\text{-}Proc_q \neq T$, or $O\text{-}Msg_q$ does not contain a vote for all processes in T, or it contains at least one NO vote. By SP-VSC3, $q \in O\text{-}Proc_q$ and by hypothesis, $q \in O\text{-}Proc_p$. Thus by SP-VSC7 it must be that $O\text{-}Proc_q = O\text{-}Proc_p$ since the intersection of the two sets $O\text{-}Proc_q$ and $O\text{-}Proc_p$ has at least q in common. So, it is not the case that $O\text{-}Proc_q \neq T$. By SP-VSC6, it must also be the case that $O\text{-}Msg_q = O\text{-}Msg_p$, contradicting the hypothesis.

ACP2. For contradiction, assume that for some correct process p the transformation results in $decide_p = COMMIT$ even though some process q had $vote_q = NO$. By construction, $I\text{-}Msg_q = (q, NO)$. Since p decides $COMMIT$, $O\text{-}Msg_p$ must contain YES messages from all processes in T, including q. Thus, $(q, YES) \in O\text{-}Msg_p$ and by SP-VSC4, $(q, YES) \in \bigcup_{p \in T} I\text{-}Msg_p$. In other words, there must exist some process r such that $(q, YES) \in I\text{-}Msg_r$. Since each input set $I\text{-}Msg_p$ is constructed to contain only the vote of p, and by SP-VSC5, it must be that $r = q$. This is a contradiction since by assumption, q had voted NO.

ACP3. Assume that $vote_p = YES$ for all process $p \in T$ and there are no failures during the execution of the algorithm solving SP-VSC. In other words, for all $p \in T$, we have $I\text{-}Msg_p = (p, YES)$. SP-VSC3 guarantees that $O\text{-}Proc_p = T$ for all $p \in T$ and that $p \in O\text{-}Proc_p$. Thus, by SP-VSC6 and SP-VSC7, respectively, we have $O\text{-}Msg_q = O\text{-}Msg_p$ and $O\text{-}Proc_p = O\text{-}Proc_q = T$ for all processes $p, q \in T$. SP-VSC4 and SP-VSC5 together require that $O\text{-}Msg_p = \bigcup_{q \in T} I\text{-}Msg_q$ for all $p \in T$. These define exactly the conditions for deciding $COMMIT$ at each process.

ACP4. From the structure of the transformation, it is clear that once process p assigns to its variable $decide_p$, it cannot modify it further. Thus, every process decides at most once. □

An important property of fault-tolerant distributed algorithms has to do with the ability of correct processes to make progress in the presence of failures in other components of the system. If an algorithm is such that correct processes are guaranteed to terminate their operations despite any possible failure scenario, it is called *nonblocking* [14]. An immediate consequence of the reduction in Theorem 6.1 is the following impossibility result.

Corollary 6.1 (Impossibility of Nonblocking SP-VSC) *In a system where communication or total process failures are possible, there exists no nonblocking algorithm that solves the SP-VSC problem.*

PROOF: As we have defined it, SP-VSC includes the Termination Property requiring each process p to either output both sets $O\text{-}Proc_p$ and $O\text{-}Msg_p$ or to crash. Thus, the transformation of Figure 3 would result in an algorithm that satisfies not only Properties ACP1–ACP4, but also the following

ACP5. Every correct process eventually decides

making it a nonblocking solution for ACP. It is well known that in systems that admit either the possibility of communication failures or the total failure of process, nonblocking solutions for ACP do not exist. □

7 Related Work

In [29] Schiper and Ricciardi describe how strong-partial group membership semantics can be implemented based on weak-partial semantics through the use of "process signatures." The idea is to extend process names by including a component that is derived from the identifier of the view in which they appear. In other words, processes are renamed at every view change. While, from an external observer's point of view, concurrent views are indeed disjoint with respect to these extended names, the technique is not effective for use from within the system: a process that installs a view v can never be sure which of the other processes in $comp(v)$ share v with it.

The relationship between view synchrony and atomic commitment has been studied in several other works. In [30] Schiper and Sandoz show how uniform view-synchronous multicast with a linear membership service can be used to implement atomic commitment. In [20] Guerraoui and Schiper show how both view-synchronous communication and atomic commitment can be implemented from a single primitive called *dynamic terminating multicast*. Inherent cost results for view-synchronous communication are obtained in [31] for the linear membership semantics relating it to the consensus problem.

8 Discussion

To better appreciate the results of Section 6, it is useful to consider upper bound costs in terms of concrete algorithms for ACP. Two-Phase Commit (2PC) and Three-Phase Commit (3PC) are canonical algorithms for ACP representing the blocking and nonblocking classes, respectively [10]. In the presence of communication failures, 3PC can be made nonblocking in one of the partitions; in all others it will block. In their "coordinator-based" versions, 2PC and 3PC require 3 and 5 tandem end-to-end message delays, respectively, in failure-free executions. We feel that, even if blocking were not an issue, these time costs may be unacceptable for view termination in large-scale distributed systems. Precisely the characteristics of such systems — large end-to-end message delays and frequent view changes due to virtual or real partitions — may render VSC with strong-partial semantics too expensive. It is for this reason that in the Relacs system, we implement *quasi-strong* semantics where concurrent views may overlap as long as they are proper subsets of each other. Not only is this semantics useful for application development, it can be achieved at a cost of 2 tandem end-to-end message delays without blocking even in the presence of communication failures [5].

References

1. Y. Amir, D. Dolev, S. Kramer and D. Malki. Membership Algorithms in Broadcast Domains. In *Proc. 6th Intl. Workshop on Distributed Algorithms*, A. Segall and S. Zacks (Eds.), Haifa, Israel, Lecture Notes in Computer Science, vol. 647, Springer-Verlag, November 1992, 292–312.

2. Y. Amir, D. Dolev, S. Kramer and D. Malki. Transis: A Communication Sub-System for High Availability. In *Proc. 22nd Annual International Symposium on Fault-Tolerant Computing Systems*, July 1992, 76–84.

3. Ö. Babaoğlu and A. Schiper. On Group Communication in Large-Scale Distributed Systems. In *Proc. ACM SIGOPS European Workshop*, Dagstuhl, Germany, September 1994. Also appears as *ACM SIGOPS Operating Systems Review*, 29(1):62–67, January 1995.

4. Ö. Babaoğlu, A. Bartoli and G. Dini. Replicated File Management in Large-Scale Distributed Systems. In *Proc. 8th Int. Workshop on Distributed Algorithms*, G. Tel and P. Vitányi (Eds.), Lecture Notes in Computer Science, vol. 857, Springer-Verlag, Berlin, September 1994, 1–16.

5. Ö. Babaoğlu, R. Davoli and A. Montresor. Efficient Algorithms for Group Membership and View-Synchronous Communication in the Presence of Partitions. Technical Report, Department of Computer Science, University of Bologna, April 1995.

6. Ö. Babaoğlu, R. Davoli, L.A. Giachini and M.G. Baker. Relacs: A Communication Infrastructure for Constructing Reliable Applications in Large-Scale Distributed Systems. In *Proc. 28th Hawaii International Conference on System Sciences*, Maui, January 1995, vol. II, 612–621.

7. Ö. Babaoğlu, R. Davoli, L.A. Giachini and P. Sabattini. The Inherent Cost of Strong-Partial View-Synchronous Communication. Technical Report UBLCS-95-11, Department of Computer Science, University of Bologna, April 1995.

8. Ö. Babaoğlu and S. Toueg. *Non-Blocking Atomic Commitment* In *Distributed Systems*, Sape J. Mullender (Ed.), Addison-Wesley-ACM Press, New York, 1993, 147–168.

9. K.P. Birman and T.A. Joseph. Exploiting Virtual Synchrony in Distributed Systems. In *Proc. 11th ACM Symposium on Operating Systems Principles*, 1987, 123–138.

10. P.A. Bernstein, V. Hadzilacos and N. Goodman. *Concurrency Control and Recovery in Database Systems*. Addison-Wesley, Reading, Massachusetts, 1987.

11. K. Birman, The Process Group Approach to Reliable Distributed Computing, *Communication of the ACM*, 9(12):36–53, December 1993.

12. T.D. Chandra and S. Toueg. Unreliable Failure Detectors for Asynchronous Systems. In *Proc. 10th ACM Symposium on Principles of Distributed Computing*, August 1991, 325–340.

13. D.R. Cheriton and W. Zwaenepoel. Distributed Process Groups in the V Kernel. *ACM Trans. Computer Systems*. 3(2):77–107, May 1985.

14. C. Dwork and D. Skeen. The Inherent Cost of Nonblocking Commitment. In *Proc. 2nd ACM Symposium on Principles of Distributed Computing*, Montreal, Canada, August 1983, 1–11.

15. P.E. Ezhilchelvan, R.A. Macedo and S.K. Shrivastava. Newtop: A Fault-Tolerant Group Communication Protocol. Technical Report, Computer Laboratory, University of Newcastle upon Tyne, Newcastle upon Tyne, United Kingdom, August 1994.

16. P. Felber, C. Malloth, A. Schiper and U. Wilhelm. Phoenix: A Group-Oriented Infrastructure for Large-Scale Distributed Systems. Technical Report, EPFL-LSE, Lausanne, Switzerland.

17. M.J. Fischer, N.A. Lynch, and M.S. Paterson. Impossibility of Distributed Consensus with One Faulty Process. *Journal of ACM*, 32(2):374–382, April 1985.

18. R. Friedman and R. van Renesse. Strong and Weak Virtual Synchrony in Horus. Technical Report TR95-1491, Department of Computer Science, Cornell University, Ithaca, New York, March 1995.

19. J.N. Gray. Notes on Database Operating Systems. In *Operating Systems: An Advanced Course*, R. Bayer, R.M. Graham and G. Seegmuller (Eds.), Lecture Notes in Computer Science, vol. 60, Springer-Verlag, 1978.

20. R. Guerraoui and A. Schiper. Transaction model vs. Virtual Synchrony model: bridging the gap. To appear in *Distributed Systems: From Theory to Practice*, K. Birman, F. Cristian, F. Mattern, A. Schiper (Eds.), Springer Verlag, LNCS, 1995.

21. V. Hadzilacos. On the Relationship Between the Atomic Commitment and Consensus Problems. In *Fault-Tolerant Distributed Computing*, B. Simons and A. Z. Spector (Eds.), Lecture Notes in Computer Science, vol. 448, Springer-Verlag, New York, 1990, 201–208.

22. F. Jahanian and W.M. Morgan. Strong, Weak and Hbrid Group Membership. In *Proc. 2nd IEEE Workshop on the Management of Replicated Data*, November 1992, 34–38.

23. M.F. Kaashoek and A.S. Tanenbaum. Group communication in the Amoeba distributed operating system. In *Proc. 11th International Conference on Distributed Computer Systems*, IEEE Computer Society Press, Arlington, Texas, May 1991, 222–230.

24. L. Moser, Y. Amir, P. Melliar-Smith and D. Agarwal. Extended Virtual Synchrony. In *Proc. 14th International Conference on Distributed Computing Systems*, IEEE Computer Society Press, Poland, June 1994,56–65.

25. L.L. Peterson, N.C. Bucholz, and R.D. Schlichting. Preserving and using context information in interprocess communication. *ACM Transactions on Computer Systems*, 7(3):217–246, August 1989.

26. R. van Renesse, K. Birman, R. Cooper, B. Glade and P. Stephenson. The Horus System. In *Reliable Distributed Computing with the Isis Toolkit*, K.P. Birman, R. van Renesse (Ed.), IEEE Computer Society Press, Los Alamitos, CA, 1993, 133–147.

27. A. Ricciardi and K. Birman. Using Process Groups to Implement Failure Detection in Asynchronous Environments. In *Proc. 10th ACM Symposium on Principles of Distributed Computing*, August 1991, 341–351.

28. A. Ricciardi, A. Schiper and K. Birman. Understanding Partitions and the "No Partition" Assumption. In *Proc. 4th IEEE Workshop on Future Trends of Distributed Systems*, Lisboa, September 1993.

29. A. Schiper and A. Ricciardi. Virtually-Synchronous Communication Based on a Weak Failure Suspector. In *Proc. 23rd International Symposium on Fault-Tolerant Computing Systems*, Toulouse, France, June 1993, 534–543.

30. A. Schiper and A. Sandoz. Uniform Reliable Multicast in a Virtually Synchronous Environment. In *Proc. 13th International Conference on Distributed Computing Systems*, May 1993, 501–568.

31. A. Schiper and A. Sandoz. Primary Partition "Virtually-Synchronous Communication" Harder than Consensus. In *Proc. 8th Int. Workshop on Distributed Algorithms*, G. Tel and P. Vitányi (Eds.), Lecture Notes in Computer Science, vol. 857, Springer-Verlag, Berlin, September 1994, 38–52.

Revisiting the relationship between non-blocking atomic commitment and consensus

Rachid Guerraoui

Département d'Informatique
Ecole Polytechnique Fédérale de Lausanne
1015 Lausanne, Switzerland
e-mail: guerraoui@di.epfl.ch

Abstract. This paper discusses the relationship between the *Non-Blocking Atomic Commitment problem (NB-AC)* and the Consensus problem in asynchronous systems with *unreliable* failure detectors. We first confirm that NB-AC is harder than Consensus. In contrast to Consensus, NB-AC is impossible to solve with unreliable failure detectors even with a single crash failure. We define a weaker problem than NB-AC, called *Non-Blocking Weak Atomic Commitment (NB-WAC)*, which is sufficient to solve for most practical situations. A fundamental characteristic of NB-WAC is its *reducibility* to Consensus. The previous results on solving Consensus with unreliable failure detectors apply therefore to NB-WAC. An interesting intermediate result of this reducibility is that Uniform Consensus and Consensus are equivalent problems. We show actually that any algorithm that solves Consensus with unreliable failure detectors also solves Uniform Consensus.

1 Introduction

To ensure transaction failure atomicity in a distributed system, an agreement problem must be solved among a set of participating processes. This problem, called the Atomic Commitment problem (AC), requires the participants to agree on an outcome for the transaction: *commit* or *abort*. When it is required that every correct participant eventually reach an outcome despite the failure of other participants, the problem is called *Non-Blocking Atomic Commitment (NB-AC)*. Solving this problem enables correct participants to relinquish resources (e.g locks) without waiting for crashed participants to recover. The *Two Phase Commit (2PC)* algorithm, for example, solves AC but not NB-AC [2], whereas the *Three Phase Commit* algorithm of [15] solves NB-AC in synchronous systems (when communication delays and process relative speeds are bounded). In this paper we compare the NB-AC problem and the Consensus problem in asynchronous systems with crash failures and reliable channels, augmented with (possibly unreliable) failure detectors [4].

Consensus and NB-AC are similar problems in that they are both non-blocking agreement problems. The so-called *FLP impossibility result*, which states that it is impossible to solve any non-trivial agreement in an asynchronous system even with a single crash failure, applies to both problems [7]. The starting point of this paper is the fundamental result of Chandra and Toueg [4], which states that Consensus is solvable in asynchronous systems with unreliable failure detectors. An interesting question is then whether NB-AC can also be solved in asynchronous systems with unreliable failure detectors.

The answer to this question is "No", and this is not surprising because the NB-AC problem has been considered harder than Consensus [6, 12]. However, in contrast to initial intuition, the reason NB-AC is harder than Consensus is not its *Uniform Agreement* condition[1]. We show that Uniform Consensus (Consensus + *Uniform Agreement*) and Consensus are equivalent problems with respect to unreliable failure detectors. The difficulty in solving NB-AC is actually its *Non-Triviality* condition (*commit* must be decided if all participants vote *yes*, and *there is no failure*). This condition, usually only intended to avoid trivial solutions to the problem, requires precise knowledge about failures which unreliable failure detectors cannot provide.

Nevertheless, with a weaker non-triviality condition (*commit* must be decided if all participants vote *yes*, and *no participant is ever suspected*), we define a problem weaker than NB-AC, called *NB-WAC (Non-Blocking Weak Atomic Commitment)*. This problem is in fact adequate in real-world transactional systems. A fundamental characteristic of NB-WAC is that it is *reducible* to Consensus in asynchronous systems with unreliable failure detectors, i.e. whenever Consensus is solvable, NB-WAC is also solvable. The results of Chandra and Toueg on solving Consensus with unreliable failure detectors [4] therefore apply to NB-WAC: (1) NB-WAC is solvable with failure detector class $\mathcal{S}$ if at least one participant is correct, and (2) NB-WAC is solvable with failure detector class $\Diamond\mathcal{S}$ if there is a majority of correct participants.

The rest of the paper is organized as follows. In Section 2 we describe our system model. In Section 3 we define NB-AC and show that it is harder than Consensus. In Section 4 we show that Consensus and Uniform Consensus are equivalent with respect to unreliable failure detectors. In Section 5 we define NB-WAC and show that it is reducible to Consensus. Finally, Section 6 summarizes the main contributions of this paper and discusses related and future work.

2 Model

Our model of asynchronous computation with failure detection is the one described in [4]. In the following, we only recall some informal definitions and results that are needed in this paper.

---

[1] The *Uniform Agreement* condition forbids any two participants (correct or not) to decide differently. NB-AC requires *Uniform Agreement* whereas Consensus requires only *Agreement* (two *correct* participants cannot decide differently).

2.1 Processes

We consider a distributed system composed of a finite set of processes $\Omega = \{p_1, p_2, \ldots, p_n\}$ completely connected through a set of channels. Communication is by message passing, *asynchronous* and *reliable*. Processes fail by crashing; Byzantine failures are not considered. Asynchrony means that there is no bound on communication delays or process relative speeds. A reliable channel ensures that a message, sent by a process p_i to a process p_j, is eventually received by p_j, if p_i and p_j are correct (i.e. do not crash). To simplify the presentation of the model, it is convenient to assume the existence of a discrete global clock. This is merely a fictional device inaccessible to processes. The range of clock ticks is the set of natural numbers. A history of a process $p_i \in \Omega$ is a sequence of events $h_i = e_i^0 \cdot e_i^1 \cdots e_i^k$, where e_i^k denotes an event of process p_i occured at time k. Histories of correct processes are infinite. If not infinite, the process history of p_i terminates with the event $crash_i^k$ (process p_i crashes at time k). Processes can fail at any time, and we use f to denote the number of processes that may crash. We consider systems where at least one process is correct (i.e. $f < |\Omega|$).

A failure detector is a distributed oracle which gives hints on failed processes. We consider algorithms that use failure detectors. An algorithm defines a set of *runs*, and a run of algorithm A using a failure detector $\mathcal{D}$ is a tuple $R = < F, H_{\mathcal{D}}, I, S, T >$: I is an initial configuration of A; S is an infinite sequence of events of A (made of process histories); T is a list of increasing time values indicating when each event in S occured; F is a failure pattern that denotes the set $F(t)$ of processes that have crashed at any time t; H is a failure detector history, which gives to each process p and at any time t, a (possibly false) view $H(p, t)$ of the failure pattern: $H(p, t)$ denotes a set of processes, and $q \in H(p, t)$ means that process p *suspects* process q at time t.

2.2 Failure detector classes

Failure detectors are abstractly characterized by *completeness* and *accuracy* properties [4]. Completeness characterizes the degree to which crashed processes are permanently suspected by correct processes. Accuracy restricts the false suspicions that a process can make. Two completeness properties have been identified. *Strong Completeness*, i.e. there is a time after which every process that crashes is permanently suspected by *every* correct process, and *Weak Completeness*, i.e. there is a time after which every process that crashes is permanently suspected by *some* correct process. Four accuracy properties have been identified. *Strong Accuracy*, i.e. no process is suspected before it crashes; *Weak Accuracy*, i.e. some correct process is never suspected; *Eventual Strong Accuracy*, i.e. there is a time after which correct processes are not suspected by any correct process; and *Eventual Weak Accuracy*, i.e. there is a time after which some correct process is never suspected by any correct process.

A failure detector class is a set of failure detectors characterized by the same completeness and the same accuracy properties (Figure 1). For example, the failure detector class $\mathcal{P}$ is the set of failure detectors characterized by *Strong*

Completeness	Accuracy			
	Strong	**Weak**	**◇ Strong**	**◇ Weak**
Strong	P	S	$◇P$	$◇S$
Weak	Q	W	$◇Q$	$◇W$

Fig. 1. Failure detector classes

Completeness and *Strong Accuracy*. Failure detectors characterized by *Strong Accuracy* are *reliable*: no false suspicions are made. Otherwise, they are *unreliable*. For example, failure detectors of S are *unreliable*, whereas failure detectors of P are *reliable*.

2.3 Reducibility and transformation

An algorithm A *solves* a problem B if every run of A satisfies the specification of B. A problem B is said to be *solvable with* a class C if there is an algorithm which solves B using any failure detector of C. A problem B^1 is said to be *reducible to* a problem B^2 with class C, if any algorithm that solves B^2 with C can be transformed to solve B^1 with C. If B^1 is not reducible to B^2, we say that B^1 is *harder than* B^2.

A failure detector class C^1 is said to be *stronger than* a class C^2, (written $C^1 \succeq C^2$), if there is an algorithm which, using any failure detector of C^1, can emulate a failure detector of C^2. Hence if C^1 is stronger than C^2 and a problem B is solvable with C^2, then B is solvable with C^1. The following relations are obvious: $P \succeq Q, P \succeq S, ◇P \succeq ◇Q, ◇P \succeq ◇S, S \succeq W, ◇S \succeq ◇W, Q \succeq W$, and $◇Q \succeq ◇W$. As it has been shown that any failure detector with *Weak Completeness* can be transformed into a failure detector with *Strong Completeness* [4], we also have the following relations: $Q \succeq P, ◇Q \succeq ◇P, W \succeq S$, and $◇W \succeq ◇S$. Classes S and $◇P$ are incomparable.

2.4 Consensus

In the Consensus problem (or simply Consensus), every participant *proposes* an input value, and correct participants must eventually *decide* on some common output value. Consensus is specified by the following conditions. *Agreement:* no two correct participants decide different values; *Uniform-Validity:* if a participant decides v, then v must have been proposed by some participant; *Termination:* every correct participant eventually decides. Chandra and Toueg have stated the following two fundamental results [4] :

1. If $f < |\Omega|$, Consensus is solvable with S.
2. If $f < [|\Omega|/2]$, Consensus is solvable with $◇S$.

3 NB-AC is harder than consensus

In this Section, we show that the Non-Blocking Atomic Commitment problem (or simply NB-AC) is not solvable in asynchronous systems with unreliable failure detectors. This impossibility result holds even with the assumption that at most one process may crash. Hence NB-AC is harder than Consensus.

3.1 The Non-Blocking Atomic Commitment problem

Atomic commitment problems are at the heart of distributed transactional systems. A transaction originates at a process called the Transaction Manager (abbreviated TM), which accesses data by interacting with various processes called Data Managers (abbreviated DM). The TM initially performs a *begin-transaction* operation, then various *write* and *read* operations (by translating writes and reads into messages sent to the DMs), and finally an *end-transaction* operation. To ensure the so-called *failure atomicity* property of the transaction, all DMs on which write operations have been performed, must resolve an *Atomic Commitment* problem (as part of the *end-transaction* operation). These DMs are called participants in the problem. In this paper we assume that the participants know each other, and know about the transaction [1].

The atomic commitment problem requires the participants to *reach* a common outcome for the transaction among two possible values: *commit* and *abort*. We will say that a participant *AC-decides commit* (respectively *AC-decides abort*). The write operations performed by the DMs become permanent if and only if participants AC-decide *commit*. The outcome AC-decided by a participant depends on *votes (yes* or *no)* provided by the participants. We will say that a participant *votes yes* (respectively *votes no*). Each vote reflects the ability of the participant to ensure that its data updates can be made permanent. We do not make any assumption on how votes are defined, except that they are not predetermined. For example, a participant votes *yes* if and only if no concurrency control conflict has been locally detected, and the updates have been written to stable storage. Otherwise the participant votes *no*. A participant can AC-decide *commit* only if all participants vote *yes*. In order to exclude trivial situations where participants always AC-decide *abort*, it is generally required that *commit* must be decided if all votes are *yes* and *no participant crashes* [2].

We consider the *Non-Blocking Atomic Commitment problem (NB-AC)* in which a correct participant AC-decides even if some participants have crashed. NB-AC is specified by the following conditions:

- **Uniform-Agreement:** No two participants AC-decide different outcomes.
- **Uniform-Validity:** If a participant AC-decides *commit*, then all participants have voted *yes*.
- **Termination:** Every correct participant eventually AC-decides.
- **NonTriviality:** If all participants vote *yes*, and there is no failure, then every correct participant eventually AC-decides *commit*.

Uniform-Agreement and *Uniform-Validity* are safety conditions. They ensure the *failure atomicity* property of transactions. *Termination* is a liveness condition which guarantees non-blocking. *NonTriviality* excludes trivial solutions to the problem where participants always AC-decide *abort*. This condition can be viewed as a liveness condition from the application point of view since it ensures progress (i.e. transaction commit) under reasonable expectations: when no crash and no participant votes *no*.

3.2 Impossibility of solving NB-AC

We show that NB-AC is harder than Consensus since even when assuming a single crash, unreliable failure detectors are not strong enough to solve NB-AC. We state this result for classes S and $\Diamond P$ (Sect 2.3). Hence the result holds for $\Diamond S$, $\Diamond Q$, W, and $\Diamond W$.

Theorem 1. *If $f > 0$, NB-AC cannot be solved with either $\Diamond P$ or S.*

PROOF. (By contradiction[2]). Consider an algorithm A which solves NB-AC using any failure detector of $\Diamond P$ (respectively of S). Consider a failure detector $\mathcal{D}$ of $\Diamond P$ (respectively of S) and a run $R = < F, H_{\mathcal{D}}, I, S, T >$ of A. In R, all participants vote *yes*. One participant p_1 crashes immediately without sending any message, and all other participants are correct. Consider a correct participant p_2. If p_2 does not AC-decide, then the *Termination* condition of NB-AC is violated in run R: a contradiction. Assume thus a time t at which p_2 AC-decides either (1) *commit* or (2) *abort*. Consider both cases:

1. p_2 *AC-decides commit at time t.* Consider a run $R^1 = < F, H_{\mathcal{D}}, I^1, S, T >$ of A, identical to R, except that p_1 votes *no* (instead of *yes*). Participant p_2 executes exactly the same events in R^1 as in R, and AC-decides *commit* at time t (R^1 is indistinguishable from R to p_2). As one participant (p_1) has voted *no*, the *Uniform-Validity* condition of NB-AC is violated in run R^1 of A: a contradiction.
2. p_2 *AC-decides abort at time t.* Consider a run $R^2 = < F^2, H_{\mathcal{D}}^2, I^2, S^2, T^2 >$ of A. In R^2, all participants (including p_1) are correct, and all messages from p_1 are delayed until after $t' > t$. Assume that $H_{\mathcal{D}}^2$ is identical to $H_{\mathcal{D}}$, except that after $t' > t$, $p1$ is never suspected in $H_{\mathcal{D}}^2$. As no participant crashes in R_3, then $H_{\mathcal{D}}^2$ satisfies *Strong Completeness*. Consider accuracy.
   - If $\mathcal{D}$ is of class $\Diamond P$, $H_{\mathcal{D}}$ satisfies *Eventual Strong Accuracy*, i.e. there is a time after which correct participants are never suspected by any correct participant. As $H_{\mathcal{D}}^2$ is identical to $H_{\mathcal{D}}$, except that p_1 is never suspected by any participant after time t', then $H_{\mathcal{D}}^2$ satisfies *Eventual Strong Accuracy*.
   - If $\mathcal{D}$ is of class S, $H_{\mathcal{D}}$ satisfies *Weak Accuracy*, i.e. some correct participant p_k is never suspected in $H_{\mathcal{D}}$. As $p_k \neq p_1$ (p_1 crashes in R), then p_k is never suspected in $H_{\mathcal{D}}^2$. Hence $H_{\mathcal{D}}^2$ satisfies *Weak Accuracy*.

---

[2] The intuitive idea of this proof was given in [5].

Until time t, participant p_2 executes exactly the same events as in R and AC-decides *abort* at t (until time t, R^2 is indistinguishable from R to p_2). As all participants are correct and all have voted *yes*, the *NonTriviality* condition of NB-AC is violated in run R^2 of A: a contradiction. □

By the relations between failure detector classes (Sect. 2.3), we have the following Corollary.

Corollary 1. *If $f > 0$, NB-AC is not solvable with either $\Diamond Q$, S, $\Diamond S$, or $\Diamond W$.*

Intuitively, the reason why NB-AC is not solvable with unreliable failure detectors is that NB-AC requires precise knowledge about failures. Assume a participant p which neither knows that all participants have voted *yes*, nor that some participant has voted *no*. Participant p cannot wait indefinitely for the votes of all participants (some may have crashed), and p cannot AC-decide *abort* unless it knows that some participant has crashed. An unreliable failure detector (which can make false failure suspicions) does not give p such knowledge and is therefore not strong enough to solve NB-AC. The need for precise knowledge about failures is contained in the *NonTriviality* condition of NB-AC. It is surprising that a condition which is intended to eliminate trivial solutions, introduces a significant difficulty in the problem. In Section 5, we weaken the *NonTriviality* condition, still precluding trivial solutions, so that the new weaker problem has solutions with unreliable failure detectors.

4 Uniform Consensus equivalent to Consensus

Generally, Atomic Commitment problems have been considered harder than Consensus because of their *Uniform Agreement* condition (not because of their *NonTriviality* condition) [6, 12]. Broadly speaking, Consensus enables two participants to decide differently as long as at least one of them crashes, whereas Atomic Commitment problems forbid two participants from ever AC-deciding differently (whether they crash or not).

In what follows, we show that in asynchronous systems with unreliable failure detectors, *Uniform Consensus* (Consensus + *Uniform Agreement*) is *reducible* to Consensus, i.e whenever Consensus is solvable, Uniform Consensus is also solvable.

4.1 Uniform Consensus reducible to Consensus with unreliable failure detectors

The Uniform Consensus problem is specified by the *Uniform-Validity* and *Termination* conditions of Consensus (Sect 2.4), and the following *Uniform-Agreement* condition:

– **Uniform-Agreement:** No two participants (correct or not) decide different values.

First, we consider unreliable failure detector classes characterized by *Strong Completeness*. These are $\Diamond \mathcal{P}$, $\mathcal{S}$, and $\Diamond \mathcal{S}$ (Figure 1). We will come back in Corollary 2 to classes characterized by *Weak Completeness*.

To show that Uniform Consensus is reducible to Consensus with $\Diamond \mathcal{P}$ (respectively $\mathcal{S}$, $\Diamond \mathcal{S}$), it suffices to show that, if there is an algorithm A that solves Consensus with $\Diamond \mathcal{P}$ (respectively $\mathcal{S}$, $\Diamond \mathcal{S}$), then we can construct an algorithm A' that solves Uniform Consensus with $\Diamond \mathcal{P}$ (respectively $\mathcal{S}$, $\Diamond \mathcal{S}$). Theorem 2 below is even stronger as it claims that A' is A itself.

Theorem 2. *Any algorithm that solves Consensus with $\Diamond \mathcal{P}$ (respectively $\mathcal{S}$, $\Diamond \mathcal{S}$), also solves Uniform Consensus with $\Diamond \mathcal{P}$ (respectively $\mathcal{S}$, $\Diamond \mathcal{S}$).*

PROOF. We show that there is a failure detector $\mathcal{D}$ of $\Diamond \mathcal{P}$ (respectively of $\mathcal{S}$, $\Diamond \mathcal{S}$) such that, if an algorithm A using $\mathcal{D}$ has a run R where Uniform Consensus is not solved, A has also a run R^1 where Consensus is not solved.

Consider a run $R = < F, H_{\mathcal{D}}, I, S, T >$ of A such that the *Uniform Agreement* condition is not satisfied in R but the specification of Consensus is satisfied (otherwise it is obvious that R^1 is R itself). In run R, two participants p_i and p_j decide different values and at least one of them crashes, say p_i. Assume p_i decides v_i at time t_i, and p_j decides v_j at time t_j ($v_i \neq v_j$).

Consider a run $R^1 = < F^1, H_{\mathcal{D}}^1, I^1, S^1, T^1 >$ with the same failure pattern as in R, except that p_i and p_j are correct in R^1. Delay in R^1 the reception of all messages from p_i and p_j, not received in R before $max(t_i, t_j)$, until $t' > max(t_i, t_j)$. Assume that $H_{\mathcal{D}}^1$ is identical to $H_{\mathcal{D}}$ until t', and after t' no correct participant is ever suspected and every participant that crashes is permanently suspected. It is thus clear that $H_{\mathcal{D}}^1$ satisfies *Strong Completeness, Eventual Strong Accuracy* and *Eventual Weak Accuracy*. As $H_{\mathcal{D}}^1$ does not contain any suspicion other than those in $H_{\mathcal{D}}^1$, if $H_{\mathcal{D}}$ satisfies *Weak Accuracy* (i.e. if $\mathcal{D}$ is of $\mathcal{S}$), $H_{\mathcal{D}}^1$ also satisfies *Weak Accuracy*.

In run R^1, participant p_i executes the same events as in R until time t_i, and decides v_i (until t_i, run R^1 is indistinguishable from R to p_i). Similarly, participant p_j executes the same events as in R until t_j, and decides v_j (until time t_j, R^1 is indistinguishable from R to p_j). Hence in run R^1, two correct participants decide differently. □

It is worthwhile to note that the algorithms described in [4], which was initially designed to solve Consensus with $\mathcal{S}$ and $\Diamond \mathcal{S}$, also solve Uniform Consensus.

By the relations between failure detector classes (Sect. 2.3), we have Corollary 2 below.

Corollary 2. *Uniform Consensus is reducible to Consensus with $\Diamond \mathcal{P}$ (respectively $\Diamond \mathcal{Q}$, $\mathcal{S}$, $\mathcal{W}$, $\Diamond \mathcal{S}$, $\Diamond \mathcal{W}$).*

Corollary 3 follows from the previous results on solving Consensus (Sect 2.4) and the relations between failure detector classes (Sect. 2.3).

Corollary 3. *If $f < |\Omega|$, Uniform Consensus is solvable with either $\mathcal{S}$ or $\mathcal{W}$, and if $f < [|\Omega|/2]$, Uniform Consensus is solvable with either $\diamond\mathcal{S}$, $\diamond\mathcal{P}$, $\diamond\mathcal{Q}$, $\mathcal{W}$, or $\diamond\mathcal{W}$.*

4.2 Uniform Consensus versus Consensus with reliable failure detectors

In this section we show that Theorem 2 does not hold with $\mathcal{P}$ (hence it does not hold with $\mathcal{Q}$).[3] We give an algorithm A that solves Consensus with any failure detector of $\mathcal{P}$, but there is a failure detector $\mathcal{D}$ of $\mathcal{P}$, such that A does not solve Uniform Consensus using $\mathcal{D}$. The algorithm is described by the function $consensus(v_i)$ in Figure 2, called by every participant p_i, where v_i represents the input value *proposed* by p_i. Function *consensus()* terminates by the execution of a "**return** *outcome*" statement, where *outcome* is the decision value (line 8): when p_i executes **return** *outcome*, p_i decides *outcome*. Participant p_i is informed by its local failure detector module, $\mathcal{D}_i$, of failure suspicions: the notation $p_j \in \mathcal{D}_i$ (line 3) indicates that p_i suspects p_j.

```
    function consensus(v_i)
1       j:=1 ;
2       while j < i
3           wait until [received (p_j, v_j, decide) or p_j ∈ D_i] ;
4               if received (p_j, v_j, decide) then
5                   v_i:=v_j ;
6           j:=j + 1 ;
7       send (p_i, v_i, decide) to all ;
8       return v_i ;
```

Fig. 2. An algorithm which solves Consensus but not Uniform Consensus

The basic idea of the algorithm is the following. Participant p_1 immediately sends the decision message $(p_1, v_1, decide)$ (line 7) (bypassing lines 2-6), and decides v_1 (line 8). If p_2 does not suspect p_1 before it receives $(p_1, v_1, decide)$, then p_2 adopts v_1 (line 5). Then p_2 sends $(p_2, v_2, decide)$ $(v_1 = v_2)$ to all (line 7), and decides v_1 (as did p_1) (line 8). Participant p_3 waits until it receives $(p_1, v_1, decide)$ or it suspects p_1, and it receives $(p_2, v_2, decide)$ or it suspects p_2. In the case where p_3 receives both messages and $v_1 \neq v_2$, p_3 adopts v_2. More generally, participants decide on the input value proposed by the participant p_k, such that k is the smallest index among participants that are never suspected.

---

[3] Note that this does not mean that Uniform Consensus is not reducible to Consensus.

Theorem 3.1. *The algorithm in Figure 2 solves Consensus with* $\mathcal{P}$.

PROOF. We show that the three conditions of Consensus are satisfied.

1. *Agreement.* Assume that a correct participant p_i decides v. As p_i is correct, then by the *Strong Accuracy* property of $\mathcal{D}$, no participant suspects p_i. Since p_i must have sent its decision message $(p_i, v, decide)$ (line 7) before deciding (line 8), then by the reliable channels assumption, every correct participant receives $(p_i, v, decide)$. Hence every participant p_k such that $i < k$ must have received $(p_i, v, decide)$ (line 4) before deciding. Thus p_k decides v (line 5).
2. *Validity.* Every outcome decided by some participant is, by construction, an input proposed by some participant (line 1).
3. *Termination.* We show by induction on i that every correct participant p_i eventually decides. If p_1 is correct then it sends a decision message (line 7) and decides (line 8). Assume that for every $k > 1$, if p_k is correct then it eventually decides, and consider p_{k+1}. As every correct participant must have sent a decision message (line 7) before deciding (line 8), then by the *Strong Completeness* property of $\mathcal{D}$ and the reliable channels assumption, p_{k+1} cannot remain blocked undefinitely at the while statement of line 2. For every $j < (k+1)$, either p_{k+1} receives the decision message $(p_j, v_j, decide)$, or p_{k+1} suspects p_j. Consequently, if p_{k+1} is correct, then p_{k+1} eventually decides. □

Theorem 3.2. *The algorithm in Figure 2 does not solve Uniform Consensus with* $\mathcal{P}$.

PROOF. We show that there is a failure detector $\mathcal{D}$ of $\mathcal{P}$, and a run of the algorithm where the *Uniform Agreement* condition is violated. Consider the run $R = \langle F, H_{\mathcal{D}}, I, S, T \rangle$ such that p_1 and p_2 have different input values. Assume that in $H_{\mathcal{D}}$, every process that crashes is permanently suspected and no correct participant is ever suspected. Hence $H_{\mathcal{D}}$ satisfies *Strong Completeness* and *Strong Accuracy*. Assume that p_1 crashes immediatly after deciding v_1 (line 8), and its decision message $(p_1, v_1, decide)$ (line 7) never arrives at p_2. Hence p_2 suspects p_1 and decides v_2 $(v_2 \neq v_1)$. Thus p_1 and p_2 decide differently in run R. □

By the relations between failure detector classes $\mathcal{P}$ and $\mathcal{Q}$, Theorem 3.1 and Theorem 3.2 apply also to $\mathcal{Q}$. Clearly, the algorithm in Figure 2 does not solve Consensus with unreliable failure detectors. Indeed, if p_1 and p_2 are correct and p_2 falsely suspect p_1, both may decide different values.

5 NB-WAC reducible to Consensus

In this Section, we define the Non-Blocking Weak Atomic Commitment problem (or simply NB-WAC) by weakening the *NonTriviality* condition of NB-AC. Then we show that in asynchronous systems with unreliable failure detectors, NB-WAC is reducible to Uniform Consensus. This implies, by Theorem 2, that NB-WAC is also reducible to Consensus.

5.1 The Non Blocking Weak Atomic Commitment problem

NB-WAC is specified by the *Uniform-Agreement, Uniform-Validity* and *Termination* conditions of NB-AC (Sect 3.1) and by the following *NonTriviality* condition:

- **NonTriviality:** If all participants vote *yes*, and no participant is ever suspected, then every correct participant eventually AC-decides *commit*.

As all failure detector classes we consider ensure *Weak Completeness* (every participant that crashes is eventually suspected), the *NonTriviality* condition of NB-WAC is weaker than the *NonTriviality* condition of NB-AC. Nevertheless, the *NonTriviality* condition of NB-WAC still eliminates trivial solutions to the problem where participants always AC-decide *abort*.[4] Note that an algorithm that solves NB-WAC may lead to always abort transactions with an underlying failure detector that always suspects some process. In practice however, failure detectors do not behave this way. Failure detectors are usually implemented using time-outs and suspect processes only after time-out expirations. The expiration of a time-out (either correct or false suspicion) is generally considered, in real-world transactional systems, a sufficient reason to *abort* a transaction [2].

5.2 NB-WAC reducible to Uniform Consensus

The reduction algorithm described by the function *atomicCommitment()* in Figure 3, transforms any algorithm that solves Uniform Consensus with $\Diamond\mathcal{P}$ (respectively $\mathcal{S}$, $\Diamond\mathcal{S}$), into an algorithm that solves NB-WAC with $\Diamond\mathcal{P}$ (respectively $\mathcal{S}$, $\Diamond\mathcal{S}$).

We assume that participants know each others, and every participant p, either crashes, or calls the function *atomicCommitment()*. The vote of participant p_i is denoted $vote_i$, and we represent a Uniform Consensus algorithm by the function *uniformConsensus()* (called at line 5 and 7). The values proposed and returned by *uniformConsensus()* are *commit* and *abort*. Function *atomicCommitment()* terminates by the execution of a "**return** *outcome*" statement, where *outcome* is either *commit* or *abort* (lines 6 and 8): when p_i executes **return** *outcome*, p_i AC-decides *outcome*. Participant p_i is informed by its local failure detector of crash suspicions: the notation $p_j \in \mathcal{D}_i$ (line 3) ($\mathcal{D}_i \in \{\Diamond\mathcal{P}_i, \mathcal{S}_i, \Diamond\mathcal{S}_i\}$) indicates that p_i suspects p_j.

The basic idea of the algorithm is the following. Every participant sends its vote to all participants (including itself). A participant that either receives a vote *no* or suspects another participant, starts Uniform Consensus by proposing *abort* (line 5), and AC-decides the outcome returned by Uniform Consensus (line 6). Every participant that receives *yes* votes from all participants, starts Uniform

---

[4] Coan and Welch have discussed in [5] the benefits of defining a weak *NonTriviality* condition in order to develop randomized Non Blocking Atomic Commitment protocols.

```
    function atomicCommitment(vote_i)
1       send (p_i, vote_i) to all
2       for j = 1 to n
3           wait until [received (p_j, vote_j) or p_j ∈ D_i] ;
4               if p_j ∈ D_i or vote_j = abort then
5                   outcome_i := uniformConsensus(abort) ;
6                   return outcome_i ;
7       outcome_i := uniformConsensus(commit) ;
8       return outcome_i ;
```

Fig. 3. An algorithm that reduces NB-WAC to Uniform Consensus

Consensus by proposing *commit* (line 7), and AC-decides the outcome returned by Uniform Consensus (line 8).

Theorem 4. *The algorithm in Figure 3 reduces NB-WAC to Uniform Consensus with either $\Diamond\mathcal{P}$, $\mathcal{S}$, or $\Diamond\mathcal{S}$.*

PROOF. We show that the four conditions of NB-WAC are satisfied.

1. *Uniform Agreement.* Any participant that AC-decides *outcome* (lines 6 and 8), must have decided *outcome* through Uniform Consensus (lines 5 and 7). By the *Uniform Agreement* condition of Uniform Consensus, no two participants can decide differently.
2. *Uniform Validity.* A participant AC-decides *outcome*, only if it decides

   outcome through Uniform Consensus. By the *Validity* condition of Uniform Consensus, a participant decides *commit* only if some participant p has proposed *commit* (in line 7). To reach line 7, p must have received *yes* votes from all.
3. *Termination.* There are two cases to consider for any correct participant p: (3.1) p receives *yes* votes from all, and (3.2) p does not. In case (3.1), p starts Uniform Consensus (line 7). In case (3.2), if p receives any vote *no*, p starts Uniform Consensus (line 5). Otherwise, as every correct participant sends its vote, then by the assumption of reliable channels and the *Eventual Strong Completeness* property of $\Diamond\mathcal{P}$ (respectively $\mathcal{S}$, $\Diamond\mathcal{S}$), p eventually suspects some participant and starts Uniform Consensus (line 5). Hence every correct participant starts Uniform Consensus. By the *Termination* condition of Uniform Consensus, every correct participant eventually decides and thus AC-decides.
4. *NonTriviality.* If there are no suspicions and all votes are *yes*, then every participant which starts Uniform Consensus proposes *commit* (line 7). By the *Uniform-Validity* condition of Uniform Consensus, every correct participant decides *commit* and thus AC-decides *commit* (line 8). □

By Corollary 3 and the relations between failure detector classes (Sect 2.3), we have Corollary 4.

Corollary 4. *If $f < |\Omega|$, NB-WAC is solvable with either $\mathcal{S}$ or $\mathcal{W}$, and if $f < [|\Omega|/2]$, NB-WAC is solvable with either $\Diamond\mathcal{S}$, $\Diamond\mathcal{P}$, $\Diamond\mathcal{Q}$, or $\Diamond\mathcal{W}$.*

NB-WAC algorithms can be obtained by combining the reduction algorithm of Figure 3 and the algorithms solving Consensus with $\mathcal{S}$ and $\Diamond\mathcal{S}$ [4]. In comparison, the algorithms described in [1, 15] for example can be seen as algorithms that use $\mathcal{P}$. Elsewhere, we have described centralized and decentralized *Three Phase Commit* algorithms using $\Diamond\mathcal{S}$ [9, 10].

6 Concluding Remarks

The importance of this work is in extending the applicability field of the results of Chandra and Toueg [4] on solving problems in asynchronous systems (with crash failures and reliable channels) augmented with unreliable failure detectors. The applicability of these results to problems other than Consensus has been discussed in [4, 11, 13, 14]. To our knowledge, it is however the first time that (non-blocking) atomic commitment problems are discussed in asynchronous systems with unreliable failure detectors.

By weakening the *NonTriviality* condition of atomic commitment, we have defined a problem, called Non-Blocking Weak Atomic Commitment (NB-WAC), which is adequate in practical transactional systems. We have shown that (1) Uniform Consensus is reducible to Consensus, and (2) NB-WAC is reducible to Uniform Consensus. As a consequence, the results of Chandra and Toueg on solving Consensus with unreliable failure detectors apply to NB-WAC.

We would like to define, in terms of failure detector characteristics, lower bounds on fault-tolerance for NB-WAC. It has been stated that $\Diamond\mathcal{W}$ is the weakest failure detector class that can solve Consensus [3], and $\Diamond\mathcal{P}$ cannot solve Consensus if more than a majority of participants can fail [4]. An interesting question is whether these lower bounds are relevant for NB-WAC. Furthermore, one may wonder if the *NonTriviality* condition defined in this paper is the strongest one that makes the problem solvable with unreliable failure detectors. Finally, we have not considered unreliable failure detectors with a known bounded number of false suspicions. Whether NB-WAC is reducible to Consensus with these failure detectors is an open question.

Acknowledgement

I am deeply grateful to André Schiper for his crucial help. The presentation of the paper was greatly improved by the suggestions of Aleta Ricciardi and the referees. I would also like to thank Tushar Chandra, Vassos Hadzilacos, Mikel Larrea and Sam Toueg for interesting discussions.

References

1. O. Babaoglu and S. Toueg. Non-Blocking Atomic Commitment. In *Distributed Systems*, pages 147-166. Sape Mullender ed, ACM Press, 1993.
2. P.A. Bernstein, V. Hadzilacos, and N. Goodman. *Concurrency Control and Recovery in Database Systems*. Addison Wesley, 1987.
3. T. Chandra, V. Hadzilacos and S. Toueg. The Weakest Failure Detector for Solving Consensus. *Proceedings of the 11th ACM Symposium on Principles of Distributed Computing*, pages 147-158. ACM Press, 1992.
4. T. Chandra and S. Toueg. Unreliable failure detectors for reliable distributed systems. Technical Report, Department of Computer Science, Cornell Univ, 1994. A preliminary version appeared in the *Proceedings of the 10th ACM Symposium on Principles of Distributed Computing*, pages 325-340. ACM Press, 1991.
5. B. Coan and J. Welch. Transaction commit in a realistic timing model. *Distributed Computing*, pages 87-103. 4(2), 1990.
6. D. Dolev and R. Strong. A Simple Model For Agreement in Distributed Systems. In *Fault-Tolerant Distributed Computing*, pages 42-50. B. Simons and A. Spector ed, Springer Verlag (LNCS 448), 1987.
7. M. Fischer, N. Lynch, and M. Paterson. Impossibility of Distributed Consensus with One Faulty Process. *Journal of the ACM*, pages 374-382. (32) 1985.
8. J. Gray. A Comparison of the Byzantine Agreement Problem and the Transaction Commit Problem. In *Fault-Tolerant Distributed Computing*, pages 10-17. B. Simons and A. Spector ed, Springer Verlag (LNCS 448), 1987.
9. R. Guerraoui, M. Larrea and A. Schiper. Non-Blocking Atomic Commitment with an Unreliable Failure Detector. To appear in *Proceedings of the 14th IEEE Symposium on Reliable Distributed Systems*, 1995.
10. R. Guerraoui and A. Schiper. The Decentralized Non-Blocking Atomic Commitment Protocol. To appear in *Proceedings of the 7th IEEE Symposium on Parallel and Distributed Processing*, 1995.
11. R. Guerraoui and A. Schiper. Transaction model vs Virtual Synchrony model: bridging the gap. In *Distributed Systems: From Theory to Practice*, pages 121-132. K. Birman, F. Mattern and A. Schiper ed, Springer Verlag (LNCS 938), 1995.
12. V. Hadzilacos. On the relationship between the atomic commitment and consensus problems. In *Fault-Tolerant Distributed Computing*, pages 201-208. B. Simons and A. Spector ed, Springer Verlag (LNCS 448), 1987.
13. L. Sabel and K. Marzullo. Election Vs. Consensus in Asynchronous Systems. Technical Report TR95-1488, Cornell Univ, 1995.
14. A. Schiper and A. Sandoz. Primary Partition "Virtually-synchronous Communication" Harder than Consensus. *Proceedings of the 8th International Workshop on Distributed Algorithms*, pages 39-52. Springer Verlag (LNCS 857), 1994.
15. D. Skeen. NonBlocking Commit Protocols. In Proceedings of the *ACM SIGMOD International Conference on Management of Data*, pages 133-142. ACM Press, 1981.

Dissecting Distributed Coordination*

Aleta Ricciardi[1]

The University of Texas at Austin, Austin TX 78712, USA

Abstract. This paper derives necessary and sufficient communication for distributed applications that perform certain actions *uniformly* in asynchronous systems. We show there is an essential structure of information flow in any solution to Uniform Coordination, suggesting message-minimal solutions. We show it is necessary for processes to conspire against each other to make progress, and we show this conspiracy requires processes to stop communicating with each other. This, we show, renders Uniform Coordination insensitive to channel delivery guarantees. We introduce the notion of *exempting* processes from coordinating. We show that 'primary partition' behavior (Isis) arises from the desire to make exempt an process indistinguishable from a crashed process. Defining weaker exemptions for distributed coordination problems gives rise to many problems solvable in asynchronous systems as well as in systems that partition. **Keywords:** Agreement, asynchronous, exemption, failures, uniformity.

1 Introduction

Distributed computing systems can broadly be viewed as alternating periods of coordination and autonomy. Coordination can occur intermittently or more frequently, and each instance will have different requirements regarding when the coordinated activity must complete, which processes must participate, and conditions under which some may later be deemed exempt. Research has tended to focus on Distributed Consensus, a simple yet strict coordination problem, and the inability of attaining it in asynchronous systems [7]. Recent work has found ways around the impossibility result: Chandra, Hadzilacos and Toueg augment the asynchronous environment with failure detectors, giving minimal conditions these must satisfy to assist a group of processes solve Consensus [3], while randomized techniques (*e.g.,* [6]) give probabilistic solutions. This paper and others (*e.g.,* [12, 15]) consider weaker coordination problems that are, without external assistance, solvable in asynchronous environments.

This work puts forth the notion that very useful coordination can be achieved with minor changes to provably unsolvable problems (*e.g.,* Consensus, Atomic Broadcast). Specifically, we view the requirement that all non-crashed[2] processes

---

* This research is supported by the NSF under grant number ASC-9318151, and a University Research Institute Summer Research Award from the Univerisity of Texas.

[2] We adopt the view (proposed in [7]) that any interesting algorithm would have all non-crashed processes decide.

reach a consistent decision as a direct way of simply *exempting* crashed processes from having to make a decision. Certainly, a coordination problem must exempt crashed processes from acting, but requiring that all non-crashed processes must act is perhaps too severe. It has been shown that systems can reach agreement with some non-crashed processes not deciding, and that one can make these executions indistinguishable from those in which the non-deciding processes do crash [15, 16].

To achieve indistinguishability, processes that are not known to decide and do not crash must be forced to behave as if they were crashed – they must (at least) be prevented from making further decisions. This induces a 'primary partition', a unique subset of processes that continues making decisions and prevents others from doing so. We show that a set of processes can effectively crash a member only by refusing to communicate with it. By being *shunned* in this way, a process is denied information essential to it making further decisions. The need for this information arises from the safety condition and the need to exact control over processes. Using results from Chandy and Misra [5], we derive the essential communication structure for any solution, then use this to determine which information must be kept from a process to disable it. We show primary partition behavior (implemented in systems like Isis [2]) is directly attributable to any exemption that requires a process to cease taking actions if it is exempt from taking any action.

Thinking of distributed coordination in terms of behavior that should be prevented if a process does not participate in a given coordinated activity is new and may lead to more appropriate, balanced coordination problems. For example, broader notions of exemption accurately describe coordination problems that can make progress in multiple sides of a partition. This is especially important for computations that occur over wide-area networks, which are (now and for the foreseeable future) prone to partition. Even in LANs, Transis [1] and Horus [17] permit some progress during a partition; for efficiency and correctness it is important to know which actions need not be resolved at merge time.

2 Asynchronous System Model

The system consists of an infinite domain of process identifiers, Proc, though at any point in time only a finite subset of them are executing. The system also has a network of channels between processes. Processes communicate with each other only by passing messages through the network. The system is asynchronous in that there is no common global clock, and messages may be arbitrarily long in transit. A process p fails by crashing, but otherwise follows its assigned protocol. While messages between processes may be lost (though not corrupted), every message sent has some non-zero probability of being received. If two processes p and q both never fail, every message from p will eventually reach q. In this environment no process can determine whether a process is unresponsive because it is crashed or because of transient performance factors.

Each process has local state that changes whenever the processes executes an *event*; of particular interest are the events $crash_p$ (used to model p crashing), $send_p(q, m)$ (p sends m to q) and $recv_q(p, m)$ (q receives m from p). After each event, a process makes all logical inferences from its new local state. A history for process p, h_p, is a sequence of events beginning with the event $start_p$. A *cut* over $S \subset$ Proc is a tuple of finite process histories, one for each $p \in S$. We assume inter-event causality [10] and consistent cuts [4] are understood.

A *system run* is a tuple of infinite process histories, one for each process that ever executes.[3] For each run of the system, the initial system composition S_0 is the set of all processes whose *start* events are not causally related; the initial cut consists only of all the $start_p$ events for $p \in S_0$.

Just as inter-event causality reflects progress made between events, the causal relation between two cuts reflects progress made between global states. Formally, given c over S and c' over S', $c \leq c'$ if and only if $S \cap S' \neq \emptyset$ and, for any process in the intersection, its history component in c is a prefix of its history component of in c'. Two cuts c and c' are *indistinguishable* to process p (written $c \sim_p c'$) when p's history component (state) in both is identical.

2.1 Distributed, Coordinated Actions

As in [12], we are concerned with applications in which specific events must occur at all processes if at any, and designate a special set of events, called *actions*. While the set of actions can be described (*e.g.*, withdrawals from accounts at the Black Hole Savings and Loan) the specific actions to appear in any execution are not known *a priori* (*e.g.*, from which account, how much, and when). An action will arise unpredictably at a single process in any given run. If α arises at p in run ρ we say p *owns* α in ρ; p_α denotes the owner of α. The particular event whereby a process learns about the existence of an action does not have any externally observable effect on that process.

2.2 The Formal Language

We use a logic supporting temporal and knowledge modalities to define the problem. Formulas are evaluated on consistent cuts. When formula φ holds on cut c, we write $c \models \varphi$. The modalities have the following semantics:
Time. $\Box\varphi$ (always) holds on c if and only if φ holds on c and on all c' such that $c \leq c'$. $\Diamond\varphi$ (inevitably - branching time) holds on c if and only if φ holds on *some* $c \leq c'$, in *every* run that includes c. $\Box$ and $\Diamond$ are not duals. $\ominus\varphi$ (in the past) holds on c if φ holds on some $c' \leq c$.
Knowledge. [9] $K_p\varphi$ (p knows) holds on c if and only if φ holds on all cuts $c' \sim_p c$. The event $learn_p(\varphi)$ refers to the place in p's history on the earliest cut satisfying $K_p\varphi$.

Crashed processes cannot 'know' anything; that is $K_p\varphi \Rightarrow \neg\text{CRASHED}(p)$. $learn_p(\varphi)$ can easily be affixed with an index if $K_p\varphi$ is not stable, though this will not be necessary in our discussions.

---

[3] Histories of crashed processes have infinitely many trailing *crash* events.

3 Uniform Distributed Coordination

Loosely stated, Uniform Agreement [8] requires all processes to reach agreement on a value, if any process decides on that value; non-uniform agreement only requires consistent behavior from the processes that never crash. Uniformity is more appropriate for our concerns. In asynchronous systems that experience only crash failures, up to the point a process crashes it behaves 'correctly' (Gopal and Toueg point out, too, that non-uniform agreement originally considered malicious failures [11]). For a participating process, deciding whether to ignore the actions of processes that will later be deemed incorrect is akin to predicting the future. As well, some applications require that the external world never be able to discern any inconsistency among the processes participating in the agreement protocol. Whenever a group of processes cooperate to implement a service that must appear as if it were being run by a single, fault-tolerant process (*e.g.*, key distribution services, controllers), the actions of *all* processes will be important, not just the ones that never crash. Non-uniform agreement exempts processes that will later be deemed faulty from behaving consistently, even before they encounter a fault.

We use the following formulas to define Uniform Coordination; they are all stable (*i.e.*, $\varphi \Rightarrow \Box\varphi$). SEND$_p(q, m)$ holds on c if and only if $send_p(q, m)$ is an event in c. SEND$_p^*(q, m)$ holds when there is a sequence of processes $p = p_0, ..., p_k = q$ and messages, $m_0, ..., m_{k-1} = m$ such that SEND$_{p_i}(p_{i+1}, m_i)$ holds on c and (the contents of) each m_1 implies (the contents of) m_0. We say m *acknowledges* m_0 and use ack(m_0) for m to make this explicit. Similarly define RECV$_q(p, m)$ and RECV$_q^*(p, m)$. CRASHED(p) holds on c if $crash_p$ is an event in c. BEFORE(e_1, e_2) holds on c if $e_1 \to e_2$ in c. DID$_p(\alpha)$ holds on c if $do_p(\alpha)$ is an event in p's history component of c. 'α' holds on c if some non-crashed process knows the action α has arisen.

For the problems we consider, actions to be taken uniformly arise unpredictably in that processes receive stimuli from the external world. Because processes may crash and the external stimuli alerting a process to an action may occur only once, the existence of an action is tied to it being known by a (non-crashed) process. We associate an action's initial existence with its owner's knowledge of it, 'α' $\Rightarrow \Diamond K_{p_\alpha}$'$\alpha$', and state that p_α is necessarily the first process to learn 'α' : BEFORE$(learn_{p_\alpha}($'α'$), learn_q($'α'$))$ for all other q.

3.1 Process Exemptions

The nature of asynchronous environments leads to a number of necessary components to *any* solution to Uniform Coordination. We must consider these before giving a complete formal specification for the problem. The non-triviality condition we will put forth forces each process to attempt to execute all actions it knows about, and the safety condition will force these actions to be done uniformly. In so doing, the safety condition will explicitly quantify a set of processes *obliged* to do each action, as well as conditions under which some of these processes may later be deemed exempt. An obvious exemption is the crash of an obliged process, but asynchrony necessitates others.

The usual statement for many distributed coordination problems requires all 'correct' processes to take the same actions, which is one way of exempting crashed processes. While crashed processes must be exempt, this particular statement is problematic. For example, the need to distinguish crashed from non-crashed processes is often cited as the reason behind Consensus and Atomic Broadcast. As well, a solution must store all values that have been decided. Each value must be store indefinitely, so that a non-crashed process, no matter how slow, can retrieve it, and it must stored at multiple sites to persist despite process crashes.

The Uniform Coordination problem described here and in [12], and the Group Membership Problem described in [15] broaden the notion of exemptions so that solutions are not required to determine the set of crashed processes exactly, or save actions indefinitely. In theory, an exemption could be granted for any reason, though we focus on process crashes and 'apparent crashes'. An exemption can limit the future behavior of a process : it can be terminal (once a process is declared exempt from taking any action, it can never take another action), restrictive (a process can only take actions from some subset), or conditional (a process is unable to take actions until some other condition is met).

Uniform Coordination, as well as the coordination achieved in Isis, produce runs that are indistinguishable from those in which the exempt processes actually crashed; that is, we are interested in a terminal exemption. Terminal exemptions allow one to reach meaningful agreement in asynchronous systems by not equating exemption with accurate failure determination.

Definition 1. A process p is *disabled*, and the formula DIS'D(p) holds, exactly when p will never take any action it has not already taken,

$$\text{DIS'D}(p) \stackrel{\text{def}}{=} \forall \alpha : \Big(\neg\text{DID}_p(\alpha) \Rightarrow \Box\neg\text{DID}_p(\alpha) \Big) . \tag{1}$$

It follows that a crashed process is disabled.

3.2 Permission for Actions

Assume process p wishes to perform action α and let S_α be the set obliged to do α along with p (Section 3.4 discusses this). Since α is initially known only to p_α, the action should be *announced* to the obligation set, S_α, for no member of S_α can take an action it does not know about. For now let $Annc_p(S_\alpha)$ be a loose way of p propagating knowledge of α (*e.g.*, multi-cast that is not failure atomic). Intuitively Algorithm 1 (Figure 1) is not safe because p cannot guarantee it will not crash between doing α and announcing it.

To effect a terminal exemption, the system must have some means of making exempt processes appear crashed. In the context of Uniform Coordination, that means exempt processes may take only finitely many actions. The notion of *permission* to take an action arises from the need to make some processes appear crashed; that is, terminally exempt processes must have their ability to take new actions revoked. In the absence of an omnipotent external entity, granting permission and revoking it falls to the members of S_α. In this way Algorithm 2 is not safe for two reasons: first there is no way of preventing p from ever taking actions, and second the network cannot guarantee any member of S_α will receive this particular announcement; should p fail immediately after taking α, knowledge of the action may be lost forever.[4]

/* Alg 1 */	/* Alg 2 */	/* Alg 3 */
do α;	$Annc(S_\alpha, \alpha)$;	$Annc(S_\alpha, \alpha)$;
$Annc(S_\alpha, \alpha)$.	do α.	when $K_p \text{PERMIT}_p(\alpha)$
		do α.

Figure 1. Possible Uniform Coordination Solutions.

Thus, while announcing an action seems necessary, it is not sufficient. A process must also receive some assurance before taking an action implying it will be taken uniformly; again, lacking some sort of oracle, this assurance ultimately comes from S_α. The formula $\text{PERMIT}_p(\alpha)$ holds whenever it is 'safe' for p to take α. Section 4.1 derives minimal conditions for defining $\text{PERMIT}_p(\alpha)$, and therefore safety. $\text{PERMIT}_p(\alpha)$ and $\text{DID}_p(\alpha)$ interact as expected, and liveness will prevent $\text{PERMIT}_p(\alpha)$ from being identically false. We stipulate that initially no actions are permitted, that if a process takes an action, it has permission for it, and that actions known to be permitted are eventually taken, provided a process does not crash.

3.3 Specification

Elsewhere [14] we have argued that many important problems in distributed computing can be specified by variants on three clauses : Uniformity, Sequence, and Termination. Here, we focus on the Uniformity clause which is the basis of other coordination problems. Variations on the Uniformity clause will define the set of processes obliged to take an action, and the exemption, which for our purposes, is DIS'D(). We are concerned with properties of all solutions to Uniform Coordination, and so confine the discussion to the set of system runs generated by them. Hereafter, when we prove or require $c \models \varphi$, it should be understood in the context only of these runs, not the set of all runs of an asynchronous system.

The clause specifying Uniformity is similar to that in [12], but refers to knowledge of permission rather than action. Since a process must eventually act if it knows it has permission and cannot act without permission, using $K_p \text{PERMIT}_p(\alpha)$ is equivalent and more direct. The Uniformity condition requires that if one member of S_α gets permission to take an action, then all other

---

[4] It will be clear later (Theorem 16) that even if the network guarantees delivery, Algorithm 2 is not safe. The members of S_α may already have decided to 'shun' p so that p not waiting for permission violates safety. The need to shun arises the need to prevent exempt processes from taking future actions.

processes in that set are obliged to (try to) get permission for it also; the only processes exempt from taking uniform actions are those that crash or become otherwise disabled,

$$p \in S_\alpha \wedge K_p \text{PERMIT}_p(\alpha) \;\Rightarrow\; \bigwedge_{q \in S_\alpha} \Diamond \Big(K_q \text{PERMIT}_q(\alpha) \vee \text{DIS'D}(q) \Big) . \qquad (2)$$

Formula 2 does not require p to know which of the two clauses, $K_q\text{PERMIT}_q(\alpha)$ or $\text{DIS'D}(q)$, will hold before p has permission to take α. This allows runs of limited divergence (see Figure 2), in which processes with no intention of adhering to the uniformity constraint for actions initiated by other processes are, for a finite period, permitted to execute their own actions. While the actions these 'outlaw' processes take must, of course, be taken by all others that are never disabled, an outlaw process need not conform to any other process's behavior. A strong Termination clause (see [14]) would prevent such behavior.

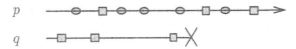

Figure 2. Process q displays finite divergence.

The non-triviality and liveness clauses state that knowledge of an action forces a process to try to take it, and preclude solutions in which all processes take a finite number of actions then quit.

3.4 Obligation Sets

A coordination problem will define obligation sets to reflect the desired degree of system-wide uniform coordination. For example, S_α can be static, or it can be dynamic [12]; it can be defined according to a single process (like p_α) or many processes. It should also be noted that obligation sets are closely related to the exemption. Our DIS'D() exemption is defined in terms of denying a process permission for all future actions. If the obligation set of a future action is not related to that of a pending action, drastic measures are needed to ensure DIS'D(). Here, we consider a static set of processes that are mutually bound to execute the same set of actions. As Corollary 15 shows, there will always be a need to add processes; it is beyond the scope of this paper to deal with those additions, and how they affect the underlying coordination problem.

4 Results

As Propositions 2 and 3 are similar to well-known results by Chandy and Misra [5], we do not include their proofs here (see the full paper [13]).

Proposition 2. *Knowledge of actions is propagated by communication,*

$$K_p `\alpha' \Leftrightarrow \begin{cases} \neg\text{CRASHED}(p) & p = p_\alpha \\ \text{RECV}_p^*(p_\alpha, ack(`\alpha')) \wedge \neg\text{CRASHED}(p) & p \neq p_\alpha \end{cases}.$$

We no longer explicitly state or prove the disclaimer that process knowledge depends on the process not having crashed. From Proposition 2, if p_α never sends a message mentioning 'α', then no process will ever know 'α', meaning that $Anncp_\alpha(S, \alpha)$ involves p_α sending messages to each member of S. Thus, $Anncp_\alpha(S, \alpha)$ is $\forall p \in S : send_{p_\alpha}^*(p, \alpha)$, or more generally $Mcastp_\alpha(S, \alpha)$.

Proposition 3. *A process's knowledge of an action is itself a local formula,*[5]

$$K_p K_q `\alpha' \Leftrightarrow \text{RECV}_p^*(q, ack(`\alpha')) \wedge \neg\text{CRASHED}(p).$$

The next theorem states that before a process can take an action, it must be able to account for all other obliged processes (either a process knows about the action or will be disabled). This is stronger than the Uniformity statement itself which only requires p to know that eventually one of the two will hold, and is directly attributable to the asynchronous system (though see Footnote 4).

Theorem 4. *[Accountability Theorem] If process p knows it has permission to take action α, then either p knows $K_q `\alpha'$ or p knows $\Diamond\text{DIS'D}(q)$ for every $q \in S$,*

$$K_p\text{PERMIT}_p(\alpha) \Rightarrow \bigwedge_{q\in S} K_p K_q `\alpha' \vee K_p \Diamond\text{DIS'D}(q). \tag{3}$$

Proof. Formula 3 differs from the Uniformity statement in that not only must p know that eventually q will learn about α (Proposition 5), but that "eventually" is not good enough (Proposition 6); p must have definitive evidence that q already knows about α. Moreover, in this case, the knowledge operator distributes over the disjunction meaning that p must know one way or the other whether q will be disabled or already knows about the action (Proposition 7).

Proposition 5. *Before $p \in S$ can know it has permission for α, it must know every $q \in S$ will eventually know that α has arisen or will eventually be disabled,*

$$K_p\text{PERMIT}_p(\alpha) \Rightarrow K_p\Diamond\Big(K_q `\alpha' \vee \text{DIS'D}(q)\Big).$$

Proof. Replacing $K_q\text{PERMIT}_q(\alpha)$ with $K_q `\alpha'$ in Formula 2 is legitimate because $K_q(P \vee Q) \wedge (P \Rightarrow P_1) \Rightarrow K_q(P_1 \vee Q)$, and because $K_q\text{PERMIT}_q(\alpha) \Rightarrow K_q `\alpha'$. $\square_{Pr5}$

Proposition 6. *A process cannot know only that another process will eventually know about an action, $K_p\Diamond K_q `\alpha' \Rightarrow K_p K_q `\alpha'$.*

---

[5] The LHS should be $K_p\ominus K_q `\alpha'$ to capture the possibility that q may be crashed, though we avoid this formulation for readability.

Proof. The proof is by contradiction. Suppose $c \models K_p \Diamond K_q `\alpha` \land \neg K_p K_q `\alpha`$, and define $\mathsf{knows}(c, `\alpha`) \overset{\text{def}}{=} \{r \in \mathsf{S} \mid c \models K_r `\alpha`\}$. Then p can imagine a $c' \geq c$ such that all channels are empty[6] on c' and

$$c' \models \bigwedge_{r \in \mathsf{knows}(c, `\alpha`)} \mathrm{CRASHED}(r) \land \neg\mathrm{CRASHED}(q) \land \neg K_q `\alpha` \, .$$

After c', q can never learn 'α', so that c cannot satisfy $K_p \Diamond K_q `\alpha`$. $\square_{Pr6}$

Proposition 7. *To know of a remote process's eventual knowledge of an action or its eventual demise, is to either know that it already knows about the action or to know that it will eventually be disabled,*

$$K_p \Diamond \Big(K_q `\alpha` \lor \mathrm{DIS'D}(q) \Big) \Rightarrow K_p K_q `\alpha` \lor K_p \Diamond \mathrm{DIS'D}(q) \, .$$

Proof. By way of contradiction, we construct a $\sim_p$-equivalent cut on which $\Diamond\Big(K_q `\alpha` \lor \mathrm{DIS'D}(q) \Big)$ does not hold. Assume

$$c \models K_p \Diamond \Big(K_q `\alpha` \lor \mathrm{DIS'D}(q) \Big) \land \neg K_p K_q `\alpha` \land \neg K_p \Diamond \mathrm{DIS'D}(q) \, ,$$

and let $\mathsf{knows}(c, `\alpha`)$ be as in Proposition 6. Construct c_1 from c by crashing all processes (except p) in $\mathsf{knows}(c, `\alpha`)$ and dropping any message currently in transit to q. Further impose that 'α' does not arise again in any completion of c_1. Let c_2 be identical to c_1 except that p crashes immediately next. That is, $c_2 \models \Box\neg K_q `\alpha`$ and so $c_1 \models \neg\Diamond K_q `\alpha`$. To satisfy the hypothesis, $\Diamond\mathrm{DIS'D}(q) \land \neg K_q \Diamond\mathrm{DIS'D}(q)$ must hold on c_1.

Lacking an omniscient, omnipotent entity, it must be that some subset of S jointly control $\mathrm{DIS'D}(q)$ (and therefore $\Diamond\mathrm{DIS'D}(q)$). By definition $\Diamond\mathrm{DIS'D}(q)$ holds only if inevitably, q will never learn it has permission to take new actions; intuitively, these controlling processes somehow prevent q from learning it has permission. Since p does not know $\Diamond\mathrm{DIS'D}(q)$, p can imagine the q-controlling processes have not yet decided to disable q. Since failures are independent, p can also imagine a completion of c_1 in which these (and any future) q-controlling processes crash before deciding to disable q and that q itself can learn they are disabled! Nothing now prevents q from learning it has permission for new actions, the ability to disable q is lost, and q will never learn 'α'. That is, $\exists c_1 \sim_p c$, such that $c_1 \models \neg\Diamond K_q `\alpha` \land \neg\Diamond\mathrm{DIS'D}(q)$ if and only if $c_1 \models \neg\Big(\Diamond K_q `\alpha` \lor \Diamond\mathrm{DIS'D}(q) \Big)$ implying $c_1 \models \neg\Diamond\Big(K_q `\alpha` \lor \mathrm{DIS'D}(q) \Big)$. $\square_{Pr7}$ and $\square_{Th4}$

Proposition 8. *If process p knows it has permission to take action α, then p received a message implying $K_q `\alpha`$, or p knows $\Diamond\mathrm{DIS'D}(q)$, for $q \in \mathsf{S}$,*

$$K_p \mathrm{PERMIT}_p(\alpha) \Rightarrow \neg\mathrm{CRASHED}(p) \land \bigwedge_{q \in \mathsf{S}} \mathrm{RECV}_p^*(q, ack(`\alpha`)) \lor K_p \Diamond\mathrm{DIS'D}(q) \, .$$

Proof. Apply Proposition 3 to Theorem 4. $\square$

---

[6] The proposition holds even when channels guarantee delivery. (Theorem 16).

4.1 Permission Revisited

At this point, a very simple definition of permission is evident. Given what must be true for a process to know it has permission, we can reason conversely and describe the condition that immediately causes a process to know it has permission. Theorem 4 and Proposition 8 mean that knowledge of permission is tied to a process receiving a message from each of the members of S that the requester does not know will eventually be disabled. That is, we can strip the K_p knowledge operators from Formula 3 to obtain

$$\text{PERMIT}_p(\alpha) \Rightarrow \bigwedge_{q \in S} K_q \text{`}\alpha\text{'} \vee \Diamond \text{DIS'D}(q) .$$

The simplest, non-trivial definition of permission makes this an equivalence.

Definition 9. Permission for p to take α holds exactly when ever member of S has either learned about α or will inevitably be disabled,

$$\text{PERMIT}_p(\alpha) \stackrel{\text{def}}{=} \bigwedge_{q \in S} K_q \text{`}\alpha\text{'} \vee \Diamond \text{DIS'D}(q) .$$

As per Section 3.2, initially no actions are permitted because no actions are initially known, and because processes do not immediately crash themselves. While this definition does not discriminate between members of S, specific applications would likely restrict permission depending on, say, a process's role within the obligation set. $\text{PERMIT}_p(\alpha)$ can hold even after p has crashed or been disabled, though if p is crashed it cannot act. When p is disabled but not crashed, knowledge of $\text{PERMIT}_p(\alpha)$ must be kept from p, and the next section derives necessary conditions to ensure this.

4.2 Disabling a Process

In this section, we derive the necessary conditions for preventing a process from learning it may have permission, thereby disabling the process. Proposition 8 and the definition of permission mean that if q is disabled (yet not crashed) there is some member of S for which q can never account. Proposition 10 instantiates $\text{PERMIT}_p(\alpha)$ to make Proposition 8 an equivalence, and Theorem 11 shows that a process is disabled if it can never account for one of the other participants.

Proposition 10.

$$K_p \text{PERMIT}_p(\alpha) \Leftrightarrow \neg\text{CRASHED}(p) \wedge \left(\bigwedge_{q \in S} \text{RECV}_p^*(q, ack(\text{`}\alpha\text{'})) \vee K_p \Diamond \text{DIS'D}(q) \right).$$

Proof. For the "$\Leftarrow$" direction, apply Proposition 3 and propositional logic. □

Theorem 11. *If $p \in S$ is not crashed, then it is disabled if and only if for every action it may ever be required to take, there is some $q \in S$ for which p can never account,*

$$p \in S \wedge \neg\text{CRASHED}(p) \Rightarrow$$
$$\left(\text{DIS'D}(p) \Leftrightarrow \forall\alpha : \left(\Diamond K_p\text{'}\alpha\text{'} \wedge \neg K_p\text{PERMIT}_p(\alpha) \Rightarrow \right.\right.$$
$$\left.\left. \bigvee_{q\in S} \Box\neg\text{RECV}_p^*(q, ack(\text{'}\alpha\text{'})) \wedge \Box\neg K_p\Diamond\text{DIS'D}(q) \right) \right) . \quad (4)$$

Proof. Let $A_\alpha \stackrel{\text{def}}{=} K_p\text{PERMIT}_p(\alpha)$, and let

$$B_\alpha \stackrel{\text{def}}{=} \bigwedge_{q\in S} \text{RECV}_p^*(q, ack(\text{'}\alpha\text{'})) \vee K_p\Diamond\text{DIS'D}(q) .$$

Proposition 8 says $A_\alpha \Rightarrow B_\alpha$, and Proposition 10 says $A_\alpha \Leftrightarrow \neg\text{CRASHED}(p) \wedge B_\alpha$.
"$\Rightarrow$" Assuming $\text{DIS'D}(p)$ and $\neg\text{CRASHED}(p)$, let α be any action such that $\Diamond K_p\text{'}\alpha\text{'} \wedge \neg A_\alpha$.

a) Because p cannot be prevented from taking α if A_α holds, $\text{DIS'D}(p) \wedge \neg A_\alpha \Rightarrow \Box\neg A_\alpha$.

b) Manipulating Proposition 10, means $\neg A_\alpha \Leftrightarrow \neg B_\alpha \vee \text{CRASHED}(p)$ is valid, as is $\neg A_\alpha \wedge \neg\text{CRASHED}(p) \Rightarrow \neg B_\alpha$, since the other disjunct cannot hold. Then $\Box$-generalization gives

$$\Box\neg A_\alpha \wedge \Box\neg\text{CRASHED}(p) \Rightarrow \Box\neg B_\alpha .$$

c) Let $\text{awol}_p(c, \alpha)$ be the subset of S that p cannot account for regarding α at cut c. Expanding B_α gives

$$\Box(\neg B_\alpha) \Leftrightarrow \Box\left(\bigvee_{q\in S} \neg\text{RECV}_p^*(q, ack(\alpha)) \wedge \neg K_p\Diamond\text{DIS'D}(q) \right) ,$$

and so $\Box\neg B_\alpha$ holds exactly when $|\text{awol}_p(c', \alpha)| \geq 1$ for $c' \geq c$. As processes are never added to $\text{awol}_p(c, \alpha)$, there must be some q that is in every $\text{awol}_p(c', \alpha)$,

$$\Box\neg B_\alpha \Leftrightarrow \bigvee_{q\in S} \Box\neg\text{RECV}_p^*(a, ack(\text{'}\alpha\text{'})) \wedge \Box\neg K_p\Diamond\text{DIS'D}(q) .$$

d) Finally, whether p eventually crashes is irrelevant if p is already disabled: $\Box\neg A_\alpha \wedge \neg\text{CRASHED}(p) \Rightarrow \Box\neg B_\alpha$. To see this, suppose, by way of contradiction, that if p eventually crashes, B_α will eventually hold. Proposition 10 says if B_α ever holds then so does A_α, contradicting $\Box\neg A_\alpha$.

"$\Leftarrow$" Assume $\neg A_\alpha \wedge \neg\text{CRASHED}(p) \wedge \Box\neg B_\alpha$, for all α that p will learn about. Proposition 10 is equivalent to $\neg B_\alpha \vee \text{CRASHED}(p) \Leftrightarrow \neg A_\alpha$. $\Box$-generalization then gives $\Box(\neg B_\alpha \vee \text{CRASHED}(p)) \Leftrightarrow \Box\neg A_\alpha$. By hypothesis, $\Box\neg B_\alpha$ holds, and by introduction, so does $\Box(\neg B_\alpha \vee \varphi)$ for any formula φ, in particular, $\neg\text{CRASHED}(p)$. Since $\Box\neg A_\alpha$ holds, so does $\Box\neg\text{DID}_p(\alpha)$, and therefore $\text{DIS'D}(p)$. $\qquad\Box$

Theorem 11 implies that q, acting alone, can disable p by guaranteeing p never receives messages (from q) acknowledging actions p is trying to take; in Formula 4 we use $\Box\neg\text{SEND}_q^*(p, \text{ack}(+))$ to reflect q's intentional decision to disable p by ceasing to send acknowledgments to p. This is not enough, for any system can then partition so that all subsets ignore the others giving no guarantee any are disabled.

$$\text{DIS'D}(p) \iff \exists q \in S : \Box\neg\text{SEND}_q^*(p, \text{ack}(+)) \land \Box\neg K_p \Diamond \text{DIS'D}(q) \iff$$
$$\exists q \in S : \Box\neg\text{SEND}_q^*(p, \text{ack}(+)) \land$$
$$\Box\neg K_p \Big(\exists r \in S : \Box\neg\text{SEND}_r^*(q, \text{ack}(+)) \land \Box\neg K_q \Diamond \text{DIS'D}(r) \Big).$$

Not only should p never receive future acknowledgments from q, but p should also never learn of a successful effort by any other process(es) to disable q. In a system consisting of only p and q, if p really is disabled, the system is asymmetric (q can disable p but not vice versa). A symmetric system of two processes cannot progress if either tries to disable the other; in larger systems this implies a coordinated conspiracy to keep information from p. The most stringent conspiracy would involve $(n-1)$ processes (for $n > 2$), but a *majority* suffices.[7] For Uniform Coordination, majorities determine which set of processes is not disabled; that is, which subset form the primary partition.

We say q *is shunning* p once q has intentionally ceased sending messages of any sort to p,[8] and denote it by $\text{SHUN}_q(p)$. As $\text{SHUN}_q(p)$ and $\text{CRASHED}(q)$ achieve the same end regarding p, and to p they are indistinguishable, we obtain,

$$\text{SHUN}_q(p) \lor \text{CRASHED}(q) \iff \Box\neg\text{SEND}_q^*(p, +).$$

The next propositions prove that q can disable p if and only if it actively conspires with a majority of p's (*i.e.*, their) cohorts to shun p, and that q only learns this by communicating with this majority. Let M be a majority of S.

Proposition 12. *A process (that is not crashed) is disabled exactly when a majority of participants cease communicating with it,*

$$\text{DIS'D}(p) \iff \exists M \subseteq S \bigwedge_{q \in M} \Box\neg\text{SEND}_q^*(p, +).$$

Proof. For the "$\Rightarrow$" direction, it should be clear that safety is violated if fewer than a majority are needed. The "$\Leftarrow$" direction follows from Theorem 11. $\quad\Box$

Proposition 13. *The fact "q is shunning p" is local to q, as is q's intent to eventually shun p,*

a) $K_r \text{SHUN}_q(p) \iff \text{RECV}_r^*(q, ack(\text{SHUN}_q(p)))$
b) $K_r \Diamond \text{SHUN}_q(p) \iff \text{RECV}_r^*(q, ack(\Diamond \text{SHUN}_q(p))).$

---

[7] In general, one requires a quorum; in a symmetric system that is a majority.
[8] Censoring q will also achieve the desired effect: q can only send messages to p that do not mention things that conflict with an attempt to disable p. For simplicity, we assume shunning involves all communication.

Proof. Similar to Proposition 2. □

Proposition 14. *A remote process r knows another process q has ceased communicating (resp. intends to cease communicating) with p if and only if q has explicitly mentioned* $\text{SHUN}_q(p)$ *(resp.* $\diamond\text{SHUN}_q(p)$*) to r,*

$$a)\ K_r\Box\neg\text{SEND}_q^*(p,+) \Leftrightarrow \text{RECV}_r^*(q, ack(\text{SHUN}_q(p)))$$
$$b)\ K_r\diamond\Box\neg\text{SEND}_q^*(p,+) \Leftrightarrow \text{RECV}_r^*(q, ack(\diamond\text{SHUN}_q(p)))$$

Proof. a). The "⇐" direction is trivial. For the "⇒" direction, $K_r\Box\neg\text{SEND}_q^*(p,+)$ $\Leftrightarrow K_r(\text{SHUN}_q(p) \vee \text{CRASHED}(q))$. Now, assuming the contradiction, every $c' \sim_r c$ satisfies $\neg\text{RECV}_r^*(q, ack(\text{SHUN}_q(p))) \wedge (\text{SHUN}_q(p) \vee \text{CRASHED}(q))$. Construct c_1 from any such c' by rolling q back to the last event, call it e_q, that causally influenced r. Since r has not received a message originating at q indicating $\text{SHUN}_q(p)$, that event or q's crash, whichever holds on c, must have happened after e_q. However, $c_1 \sim_r c$ and $c_1 \models \neg\text{SHUN}_q(p) \wedge \neg\text{CRASHED}(q)$.

The proof of b) follows from Proposition 13 and the proof of a). □

Corollary 15. *Before a process r can know another process p will eventually be disabled, it must know a majority of p's cohorts will eventually shun p,*

$$K_r\diamond\text{DIS'D}(p) \Leftrightarrow K_r\diamond\Big(\exists M \subseteq S \bigwedge_{q\in M} \Box\neg\text{SEND}_q^*(p,+)\Big) \Leftrightarrow$$
$$K_r\Big(\exists M \subseteq S \diamond \bigwedge_{q\in M} \Box\neg\text{SEND}_q^*(p,+)\Big) \Leftrightarrow$$
$$\exists M \subseteq S \bigwedge_{q\in M} \text{RECV}_r^*(q, ack(\diamond\text{SHUN}_q(p)))\ .$$

Proof. That r must know the majority exists (and not that it will eventually) follows by an argument similar to that of Proposition 6. □

Theorem 16. *Uniform Coordination is equally hard when channels guarantee delivery as when they do not.*

Proof. (Sketch. See [14]) Proposition 12 shows processes must invoke shunning to disable each other; disabling arises because of the desire to make exempt processes appear crashed, and this requires some mechanism by which processes can revoke another's ability to take actions. As a result, even when channels may guarantee delivery, no process can know a message it sends will be received – the destination may be shunning it – which is exactly the case when channels do not guarantee delivery. □

4.3 A Solution to Uniform Coordination

Figure 3 gives a solution to Uniform Coordination. The majority requirement for disabling a process percolates up to $\text{PERMIT}_p(\alpha)$: a process that has not received $ack('\alpha')$s from a majority cannot then disable that unresponsive majority. The message $\diamond\text{shun}(T)$ is the request to shun processes in T, and the statement "await x messages" prevents a process from continuing until it has received at least x messages, though it may elect to wait for more responses.

/* Alg 4 : Initiator p */	/* Alg 4 : Respondent q - action */
choose α from task list; $Mcast_p(S, \alpha)$; await $recv_p^*(q, \text{`}\alpha\text{'})$ for $q \in M \subset S$; $T = \{q \in S - M \mid \neg K_p \Diamond \text{DIS'D}(q)\}$ $Mcast_p(M, \Diamond\text{shun}(T))$ await $recv_p^*(q', \text{ack}(\Diamond\text{shun}(T)))$ for $q' \in$ $M' \subseteq M$, still a majority of S /* $K_p \Diamond \text{DIS'D}(r)$ for $r \in S - M$ */ do α;	$recv_q^*(p, \text{`}\alpha\text{'})$;   if promised $\Diamond\text{SHUN}_q(p)$ then choose fairly      a. $send_q(p, \text{ack}(\text{`}\alpha\text{'}))$; add α to task list; b. begin shunning p; else $send_q(p, \text{ack}(\text{`}\alpha\text{'}))$; add α to task list; /* Alg 4 : Respondent q - shun */ $recv_q^*(p, \Diamond\text{shun}(T))$; if promised $\Diamond\text{SHUN}_q(p)$ then choose fairly a. $send_q(p, \text{ack}(\Diamond\text{shun}(T)))$; add T to shun list; b. begin shunning p; else $send_q(p, \text{ack}(\Diamond\text{shun}(T)))$; add S to shun list;

Figure 3. Solution to Uniform Coordination.

A majority must agree to shun a process to actually disable it, but processes may begin shunning without further communication; while it must be done 'uniformly' a process does not need permission to take the action $shun(p)$. This follows because, in contrast to $do_q(\alpha)$, q shunning r and q crashing both achieve the promised effect.

5 Conclusions

This paper describes necessary and sufficient conditions for a group of autonomous processes to take actions uniformly in asynchronous systems. In the absence of infinite storage space and failure detectors of guaranteed strength, communication and its lack are vital in ensuring both safety and liveness. That the relatively weak Uniformity problem requires majority agreement is due to the desire to *simulate* exempting processes from acting only if they have crashed; exempt processes must appear, for all intents and purposes, as if they had failed.

Terminal exemptions induce a primary partition behavior, but we can imagine coordination problems for which exemptions need not be terminal. These are exactly the problems in which progress can be made in multiple sides of a partition. Thus, it seems fruitful to understand coordination problems in terms of limiting the behavior of processes that, during certain periods, cannot be accounted for. Knowing what is possible during partitions is especially important in wide-area and cellular networks in which connectivity guarantees, due to cost and technology limitations, are less certain.

Finally, solutions to Uniform Coordination will eventually need to add processes and redefine obligation sets if runs are to be infinite. Since our exemption is terminal, once a minority are *either* crashed *or* disabled, we have reached the 'natural' limits. Individual problems will decide when and how to define the new obligation set to reflect the degree of system-wide coordination desired.

References

1. Y. Amir, D. Dolev, S. Kramer, and D. Malki. Transis: A Communication Sub-System for High Availability. In *22nd FTCS*, pages 76–84. IEEE, 1992.
2. K. P. Birman and R. van Renesse. *Reliable Distributed Computing with the Isis Toolkit*. IEEE Computer Society Press, 1994.
3. T. D. Chandra, V. Hadzilacos, and S. Toueg. The Weakest Failure Detector for Solving Consensus. In *11th PODC*, pages 147–158. ACM, 1992.
4. K. M. Chandy and L. Lamport. Distributed Snapshots: Determining Global States of Distributed Systems. *ACM TOCS*, 3(1):63–75, 1985.
5. K. M. Chandy and J. Misra. How Processes Learn. *Distributed Computing*, 1(1):40–52, 1986.
6. B. Chor and C. Dwork. Randomization in Byzantine Agreement. *Advances in Computer Research*, 5:443–497, 1989.
7. M. J. Fischer, N. A. Lynch, and M. S. Paterson. Impossibility of Distributed Consensus with One Faulty Process. *JACM*, 32(2):374–382, 1985.
8. A. Gopal and S. Toueg. Reliable Broadcast in Synchronous and Asynchronous Environments. In *3rd WDAG – LNCS 392*, pages 110–123. Springer Verlag, 1989.
9. J.Y. Halpern and Y. Moses. Knowledge and Common Knowledge in a Distributed Environment. *JACM*, 37(3):549–587, 1990.
10. L. Lamport. Time, Clocks and the Ordering of Events in a Distributed System. *Communications of the ACM*, 21(7):558–565, 1978.
11. L. Lamport, R. Shostak, and M. Pease. The Byzantine Generals Problem. *ACM Transactions on Programming Languages and Systems*, 4(3):382–401, 1982.
12. D. Malki, K. P. Birman, A. Ricciardi, and A. Schiper. Uniform Actions in Asynchronous Distributed Systems. In *13th PODC*, pages 274–284. ACM, 1994.
13. A. Ricciardi. Dissecting Distributed Coordination in Asynchronous Systems. Technical Report ECE-PDS-9502, The Univerisity of Texas, 1995.
14. A. Ricciardi. Sequential Distributed Coordination. Technical Report ECE-PDS-9503, The Univerisity of Texas, 1995.
15. A. Ricciardi and K. Birman. Using Process Groups to Implement Failure Detection in Asynchronous Environments. In *10th PODC*, pages 341–351. ACM, 1991.
16. L. Sabel and K. Marzullo. Simulating Fail-Stop in Asynchronous Distributed Systems. In *13th Symposium on Rel. Dist. Sys.*, pages 138–47. IEEE, 1994.
17. R. van Renesse, T. Hickey, and K. Birman. Design and Performance of Horus: A Lightweight Group Communications System. Technical Report 94-1441, Cornell University, 1994.

Optimal Broadcast with Partial Knowledge

(Extended Abstract)

Baruch Awerbuch [*]   Shay Kutten [†]   Yishay Mansour [‡]

David Peleg [§]

June 28, 1995

Abstract

This work concerns the problem of broadcasting a large message efficiently when each processor has partial prior knowledge about the contents of the broadcast message. The partial information held by the processors might be out of date or otherwise erroneous, and consequently, different processors may hold conflicting information.

The problem of Broadcast with Partial Knowledge (BPK) was introduced in the context of Topology Update - the task of updating network nodes about the network topology after topological changes. Awerbuch, Cidon, and Kutten gave a message optimal solution for BPK, yielding a message optimal Topology Update algorithm. However, the time complexity of both algorithms was not optimal. The time complexity was subsequently improved in two follow up papers, but the best known time complexity was still higher than optimal by at least a logarithmic factor.

In this paper we present a time-optimal, communication-optimal algorithm for BPK. The algorithm is randomized, and, similar to previous randomized algorithms, it does not require the additional knowledge assumptions essential for deterministic solutions. In addition to the theoretical interest in optimality, a logarithmic factor is often important in practice, especially when using the procedure as a component within a periodically activated Topology Update algorithm.

[*]Johns Hopkins University, Baltimore, MD 21218, and MIT Lab. for Computer Science (baruch@blaze.cs.jhu.edu). Supported by Air Force Contract TNDGAFOSR-86-0078, ARPA/Army contract DABT63-93-C-0038, ARO contract DAAL03-86-K-0171, NSF contract 9114440-CCR, DARPA contract N00014-J-92-1799, and a special grant from IBM.

[†]IBM T.J. Watson Research Center P.O. Box 704, Yorktown Heights, NY 10598 (kutten@watson.ibm.com).

[‡]Department of Computer Science, Tel Aviv University, Tel Aviv 69978, Israel (mansour@math.tau.ac.il).

[§]Department of Applied Mathematics and Computer Science, The Weizmann Institute, Rehovot 76100, Israel (peleg@wisdom.weizmann.ac.il). Supported in part by an Allon Fellowship, by a Walter and Elise Haas Career Development Award and by a Bantrell Fellowship.

1 Introduction

1.1 Motivation

Many tasks in distributed computing deal with concurrently maintaining the "view" of a common object in many separate sites of a distributed system. This object may be the topology of a communication network (in which case the view is a description of the underlying network graph), or certain resources held at the system sites (in which case the view is an inventory listing the resources held at each site), or even a general database. The objects considered here are dynamic in nature, and are subject to occasional changes (e.g., a link fails, a resource unit is consumed or released, a database record is modified). It is thus necessary to have an efficient mechanism for maintaining consistent and updated views of the object at the different sites.

One obvious algorithm for maintaining updated views of a distributed object is the *Full Broadcast* algorithm. This algorithm is based on initiating a broadcast of the entire view of the object whenever a change occurs. Due to the possibility of message pipelining, the time complexity of this algorithm is relatively low. On the other hand, this algorithm might be very wasteful in communication, since the object may be rather large.

Consequently, it is clear that a successful consistency maintenance strategy should strive to utilize the fact that the processors already have a correct picture of "most" of the object, and need to be informed of relatively few changes. Viewed from this angle, the problem can be thought of as having to broadcast the entire view of the object, while taking advantage of prior partial knowledge available to the processors of the system.

On the other extreme there is the *Incremental Update* strategy, in which only "necessary" information is transmitted. This strategy is at the heart of the algorithms suggested for handling the topology update problem ([ACK90, MRR80, SG89, BGJ+85]). Unfortunately, it is not obvious how to employ information pipelining with this method, as demonstrated in the sequel. This increases the time complexity.

The purpose of this work is to study the problem of updating a distributed database, under minimal assumptions. That is, we do not assume any initial coordination and allow only small amount of space. Under such conditions, we look for efficient solutions to the problem with respect to communication and time overheads. In this setting, it turns out that the main bottleneck of the database update problem can be characterized as a fairly simple "communication complexity" problem, called *Broadcast with Partial Knowledge*.

The problem of Broadcast with Partial Knowledge was introduced in the context of Topology Update - the task of updating network nodes about the network topology after topological changes. Awerbuch, Cidon, and Kutten gave a message optimal solution, thus yielding a message optimal Topology Update algorithm. However, the time complexity (of both the broadcast with partial knowledge, and the topology update) was not optimal. The time complexity was subsequently improved in two follow up papers, one providing a randomized algorithm (using fewer assumptions on knowledge) [ACK+91], and one giving a deterministic algorithm (using a stronger knowledge assumption, and with time complexity higher by a polylogarithmic factor)[AS91]. The time complexity of the randomized algorithm of [ACK$^+$91] was still higher than optimal by at least a logarithmic factor. While this may not seem a large factor from the theoretical point of view, it is still interesting to find out that an optimal algorithm is possible. From the practical point of view, getting rid of a logarithmic factor is often important, especially in the context of the practically significant Topology Update problem.

In this paper we present a time optimal algorithm. The algorithm is randomized, and, similar to the previous randomized algorithm of [ACK$^+$91], does not require the additional knowledge required by any possible deterministic algorithm. The message complexity of the algorithm is optimal too. The improvement in the time complexity is obtained by "simulating" the previous algorithm but in a less synchronized manner. This enables full pipelining, while in the previous algorithm there may have been times nodes could not transmit between "phases".

1.2   The model and the problem

The *Broadcast with Partial Knowledge* problem can be formulated as follows. Consider an asynchronous communication network, consisting of $n+1$ processors, $p_0, \ldots, p_n$, with each processor p_i has an m-bit *local input* w_i, and processor p_0 is distinguished as the *broadcaster*. In a correct solution to the problem all the processors write in their local output the value of the broadcaster's input, $w = w_0$.

This formulation of the problem can be interpreted as follows. The input w_i is stored at processor p_i and describes the local representation of the object at processor p_i. The correct description of the object is $w = w_0$, held by the broadcaster. The local descriptions w_i may differ from the correct one as a result of changes in the object. In particular, every two processors may have different descriptions due to different messages they got from the broadcaster in the past, as a result of message losses, topology changes and the asynchronous nature of the network. Our goal is to inform all the processors throughout the network about the correct view of the object w, and to use the processor's local inputs given to each processor in order to minimize the time and communication complexities.

In this paper, we provide a randomized solution for the hardest version of this problem, in which each processor only knows its own input, and has no information regarding inputs of other processors. A weaker version of the problem is based on making the rather strong "neighbor knowledge" assumption, namely, assuming that each processor correctly knows the inputs of all its neighbors, in addition to its own. This assumption is justified in [ACK90], where it is shown that neighbor-knowledge comes for free in context of database and topology update protocols. Even for this weaker problem, none of the previously known solutions are optimal *both* in communication and time. Following the randomized algorithm of [ACK$^+$91], a deterministic algorithm was given for the weaker problem [AS91]. The complexity of that algorithm is larger than that of the randomized algorithm presented here by a polylogarithmic factor.

In order to quantify the possibility of exploiting local knowledge, we first introduce a new measure that captures the level of "information" of the knowledge held by each processor. Let the *discrepancy* δ_i of the input w_i held by processor p_i be the number of bits in which w_i, the local description at p_i, differs from the broadcaster's input w, which is the correct description of the object. Define also the *total discrepancy* $\Delta = \sum_i \delta_i$, the *average discrepancy* $\delta_{av} = \Delta/n$, and the *maximum discrepancy* $\delta_{max} = \max_i\{\delta_i\}$.

Our goal is to study the relationships between these discrepancies and the complexity of broadcast algorithms, following the intuition that the complexity of broadcast protocols should be proportional to discrepancy of processors' inputs, i.e., if the views of most processors are "almost correct", then the overhead of the protocol should be small. We therefore express the communication and time complexity of our solution as a function of m, n and δ_{av}. The complexities are measured in the bit complexity model.

1.3 Basic solutions

The first obvious solution to the *Broadcast with Partial Knowledge* problem is the aforementioned *Full Broadcast* protocol, which is wasteful in communication, i.e. requires $\Omega(nm)$ bits. On the other hand it is rather fast, since the broadcast can be done in a pipelined fashion and thus can terminate in $O(n + m)$ time. Thus, one would like to improve on this algorithm with respect to communication complexity, aiming towards reducing this complexity to be close to the total discrepancy Δ, while maintaining near-optimal time complexity.

The *Incremental Update* strategy proposed in [ACK90] poses an alternative approach. It can be applied only under the strong assumption of "neighbor knowledge": each node is assumed to "know" the value of the database at its neighbor. The essence of this strategy is that a node with "correct" view transmits to its neighbor a "correction" list, which contains all the positions where neighbor's input is erroneous. When the neighbor received all the corrections, it can assume that the rest of its input is correct, and start using it for correcting its own neighbors who are further away from the source. Thus a "correction wave" propagates through the network from the source, till all nodes are corrected. Note that there is almost no pipelining possible in this algorithm as described above, since a node can start transmitting only after it done with the receiving. Even in the simple case of a path network the protocol may require $\Omega(\Delta)$ time. As mentioned above, in the follow-up paper [AS91] the complexity of this strategy (for the "neighbor knowledge" variant of the problem) was improved significantly (although still not matching the lower bound), using a very sophisticated partitioning of the information, and a recursive implementation.

1.4 Our results

In this paper, we provide an efficient randomized solution to the Broadcast with Partial Knowledge problem. It has success probability at least $1 - \epsilon$, and uses $O(\Delta \log m + n \log \frac{n}{\epsilon})$ communication and $O(n + m)$ time, where ϵ is a parameter to the algorithm. The algorithm can be easily adapted to be executed on trees, rather than on a line (which is the "worst-case" tree) as described here. Thus in an arbitrary topology network, performing the algorithm on a shortest-path tree yields the same message complexity, with the time complexity being $O(D + m)$, where D

Algorithm	Communication	Time	
Full broadcast (folklore)	nm	$n + m$	
Incr. Update [ACK90]	$n + \Delta \log m$	$n + \Delta \log m$	NK
[ACK+91]	$\Delta \log m + n \log \frac{n}{\epsilon}$	$n \log \delta_{av} m + \log \frac{1}{\epsilon}\}$	
[AS91]	$(\delta_{av} + 1)n \log m$	$(n + m) \log^3 m$	NK
Our algorithm	$\Delta \log m + n \log \frac{n}{\epsilon}$	$n + \log \frac{n}{\epsilon} + \min\{m, \Delta \log m\}$	
Lower bounds [ACK+91]	$n + n\delta_{max} \log(m/\delta_{max})$	$n + \delta_{max} \log(m/\delta_{max})$	

Figure 1: Comparison of protocols and lower bounds. "NK" stands for the neighbor knowledge assumption.

is the network diameter. Note that in all cases, we allow the inputs stored at the various processors to differ in arbitrary ways, subject to the discrepancy constraints.

Our upper bounds are derived using linear codes. Such codes were used before in constructing distributed algorithms for solving various problems. In particular they are used in a similar way by [ACK+91]. Metzner [Met84] uses Reed-Solomon and random codes to achieve efficient retransmission protocols in a complete network. Ben-Or, Goldwasser and Wigderson [BGW88] use BCH codes to guarantee privacy in a malicious environment. Rabin [Rab89] uses codes to achieve a reliable fault-tolerant routing with a low overhead.

In [ACK+91] it was shown that when the average discrepancy is δ_{max}, the communication complexity is at least $\Omega(\Delta \log(\frac{m}{\delta_{max}}))$ and the time complexity is at least $\Omega(n + \delta_{max} \log(\frac{m}{\delta_{max}}))$. It is also argued there that in the case that no information is known about the discrepancies, any deterministic protocol would send $\Omega(nm)$ bits, even if there are *no* discrepancies at all.

1.5 Applications

One application of our work is to the classical network problem of Topology Update, which is at the heart of many practical network protocols [MRR80, BGJ+85, ACG+90]. In Topology Update, initially, each processor is aware of the status of its adjacent links, i.e., whether each link is up or down, but may not be aware of the status of other links. The purpose of the protocol is to supply each processor with this global link status information.

The topology update algorithm of [ACK90] is based on the *Incremental Update* strategy. The possibility of recurring network partitions and reconnections significantly complicates implementation of this strategy. Nevertheless, the resulting broadcast procedure is efficient in terms of communication (although not in time), and leads to essentially communication-optimal topology update protocols [ACK90].

A consequence of [ACK90] that is most significant for our purposes is the observation that it is possible to relate the complexities of the problem of Broadcasting with Partial Knowledge to those of Topology Update, effectively reducing the latter problem to the former. Namely, given *any* solution for the Broadcast with Partial Knowledge problem, one can construct a topology update protocol with a similar overheads in both communication and time.

Reference	Amortized Commun.	Quiescence Time
Full broadcast ([AAG87])	VE	$V + E$
Incr. Update [ACK90]	$V \log E$	$V^2 \cdot \log E$
Our upper bound	$V \log E$	$E + V \log V$
Lower bounds	$V \log E$	E

Figure 2: Applications of Partial Knowledge Broadcast protocols to topology update.

Figure 2 summarizes the complexities of protocols to the topology update task obtained by applying various Broadcast with Partial Knowledge algorithms (with V, E denoting the number of vertices and edges in the network, respectively).

It is worth pointing out that our complexity results are presented in the bit complexity model, whereas the results in [ACK90] are presented in the message complexity model which charges only one complexity units for a message of size $O(\log n)$ bits.

Our algorithm may also be applicable for dealing with the issue of self stabilization [Dij74, ASY90, KP90, APV91]. The self-stabilization approach is directed at dealing with intermittent faults that may change the memory contents of nodes, and cause inconsistency between the local states of nodes. Dijkstra's example [Dij74] is that of a token passing system, where it is required that exactly one of the nodes holds a *token* at any given time. The faults may cause an illegal situation in which no node holds a token (each "assumes" that some other has it) or alternatively, that several nodes hold a token. Overcoming such faults requires the nodes to continuously check the states of their neighbors, and possibly to correct them when necessary. It is conceivable that the faults cause only partial changes in memory, so our algorithm can be used to mend the situation. Note that in this context, it is essential that we do not make the "neighbor knowledge" assumption.

1.6 Organization of the paper

The rest of the paper is structured as follows. In section 2 we review for later use some necessary material concerning universal hash functions and coding theory. This background is mostly the same as in [ACK+91]. In Section 3, we first describe the algorithms of [ACK+91], that motivate and help in the proof of the new result, which is algorithm BPart in Subsection 3.4. The full proof of the new result is given in [ACK+95], but we do point out similarities between the proofs and parts of the proof of the previous algorithms. This is possible since the new algorithm is basically a simulation of the previous algorithms, but with enhanced pipelining. It is hoped that the new pipelining technique can be used to help pipeline other phase based algorithms.

2 Preliminaries

2.1 Universal hash functions

Universal hash functions have found many interesting applications since their introduction by Carter and Wegman [WC79]. A family of functions $\mathcal{F} = \{h : A \to B\}$ is called a *universal hash function* if for any $a_1 \neq a_2 \in A$ and $b_1, b_2 \in B$ the following holds:

$$Prob[h(a_1) = b_1 \text{ and } h(a_2) = b_2] = \frac{1}{|B|^2}$$

where the probability is taken over the possible choices of h, which is randomly and uniformly chosen from $\mathcal{F}$.

There are many families of simple universal hash functions. One example can be constructed as follows. Let p be a prime and let $B = Z_p$. (Note $|B| = p$.) Then

$$H = \{h_{\alpha,\beta}(x) = (\alpha x + \beta) \bmod p \mid \alpha, \beta \in Z_p\}$$

is a family of universal hash functions.

In the above example the encoding of a hash function requires only two elements from Z_p, and also p, therefore we can describe such a hash function using only $O(\log|B|)$ bits. (Note that the encoding of h does not depend on A.) Later, when using a universal hash function, it is assumed that it can be represented with $O(\log|B|)$ bits.

Another way to view the parameters is the following. We are interested in a family of universal hash functions $\mathcal{F}_\epsilon$, that has the following property: given any two distinct elements, the probability that a random hash function $h \in \mathcal{F}_\epsilon$ maps them to the same point, is bounded by ϵ. From the properties of the universal hash function this occurs with probability $1/|B|$. Therefore, choosing $\epsilon = 1/|B|$, we conclude that there is a family of hash functions $\mathcal{F}_\epsilon$ whose encoding size is $O(\log\frac{1}{\epsilon})$.

2.2 Information theoretic background

The tools developed later on are based on some basic results from coding theory. A code $C_{m,d} : \{0,1\}^m \mapsto \{0,1\}^{m+r}$ is a mapping that transforms an input word $w \in \{0,1\}^m$ into a codeword $C_{m,d}(w) = \hat{w} \in \{0,1\}^{m+r}$. The codes considered in this paper are standard "check-bit" codes, namely, the resulting codeword $\hat{w}$ is assumed to be of the form $\hat{w} = w \| \rho$, where $\rho \in \{0,1\}^r$ is a "trail" of r check bits concatenated to the input word w, called the *syndrom*. Denote the check bit syndrom that the code $C_{m,d}$ attaches to a word w by $C^*_{m,d}(w)$. The lengths of the entire codeword and the check bit syndrom are denoted in the sequel by $|C_{m,d}(w)|$ and $|C^*_{m,d}(w)|$, respectively.

A code $C_{m,d}$ is said to be *d-correcting* if the original word w can be correctly decoded from any word z that differs from the codeword $C_{m,d}(w)$ in no more than d places.

The following theorem states the properties possessed by the code necessary for our purposes.

Theorem 2.1 ([ACK+91]) For any m and $d \leq m/3$, there exists a check-bit code $C_{m,d}$ with the following properties:

1. The check bit syndrom is of length $|C^*_{m,d}(w)| = O(d \log m)$.

2. The code $C_{m,d}$ is d-correcting.

3. The encoding and decoding operations ($C_{m,d}$ and $C^{-1}_{m,d}$, respectively) require time polynomial in m and d.

In order to prove the theorem, [ACK+91] modified BCH codes slightly. All codes $C_{m,d}$ referred to later on in the paper are meant to be check-bit codes that satisfy the properties in Theorem 2.1. The subscripts m, d are omitted whenever m and d are clear from the context.

3 Upper bounds

We develop our solution in a modular fashion via a number of steps. The first three steps follow [ACK+91]. The first step is a simple algorithm named MAXIMUM, presented in Subsection 3.1, which is based on the assumption that the maximum discrepancy δ_{max} is known to the broadcaster. Next, Subsection 3.2 presents the algorithm AVERAGE, which assumes only knowledge of the average discrepancy. Then, in Subsection 3.3 it is shown that the assumptions about knowledge of the discrepancy can be eliminated at the cost of increasing the time complexity by a factor of $\log \delta_{av}$. Finally, in Subsection 3.4 we present our new algorithm, based on condensing the previous algorithm, so that its time complexity becomes optimal again.

3.1 Algorithm MAXIMUM

This section handles broadcast in the case where the maximum discrepancy δ_{max} is known, and presents a straightforward broadcasting algorithm MAXIMUM, which assumes that the broadcaster "knows" δ_{max}. The algorithm requires $O(n\delta_{max} \log m)$ communication and $O(n + \delta_{max} \log m)$ time.

We should note that this algorithm is not efficient, since the maximum discrepancy can be very far from the average discrepancy. This algorithm is presented, in order to be used in the next section as a subroutine.

For simplicity, it is assumed that the network is a simple path, namely, the $n + 1$ processors $p_0, \ldots, p_n$ are arranged on a line, with a bidirectional link connecting processor p_i to processor p_{i+1}, for every $0 \leq i < n$. Note that this does not restrict generality in any way, since the path is the worst topology for broadcast, and moreover, there exists an easy transformation from every other network to a path network by using a depth-first tour ([Eve79]).

Algorithm MAXIMUM works as follows: The *broadcaster* encodes the broadcast message w using the code $C = C_{m,\delta_{max}}$. (Note that this code C is fixed and known to all other processors.) The broadcaster broadcasts only the check bit syndrom $C^*(w)$. The broadcasting proceeds in full pipelining. I.e., each processor p_i for $i < n$ that receives the first bit of $C^*(w)$ immediately forwards it to processor p_{i+1}, without waiting for the entire value of $C^*(w)$.

Once a processor p_i has received the complete message $\rho = C^*(w)$, it concatenates it to its own input w_i, thus obtaining a complete (but possibly corrupted) codeword $\hat{w}_i = w_i \| \rho$ and decodes this codeword by computing $o_i = C^{-1}(\hat{w}_i)$, which is taken to be the output.

Lemma 3.1 ([ACK+91]) If the input w_i of processor p_i is different from w in at most δ_{max} places, then $o_i = w$.

Lemma 3.2 ([ACK+91]) The time Complexity of Algorithm MAXIMUM is $n + O(\delta_{max} \cdot \log m)$, and its communication complexity is $O(n \cdot \delta_{max} \log m)$.

We complete the description by noting that both the time and communication complexities can be improved for large δ_{max}. Specifically, if $\delta_{max} \log m > m$, then a full broadcast of the information is more efficient (namely, send w to all the processors). Therefore we have

Theorem 3.3 ([ACK+91]) Given the value of δ_{max}, there is a deterministic algorithm for performing broadcast with partial information, that requires $n + O(\min\{m, \delta_{max} \cdot \log m\})$ time and has communication complexity $O(n \cdot \min\{m, \delta_{max} \cdot \log m\})$.

A similar result holds when the broadcaster knows only an upper bound d on the discrepancies, where the same complexities hold except with d replacing δ_{max}. When the upper bound is "accurate", namely $d = O(\delta_{max})$, the complexities remain the same.

Note that the communication complexity of this algorithm is not good when there are differences between the discrepancies of nodes. For example, consider the case that one one has a high discrepancy. This forces the algorithm to send a long check bit syndrom also to the other nodes on the way, although they have low discrepancies. The algorithm of the next subsection manages to fix this problem, even though it relies on a weaker assumption.

3.2 Algorithm AVERAGE

In this section we replace the assumption of known δ_{max} with the assumption that the average discrepancy δ_{av} is known. Note that no assumptions are made about how the discrepancies are distributed. In particular, it may be that some processors have large discrepancies while others have the correct value. For simplicity of notation, we assume throughout the section that $\delta_{av} \geq 1$, or $\Delta \geq n$.

The broadcast algorithm AVERAGE presented in this section is randomized, i.e., it guarantees the correctness of the output of each processor with high probability. The communication complexity of Algorithm AVERAGE depends linearly on the average discrepancy δ_{av}, while its time complexity is still linear in m. Both complexities apply to the worst case scenario.

We begin with a high level description of Algorithm AVERAGE. The algorithm works in phases, and invokes Algorithm MAXIMUM of Section 3.1 at each phase. At every phase of the execution, each processor can be in one of two states, denoted $\mathcal{K}$ and $\mathcal{R}$. Initially, only the broadcaster is in state $\mathcal{K}$, while the other processors are in state $\mathcal{R}$. Intuitively, a processor p_i switches from state $\mathcal{R}$ to state $\mathcal{K}$ when it concludes that his current guess for w is equal to the "real" broadcast word w.

The phases are designed to handle processors with increasingly larger discrepancies. More specifically, let us classify the processors into classes $C_1, \ldots, C_\mu$, $\mu = \left\lceil \log(\frac{m}{\delta_{av} \log m}) \right\rceil$, where the class C_l contains all processors p_i whose discrepancy δ_i falls in the range $2^{l-1}\delta_{av} < \delta_i \leq \min\{m, 2^l\delta_{av}\}$ for $2 \leq l \leq \mu - 1$, $\delta_i \leq 2\delta_{av}$ for $l = 1$, and the rest in C_μ (i.e., $\delta_i \geq \frac{m}{\log m}$). Then each phase $l \geq 0$ is responsible for informing the processors in class C_l. This is done by letting the processors in state $\mathcal{K}$ broadcast to the other processors.

Note that the $\mathcal{K}$ and $\mathcal{R}$ states reflect, in a sense, only the processors' "state of mind", and not necessarily the true situation. It might happen that a processor switches prematurely to state $\mathcal{K}$, erroneously believing it holds the true value of the input w. Such an error might subsequently propagate to neighboring processors as well. Our analysis will show that this happens only with low probability.

By a simple counting argument, the fraction of processors whose discrepancy satisfies $\delta_i \geq k\delta_{av}$ is bounded above by $\frac{1}{k}$, for every $k \geq 1$. The first phase attempts to correct the inputs of processors from C_1, while in general, the l-th phase attempts to correct the processors in C_l. By the previous argument, at least half of the processors are in C_1, and furthermore, $\sum_{j=l}^{\mu} |C_j| \leq \frac{n}{2^l}$. Assuming that all the processor that shifted from $\mathcal{R}$ to $\mathcal{K}$ had the correct value, then after the l-th phase, at most $\frac{n}{2^l}$ processors are in state $\mathcal{R}$.

Let us now describe the structure of a phase l in more detail. At the beginning of phase l, the current states of the processors induces a conceptual partition of the line network into consecutive intervals $I_1, \ldots, I_t$, with each interval $I = (p_i, p_{i+1}, \ldots)$ containing one or more processors, such that the first processor p_i is in state $\mathcal{K}$, and the rest of the processors (if any) are in state $\mathcal{R}$.

The algorithm maintains the property that each processor knows its state, as well as the state of its two neighbors, hence each processor knows its relative role in its interval, as either a "head" of the interval, an intermediate processor, or a "tail" (i.e., the last processor of the interval).

Suppose that processor p_i is in state $\mathcal{K}$ at the beginning of phase $l < \mu$ and is the "head" of some interval I. If p_{i+1} is also in state $\mathcal{K}$, then the interval I contains only p_i, and thus p_i has finished its part in the algorithm. Otherwise, interval I contains at least one processor in state $\mathcal{R}$. In this case, processor p_i is assigned the role of the *broadcaster* with respect to its interval in phase l. More specifically, it needs to inform its value to all processors of class C_l in its interval I. Hopefully, this results in the further partition of interval I into subintervals for the next phase.

Processor p_i performs this task by using Algorithm MAXIMUM of Section 3.1, with parameter $d_l = 2^l\delta_{av}$. To be more specific, if p_i's interval I contains other processors (i.e., processor p_{i+1} is in state $\mathcal{R}$) then p_i computes $C^*_{m,d_l}(o_i)$ and sends it to p_{i+1}. (In case $l = \mu$, processor p_i sends o_i.) As we shall see, with high probability $o_i = w$ for any processor i that is in state $\mathcal{K}$. Therefore, later in this informal description we substitute $C^*_{m,d_l}(w)$ for $C^*_{m,d_l}(o_i)$. Consider any intermediate processor p_j (in state $\mathcal{R}$) in interval I that receives a message simply forwards the message (using pipelining). The tail processor of the interval (i.e., the one whose successor is in state $\mathcal{K}$) does nothing.

It remains to explain when a processor decides to change its state from $\mathcal{R}$ to $\mathcal{K}$. This task requires an *initialization* phase, in which the broadcaster chooses a random universal hash function $h \in \mathcal{F}_{\epsilon/n\mu}$ and sends both the description of h and the hashed value of the broadcast message, i.e., the pair

$$\mathcal{H}(w) = \langle h, h(w) \rangle,$$

to all processors. Since the description of h requires $O(\log \frac{n\mu}{\epsilon})$ bits, the size of the message is $O(\log \frac{n\mu}{\epsilon}) = O(\log \log m + \log \frac{n}{\epsilon})$. The pair $\mathcal{H}(w)$ will later serve each processor to test whether its new computed value of w is correct.

Specifically, as said above, in phase $l < \mu$ each processor p_j in state $\mathcal{R}$ receives $\rho_l = C^*_{m,d_l}(w)$. It concatenates it to w_j and computes

$$g_j(l) = C^{-1}_{m,d_l}(w_j C^*_{m,d_l}(w)),$$

which is its "guess" for w. It then tests whether $h(g_j(l)) = h(w)$.

In case of equality, the processor deduces that its current guess is correct. It then changes its state from $\mathcal{R}$ to $\mathcal{K}$, and sets its output to be $o_j = g_j(l)$. At the last phase, $l = \mu$, when a processor p_j receives value o_i, from some processor p_i, then p_j sets $o_j = o_i$. The algorithm ends after phase μ.

Lemma 3.4 ([ACK$^+$91]) The probability that some processor produces an incorrect output is bounded above by ϵ.

Now, we analyze the communication and time complexity of the protocol. We first show that if no node mistakenly outputs an incorrect value, then both time and communication complexities are small.

Lemma 3.5 ([ACK$^+$91]) Assuming that no processor outputs an incorrect value, the time complexity of Algorithm AVERAGE is $O(n + m + \log \frac{1}{\epsilon})$, and its communication complexity is $O(\Delta \log m + n \log \frac{n}{\epsilon})$.

Note that ϵ can always be chosen so as to make the failure probability polynomially small in m, without degrading the time or communication complexities of the algorithm. Consequently we have

Theorem 3.6 Given an average discrepancy δ_{av} and $0 < \epsilon < 1$, Algorithm AVERAGE solves the broadcast with partial knowledge problem correctly with probability $1 - \epsilon$. In the case that the solution is correct, the time complexity is $O(n + m + \log \frac{1}{\epsilon})$ and the communication complexity is $O(\delta_{av} \cdot n \cdot \log m + n \log \frac{n}{\epsilon})$ bits.

In case algorithm AVERAGE fails, and the output is incorrect, we can guarantee only trivial bounds on the time and communication complexities of the algorithm. These bounds are derived from bounding the number of phases by $\log m$, and the number of bits in a message by m. This gives a worst case bounds of $O((n+m)\log m)$ time and $O(nm)$ communication. However, ϵ can be selected so as to equate the expected complexity (over all executions) with the high probability complexity (i.e. over the executions that have a correct output) . Consequently we have

Corollary 3.7 Algorithm AVERAGE has expected time complexity $O(n + m)$ and expected communication complexity of $O(\Delta \log m + n \log nm)$ bits.

3.3 Unknown discrepancy

In the case that δ_{av} is not known in advance, we can solve the problem by initiating Algorithm AVERAGE with a guessed average discrepancy $\hat{\delta}_{av} = 1$. Call this Algorithm UNKNOWN. In such a case, in the $\log \delta_{av}$ first phases of Algorithm AVERAGE, it may happen that no processor changes to $\mathcal{K}$. The communication complexity essentially remain the same, since the additional $O(\delta_{av} \cdot n) = O(\Delta)$ bits are absorbed in the previous bound. However, the time complexity does increase in this case by an additive factor of $O(n \log \delta_{av})$.

Theorem 3.8 ([ACK$^+$91]) Given $0 < \epsilon < 1$, Algorithm UNKNOWN solves the broadcast with partial knowledge correctly with probability $1 - \epsilon$. In the case that the solution is correct, the time complexity is $O(n \log \delta_{av} + m + \log \frac{1}{\epsilon})$ and the communication complexity is $O(\Delta \log m + n \log \frac{n}{\epsilon})$ bits.

In a similar way to the previous subsection, we can bound the expected complexities by choosing ϵ appropriately.

Corollary 3.9 ([ACK$^+$91]) Algorithm UNKNOWN has expected time complexity $O(n \log \delta_{av} + m)$ and expected communication complexity of $O(\Delta \log m + n \log nm)$ bits.

3.4 Optimal Time Complexity

Intuitively, the main reason that the time in the algorithm of the previous subsection is not optimal is the fact that there can be "time spaces" between the phases. In this section we describe a simulation of Algorithm UNKNOWN in which the information transmitted is fully pipelined. For the sake of clarity we describe the whole algorithm below.

Algorithm BPART

We assume that $\Delta \log m < mn$. If this assumption does not hold, then the algorithm might fail, at which time full broadcast can be engaged, since the maximum complexity must be paid in any case.

The algorithm requires an initialization phase similar to the one of Algorithm AVERAGE, in which a random universal hash function $h \in \mathcal{F}_{\epsilon/n\mu}$ is chosen and the pair $\mathcal{H}(w)$ is sent to all processors.

The main part of the algorithm proceed as follows. Set $\mu = \log m - \log \log m$. The source transmits the encoding $w(i) = C_{m,2^i}(w)$ of its vector w in all codes $C^*_{m,2^i}$ of all levels $0 \leq i \leq \mu$, one after another. Hence the sequence transmitted by the source is of the form

$$\xi(w) = \langle w(0), w(1), \ldots, w(\mu), w \rangle.$$

Essentially, this information is to be forwarded along the line to all processors. Observe that a naive implementation of this would require communication complexity nm and time $m + n$. The communication complexity is minimized by stopping the flood of bits into a node p_j once this node is able to correctly decode the entire source's vector ξ (with high probability), i.e., to produce an output o_j such that

$h(w) = h(o_j)$. This is done in the same way as in Algorithm UNKNOWN, as described below.

During the main part of the algorithm, each processor p_j on the line does the following. It initially enters state $\mathcal{R}$, intuitively signifying the fact that its data may be outdated. It then receives the sequence $\xi(o_{j-1})$ from its predecessor p_{j-1}, constructs its own output o_j and sequence $\xi(o_j)$, and sends this sequence to its successor. The incoming sequence is received and processed entry by entry, as long as p_j is in state $\mathcal{R}$.

Each arriving entry $o_{j-1}(i) = C^*_{m,2^i}(o_{j-1})$, $0 \leq i \leq \mu$, is processed as follows. First, the entry is stored as $o_j(i)$, and forwarded to p_{j+1}. In addition, p_j concatenates $o_{j-1}(i)$ to w_j, and computes its "guess" for w,

$$g_j(i) = C^{-1}_{m,2^i}(w_j \cdot C^*_{m,2^i}(o_{j-1})),$$

It then tests whether $h(g_j(i)) = h(w)$.

In case of equality, the processor does the following. First, it changes its state from $\mathcal{R}$ to $\mathcal{K}$, and informs its predecessor p_{j-1} to stop sending the rest of the sequence $\xi(o_{j-1})$. Next, it sets its output to be $o_j := g_j(i)$, and computes the rest of the sequence $\xi(o_j)$ locally (in order to be able to continue sending it to its successor on the line).

Note that p_j may fail in its tests in all stages $i \leq \mu$. In this case, it will receive the entire sequence $\xi(o_{j-1})$ from its predecessor, including o_{j-1} in its last entry, and adopt this value for o_j.

Let us now bound the probability of failure.

Lemma 3.10 The probability that some processor produces an incorrect output is bounded above by ϵ.

Finally, we analyze the communication and time complexity of the protocol.

Theorem 3.11 Assuming that no processor outputs an incorrect value, the communication complexity of Algorithm BPART is $O(\Delta \log m + n \log \frac{n}{\epsilon})$.

Theorem 3.12 Assuming that no processor outputs an incorrect value, the time complexity of Algorithm BPART is $O(n + \log \frac{n}{\epsilon} + \min\{m, \Delta \log m\})$.

As before, we bound the expected complexities by choosing ϵ appropriately.

Corollary 3.13 Algorithm BPART has expected time complexity $O(n + m)$ and expected communication complexity $O(\Delta \log m + n \log nm)$.

References

[AAG87]   Yehuda Afek, Baruch Awerbuch, and Eli Gafni. Applying static network protocols to dynamic networks. In 28th *Annual Symposium on Foundations of Computer Science*, October 1987.

[ACG+90]   Baruch Awerbuch, Israel Cidon, Inder Gopal, Marc Kaplan, and Shay Kutten. Distributed control for paris. In *Proc. 9th ACM Symp. on Principles of Distributed Computing*, 1990. To appear.

[ACK90]   Baruch Awerbuch, Israel Cidon, and Shay Kutten. Optimal maintenance of replicated information. In *Proc. 31st IEEE Symp. on Foundations of Computer Science*. Comp. Soc. of the IEEE, IEEE, 1990.

[ACK+91]   Baruch Awerbuch, Israel Cidon, Shay Kutten, Yishay Mansour, and David Peleg. Broadcast with partial knowledge. In *Proc. 10th ACM Symp. on Principles of Distributed Computing*, 1991.

[ACK+95]   Baruch Awerbuch, Israel Cidon, Shay Kutten, Yishay Mansour, and David Peleg. Optimal broadcast with partial knowledge. Manuscript, available on request. 1995.

[APV91]   Baruch Awerbuch, Boaz Patt-Shamir, and George Varghese. Self-stabilization by local checking and correction. In *Proc. 32nd IEEE Symp. on Foundations of Computer Science*, pages 268–277, October 1991.

[AS91]   Baruch Awerbuch and Leonard J. Schulman. The maintenance of common data in a distributed system. In *Proc. 32nd IEEE Symp. on Foundations of Computer Science*, October 1991.

[ASY90]   Y. Afek, S.Kutten, and M. Yung. Memory-efficient self-stabilization on general networks. In *Proc. 4th Workshop on Distributed Algorithms*, Italy, September 1990.

[BGJ+85]   A. E. Baratz, J. P. Gray, P. E. Green Jr., J. M. Jaffe, and D.P. Pozefski. Sna networks of small systems. *IEEE Journal on Selected Areas in Communications*, SAC-3(3):416–426, May 1985.

[BGW88]   Michael Ben-Or, Shafi Goldwasser, and Avi Wigderson. Completeness theorem for non-cryptographic fault tolerant distributed computing. In *Proc. 20th ACM Symp. on Theory of Computing*, May 1988.

[Dij74]   Edsger W. Dijkstra. Self stabilizing systems in spite of distributed control. *Commun. of the ACM*, 17:643–644, 1974.

[Eve79]   Shimon Even. *Graph Algorithms*. Computer Science Press, 1979.

[KP90]   Shmuel Katz and Kenneth Perry. Self-stabilizing extensions for message-passing systems. In *Proc. 10th ACM Symp. on Principles of Distributed Computing*, Quebec City, Canada, August 1990.

[Met84]   J. J. Metzner. An improved broadcast retransmission protocol. *IEEE Trans. on Communications*, COM-32(6):679–683, June 1984.

[MRR80]   I. McQuillan, I. Richer, and E.C. Rosen. The new routing algorithm for the arpanet. *IEEE Trans. on Commun.*, COM-28, May 1980.

[Rab89]   M. Rabin. efficient dispersal of information for security, load balancing, and fault tolerance. *J. of the ACM*, 36(3):335–348, 1989.

[SG89]   John M. Spinelli and Robert G. Gallager. Broadcasting topology information in computer networks. *IEEE Trans. on Commun.*, May 1989. to appear.

[Tiw84]   P. Tiwari. Lower bounds on communication complexity in distributed computer networks. In 25th *Annual Symposium on Foundations of Computer Science, Singer Island, Florida*, pages 109–117, 1984.

[WC79]   M.N. Wegman and J.L. Carter. Universal classes of hash functions. *Journal of Computer and System Sciences*, 18:143–154, 1979.

[Yao79]   Andy Yao. Some complexity questions related to distributed computing. In *Proceedings of the 11th Annual ACM Symposium on Theory of Computing, Atlanta, Georgia*, pages 209–213. ACM SIGACT, ACM, April 1979.

Multi-Dimensional Interval Routing Schemes*

Michele Flammini[1,2], Giorgio Gambosi[3], Umberto Nanni[1] and Richard B. Tan[4,5]

[1] Dipartimento di Informatica e Sistemistica,
University of Rome "La Sapienza",
via Salaria 113, I-00198 Rome, Italy
{flammini,nanni}@dis.uniroma1.it

[2] Dipartimento di Matematica Pura ed Applicata,
University of L'Aquila,
via Vetoio loc. Coppito, I-67010 l'Aquila, Italy

[3] Dipartimento di Matematica,
University of Rome "Tor Vergata",
via della Ricerca Scientifica, I-00133 Rome, Italy
gambosi@mat.utovrm.it,

[4] Department of Computer Science,
Utrecht University
Padualaan 14, 3584 CH Utrecht, the Netherlands
rbtan@cs.ruu.nl

[5] Department of Computer Science
University of Sciences & Arts of Oklahoma
Chickasha, OK 73119, U.S.A.

Abstract. Interval Routing Scheme (k-IRS) is a compact routing scheme on general networks. It has been studied extensively and recently been implemented on the latest generation INMOS Transputer Router chip. In this paper we introduce an extension of the Interval Routing Scheme k-IRS to the multi-dimensional case $\langle k, d \rangle$-MIRS, where k is the number of intervals and d is the number of dimensions. Whereas k-IRS only represents compactly a single shortest path between any two nodes, with this new extension we are able to represent *all* shortest paths compactly. This is useful for fault-tolerance and traffic distribution in a network. We study efficient representations of all shortest paths between any pair of nodes for general network topologies and for specific interconnection networks such as rings, grids, tori and hypercubes. For these interconnection networks we show that for about the same space complexity as k-IRS we can represent all shortest paths in $\langle k, d \rangle$-MIRS (as compared to only a single shortest path in k-IRS). Moreover, tradeoffs are derived between the dimension d and the number of intervals k in multi-dimensional interval routing schemes on hypercubes, grids and tori.

Keywords : Compact Routing Methods, Interval Routing Schemes, Interconnection Networks, Shortest Paths, Dimensions.

---

* Work supported by the **EEC ESPRIT II** Basic Research Action Program under contract No.8141 "Algorithms and Complexity II", by the EEC "Human Capital and Mobility" **MAP** project, and by the Italian **MURST** 40% project "Algoritmi, Modelli di Calcolo e Strutture Informative".

1 Introduction

Routing messages between pairs of processors is a fundamental task in a distributed computing system. In order to exchange messages between pairs of processors in such a way as to maintain a high throughput, it is important to route messages along paths of minimum cost (shortest paths). Moreover, the distributed nature of the system requires that path information be stored somehow at each intermediate node.

As more processors are added to the system in order to increase the computing power, the underlying communication network needs to *scale* favourably along with the expansion. Moreover, as the amount of storage space at each processor is limited, the expansion of the network should not put undue burden locally by requiring excessive space for communication purposes. The *routing* methods used should also be simple and dynamically adjustable with the expansion. The underlying network structure can be quite arbitrary, so the routing methods should not rely on any fixed *topology*. More and more emphasis is given to this type of *universal routing* on arbitrary networks (see, for example, [MT90], [I91], [HKR91]).

The trivial solution is the one of storing, at each node v, a complete routing table which specifies, for each destination u, one incident link belonging to a shortest path between u and v. Such a table has size $\Theta(n \cdot \log \delta)$, where δ is the node degree and n the size of the network. Since in the general case such tables are too space-consuming for large networks, it is necessary to devise routing schemes with smaller tables. This gives rise to a need of simple scalable and topology independent *compact routing* methods.

Research activities have focused on identifying classes of network topologies where the shortest path information at each node can be succinctly stored, assuming that suitably "short" labels can be assigned to nodes and links at preprocessing time. Such labels are used to encode useful information about the network structure, with special regard to shortest paths.

In the ILS (*Interval Labelling Scheme*) ([SK82], [LT83], [LT85]), node-labels belong to the set $\{1, \ldots, n\}$, while link-labels are pairs of node-labels representing disjoint intervals of $[1..n]$. To send a message m from a source v_i to a destination v_j, m is transmitted by v_i on the (unique) link $e = (v_i, v_k)$ such that the label of v_j belongs to the interval associated to e. With this approach, one always obtains an efficient memory occupation, while the problem is to choose node and link-labels in such a way that messages are routed along shortest paths.

In [SK82], [LT83], [LT85] it is shown how the ILS approach can be applied to optimally route messages on particular network topologies, such as trees, rings, etc. The ILS approach has also been used in other papers as a basic building block for routing schemes based on network decomposition and clustering ([ABLP89], [ABLP90], [FJ86], [FJ89], [FJ90], [PU89]).

In [LT85], the approach has been extended to allow more than 1 interval to be associated to each link; in particular, a 2-ILS, i.e. a scheme associating at most 2 intervals for each edge, is proposed for 2-dimensional doubly wrapped grids. Multi-label k-ILS has been implemented on the latest generation of INMOS Transputer C104 Router Chips [I91] (for a survey of results on compact routing methods see [LT94]).

All results on ILS only handle the case where just one shortest path between each pair of nodes are represented. On the other hand, representing all shortest paths between each pair of nodes turns out to be convenient when problems related to flow control aspects such as fault tolerance and traffic load balancing are considered. The Boolean Routing approach introduced in [FGS93] explicitly aims at the efficient representation of all shortest paths. However, in this scheme different boolean predicates need to be used for each network.

In order to derive efficient ILS routing schemes for the representation of *all shortest paths*, we introduce multi-dimensional extensions of ILS, $\langle k, d \rangle$-MILS. In this extension, an ILS with associated *dimension d* has as node-labels d-tuples of integers, while each link is labelled with up to k d-tuples of intervals. The usual ILS corresponds to the case $d = 1$.

We show in this paper that with this new extension of ILS to multi-dimensional ILS it is possible to represent all shortest paths compactly in a routing table for common interconnection networks such as trees, rings, grids, tori and hypercubes, with about the same space complexity as the regular k-ILS. We also consider problems on the efficiency of the new extensions for general graphs. The problem of deriving trade-offs between dimension d and the number of intervals k is also studied. In particular, some trade-offs between these parameters are given for relevant interconnection networks such as grids, tori, and hypercubes. For example, it is easy to represent a d-dimension hypercube with a $\langle 1, d \rangle$-MILS representing all shortest paths, (i.e. with only 1 interval per link using d dimensions), whereas we show that it requires $\lceil \frac{2^{d-1}}{d} \rceil$-ILS (a much higher number of intervals and space complexity) to achieve the same task, for about the same space complexity as the normal 1-ILS.

The paper is organized as follows. The next section contains a description of the communication model used and some definitions. In section 3 we state some results for general networks. We show that the product of graphs with optimum multi-dimensional ILS is also an optimal multi-dimensional ILS. Also a complexity result on NP-hardness of multi-dimensional ILS is stated. Section 4 contains specific results on interconnection networks trees, rings, grids, tori and hypercubes. In section 5 we study the relationship between the dimension d and the number of intervals k: how it is possible to trade-off one parameter for the other in networks such as hypercubes, grids and tori. We also give tight bounds on the number of intervals and dimensions needed for hypercubes. Finally we list some open problems in the last section.

2   The Model

The model we shall use is the *point to point* communication model, where each process in the network has access only to its own local memory and communicate by sending messages via one of its neighbours. Let $G = \langle V, E \rangle$ be a graph (network) with vertex set V of size n and edge set E. An *Interval Labelling Scheme*(ILS) is a scheme of labelling each node in the graph with some unique integer in the set $\{1, ..., n\}$ and each link with a unique interval $[a, b]$, with $a, b \in \{1, ..., n\}$. Wrap-around of intervals is allowed, so if $a > b$ then $[a, b] = \{a, a+1, ..., n, 1, ..., b\}$. The set of all intervals associated with the edges of a node forms a partition of the interval $[1..n]$ (thus in reality each link needs to be labelled with only the left end-point of the interval). Messages to a destination node j are routed via the link that is labelled with the interval $[a, b]$ such that $j \in [a, b]$. An ILS is *valid* if, for all the nodes i and j of G, messages sent from i to j eventually reach j correctly. A valid ILS is sometimes called an *Interval Routing Scheme* (*IRS* for short).

We now extend the above concept to multi-dimension. For simplicity, we first define a d–dimensional ILS. A $\langle 1, d \rangle$-MILS (*multi-dimensional ILS*) $(d > 0)$ is a labelling scheme where each node of G is labelled with an element from $\mathbf{N}^d$ (where $\mathbf{N}$ is the set of non-negative integers, and d is the *dimension*) and each link is labelled with a d-tuple $([a_1, b_1], ..., [a_d, b_d])$ of intervals, $a_i, b_i \in \mathbf{N}$ for each i. In general, let $\mathbf{I}$ be the set of all closed intervals on $\mathbf{N}$, so we can consider $\mathbf{I} = \mathbf{N} \times \mathbf{N}$. Each link in a $\langle 1, d \rangle$-MILS is then labelled with a value from $\mathbf{I}^d$. To route a message to a destination node $j = (j_1, ..., j_d)$ a node checks its link-labels and finds one d-tuple of intervals $([a_1, b_1], ..., [a_d, b_d])$ that satisfies $j_i \in [a_i, b_i]$ for *each* $i, 1 \le i \le d$.

In a $\langle k, d \rangle$-MIRS each link is labelled with up to k values from $\mathbf{I}^d$, i.e. with at most k d-tuples of intervals. A message with destination $j = (j_1, ..., j_d)$ is then routed on any link with label $\{I_1, ..., I_l\}$ $(l \le k$ and $I_h \in \mathbf{I}^d, 1 \le h \le l)$ if there exists some d-tuple of intervals I_h such that $j_i \in [a_{i_h}, b_{i_h}]$ for each i, $1 \le i \le d$. A valid MILS is also called a *multi-dimensional Interval Routing scheme* (*MIRS*). Thus a regular IRS is just a $\langle 1, 1 \rangle$-MIRS.

A $\langle k, d \rangle$-MIRS is *optimum* if the route traversed by each message is via the shortest path and *overall optimum* if, for any two nodes $u, v \in V$, *all* the shortest paths from u to v are represented in the scheme. In the case where multiple paths are represented (as for an overall optimum MIRS), the labels on the edges of a given node may overlap, i.e., they do not form a partition of the vertices in V.

3 Multi-Dimensional Interval Routing On General Networks

Let $G = \langle V, E \rangle$ be a graph with $|V| = n$.

Let the nodes of G be $v_1, ..., v_n$. We can simply label node v_1 with the n-tuple $(1, 0, ..., 0)$, node v_2 with $(0, 1, 0, ..., 0)$ and so on. Now label each link with the n-tuple of intervals $([0, b_1], ..., [0, b_n])$, where $b_i = 1$ if node v_i can be reached by a shortest path via this link and $b_i = 0$ otherwise. It is easily seen that this is a valid and overall optimum $\langle 1, n \rangle$-MIRS. But we can do slightly better.

Theorem 1. *For any graph G, there is an overall optimum $\langle 1, \lceil \frac{n}{2} \rceil \rangle$-MIRS.*

Proof. Let the nodes of G be $v_1, ..., v_n$. Label node v_1 with the $\lceil \frac{n}{2} \rceil$-tuple $(1, 0, ..., 0)$, node v_2 with $(2, 0, 0, ..., 0)$, node v_3 with $(0, 1, 0, ..., 0)$, node v_4 with $(0, 2, 0, ..., 0)$ and in general node v_i with the $\lceil \frac{n}{2} \rceil$-tuple $(d_1, ..., d_{\lceil \frac{n}{2} \rceil})$ such that $d_j = 0$ for $j \ne \lceil \frac{i}{2} \rceil$, $d_{\lceil \frac{i}{2} \rceil} = 1$ if i is odd and $d_{\lceil \frac{i}{2} \rceil} = 2$ if i is even.

Now at each node v_i label each incident link e with the $\lceil \frac{n}{2} \rceil$-tuple of intervals $([a_1, b_1], ..., [a_{\lceil \frac{n}{2} \rceil}, b_{\lceil \frac{n}{2} \rceil}])$, where:

- $a_j = 0, b_j = 0$ if e is neither on a shortest path between v_i and v_{2j-1} nor on a shortest path between v_i and v_{2j};
- $a_j = 0, b_j = 1$ if e is on a shortest path between v_i and v_{2j-1} and e is not on a shortest path between v_i and v_{2j};

- $a_j = 2, b_j = 0$ if e is not on a shortest path between v_i and v_{2j-1} and e is on a shortest path between v_i and v_{2j};
- $a_j = 0, b_j = 2$ if e is on a shortest path between v_i and v_{2j-1} and also on a shortest path between v_i and v_{2j}.

It is easily seen that this scheme is overall optimum. $\qquad\square$

The space complexity of the scheme as described above requires n bits for each node-label and $2n$ bits for each link-label.

On the other hand, we can simply label each node with a value in $\{1, ..., n\}$ and, for any link, list all the nodes (at most n) optimally reachable through that link by specifying, for each such node i, the corresponding interval $[i, i]$. This gives us an overall optimum $\langle n, 1\rangle$-MIRS, which can be further improved by the following theorem.

Theorem 2. *For any graph G, there exists an overall optimum $\langle \lfloor \frac{n}{2} \rfloor, 1\rangle$-MIRS.*

Proof. We use the above $\langle n, 1\rangle$-MIRS scheme and note that we can collapse any two adjacent intervals $[i, i]$, $[i+1, i+1]$ to a single interval $[i, i+1]$. Thus we have at most $\lfloor \frac{n}{2} \rfloor$ intervals left. $\qquad\square$

The space complexity of the node-label for this scheme is $\log n$ but the link-label can be quite bad, about $n \log n$. In general, for a $\langle k, d\rangle$-MIRS, let the node-label be $(i_1, ..., i_d)$ with $i_1 \in \{1, ..., n_1\}, ..., i_d \in \{1, ..., n_d\}$. Then the size of each node-label is about $\log n_1 + ... + \log n_d = \log(n_1 \cdot n_2 \cdots n_d)$ and the size of each link-label is about $2k \log(n_1 \cdot n_2 \cdots n_d)$. We shall see in the next two sections that for specific graphs we can actually do much better.

We now consider the *Cartesian Product* of graphs. This class of graphs includes the topologies of some interconnection networks commonly used in parallel architectures, such as hypercubes, d-dimensional grids and tori.

Definition 3. Given d graphs $G_1 = (V_1, E_1), ..., G_h = (V_h, E_h)$, $h > 0$, define the *product graph* $G_1 \times ... \times G_h$, as the graph $G = (V, E)$, where:

1. $V = V_1 \times ... \times V_h$,
2. $E = \bigcup_{j=1}^{h} \{(v_{i_1,...,i_j,...,i_h}, v_{i_1,...,i'_j,...,i_h}) \mid v_{i_1} \in V_1, ..., v_{i_{j-1}} \in V_{j-1}, v_{i_j} \in V_j,$
   $v_{i_{j'}} \in V_j, v_{i_{j+1}} \in V_{j+1}, ..., v_{i_h} \in V_h, (v_{i_j}, v_{i'_j}) \in E_j\}$, where for the sake of simplicity we denote any node $(v_{i_1}, ..., v_{i_h}) \in V$ by $v_{i_1,...,i_h}$.

The definition states that each node $v_{i_1,...,i_h}$ of the resulting graph G belongs to the d dimensional space $V = V_1 \times ... \times V_h$ and that for any j, with $1 \le j \le h$, the subgraph induced by all nodes with the same $i_1, ..., i_{j-1}, i_{j+1}, ... i_h$ values is isomorphic to G_j. In Fig. 1 an example of graph product for $h = 2$ is provided.

We note here that the product of graphs with k-IRS schemes is not necessarily a k-IRS ([LT85, R88]), but this is true for Linear Interval Routing schemes ([KKR93]) and Boolean Routing schemes ([FGS94]). Happily this is also true for $\langle k, d\rangle$-MIRS.

Suppose each subgraph G_j has a $\langle k_j, d_j\rangle$-MIRS, $1 \le j \le h$, with $|V_j| = n_j$. Let $G = (V, E)$ be the product graph defined as above and

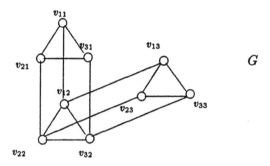

Fig. 1. Sample product

let $d = \sum_{j=1}^{h} d_j$. We label each node $v_{i_1,\ldots,i_j,\ldots,i_h} \in V$ with the d-tuple $(a_{1,1},\ldots,a_{1,d_1},a_{2,1},\ldots,a_{2,d_2},\ldots,a_{h,1},\ldots,a_{h,d_h})$, where for each j, $(a_{j,1},\ldots,a_{j,d_j})$ is the label of node $v_{i_j} \in V_j$ in the (k_j,d_j)-MIRS for G_j.

For each link $e = (v_{i_1,\ldots,i_j,\ldots,i_h}, v_{i_1,\ldots,i'_j,\ldots,i_h}) \in E$ in the product graph G, we label it with k_j d-tuples of intervals

$$(I_{1,1},\ldots,I_{1,s_j}, I_{1,s_j+1},\ldots,I_{1,s_j+d_j}, I_{1,s_{j+1}+1},\ldots,I_{1,d}),$$

$$\vdots$$

$$(I_{k_j,1},\ldots,I_{k_j,s_j}, I_{k_j,s_j+1},\ldots,I_{k_j,s_j+d_j}, I_{k_j,s_{j+1}+1},\ldots,I_{k_j,d}),$$

where $s_j = \sum_{i=1}^{j-1} d_i$, and for each i such that either $i < s_j$ or $i > s_{j+1} + 1$, $I_{1,i} = I_{1,i} = \ldots = I_{k_j,i}$ is the interval containing the i-th dimensional components of all node-labels, and $(I_{1,s_j+1},\ldots,I_{1,s_j+d_j}), \cdots, (I_{k_j,s_j+1},\ldots,I_{k_j,s_j+d_j})$ are the k_j d_j-tuples associated at node v_{i_j} to edge $e_j = (v_{i_j}, v_{i'_j}) \in E_j$ in the (k_j, d_j)-MIRS for G_j.

It is now possible to prove the following lemma:

Lemma 4. *The scheme described above correctly routes messages along their shortest paths.*

Proof. Proof omitted. □

We then have the following *product* theorem.

Theorem 5. *If each graph G_i in the set $\{G_1, G_2, \ldots, G_h\}$ has an optimum (or overall optimum) $\langle k_i, d_i \rangle$-MIRS, $1 \leq i \leq h$, then the product graph $G = G_1 \times G_2 \times \ldots \times G_h$ has an optimum (or overall optimum) $\langle k, d \rangle$-MIRS, with $k = \max(k_1, \ldots, k_h)$ and $d = d_1 + \ldots + d_h$.*

Proof. Observe that in the above construction, at each link the number of intervals is one of the k_j's of $\langle k_j, d_j \rangle$-MIRS, hence k can be no worse than one of the k_j's. The dimension of the product graph is clearly the sum of the dimensions of all the subgraphs. □

We now consider the problem of the complexity of designing $\langle k, d \rangle$-MIRS. It has been proved in [FGS95] that for any weighted graph G and any integer $k > 0$, deciding whether there exists an optimum k-IRS for G is NP-Complete, both in the case that only one shortest path and when all shortest paths must be represented. As a direct consequence of this result we obtain the following theorem.

Theorem 6. *Given a weighted graph G and two integers $k, d \geq 1$, the problem of deciding whether an optimum or overall optimum $\langle k, d \rangle$-MIRS exists for G is NP-Complete.*

Proof. By restriction to the case $d = 1$. □

4 Interconnection Networks

We now show that there exists an overall optimum MIRS for some standard interconnection networks.

Theorem 7. *Trees, Rings and Complete Graphs have overall optimum $\langle 1, 1 \rangle$-MIRS.*

Proof. For trees and complete graphs, the overall optimum MIRS is just the normal 1-IRS (see [SK82] and [LT85]), as there is only a single shortest path between each pair of nodes. We can also extend the standard optimal 1-IRS for rings to include all shortest paths by specifying the correct end-point of each interval to include the appropriate node on rings of even size. □

The space complexity for each node-label is just $\log n$ and for each link-label it is $2 \log n$.

Theorem 8. *Complete Bipartite Graphs have overall optimum $\langle 2, 1 \rangle$-MIRS.*

Proof. Let $G = (N_A \cup N_B, E)$ be a complete bipartite graph, with $E = \{(x, y) \mid x \in N_A \text{ and } y \in N_B\}$, $|N_A| = n_A$, and $|N_B| = n_B$. Nodes in N_A are labelled with labels $1, \ldots, n_A$ and nodes in N_B with labels $n_A + 1, \ldots, n_A + n_B$. For each node a in N_A with label $l_a \in \{1, \ldots, n_A\}$, and for each node b in N_B with label $l_b \in \{n_A + 1, \ldots, n_A + n_B\}$, the link connecting a to b is labelled with the 2-intervals 1-dimensional label $\{[1, n_A], [l_b, l_b]\}$. Similarly, for each node b in N_B, label each link (b, a) connecting b to a node a in N_A with $\{[n_A + 1, n_A + n_B], [l_a, l_a]\}$. It is easy to verify that such labelling covers all the shortest paths in the graph G. □

The overall optimum MIRS described above has a space complexity $\log n$ for each node-label and $4 \log n$ for each link-label.

Theorem 9. *d-grids, d-tori and d-hypercubes have overall optimum $\langle 1, d \rangle$-MIRS.*

Proof. This follows immediately from the product of *lines* (trees of degree 2) and *rings*, and applying the product Theorem 5. ☐

For the hypercubes, the space complexity of each node-label and each link-label is respectively $\log 2^d = d$ and $2 \log 2^d = 2d$. Also the ones for grids and tori are $\log n$ and $2 \log n$.

Notice that, in the case of hypercubes, since $d = \log n$, this shows that it is possible to represent all shortest paths in the network with no additional cost (in terms of space) with respect to the usual representation of one shortest path for any pair of nodes in 1-IRS. Thus we gain in flexibility of routing with the multidimensional $\langle 1, d \rangle$-MIRS. In the next section we shall see that we can obtain an even better bound with an overall optimum $\langle 1, \frac{d}{2} \rangle$-MIRS.

5 Trade-offs between k and d in $\langle k, d \rangle$-MIRS

In this section we investigate the relationship between the number of intervals k and the number of dimensions d in $\langle k, d \rangle$-MIRS. We show that for some interconnection networks there are trade-offs between these two parameters in MIRS. In particular we show how the increase of the dimensions d yields a corresponding decrease of the number of intervals k needed and vice versa.

First, some technical facts.

5.1 Technical Preliminaries

We now introduce the *matrix representations* of shortest paths [F95, FLM95] and state some of their properties that will be exploited for determining lower and upper bounds on the number of intervals needed by the MIRS.

For a graph $G = (V, E)$, and a node $v \in V$, we will denote by $I(v) \subseteq E$ the set of edges incident to v and by $I(V) = \{(v, e) \mid v \in V, e \in I(v)\}$ the set of all possible pairs of node and incident-link. Moreover, for each node u and each link $e \in I(u)$, denote by $s(u, e)$ the set of nodes v optimally reachable from u through that link (i.e. such that e belongs to some shortest path from u to v).

Definition 10. Given a graph $G = (V, E)$ and a set of pairs $P = \{(v_1, e_1), \ldots, (v_l, e_l)\} \subseteq I(V)$, the *matrix representation* of G w.r.t. P is an $n \times l$ matrix $M(P)$ such that $M(P)[j, i] = 1$ if $v_j \in s(v_i, e_i)$, otherwise $M(P)[j, i] = 0$.

Clearly there is a one-to-one correspondence between each permutation of the rows of $M(P)$ and each labelling of the nodes in G, and in $M(P)$ each maximal block of consecutive entries equal to 1 in column i corresponds to a maximal interval of integers associated at node v_i to its incident link e_i. Thus the following lemma can be easily proved.

Lemma 11. *Given $G = (V, E)$, let $M(I(V))$ be the matrix representation w.r.t. $I(V)$. Then there exists an overall optimum $\langle k, 1 \rangle$-MIRS for G if and only if there exists a circular permutation of the rows of $M(I(V))$ such that each column has at most k blocks of consecutive entries equal to 1.*

For the lower bounds on the number of intervals required by MIRS, we have the following lemma.

Lemma 12. *Given $G = (V, E)$, let $M(P)$ be the matrix representation w.r.t. $P = \{(v_1, e_1), \ldots, (v_l, e_l)\} \subseteq I(V)$, and assume that, for any two rows r_i and r_j belonging to $M(P)$, $d_H(i, j) \geq 2t$ for some $t > 0$, where $d_H(i, j)$ is the Hamming distance of rows r_i and r_j in $M(P)$. Then there is no overall optimum $\langle k, 1 \rangle$-MIRS for G with $k < \lceil \frac{n \cdot t}{l} \rceil$.*

Proof. Proof omitted. □

5.2 Hypercubes

We have seen that there is a simple overall optimum $\langle 1, d \rangle$-MIRS for hypercubes (Theorem 9). We now show that it is not possible to cover all shortest paths in the regular 1-IRS; in fact, we give a precise bound for the number of intervals required.

Theorem 13. *There is no overall optimum $\langle k, 1 \rangle$-MIRS for d-dimensional hypercubes H_d with $k < \lceil \frac{2^{d-1}}{d} \rceil$.*

Proof. Given any node $v \in H_d$, consider the matrix representation $M(P)$ w.r.t. $P = \{(v, e_i) \mid 1 \leq i \leq d\}$, where e_i is the link incident to v in the i-th dimension. It is easy to see that $M(P)$ consists of the 2^d rows that are all possible strings of d bits, thus for all pairs of rows r_i, r_j, we have $d_H(i, j) \geq 1$. Now by Lemma 12 there is no $\langle k, 1 \rangle$-MIRS for H_d with $k < \lceil \frac{2^d \cdot \frac{1}{2}}{d} \rceil = \lceil \frac{2^{d-1}}{d} \rceil$. □

We are now able to give upper bounds on the number of intervals required by $\langle k, 1 \rangle$-MIRS for H_d.

Theorem 14. *There exists an overall optimum $\langle k, 1 \rangle$-MIRS for H_d with $k = \lceil \frac{2^{d-1}}{d} \rceil$.*

Proof. Consider the matrix representation $M(I(V))$ w.r.t. $I(V)$ and for each node v let e_i be its incident link in the i-th dimension. For any circular permutation of the rows π, let $num(M(I(V), \pi))$ be the maximum number of blocks of consecutive entries equal to 1 over all the columns of $M(I(V))$.

Notice that, whatever the circular permutation π is, all columns associated to pairs (v, e_i) for a fixed dimension i have the same number of consecutive blocks of entries equal to 1, since any two such columns are either identical or just the bit-complement of the other. Thus, for a given node $v \in H_d$, with its submatrix $M(P)$ w.r.t. $P = \{(v, e_i) \mid 1 \leq i \leq d\}$ (recall that this matrix has for all of its 2^d rows all the possible strings of d bits) for each permutation π, $num(M(I(V), \pi)) = num(M(P), \pi)$.

In [RC81] it has been proved that it is possible to permute rows of $M(P)$ in such a way that $num(M(P), \pi) = \lceil \frac{2^{d-1}}{d} \rceil$. The theorem now follows from Lemma 11. □

Corollary 15. *For each i such that $1 \leq i \leq d$ there exists an overall optimum* $\langle \lceil \frac{2^{i-1}}{i} \rceil, \lceil \frac{d}{i} \rceil \rangle$*-MIRS for* H_d.

Proof. A d-dimensional hypercube H_d is given by the product of $\lfloor \frac{d}{i} \rfloor$ hypercubes of dimension i and a hypercube of dimension $(d \bmod i)$. The corollary now follows from product Theorem 5 by observing that because of Theorem 14 each of these $\lceil \frac{d}{i} \rceil$ hypercubes, of dimension at most i, admits a $\langle \lceil \frac{2^{i-1}}{i} \rceil, 1 \rangle$-MIRS. $\qquad\square$

This corollary shows what we can effectively gain by increasing the number of dimensions of an MIRS. In fact, in the 1-dimensional case we cannot aim to get better than a $\langle \frac{2^{d-1}}{d}, 1 \rangle$-MIRS, i.e. to use less than $\frac{2^{d-1}}{d}$ 1-dimensional intervals. For the 2-dimensional case we can get a $\langle \frac{2^{d/2}}{d}, 2 \rangle$-MIRS, for the 3-dimensional case a $\langle \frac{3 \cdot 2^{d/3-1}}{d}, 3 \rangle$-MIRS, and so on till we obtain a $\langle \lceil \frac{4}{3} \rceil, \frac{d}{3} \rangle$-MIRS, and finally a $\langle 1, \frac{d}{2} \rangle$-MIRS. Recalling the construction of product Theorem 5, the ratio between the space complexity in the $\langle \frac{2^{d-1}}{d}, 1 \rangle$-MIRS and in the $\langle 1, d/2 \rangle$-MIRS is $\frac{2^{d-1}}{d}$, which is almost linear in the number of nodes. The trade-off between number and dimension of intervals in edge labels for a hypercube of dimension d is shown in Fig. 2.

no. of intervals	dimension
$\frac{2^{d-1}}{d}$	1
$\frac{2 \cdot 2^{\frac{d}{2}-1}}{d}$	2
$\frac{3 \cdot 2^{\frac{d}{3}-1}}{d}$	3
$\cdots$	$\cdots$
$\frac{d}{2 \cdot \log d}$	$\frac{d}{\log d}$
$\cdots$	$\cdots$
2	$\frac{d}{4}$
1	$\frac{d}{2}$

Fig. 2. Trade-off between number of intervals and dimensions for a hypercube of dimension d (all the quantities are to be rounded to the next integer).

5.3 Grids and Tori

A grid of d dimensions can be seen as the product of d graphs $P_1, \ldots, P_d$, in which each P_i is a line of n_i nodes. Similarly, a torus is the product of d rings $R_1, \ldots, R_d$, in which each R_i has n_i nodes. If we allow the product of d graphs $G_1, \ldots, G_d$, in which each G_i is either a line or a ring of n_i nodes, then we come up with the generalized definition of d-dimensional grids in which, for a given dimension i, we have wrap-arounds or not according to whether G_i is a ring or a line. Let us call this generalized grid a *grid-torus*. By using similar techniques to those for the hypercubes, it is possible to prove the following results.

Theorem 16. *There is no overall optimum $\langle k, 1 \rangle$-MIRS for a d-dimensional grid-torus $G_1 \times \ldots \times G_d$ with $k < \left\lceil \frac{\prod_i n_i}{2 \cdot \sum_i n_i} \right\rceil$, where $n_i = |V_i|$.*

Proof. Proof omitted. ☐

Corollary 17. *Given a d-dimensional grid-torus $G_1 \times \ldots \times G_d$, where each $|V_i| = m$, there is no overall optimum $\langle k, 1 \rangle$-MIRS with $k < \lceil \frac{m^{d-1}}{2d} \rceil$.*

Similar results on the upper bounds on the number of intervals required by the schemes for the grids-tori can now be proved.

Theorem 18. *There exists an overall optimum $\langle k, 1 \rangle$-MIRS for grids-tori with $k = \prod_{i=2}^{d} n_i$.*

Proof. Proof omitted. ☐

Corollary 19. *Given a d-dimensional grid-torus $G_1 \times \ldots \times G_d$, where each $|V_i| = m$, there exists an overall optimum $\langle k, 1 \rangle$-MIRS with $k = m^{d-1}$.*

For the multi-dimensional version, in the case in which each G_i has the same cardinality, we have the following corollary.

Corollary 20. *Given a d-dimensional grid-torus $G_1 \times \ldots \times G_d$, where each $|V_i| = m$, for each i such that $1 \leq i \leq d$ there exists an overall optimum $\langle m^{i-1}, \lceil d/i \rceil \rangle$-MIRS.*

Proof. The d-dimensional grid-torus is given by the product of $\lfloor \frac{d}{i} \rfloor$ subgrids-tori of dimension k and a grid-torus of dimension $(d \bmod i)$. The corollary follows now from product Theorem 5 and Corollary 19. ☐

As in the case of hypercubes, this corollary states that by increasing the number of dimensions it is possible to go from a $\langle m^{d-1}, 1 \rangle$-MIRS to a $\langle 1, d \rangle$-MIRS (see table in Fig. 3). The ratio between the space complexity in the $\langle \frac{m^{d-1}}{d}, 1 \rangle$-MIRS and in the $\langle 1, d \rangle$-MIRS is $\frac{m^{d-1}}{d}$, which is again almost linear in the number of nodes. Also the space required by the $\langle 1, d \rangle$-MIRS is the same as the one required by a 1-IRS scheme for the d-grid, but in the $\langle 1, d \rangle$-MIRS all shortest paths between every pair of nodes are represented, while in the 1-IRS only a single shortest path between every pair is represented. Furthermore, 1-IRS only exists for grids with no wrap-around and columns (or rows, but not both) wrap-around [LT85, R88], whereas our results here apply to any grid-torus with wrap or no wrap-around in any dimension.

no. of intervals	dimension
m^{d-1}	1
$m^{\frac{d}{2}-1}$	2
...	...
m^2	$\frac{d}{3}$
m	$\frac{d}{2}$
1	d

Fig. 3. Trade-off between number of intervals and dimensions for a grid-torus of dimension d, i.e., with m^d nodes (all the quantities are to be rounded to the next integer).

6 Conclusion and Open Problems

We have introduced multi-dimensional Interval Routing schemes, which generalize the standard Interval Routing schemes to higher dimensions. With the multi-dimensional schemes we improve the routing schemes to include all shortest paths for some standard interconnection networks such as d-grids, d-tori and d-hypercubes. This is achieved with efficient space complexity.

There are still many unresolved problems with $\langle k, d \rangle$-MIRS. We list here some open problems for future research.

1. Study $\langle k, d \rangle$-MIRS for other interconnection networks.
2. The NP-Hard result stated in this paper is for the case of weighted links only. This should hold true for the uniform cost link also.
3. The trade-off between the number of intervals k and dimensions d are stated in this paper for hypercubes, grids and tori. It would be nice to obtain similar results for other graphs also. A general result between k and d for arbitrary graphs would be quite desirable.

References

[ABLP89] B. Awerbuch, A. Bar-Noy, N. Linial, and D. Peleg, Compact Distributed Data Structures for Adaptive Routing, *Proc. 21st ACM Symp. on Theory of Computing* (1989), pp. 479–489.

[ABLP90] B. Awerbuch, A. Bar-Noy, N. Linial, and D. Peleg, Improved Routing Strategies with Succinct Tables. *Journal of Algorithms*, 11 (1990), pp. 307–341.

[BLT94] E. M. Bakker, J. van Leeuwen and R. B. Tan, Some Characterization Results in Compact Routing Schemes, *Manuscript* (1994).

[BLT91] E. M. Bakker, J. van Leeuwen and R. B. Tan, Linear Interval Routing Schemes, *Tech. Rep. RUU-CS-91-7*, Dept. of Computer Science, Utrecht University (1991). Also in: *Algorithms Review* 2 (2) (1991), pp. 45–61.

143

[F95]   M. Flammini, Compact Routing Models: Some Complexity Results and Exten-
           sions, Ph. D. Thesis, Dept. of System and Computer Science, University of Rome
           "La Sapienza", 1995.

[FGS93]   M. Flammini, G. Gambosi and S. Salomone, Boolean Routing, *Proc.* 7th *Interna-
           tional Workshop on Distributed Algorithms (WDAG'93)*, Springer-Verlag *LNCS*
           725 (1993), pp. 219-233.

[FGS94]   M. Flammini, G. Gambosi and S. Salomone, On Devising Boolean Routing
           Schemes, extended abstract, in: M. Nagl (Ed.), Graph-Theoretic Concepts in
           Computer Science (WG'95), *Proceedings 21st International Workshop*, Springer-
           Verlag LNCS (1995).

[FGS95]   M. Flammini, G. Gambosi and S. Salomone, Interval Routing Schemes, *Proc.*
           12th *Symp. on Theoretical Aspects of Computer Science (STACS'95)*, Springer-
           Verlag *LNCS* 900 (1995), pp. 279-290.

[FLM95]   M. Flammini, J. van Leeuwen and A. Marchetti Spaccamela, The Complexity
           of Interval Routing on Random Graphs, to appear in *Proc.* 20th *Symposium on
           Mathematical Foundation of Computer Science (MFCS'95)* (1995).

[FJ86]   G. N. Frederickson and R. Janardan, Optimal Message Routing Without Com-
           plete Routing Tables, *Proc.* 5th *Annual ACM Symposium on Principles of Dis-
           tributed Computing* (1986), pp. 88-97. Also as: Designing Networks with Com-
           pact Routing Tables, *Algorithmica* 3 (1988), pp. 171-190.

[FJ89]   G. N. Frederickson and R. Janardan, Efficient Message Routing in Planar Net-
           works, *SIAM Journal on Computing* 18 (1989), pp. 843-857.

[FJ90]   G. N. Frederickson and R. Janardan, Space Efficient Message Routing in c-
           Decomposable Networks, *SIAM Journal on Computing* 19 (1990), pp. 164-181.

[HKR91]   H. Hofestädt, A. Klein and E. Reyzl, Performance Benefits from Locally Adaptive
           Interval Routing in Dynamically Switched Interconnection Networks, *Proc.* 2nd
           European Distributed Memory Computing Conference (1991), pp. 193-202.

[I91]   *The T9000 Transputer Products Overview Manual*, Inmos (1991).

[KKR93]   E. Kranakis, D. Krizanc and S. S. Ravi, On Multi-Label Linear Interval Routing
           Schemes, in: J. van Leeuwen (Ed.), *Graph-Theoretic Concepts in Computer Sci-
           ence (WG'93)*, *Proceedings* 19th *International Workshop*, Springer-Verlag *LNCS*
           790 (1993), pp. 338-349.

[LT83]   J. van Leeuwen and R. B. Tan, Routing with Compact Routing Tables, *Tech.
           Rep. RUU-CS-83-16*, Dept. of Computer Science, Utrecht University (1983). Also
           as: Computer Networks with Compact Routing Tables, in: G. Rozenberg and A.
           Salomaa (Eds.) *The Book of L*, Springer-Verlag, Berlin (1986), pp. 298-307.

[LT85]   J. van Leeuwen and R. B. Tan, Interval Routing, *Tech. Rep. RUU-CS-85-16*,
           Dept. of Computer Science, Utrecht University (1985). Also in: *Computer Jour-
           nal* 30 (1987), pp. 298-307.

[LT94]   J. van Leeuwen and R. B. Tan, Compact Routing Methods: A Survey, *Proc. Col-
           loquium on Structural Information and Communication Complexity (SICC'94)*,
           Carleton University Press (1994).

[MT90]   D. May and P. Thompson, *Transputers and Routers: Components for Concurrent
           Machines*, Inmos (1990).

[PU89]   D. Peleg, E. Upfal. A trade-off between space and efficiency for routing tables.
           Journal of the ACM, 36 (3) (1989), pp. 510-530.

[R88]   P. Ružička, On Efficiency of Interval Routing Algorithms, in: M.P. Chytil, L.
           Janiga, V. Koubek (Eds.), *Mathematical Foundations of Computer Science 1988*,
           Springer-Verlag *LNCS* 324 (1988), pp. 492-500.

[RC81]   J. P. Robinson and M. Cohn. Counting Sequences, *IEEE Transactions on Com-
           puters*, C-30 (1) (1981), pp. 17-23.

[SK82]   N. Santoro and R. Khatib, Routing Without Routing Tables, *Tech. Rep. SCS-TR-6*, School of Computer Science, Carleton University (1982). Also as: Labelling and Implicit Routing in Networks, *Computer Journal* **28** (1) (1985), pp. 5–8.

Data Transmission in Processor Networks

Andreas Jakoby*

Rüdiger Reischuk

Med. Universität Lübeck**

Abstract. We investigate the communication capacity and optimal data transmission schedules for processor networks connected by communication links, for example Transputer clusters. Each link allows the two processors at its endpoints to exchange data with a given fixed transmission rate τ_d. The communication itself is done in a blocking mode, that means the two processors have to synchronize before starting to exchange data and at any time each processor cannot communicate with more than one other processor.

Our efficiency analysis will be more realistic by also taking into account the setup time for a communication, which will be assumed to be a fixed constant $\tau_s > 0$. Thus, a large amount of data can be sent from one processor to a neighbour faster by a single long communication step than by a bunch of small data exchange steps: sending p data units in one step takes time $\tau_s + p \cdot \tau_d$. However, there is a tradeoff since the receiver has to wait until it has received the complete set of data before it can forward pieces to other processors.

The following prototype task called *scattering* will be considered: At the beginning one processor called the *source* possesses a set of unit size data packets, one for each processor in the network. The goal is to distribute the packets in minimal time to all recipients.

Our results concerning the complexity of this problem in arbitrary processor networks are as follows: For the general case, we give lower bounds on the minimal schedule length and show that to determine the length precisely is $\mathcal{NP}$–complete. Special classes of simple strategies are investigated in more detail. For certain networks they turn out to yield optimal schedules.

Finally, we investigate optimal schedules that can be computed efficiently and good approximation algorithms for specific regular networks like hypercubes and multidimensional grids.

1 Introduction

1.1 Motivation

When designing efficient algorithms for distributed networks one often faces a serious bottleneck due to the data distribution overhead. For example, consider

---

* supported by DFG Research Grant Re 672-2

** Institut für Theoretische Informatik, Wallstraße 40, 23560 Lübeck, Germany
email: jakoby / reischuk @ informatik.mu-luebeck.de

parallelizing matrix multiplication by distributing the computation of the scalar products among the processors. At the beginning the data typically resides at a single location like an I/O-processor. Then, often about the same amount of time is spent to distribute the matrix elements among the processors by message passing as on the numerical computation itself. Thus, it is important to perform the data transmission as fast as possible. In previous work it was generally assumed that the transmission delay over a single link is proportional to the amount of data. Under this assumption a simple receive-and-forward strategy of small data chunks is able to generate optimal schedules. Making the additional assumption that a processor can simultaneously forward a data packet and receive the next one the problem becomes trivial.

In real systems, however, like Transputer based networks the set-up time for a data transmission cannot be neglected. Establishing a connection requires some overhead. Therefore, it is faster to send a few large data chunks than a large number of small packets. Our model defined below will take this property of real systems into account. For this more realistic model we develop optimal or nearly optimal schedules for arbitrary networks and also for several specific topologies that have been proposed as efficient networks.

In a similar way, the scheduling of multiprocessor systems has been extended to a more realistic scenario by including the communication delays between processors. If the predecessor of a task is executed on a different processor the time it will be available is given by the length of the task plus the time to transmit the task. As one would expect, constructing optimal schedules in this generalized model is $\mathcal{NP}$-hard in general. This already holds for very simple networks. On the other hand, efficient approximation schemes guaranteeing a factor 2 have been obtained. These results can be found in [PY88, JKS89, JR92].

The data distribution problem considered here called *scattering* is different from the *broadcasting* and *gossiping* problem, which have been studied extensively, see [SCH81, HHL88, LP88, HJM90, BHLP92, JRS94]. For scattering there is a different piece of information that has to be transmitted to each processor. Scattering has been studied for example in [SS89, JH89, FMR90, BBP93] for different computational models, either neglecting the set–up delay or allowing multiport communication of nodes.

1.2 The Communication Model

Definition 1 *A network of processors with two-way communication links is modelled by an undirected connected graph $G = (V, E)$. The two parameters τ_s, the set-up delay, and τ_d, the transmission rate of a link, describe the communication capacity of the network. For simplicity, we may choose the time scale such that both parameters are integer values. The data transmitted within the network is modelled by a set $\mathcal{W}$ of packets. Packets have identical length and require link transmission time τ_d. Thus, a single data exchange of m packets over a link takes time*

$$t(m) = \tau_s + m \cdot \tau_d .$$

We assume that processors exchange data in synchronous rounds in a blocking mode. Such a schedule will be specified by a set S of triples

$$((u,v),w,t) \in E \times 2^{\mathcal{W}} \times \mathbb{N} ,$$

meaning that processors u,v exchange data w, a subset of packets in $\mathcal{W}$, starting at round t. For each pair of triples $((u,v),w,t) \neq ((u',v'),w',t')$ in S with $\{u,v\} \cap \{u',v'\} \neq \emptyset$ and $t \leq t'$ the following inequality has to hold:

$$t' \geq t + t(|w|) = t + \tau_s + |w| \cdot \tau_d ,$$

that is, different communication events may not interfere. The length of a schedule S is given by

$$\text{length}(S) := \max_{(e,w,t)\in S} t + t(|w|) .$$

For a schedule S and round t the set of packets $\mathcal{R}_v(t)$ received by processor v is given by

$$\mathcal{R}_v(t) := \begin{cases} \emptyset & \text{if } t = 0, \\ \mathcal{R}_v(t-1) \cup w & \text{if } ((u,v),w,t-t(|w|)) \in S, \text{ and} \\ \mathcal{R}_v(t-1) & \text{else .} \end{cases}$$

Naturally, for each tuple $((v,u),w,t) \in S$ it is required that v has already received all packets in w, that is $w \subseteq \mathcal{R}_v(t)$,
*One distinguished processor $\bar{v} \in V$ serves as the **data source**. For the specific data transmission problem considered here the set $\mathcal{W}$ contains exactly one packet p_v for each processor v. Thus the starting configuration at round 0 can be described by setting $\mathcal{R}_{\bar{v}}(0) := \{p_v | v \in V\}$.*
*A schedule S solves the data distribution problem for G iff after termination of S each processor has received its packet: $p_v \in \mathcal{R}_v(\text{length}(S))$ for all $v \in G$. Let us call the minimal length of a schedule for G the **data distribution time** of G, denoted by $\text{DDTime}(G, \tau_s, \tau_d)$, where τ_s, τ_d are the delay and capacity parameters. A schedule S is called **canonical** if*

- *each processor v receives each packet at most once,*

- *if v receives a packet $p_u \neq p_v$ it will forward p_u to a neighbour,*

- *and each v does not receive any more packets after it has received its own packet.*

Note that each schedule S can easily be transformed into a canonical schedule S' with $\text{length}(S') \leq \text{length}(S)$.

2   Bounds for Arbitrary Graphs

We start by proving a general lower bound for arbitrary networks of size n, which we call the **delay-capacity bound** for the data distribution problem. It says that the set-up delay multiplied with the minimal graph theoretic radius for graphs of outdegree 2, which is about $\log_2 n$, *plus* the communication capacity of the source for the $n-1$ packets to be sent to the other processors, which is $(n-1) \cdot \tau_d$, cannot be beaten. The proof is based on the following combinatorial lemma. Define $\log n := \lceil \log_2 n \rceil$ and $\overline{n} := 2^{\log n}$.

Lemma 1 *Given a sequence $a_1, \ldots, a_l$ of $l < \log n$ positive natural numbers that add up to at least $n-1$, then there exists an i such that*

$$a_i + \sum_{j=1}^{i} a_j > n \qquad \text{and} \qquad \lceil \log a_i \rceil \geq \lceil \log n \rceil - i .$$

Proof of Lemma 1: Let $2^{k-1} < n \leq 2^k$ then $2^i \cdot \overline{a_i} \geq \overline{n}$ implies $a_i > 2^{k-i-1}$. Assume that for all $i \in \{1, \ldots, l\}$ with $l < k$ it holds $a_i \leq 2^{k-i-1}$ then

$$\sum_{i=1}^{l} a_i < 2^{k-1} < n .$$

We conclude that there exists at least one i with $a_i > 2^{k-i-1}$. Choose a maximal i_0 with this property, then $\sum_{i=i_0+1}^{l} a_i < 2^{k-i_0-1}$. Assume that $a_{i_0} + \sum_{i=1}^{i_0} a_i \leq n$ then $\sum_{i=1}^{i_0} a_i \leq n - a_{i_0} < n - 2^{k-i_0-1}$ and therefore

$$\sum_{i=1}^{l} a_i = \sum_{i=1}^{i_0} a_i + \sum_{i=i_0+1}^{l} a_i < n - 2^{k-i_0-1} + 2^{k-i_0-1} - 1 = n - 1 .$$

∎

In a similar way the following Lemma can easily be derived.

Lemma 2 *Given a sequence $a_1, \ldots, a_k$ of positive natural numbers adding up to $2^k - 1$ with the property that for each i it holds $a_i + \sum_{j=1}^{i} a_j \leq 2^k$ and $a_i \leq 2^{k-i}$, then $a_i = 2^{k-i}$.*

Theorem 1 *Any schedule for the data distribution problem on an n-processor network has length at least the delay-capacity bound*

$$\text{DCB}(n, \tau_s, \tau_d) := \log n \cdot \tau_s + (n-1) \cdot \tau_d .$$

Proof: Let $G = (V, E)$ be an n-processor network with parameters τ_s, τ_d. By the remark above it suffices to consider canonical schedules S for G. For a node v let

$$S_{\text{send}}(v) = ((v, u_1), w_1, t_1), ((v, u_2), w_2, t_2), \ldots$$

be all communication events with sender v in chronological order at rounds t_i relative to the round in which w_1 was sent, that means $0 = t_1 < t_2 < \ldots$. Similarly for $w \subseteq W$

$$S_{\text{send}}(v, w) = ((v, u_1'), w_1', t_1'), ((v, u_2'), w_2', t_2'), \ldots$$

denotes the subsequence of all events with $w \cap w_i' \neq \emptyset$, that means messages from v containing packets in w. Note that for each i

$$t_i \geq \sum_{j=1}^{i-1} t(|w_j|) \; = \; (i-1) \cdot \tau_s + \sum_{j=1}^{i-1} |w_j| \cdot \tau_d \; ,$$

$$t_i' \geq \sum_{j=1}^{i-1} t(|w_j'|) \; ,$$

$$\text{length}(S) \geq \sum_{j=1}^{i} t(|w_j|) \; + \; \text{length}(S_{\text{send}}(u_i, w_i)) \; .$$

We will show that the assumption

$$\text{length}(S) \; < \; \log n \cdot \tau_s + (n-1) \cdot \tau_d$$

yields a contraction. Since

$$\text{length}(S) \; \geq \; |S_{\text{send}}(\bar{v})| \cdot \tau_s + (n-1) \cdot \tau_d$$

it must hold $|S_{\text{send}}(\bar{v})| < \log n$. Lemma 1 applied to

$$S_{\text{send}}(\bar{v}) \; = \; ((\bar{v}, u_1), w_1, t_1), \ldots \; ,$$

that is $n - 1 = |\mathcal{W} - \{p_{\bar{v}}\}|$ and $a_i = |w_i|$ implies that there exists a tuple $((\bar{v}, u_i), w_i, t_i) \in S_{\text{send}}(\bar{v})$ with

$$\log n \cdot \tau_s + (n-1) \cdot \tau_d \; < \; \log(2^i |w_i|) \cdot \tau_s + (\sum_{j=1}^{i} |w_j| + (|w_i| - 1)) \cdot \tau_d \; .$$

Combining this inequality with the ones for $\text{length}(S)$ yields

$$\text{length}(S_{\text{send}}(v_i, w_i)) \; < \; \log(|w_1|) \cdot \tau_s + (|w_i| - 1) \cdot \tau_d \; .$$

Since S is a canonical schedule and

$$\text{length}(S_{\text{send}}(v_i, w_i)) \; \geq \; |S_{\text{send}}(v_i, w_i)| \cdot \tau_s + (|w_i| - 1) \cdot \tau_d$$

it holds $|S_{\text{send}}(v_i, w_i)| < \log(|w_i|)$. Therefore, we can repeat this argument for the subschedule $S_{\text{send}}(v_i, w_i)$ instead of the complete schedule S to obtain a subschedule for a neighbour of v_i that starts after message w_i has been transmitted from $\bar{v}$ to u_i and so on. But this process cannot go forever since S is finite. ∎

Consider a 1-dimensional network of size n with the source as one of the two endpoints. The obvious strategy sending each packet individually from the source to its destination beginning with the packet that has to travel the longest distance takes time exactly $(2n-3) \cdot (\tau_s + \tau_d)$. This network seems to be the worst topology for data distribution. It is not hard to show that any other network of the same size can achieve this transmission time.

Lemma 3 *Every n-node network has a schedule of length $(2n - 3) \cdot (\tau_s + \tau_d)$. Such a schedule can be constructed efficiently.*

For a 1-dimensional network with the source in the middle one can alternate the strategy described above between the two directions to achieve a time bound of $n \cdot (\tau_s + \tau_d)$. Thus, a more favourable placement of the source gives an improvement by a factor about 2.

In both cases, however, there is a better method by sending packets for neighbouring processors in pairs. The source at the endpoint starts by combining the two packets to the two most distant processors v_{n-1}, v_n into a single message that is relayed to v_{n-1}, then the packets for v_{n-3}, v_{n-2}, and so on. Processor v_{n-1} takes its packet and forwards the other packet to its neighbour v_n. This strategy yields a better time bound $(n - 1) \cdot \tau_s + (2n - 3) \cdot \tau_d$. It can be shown that this bound is the best one can achieve for such a chain. For 1-dimensional networks sending messages with an even larger number of packets does not give further improvements, on the contrary we get a degradation. If the source lies in the middle the time bound $\lfloor (n + 1)/2 \rfloor \cdot \tau_s + (n - 1) \cdot \tau_d$ can be achieved.

Theorem 2 *Let L_n and C_n denote a 1-dimensional processor chain of length n with the source at one endpoint, resp. a circle of length n. Then,*

$$\mathtt{DDTime}(L_n, \tau_s, \tau_d) = (n - 1) \cdot \tau_s + (2n - 3) \cdot \tau_d ,$$

$$\mathtt{DDTime}(C_n, \tau_s, \tau_d) = \left\lfloor \frac{n + 1}{2} \right\rfloor \cdot \tau_s + (n - 1) \cdot \tau_d .$$

Thus this simple example already indicates that a variety of strategies might be suitable for optimal data distribution and it is not that easy to determine the optimal ones.

The broadcast properties of a network provide another way to obtain a lower bound on its data transmission time. The broadcast problem is simpler than the data distribution problem consider here, it requires only that a single packed located at the source reaches every processor in the network. Thus there is only one packet and a processor may duplicate it to forward it to different neighbours, one at a time.

Definition 2 *A broadcast schedule B for a network $G = (V, E)$ with source $\bar{v}$ is a sequence of subsets of edges $E_1, E_2, \ldots, E_f$ with associated subset of processors $V_0 = \{\bar{v}\}$ and $V_f = V$, where for $i > 0$ $V_i := V_{i-1} \cup \{ v \mid (u, v) \in E_i$ and $u \in V_{i-1} \}$. V_i are those processors that have received the broadcast information by round i. It is required that at each round a processor can forward this information to only one neighbour, that is $E_i \subseteq \{ (u, v) \in E \mid u \in V_{i-1} \}$ and $\forall u \in V_{i-1} : |E_i \cap (\{u\} \times V)| \leq 1$.*
Define $\mathtt{BCTime}(G)$ as the minimal length f of a broadcast schedule for G.

When a data transmission schedule terminates each node of the network has received at least one packet from the source. Thus, from a data transmission schedule one can easily obtain a broadcast schedule. A message containing packets takes time at least $\tau_s + \tau_d$ for transmission over a link in the data distribution model, whereas the time scale for the broadcast problem are units. Therefore,

Theorem 3 *For every network G holds:*

$$\text{DDTime}(G, \tau_s, \tau_d) \geq \text{BCTime}(G) \cdot (\tau_s + \tau_d) .$$

There is another interesting difference between broadcasting a single piece of information and distributing data with set-up delays in a blocking mode. For every network G one can achieve the minimal broadcasting time by choosing a suitable spanning tree of G. For the data distribution problem, however, a spanning tree may not be sufficient to achieve the optimal schedule length (see figure 1).

3 Networks Matching the Delay-Capacity Bound

In this section we will consider specific network topologies G that are best suited for the data distribution problem with set-up delays. Such a G has the property that

$$\text{DDTime}(G, \tau_s, \tau_d) = \text{DCB}(|G|, \tau_s, \tau_d) .$$

It turns out that a special family of trees are essential, the binomial trees [OW93].

Definition 3 *Binomial trees are defined inductively as follows. The graph $\text{BT}(0)$ consists of a single node. For level $k > 0$*

$$\text{BT}(k) := (V_l \cup V_r, \{\{\rho_l, \rho_r\}\} \cup E_l \cup E_r) ,$$

where $T_l = (V_l, E_l)$ and $T_r = (V_r, E_r)$ are two $\text{BT}(k-1)$–trees with roots ρ_l, resp. ρ_r. One of the two roots will serve as the root of $\text{BT}(k)$, let us choose the right one ρ_r.

$\text{BT}(k)$ has 2^k nodes. The root, which serves as the source, has outdegree k.

Theorem 4 *Binomial trees achieve the delay capacity bound, that is:*

$$\text{DDTime}(\text{BT}(k), \tau_s, \tau_d) = \text{DCB}(2^k, \tau_s, \tau_d) = k \cdot \tau_s + (2^k - 1) \cdot \tau_d .$$

An optimal schedule can be constructed in linear time.

Proof: The claim obviously holds for $k = 0, 1$. Let T be a $\text{BT}(k+1)$–tree with source $\bar{v}$ consisting of $\text{BT}(k)$–subtrees $T_l = (V_l, E_l)$, $T_r = (V_r, E_r)$ with roots ρ_l, resp. $\rho_r = \bar{v}$. Let S_l and S_r be optimal schedules for these subtrees and $\mathcal{W}_l$ be the set of packets for V_l. Then

$$S := \{ ((\rho_r, \rho_l), \mathcal{W}_l, 0) \} \cup \{ (e, w, t + t(|\mathcal{W}_l|)) \mid (e, w, t) \in S_l \cup S_r \}$$

is a schedule for T of

$$\texttt{length}(S) \;=\; \tau_s + |\mathcal{W}_l| \cdot \tau_d + k \cdot \tau_s + (2^k - 1) \cdot \tau_d \;=\; (k+1) \cdot \tau_s + (2^{k+1} - 1) \cdot \tau_d \;.$$

The lower bound of Theorem 1 implies that this schedule is optimal. This can also easily be seen directly because the root has to send $k + 1$ messages to its $k + 1$ neighbours, yielding a delay of $(k + 1) \cdot \tau_s$. $\blacksquare$

These trees have to occur as spanning trees in networks that achieve data distribution in optimal time.

Theorem 5 *A network G of size 2^k with source $\bar{v}$ achieves the delay-capacity bound iff* $\texttt{BT}(k)$ *can be embedded into G such that its root is mapped onto $\bar{v}$.*

Proof: If such a tree spans G it is obvious that the bound can be achieved. On the other hand, let S be a schedule for G with source $\bar{v}$ of length $k \cdot \tau_s + (2^k - 1) \cdot \tau_d$. Then $|S_{\texttt{send}}(\bar{v})| \leq k$. Let $S_{\texttt{send}}(\bar{v}) \;=\; ((\bar{v}, v_1), w_1, t_1), \ldots, ((\bar{v}, v_a), w_a, t_a)$, with $t_i < t_{i+1}$. Note that $w_1, \ldots, w_a$ is a partition of $\mathcal{W} \setminus \{p_{\bar{v}}\}$. Thus from Lemma 1 follows $|S_{\texttt{send}}(\bar{v})| = k$ and from Lemma 2 $|w_i| = 2^{k-i}$.
Since $t_i \geq (i - 1) \cdot \tau_s + (2^k - 2^{k-i+1}) \cdot \tau_d$ the set $S_{\texttt{send}}(v_i, w_i)$ has to distribute a set of 2^{k-i} packets within

$$\texttt{length}(S_{\texttt{send}}(v_i)) \;\leq\; (k - i) \cdot \tau_s + (2^{k-1} - i) \cdot \tau_d$$

many steps. This is only possible if $p_{v_i} \in w_i$. Therefore, the claim follows inductively. $\blacksquare$

It is not hard to see that this family of trees can be embedded into hypercubes. Thus,

Corollary 1 *For the d–dimensional hypercube H_d of size 2^d holds*

$$\texttt{DDTime}(H_d, \tau_s, \tau_d) \;=\; \texttt{DCB}(|H_d|, \tau_s, \tau_d) \;=\; d \cdot \tau_s + (2^d - 1) \cdot \tau_d \;.$$

Definition 4 *Define a $l_1 \times l_2 \times \ldots \times l_d$–grid as the induced subgraph of the infinite d-dimensional integer grid restricted to nodes with i-th coordinate in the range $[0, l_i - 1]$. Nodes of degree $2d$ are called inner nodes.*

The embedding property still holds if one enlarges a hypercube in each dimension by a factor 2.

Corollary 2 *Let G_d be a $4 \times 4 \times \ldots \times 4$–grid of dimension d of size 4^d with the source being an inner node. Then*

$$\texttt{DDTime}(G_d, \tau_s, \tau_d) \;=\; \texttt{DCB}(|G_d|, \tau_s, \tau_d) \;=\; 2d \cdot \tau_s + (4^d - 1) \cdot \tau_d \;.$$

4 $\mathcal{NP}$-Completeness Result

Next, we will investigate the complexity of the data distribution problem with set-up delays for arbitrary graphs. For the reduction one can use the 3–dimensional matching problem.

Definition 5 3–Dimensional Matching (3DM)
Given three disjoint sets A, B, C of equal size and a set $M \subseteq A \times B \times C$ of triples, decide whether M contains a matching, i.e. whether there exists a subset $M' \subseteq M$ of size $|A|$ such that no two elements of M' agree in any coordinate?

The 3DM problem is known to be $\mathcal{NP}$–complete even if the cardinality of A is a power of 2 and each element of A, B, C occurs in at most three triples.
For a given instance A, B, C, M of the 3DM problem we generate the following graph $G = (V, A)$:

- For each element $\alpha_i \in A$ let $A_i = (V_{\alpha_i}, E_{\alpha_i})$ be a BT(4)–tree with root $\alpha_i \in V_{\alpha_i}$ and let $A = (V_A, E_A) = (\bigcup_{\alpha_i \in A} V_{\alpha_i}, \bigcup_{\alpha_i \in A} E_{\alpha_i})$.
- For each element $\beta_i \in B$ let β_i''' be the root of a BT(1)–tree $T_{\beta_i'''} = (V_{\beta_i'''}, E_{\beta_i'''})$ and let $T_{\beta_i} = (V_{\beta_i}, E_{\beta_i})$ be a BT(2)–tree with root r_{β_i} then define $B_i :=$ $(\{\beta_i, \beta_i', \beta_i''\} \cup V_{\beta_i'''} \cup V_{\beta_i}, \{\{\beta_i, r_{\beta_i}\}\} \cup E_{\beta_i'''} \cup E_{\beta_i})$ and let $B = (V_B, E_B) :=$ $(\bigcup_{\beta_i \in B} V_{\beta_i}, \bigcup_{\beta_i \in B} E_{\beta_i})$.
- For each element $\gamma_i \in C$ let $C_i = (V_{\gamma_i}, E_{\gamma_i})$ be a BT(2)–tree with root $\gamma_i \in V_{\gamma_i}$ and let $C = (V_C, E_C) = (\bigcup_{\gamma_i \in C} V_{\gamma_i}, \bigcup_{\gamma_i \in C} E_{\gamma_i})$.
- For each element $\mu_i = (\alpha_i, \beta_i, \gamma_i) \in M$ let $M_i := (V_{M_i}, E_{M_i})$ with $V_{M_i} :=$ $V_{\alpha_i} \cup V_{\beta_i} \cup V_{\gamma_i} \cup \{\mu_i\}$ and

$$E_{M_i} := E_{\alpha_i} \cup E_{\beta_i} \cup E_{\gamma_i} \cup \{\{\mu_i, \alpha_i\}, \{\mu_i, \beta_i\}, \{\mu_i, \beta_i'''\}, \{\mu_i, \gamma_i\}\} .$$

For each element $\beta_i \in B$ let $M_{\beta_i} := (\mu_i, \mu_j, \mu_k) \subseteq M$ be the set of triples where β_i occurs with $i < j < k$ then let $M := (V_M, E_M)$ with $V_M := \bigcup_{\mu_i \in M} V_{\mu_i}$ and

$$E_M = \bigcup_{\mu_i \in M} E_{\mu_i} \cup \bigcup_{\beta_i \in B} \{\{\mu_i, \beta_i'\}, \{\mu_j, \beta_i'\}, \{\mu_k, \beta_i''\}\} \mid M_{\beta_i} = \{\mu_i, \mu_j, \mu_k\}\}$$

Note that each node α_i has degree 7, each node μ_i and γ_i has degree 5, and each node β_i has degree 4.

- Let $V_T = \{\alpha_1', \ldots, \alpha_{|A|}'\}$, let $A_{\alpha_i'} = (V_{\alpha_i'}, E_{\alpha_i'})$ be a BT(5)–tree with root α_i' and let $T_{\alpha_i'} = (V_{T_i'}, E_{T_i'})$ be a BT(6)–tree with root $r_{\alpha_i'}$ for each $\alpha_i' \in V_T$. Since $|A| = 2^k$ there exists a BT(k)–tree $A_T = (V_T, E_T)$ with root α_1'. So let $G(A, B, C, M) = (V, E)$ with

$$V := V_M \cup V_T \cup \bigcup_{i \in \{1, \ldots, |A|\}} \left(V_{\alpha_i'} \cup V_{T_i'}\right) \quad \text{and}$$

$$E := E_M \cup E_T \cup \bigcup_{i \in \{1, \ldots, |A|\}} \left(\{\{\alpha_i, \alpha_i'\}\} \cup E_{\alpha_i'} \cup \left\{\{\alpha_i', r_{\alpha_i'}\}\right\} \cup E_{T_i'}\right) .$$

Lemma 4 *The* BT$(k+7)$*-tree with root* α_1 *can be embedded into* $G(A,B,C,M)$ *iff* M *contains a matching.*

Theorem 6 *To decide whether an arbitrary network* G *achieves the delay-capacity bound for the data distribution problem is* $\mathcal{NP}$*-complete.*

The proof follows from theorem 5 and the fact that $|V_M| = 16 \cdot |A| + 9 \cdot |B| + 4 \cdot |C| + |M| + 96 \cdot |A| = 125 \cdot |A| + 3 \cdot |A| = 2^7 \cdot 2^k = 2^{k+7}$

Corollary 3 *The problem to compute* DDTime(G, τ_s, τ_d) *for arbitrary networks* G *is* $\mathcal{NP}$*-hard.*

5 Approximations

We have seen that a special family of trees achieves the delay-capacity bound. The complexity of the data distribution problem for arbitrary trees is unknown. However, we can at least give reasonable approximations to the optimal schedule length. For the purpose, two important subclasses of schedules will be considered in more detail.

5.1 One Block Schedule

Definition 6 *We call a schedule a* **one–block schedule** *if each node receives at most one message.*

Note that the optimal schedule for the special trees described above is a one–block schedule. The same holds for hypercubes and the d–dimensional grid of size 4^d. Thus networks that achieve the delay-capacity bound always have an optimal schedule with the one-block property. One–block schedules are easy to analyze. Let us first generalize the notion of binomial trees.

Definition 7 *For* $d \in \mathbb{N}$, $d \geq 2$, *the family of* BT$^{[d]}$*-trees is defined as follows:*

$$\text{BT}^{[d]}(k) := \begin{cases} (\{\rho\}, \{\}) & \text{if } k = 0, \\ (\{\rho\} \cup \bigcup_{j=0}^{k-1} V_j, \bigcup_{j=0}^{k-1}(E_j \cup \{\{\rho, \rho_j\}\})) & \text{if } k \leq d, \\ (\{\rho\} \cup \bigcup_{j=k-d}^{k-1} V_j, \bigcup_{j=k-d}^{k-1}(E_j \cup \{\{\rho, \rho_j\}\})) & \text{else,} \end{cases}$$

where ρ *is the root of the* BT$^{[d]}(k)$*-tree and the* (V_j, E_j) *are* BT$^{[d]}(j)$*-trees with root* ρ_j.

Theorem 7 *For a* BT$^{[d]}(k)$*-tree holds*

$$\text{DDTime}(T, \tau_s, \tau_d) \leq k \cdot \tau_s + \left(\left(1 + 2^{-\lfloor (d-1)/2 \rfloor}\right) \cdot |T| - \left\lceil \frac{k}{d} \right\rceil \right) \cdot \tau_d .$$

Such a schedule can be constructed in linear time.

Since $\log|T| \geq (k-2)/2$ this bound is at most twice the delay-capacity bound. Hence, this schedule approximates an optimal schedule for $\text{BT}^{[d]}(k)$–trees with a factor at most 2.

Proof of Theorem 7: For a $\text{BT}^{[d]}(k)$–tree $T = (V, E)$ with root ρ let

$$T_{k-1}, T_{k-2}, \ldots, T_a$$

(with $a = \max\{k - d, 0\}$) be the $\text{BT}^{[d]}(j)$–subtrees of T rooted at the sons ρ_j of ρ. Let $\mathcal{W}_j$ be the subset of packets for T_j and S be the schedule

$$S_{\text{send}}(\rho) = \{((\rho, \rho_j), \mathcal{W}_j, t_j)\}$$

with $t_j = \sum_{l=0}^{j-1} t(|\mathcal{W}_l|)$. The subschedules for these subtrees are defined recursively the same way. After $d \cdot \tau_s + (|V| - 1) \cdot \tau_d$ steps only processors in subtrees of $\text{BT}^{[d]}(k - d)$–trees are still lacking their packet. Thus, $\text{length}(S) = L(k)$ with

$$L(k) = \begin{cases} d \cdot \tau_s + (|T_k| - 1) \cdot \tau_d + L(k - d) & \text{if } k \geq d, \\ k \cdot \tau_s + (|T_k| - 1) \cdot \tau_d & \text{else,} \end{cases}$$

where T_k is a $\text{BT}^{[d]}(k)$–tree. Since

$$|T_k| - 1 = \begin{cases} \sum_{l=0}^{d-1} |T_{k-d+l}| & \text{if } k \geq d, \\ \sum_{l=0}^{k-1} |T_l| & \text{else,} \end{cases}$$

we get

$$L(k) = k \cdot \tau_s + \sum_{j=0}^{k-1} |T_j| \cdot \tau_d \leq k \cdot \tau_s + \sum_{j=0}^{\lceil k/d \rceil - 1} (|T_{k-j \cdot d}| - 1) \cdot \tau_d$$

$$\leq k \cdot \tau_s + \left((|T_k| + |T_{k-d+1}|) - \left\lceil \frac{k}{d} \right\rceil \right) \cdot \tau_d$$

$$\leq k \cdot \tau_s + \left(\left(1 + 2^{-\lfloor (d-1)/2 \rfloor}\right) \cdot |T_k| - \left\lceil \frac{k}{d} \right\rceil \right) \cdot \tau_d .$$

∎

Next let us consider balanced binary trees and generalizations of such trees.

Definition 8 *Let* leaves(T) *denote the number of leaves of a tree T and $0 < \alpha < 1$ be a rational number. A* BB(α)–*tree is a binary rooted tree T such for each internal node v its left and right subtrees T_l, T_r are of about the same size, that is:*

$$\alpha \cdot (1 + |\text{leaves}(T_l)| + |\text{leaves}(T_r)|) \leq |\text{leaves}(T_l)|$$
$$\leq (1 - \alpha) \cdot (1 + |\text{leaves}(T_l)| + |\text{leaves}(T_r)|) .$$

T is a BV(d, α)–*tree if it is either a single node, or its root has $k \leq d$ subtrees $T_1, \ldots, T_k$ and for each T_i holds: T_i is a* BV(d, α)–*tree with $|T_i| \leq (1 - \alpha) \cdot |T|$.*

For balanced trees there are good approximations for the data distribution problem.

Theorem 8 *For* BB(α)*–trees one can efficiently construct a schedule of length at most*

$$2 \cdot \log_{\frac{1}{1-\alpha}} \left(\frac{|V|+1}{2} \right) \cdot \tau_s + \left(\frac{|V|-1}{\alpha} - 2 \cdot \log_{\frac{1}{1-\alpha}} \left(\frac{|V|+1}{2} \right) \right) \cdot \tau_d \ .$$

Corollary 4 *A complete or almost complete binary tree of size n has a simple schedule for the data distribution problem of length at most*

$$2 \cdot (\log(n+1) - 1) \cdot \tau_s + (2n - 2\log(n+1)) \cdot \tau_d \ \leq \ \mathrm{DCB}(n, \tau_s, \tau_d) \ .$$

Theorem 9 *A* BV(d, α)*–tree of size n has a schedule constructable in polynomial time of length at most*

$$d \cdot \log_{\frac{1}{1-\alpha}} n \cdot \tau_s + \left(\frac{n-1}{\alpha} - \log_{\frac{1}{1-\alpha}} n \right) \cdot \tau_d \ .$$

We can, however, show that not all graphs have an optimal schedule that is a one–block schedule. For example, a 1-dimensional chain of length $n \geq 4$ with the source being one of its endpoints requires length $(n-1) \cdot \tau_s + \frac{n \cdot (n-1)}{2} \cdot \tau_d$. Again, one can show that this topology exhibits the worst case for one–block schedules.

Theorem 10 *An arbitrary connected network G of size n has a one–block schedule of length*

$$(n-1) \cdot \tau_s + \frac{n \cdot (n-1)}{2} \cdot \tau_d \ .$$

5.2 OLBS–Schedule

How can one-block schedules be generalized to allow more flexible and efficient strategies? Considering again the example of 1-dimensional chains we notice that a processor forwards a bunch of messages each containing more than one packet and that at most the last message is split into smaller pieces. The other messages are relayed without any change. Let us formalize this observation as follows.

Definition 9 *A schedule S has the* **only last block split property** *iff S is a canonical schedule and for each node v excluding the source holds:* $((v, u), w, t) \in S$ *implies that S contains a tuple* $((u', v), w', t')$ *such that either* $w' = w$ *or that this tuple is the last receive event of v. We call such a schedule an* **olbs–schedule**.

An $l_1 \times l_2 \times \ldots \times l_d$**–torus** is obtained from an $l_1 \times l_2 \times \ldots \times l_d$–grid by connecting the corresponding outer boundaries in each dimension.

Theorem 11 *A* $l_1 \times l_2 \times \ldots \times l_d$ *d–dimensional torus* T_d *has a lower bound*

$$\mathrm{DDTime}(T_d, \tau_s, \tau_d) \ \geq \ \max \left\{ (|T_d| - 1) \cdot \tau_d, \ \sum_{i=1}^{d} \left\lfloor \frac{l_i}{2} \right\rfloor \cdot \tau_s \right\} \ .$$

Proof: The lower bound $(|T_d| - 1) \cdot \tau_d$ is trivial. The second bound follows from the observation that each node of T_d has other nodes in distance $\sum_{i=1}^d \lfloor \frac{l_i}{2} \rfloor$. ∎
Now we will prove an almost matching upper bound even for grids without wrap around. The bound is basically the sum of the two arguments of the max operator, and thus at most twice as large.

Theorem 12 *The data distribution problem on an $l_1 \times l_2 \times \ldots \times l_d$–grid G_d with source in the center, that means radius $\sum_{i=1}^d \lfloor \frac{l_i}{2} \rfloor$, can be solved in time*

$$(|G_d| - 1) \cdot \tau_d \; + \; \sum_{i=1}^d \left\lceil \frac{l_i}{2} \right\rceil \cdot \tau_s \; .$$

However, such a strategy is not always sufficient, see figure 2.

Theorem 13 *There exists trees such that olbs–schedules do not achieve optimal time.*

6 Conclusions

We have defined and analysed a more realistic model for the distribution of data in processor networks with message passing in a blocking mode. It takes into account the set-up delay for a communication event between two neighbouring processors. This problem is trivial if one neglects the set-up delays and allows nonblocking information exchange.
Even synchronizing a network without set-up delays, but which operates in a blocking mode, turns out to be a nontrivial task. In [J95] we have analysed this model and determined the optimal schedule length. Optimal schedules can be constructed for arbitrary such networks in polynomial time, but this seems to require a detailed analysis of the network topology.

References

[BBP93]   S. N. Bhatt, G. Bilardi, G. Pucci, A. Ranade, A. L. Rosenberg and E. J. Schwabe, *On Bufferless Routing of Variable Length Messages in Leveled Networks*, 1st European Symp. Algorithms, 1993.

[BPRR93] S. N. Bhatt, G. Pucci, A. Ranade and A. L. Rosenberg, *Scattering and Gathering Messages in Networks of Processors*, IEEE Trans. Computers 42, 1993, 938-949.

[BHLP92] J.-C. Bermond, P. Hell, A. Liestman, and J. Peters, *Broadcasting in Bounded Degree Graphs*, SIAM J. Disc. Math. 5, 1992, 10-24.

[FMR90]   P. Fraigniaud, S. Miguet and Y. Robert, *Complexity of Scattering on a Ring of Processors*, Parallel Computing 13, 1990, 377-383.

[HHL88]   S. Hedetniemi, S. Hedetniemi, and A. Liestman, *A Survey of Gossiping and Broadcasting in Communication Networks*, Networks 18, 1988, 319-349.

[HJM90]   J. Hromkovič, C.-D. Jeschke, and B. Monien, *Optimal Algorithms for Dissemination of Information in Some Interconnection Networks*, Proc. 15th MFCS, 1990, 337-346.

[J95]   A. Jakoby, *Optimal Data Distribution in Blocking Networks*, Technical Report Universität Lübeck, in preparation.

[JH89]   S. L. Johnsson and C.-T. Ho, *Optimal Broadcasting and Personalized Communication in Hypercubes*, IEEE Trans. Computers 38, 1989, 1249-1268.

[JKS89]   H. Jung, L. Kirousis, P. Spirakis, *Lower Bounds and Efficient Algorithms for Multiprocessor Scheduling of DAGs with Communication Delays*, Proc. 1st SPAA, 1989, 254 - 264.

[JR92]   A. Jakoby, R. Reischuk, *The Complexity of Scheduling Problems with Communication Delays for Trees*, Proc. 3rd SWAT, 1992, 165-177.

[JRS94]   A. Jakoby, R. Reischuk, C. Schindelhauer, *The Complexity of Broadcasting in Planar and Decomposable Graphs*, Proc. 14th International Workshop on Graph-Theoretic Concepts in Computer Science, Herrsching, June 1994.

[LP88]   A. Liestman and J. Peters, *Broadcast Networks of Bounded Degree*, SIAM J. Disc. Math. 4, 1988, 531-540.

[OW93]   T. Ottmann and P. Widmayer, *Algorithmen und Datenstrukturen*, BI Wissenschaftsverlag, 1993.

[PY88]   C. Papadimitriou and M. Yannakakis, *Towards an Architecture-Independent Analysis of Parallel Algorithms*, Proc. 20th STOC, 1988, 510-513, see also SIAM J. Comput. 19, 1990, 322-328.

[SCH81]   P. Slater, E. Cockayne, and S. Hedetniemi, *Information Dissemination in Trees*, SIAM J. Comput. 10, 1981, 692-701.

[SS89]   Y. Saad and M. H. Schultz, *Data Communication in Parallel Architectures*, Parallel Computing 11, 1989, 131-150.

Figures

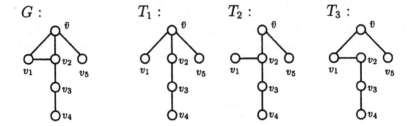

Fig. 1. A network G for which the data cannot be distributed in minimal time in a tree-like fashon, that means restricting to one of its spanning trees T_i.

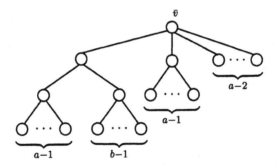

Fig. 2. The tree $T_{a,b}$: for $a = 6$, $b = 4$, $\tau_s = 4$ and $\tau_d = 2$ there is no OLBS–schedule that achieves minimal length.

Distributed Protocols Against Mobile Eavesdroppers*

P. Spirakis B. Tampakas and H. Antonopoulou

Computer Technology Institute
PO BOX 1122, 26110 Patras, Greece
e-mail: spirakis@cti.gr, tampakas@cti.gr, Antonopl@cti.gr

Abstract. We propose and study the following pursuit-evation problem in distributed enviroments: Members of a team of guards (e.g. antivirus programs) traverse the links of a network represented by a graph G, in pursuit of a fugitive (e.g. worm) which moves along the links of the graph without any other knowledge about the locations of the guards than whatever it can collect as it moves (e.g. the worm is oblivious to dynamic network behaviour). The fugitive's purpose is just to read local information at each node and to stay in the net as long as possible. When a guard meets a fugitive, the fugitive is destroyed. We combinatorially characterize and compare such problems, and we present network protocols that allow an efficient (in terms of number of guards and messages) elimination of the fugitive. Note that the problem we study is fundamentally different from distributed graph searching, since the fugitive does not know the locations of the guards. Our protocols make use of accidental meetings in random walks. The analysis and the proof techniques are based on a novel extension of multiple, parameterized random walk properties which may be of independent theoretical interest.
Keywords: Theory of Distributed Computation, Privacy and Security, Algorithms and Data Structures.

1 Introduction and the Problem

Security of networks has triggered a number of fundamental studies in recent years. [Franklin et al. 93] considered the problem of maintaining privacy in a network that is threatened by mobile eavesdroppers, i.e. by an abversary that can move its bugging equipment within the system. Mobile adversaries in the context of secure computation were introduced in [Ostrovsky, Yung 91].

We also adopt here the notion of a mobile "eavesdropper" which moves in the network without having available to it an instantaneous description of the whole network state. Unlike previous studies, however, our goal here is to describe network protocols which result in the elimination of the mobile adversary. Our assumption is that the network links can also traversed by mobile guards (e.g. antivirus software), any of which will eliminate the bug if they are both at the same node at the same time.

* This research was partially funded by the EC Basic Research Action project No 7141 (ALCOM II).

We consider the case of a single mobile bug. Note that, due to the mobility of the bug, the actual number of nodes being targeted can change over time (e.g. in each network round). Our work easily generalizes to a fixed number of mobile bugs (called fugitives from here on).

Once at a node, the (non-disrupting) bug gets to learn all incoming and outgoing messages and the memory contents. The bug can flow with message traffic (to neighbours only). It can not forge messages originating by guards (some form of electronic signature service is supported to be guarranteed by the network at a lower level).

The security problem we consider is driven by realistic assumptions about network attacks by mobile intruders (see e.g. [Securenet 92]). Thus, the fugitive does not have any (prior) knowledge of locations of guards and the guards are limited by the distributed nature of network communication and computation. Note that the problem we consider is *not* that of *distributedly* searching a graph (for definitions of graph searching see e.g. [Megiddo et al. 88]) where the fugitive is assumed to have *complete knowledge* of locations of pursuers, and (in some cases) infinite speed.

Our emphasis is on the discovery of efficient protocols (executed by network nodes) in terms of number of guards, messages and rounds, so that eventually the fugitive is eliminated. Our proposed protocols are *randomized*. Our protocols make use (and extend) properties of random walks that concern *accidental meetings*[2]. Our approach is thus more similar to distributed interception games(for sequential complexity of interception games see e.g. [Reif 79]).

Because our protocols use random walks, we restrict our attention to non-bipartite, undirected graphs (networks) to ensure that the random walks will be ergodic (and thus any random walk will converge to a limiting probability distribution on the vertices of the graph). We also assume that the network is *synchronous* and thus the fugitive must make a move at each clock tick.

2 The Basic Protocol and its Variations

The main idea of our protocol is to partition the guards into two groups: the *waiting guards* and the *searchers*. The waiting guards are spread into the network by a randomized protocol and occupy some (randomly selected) final positions and stay there. They act as traps. If the fugitive passes from any of these positions, it is eliminated. This part of the protocol is called the *spreading protocol*.

Due to the *randomized nature* of the spreading protocol the fugitive cannot guess the final positions of the waiting guards even if it knows the protocol. Notice that the final positions of the waiting guards partition the network into statistically similar pieces. Since the fugitive may stay inside such a piece (or even oscillate between two nodes) forever, the searchers are used to counteract this.

---

[2] An one page abstract of this line of research appeared as a short paper in PODC 94 [Spirakis,Tampakas,94].

Each searcher is doing a *random walk*. The collection of random walks will intercept any position , that the fugitive could keep, in small time (polynomial in the size of the network). The fugitive cannot guess the current positions of the searchers, due to the random, independent, choises that they make during their walks.

Notice that it is important that guards are able to erase information and that their source of randomness be on-line. Otherwise the fugitive would know all past and/or future network behaviour as soon as each node is visited by the bug at least once. Note also that just one searcher (and no other guards) are not enough, since the fugitive may possibly read incoming messages at the node it currently occupies and then it will escape in a direction different than that of the incoming messages. (In actual networks of today, in order for the anti-virus software to move from a node to a neighbour, the nodes must first exchange send/receive messages of a certain *type*. This may alert the fugitive/eavesdrpopper software).

However, by trying to escape, the fugitive may either coincide at a node with another searcher, or fall into a node trapped by a waiting guard. In both cases, the fugitive will be eliminated. (Actually the fugitive may also be eliminated by having the searchers accidentally occupy all neighbours of the node that the fugitive is currently and then move one searcher into that node. This is like the traditional graph searching paradigm but we will show that the formerly described cases have higher probability to happen soon).

Note that the searchers do not communicate with each other when they search. This prevents the bug from learning the searchers "plans".

The perfomance of the basic protocol can be significantly strengthened if we allow each of the waiting guards to repeat the execution of the spreading protocol after waiting for some time. The waiting time for each waiting guard could be either a fixed amount of time (equal to the mean time for a random walk to visit all the graph nodes) or randomly and uniformly selected for each waiting guard from an interval of the above mean value. We call this strengthening of the basic protocol, the *strong* protocol.

In the sequel we will show the following claim: Our *strong* protocol guarantees elimination of the bug in small polynomial expected number of rounds ,even with just *one* waiting guard and *two* searchers.

Other interesting variations of the basic protocol include having either **(a)** the waiting guards select final positions not uniformly randomly but with some bias to certain "good" positions e.g. at articulation points, at dense subgraphs or at main passages or **(b)** the searchers may do their random walks each just inside the graph parts created by the positions of the guards or even they may move in some statistically coordinated way. Some of these variations are dealt with in subsequent sections.

3 Notation and preliminaries

Let w be the number of waiting guards and s be the number of searchers. Let $t(w, s)$ be the random variable indicating the time (number of rounds) needed by the protocol to eliminate the fugitive and $\bar{t}(w, s)$ its expected value. Let G be the (undirected) graph of the network, with vertex set V and edge set E, where $|V| = n$ and $|E| = m$.

Concider G fixed and the protocol fixed. A (possible randomized) strategy S for the fugitive on G consists of decisions which tell the fugitive where to go in the next clock tick, based on the knowledge it has acquired so far.

An optimal (for the fugitive) strategy is one in which $\bar{t}(w, s)$ is maximal. A random (for the fugitive) strategy is one in which the fugitive selects, for its next move, equiprobably at random any neighbouring node from which no intercepting messages are currently coming.

The *hitting time* $H_G(x, y)$ from x to y is defined to be the expected number of steps for a random walk on G (as defined by the protocol of searchers) beginning at vertex x to reach vertex y for the first time.

Let $Y = \{y_1, \ldots, y_k\}$ be a subset of V. The hitting time $H_G(x, Y)$ is defined as the expected number of steps for a random walk on G beginning at vertex x to reach any of the vertices in Y for the first time.

Let $T_{G,S}(w, s)$ be the expected number of clock ticks (after the end of the spreading protocol) at which the fugitive, moving with strategy S, will fall into a node trapped by a waiting guard.

Let $M_{G,S}(w, s)$ be the expected number of clock ticks (after the end of the spreading protocol) at which the fugitive , having strategy S, will meet a searcher at a node.

Let $F_G(w)$ be the time (number of clock ticks) required for the spreading protocol. Clearly,

Lemma 1
For the optimal strategy S, $\bar{t}(w, s) \leq F_G(w) + \min\{T_{G,S}(w, s), M_{G,S}(w, s)\}$

4 Analysis of the Basic Protocol

4.1 The Spreading Protocol

The spreading protocol, in its basic form, is just a random walk for each waiting guard. The random walks may start from the same or different vertices and they are independent of each other. Each walk is then a *Markov Chain*, irreducible, and its stationary probability π satisfies, for each vertex x, $\pi(x) = d(x)/2m$, where $d(x)$ is the degree of x [Aleliunas et al, 79].

For each particular walk, the mean time to visit all the vertices of G at least once is $\sum_{x \in V} \mu(x)$ where $\mu(x)$ is the mean recurrence time of vertex x. But $\mu(x) = 1/\pi(x)$. Thus $\sum_{x \in V} \mu(x) \leq 2mn = O(n^3)$.

Since the walks are independent, if we wish to allow for each of them to hit all vertices of G at least once, we get (by tails of maximum of w random variables):

Lemma 2
All random walks will have visited all of G at least once in at most $O(n^3 \log w)$

expected time. Thus, in $O(n^3 \log w)$ expected time, each waiting guard is placed in a random node of the network.

$\square$

4.2 The Searching Part

Consider $s \geq 2$. What is an optimal strategy for the fugitive? It does not know the current positions of the searchers. It may only understand the case where a particular searcher will come to the node at which the fugitive stays, in the next clock tick. Call it an alerting searcher. Also the fugitive cannot assume anything about the positions of the waiting guards, other than that they are random (by Lemma 2). Assume that the optimal strategy forces the fugitive to stay at a local set A of nodes of G, and only change positions within A, if need be. By a theorem of [Tetali, Winkler,91] any node of A will be hit by at least one of the non-alerting searchers in $\Theta(n^3)$ clock ticks. By Lemma 2, the probability that A does not contain any waiting guard is $(1 - \frac{|A|}{n})^w \leq e^{\frac{-|A|w}{n}}$

Definition:
The set of nodes, A, indicated by the strategy S as the only set of nodes to be visited by the fugitive, is called the *set of places*.

Definition:
The set of places is *safe* if it does not contain any waiting guard.

We then get

Lemma 3:
For any strategy S and any $w \geq 2$, the probability that A is safe is less than $e^{\frac{-|A|w}{n}}$

Consider now the case of a safe set A chosen by an optimal strategy. As it is indicated in [Tetali, Winkler,91] any node of A will be hit by a single non-alerting searcher in an expected time of $\Theta(n^3|A|)$.
Since there are s searchers moving independently at random, we get (detailed proof in full paper) that:

Lemma 4:
For any particular subset A of V fixed by the optimal strategy to be the set of places, the $M_{G,S}(w,s) = \Theta((n/s)^3|A|)$.

Consider the graph G arbitrarily partitioned into b *connected* sets of nodes $V_1, \ldots, V_b$ of (almost) equal cardinality (the ratio of max over min cardinality in the V_i sets is bounded by a constant) and select the parameter b to be the maximum integer such that $\gamma b \log b \leq w$ for some fixed $\gamma > 2$. Then, by Lemma 2 and by the analogy of placing w balls randomly into b bins, we get:

Lemma 5:

Each V_i contains at least one waiting guard with probability tending to 1, provided $w \to \infty$ as $n \to \infty$.

Proof sketch: A particular V_i will not get any waiting guard with probability

$$(1 - \frac{1}{b})^w \leq (1 - \frac{1}{b})^{\gamma b \log b} \leq \frac{1}{b^\gamma}$$

Then $Prob\{\exists V_i$ which does not get any waiting guard $\} \leq b b^{-\gamma} = b^{-\gamma+1}$

□

An optimal strategy will have $T_{G,S} \leq \max H_G(x, Y)$ where $x \in V$ and Y is the set of positions $Y = \{Y_1, \ldots, Y_b\}$ of the waiting guards in $V_1, \ldots, V_b$. But then, because of Lemma 5, if G_i is the graph induced by V_i,

$$\max_{(x \in V)} H_G(x, Y) \leq \max_{(i)} \max_{(x \in V_i)} H_{G_i}(x, Y_i)$$

But $H_{G_i}(x, Y_i) \leq \Theta((n/b)^3)$ for any $x \in V_i$ and any Y_i, by [Brightwell,Winkler,90]. Thus,

Lemma 6:
For the optimal strategy, $T_{G,S}(w, s) \leq \Theta((n/b)^3)$, where $b = \Theta(w/\log w)$.

From Lemmas 1, 4, 6 we get :

Theorem 1:
For our basic protocol and any optimal strategy S of the fugitive with safe set A:

$$\bar{t}(w, s) \leq O(n^3 \log w + \min\{(\frac{n}{s})^3 |A|, (\frac{n \log w}{w})^3\})$$

□

5   Analysis of the Strong Protocol

We consider here the Strong Protocol with Fixed Waiting Time

Definition:
Let a *round* be the maximum period of time that the waiting guards stay at their currently chosen position.

Lemma 7:
Consider any set of nodes A. Then the probability that A remains safe for R rounds is at most $e^{\frac{-|A|w}{n}R}$.

Proof sketch: By Lemma 3 and the intependence of moves of the waiting guards when they change position.

□

Corollary:

For $R \geq n$ and any $w \geq 2$, any particular set A with $|A| \geq \log n$ will remain safe for R rounds with probability at most $(1/n)^w$.

In order to find a bound for the expected value of $T_{G,S}(w, s)$ we must examine the structure of the set of places A. Since the fugitive can base its next move only on the basis of avoiding an alerting searcher, we have that:

Lemma 8:

For any strategy S, the set A is optimally chosen when the fugitive *randomly* selects a neighbour node to move, other than the node of an alerting searcher.

Proof sketch: Note that sets A of size at least $\log n$ tend not to remain safe. Thus, either the fugitive will choose to stay at a very small set (almost not moving) or it will move at random to avoid recognized threats (since the waiting guards are at random places). The choise of the fugitive to stay at a very small set is not optimal, because then single random walks of the searchers will hit it quickly.

$\square$

Definition:

Let a *randomly avoiding* strategy be a strategy that satisfies Lemma 8.

Note now that if we partition the graph into the sets V_i, each V_i "periodically" will get waiting guards with probability $\rightarrow 1$, after $R \geq n$ rounds, even if w is fixed.

By arguing then as in Lemma 5 and 6 we get our main theorem:

Theorem 2:

For the Strong Protocol and any optimal strategy of the fugitive (including the *randomly avoiding* strategy) we get:

- The expected time to eliminate the bug after $R \geq n$ spreading rounds is

$$\min\{(\frac{n}{s})^3 \log n, (\frac{n \log w}{w})^3\})$$

- Each Spreading part has expected time $O(n^3 \log w)$

This holds for any $w \geq 1$ and $s \geq 2$.

For example, for $w, s = \sqrt{n}$, the time to eliminate the bug, after the R spreading rounds, is $O(n^{3/2} \log n)$.

6 Conclusions and Open Problems

Because of a theorem of [Gillman, 93], our result is considerable improved if G is an expander graph, because then the sample average number of visits to any set of vertices converges quickly to the stationary probability of A. One way to exploit this on arbitrary graphs, is to have the guards initially choose dense subgraphs of G (see e.g. [Kortsarz,Peleg,93]) and then have the spreading protocol to distribute the waiting guards randomly at the borders of the dense graphs, and the searcher be partitioned into each dense graph. We are currently examining such protocol variations, which at least heuristically, seen to behave better for mobile eavesdroppers of limited capabilities.

Acknowledgments: We wish to thank Moti Yung for inspiring us to work on privacy issues in distributed computing. We also thank the anonymous referees of WDAG 9 for their useful remarks.

References

[Aleliunas et al, 79] R. Aleliunas, R. Karp, R. Lipton, L. Lovasz, C. Rackoff, *"Random walks, universal traversal sequences and the complexity of maze problems"*, 20th ACM FOCS, pp. 218–223.

[Brightwell,Winkler,90] G. Brightwell and P. Winkler, *"Maximum hitting time for random walks on graphs"*, J. Random Structures and Algorithms, No.3(1990), pp. 263–276.

[Franklin et al. 93] M. Franklin, Z. Galil and M. Yung, , *"Eavesdropping Games: A Graph-Theoretic Approach to Privacy in Distributed Systems"*, ACM FOCS 1993, 670–679.

[Gillman, 93] D. Gillman, *A Chernoff bound for random walks on expander graphs"*, ACM FOCS 93, pp. 680–691.

[Kortsarz,Peleg,93] G. Kortsarz, D. Peleg, *" On Choosing a Dense Subgraph"* ACM FOCS 93, pp. 692–701.

[Megiddo et al. 88] N. Megiddo, S. Hakimi, M. Garey, D. Johnson and C. Papadimitriou, *"The Complexity of Searching a Graph"*, JACM 35 (1988), 18–44.

[Ostrovsky, Yung 91] R. Ostrovsky and M. Yung, *"Robust Computation in the presence of mobile viruses"*, ACM PODC 1991, 51–59.

[Reif 79] J.H. Reif, *"Universal Games of Incomplete Information"*, ACM STOC 11 (1979) pp. 288-308.

[Securenet 92] CEC RACE II Programme SECURENET (R 2057) *"Network Security and Protection"*, Final Report, 1992.

[Spirakis,Tampakas,94] P.Spirakis and B. Tampakas, *"Distributed Pursuit-Evation: Some aspects of Privacy and Security in Distributed Computing"*, short paper, ACM PODC 94.

[Tetali, Winkler,91] P. Tetali and P. Winkler, *" On a Random Walk problem arising in Self-stabilizing Token Management"*, ACM PODC 91, pp. 273–280.

Universal Constructions for Large Objects *

James H. Anderson and Mark Moir

Dept. of Computer Science, University of North Carolina at Chapel Hill

Abstract

We present lock-free and wait-free universal constructions for implementing large shared objects. Most previous universal constructions require processes to copy the entire object state, which is impractical for large objects. Previous attempts to address this problem require programmers to explicitly fragment large objects into smaller, more manageable pieces, paying particular attention to how such pieces are copied. In contrast, our constructions are designed to largely shield programmers from this fragmentation. Furthermore, for many objects, our constructions result in lower copying overhead than previous ones.

Fragmentation is achieved in our constructions through the use of *load-linked*, *store-conditional*, and *validate* operations on a "large" multi-word shared variable. Before presenting our constructions, we show that these operations can be efficiently implemented from similar one-word primitives.

1 Introduction

This paper extends recent research on *universal* lock-free and wait-free constructions of shared objects [3, 4]. Such constructions can be used to implement any object in a lock-free or a wait-free manner, and thus can be used as the basis for a general methodology for constructing highly-concurrent objects. Unfortunately, this generality often comes at a price, specifically space and time overhead that is excessive for many objects. A particular source of inefficiency in previous universal constructions is that they require processes to copy the entire object state, which is impractical for large objects. In this paper, we address this shortcoming by presenting universal constructions that can be used to implement large objects with low space overhead.

We take as our starting point the lock-free and wait-free universal constructions presented by Herlihy in [4]. In these constructions, operations are implemented using "retry loops". In Herlihy's lock-free universal construction, each process's retry loop consists of the following steps: first, a shared object pointer is read using a *load-linked* (LL) operation, and a private copy of the object is made; then, the desired operation is performed on the private copy; finally, a *store-conditional* (SC) operation is executed to attempt to "swing" the shared object pointer to point to the private copy. The SC operation may fail, in which case these steps are repeated. This algorithm is not wait-free because the SC of each loop iteration may fail. To ensure termination, Herlihy's wait-free construction employs a "helping" mechanism, whereby each process attempts to help other processes by performing their pending operations together with its own. This mechanism ensures

---

*Work supported, in part, by NSF contract CCR 9216421, and by a Young Investigator Award from the U.S. Army Research Office, grant number DAAHO4-95-1-0323.

that if a process is repeatedly unsuccessful in swinging the shared object pointer, then it is eventually helped by another process (in fact, after at most two loop iterations).

As Herlihy points out, these constructions perform poorly if used to implement large objects. To overcome this problem, he presents a lock-free construction in which a large object is fragmented into blocks linked by pointers. In this construction, operations are implemented so that only those blocks that must be accessed or modified are copied.

Herlihy's lock-free approach for implementing large objects suffers from three short-comings. First, the required fragmentation is left to the programmer to determine, based on the semantics of the implemented object. The programmer must also explicitly determine how copying is done. Second, Herlihy's approach is difficult to apply in wait-free implementations. In particular, directly combining it with the helping mechanism of his wait-free construction for small objects results in excessive space overhead. Third, Herlihy's large-object techniques reduce copying overhead only if long "chains" of linked blocks are avoided. Consider, for example, a large shared queue that is fragmented as a linear sequence of blocks (i.e., in a linked list). Replacing the last block actually requires the replacement of every block in the sequence. In particular, linking in a new last block requires that the pointer in the previous block be changed. Thus, the next-to-last block must be replaced. Repeating this argument, it follows that every block must be replaced.

Our approach for implementing large objects is also based upon the idea of fragmenting an object into blocks. However, it differs from Herlihy's in that it is array-based rather than pointer-based, i.e., we view a large object as a long array that is fragmented into blocks. Unlike Herlihy's approach, the fragmentation in our approach is not visible to the user. Also, copying overhead in our approach is often much lower than in Herlihy's approach. For example, we can implement shared queues with constant copying overhead.

Our constructions are similar to Herlihy's in that operations are performed using retry loops. However, while Herlihy's constructions employ only a single shared object pointer, we need to manage a collection of such pointers, one for each block of the array. We deal with this problem by employing LL, SC, and *validate* (VL) operations that access a "large" shared variable that contains all block pointers. This large variable is stored across several memory words.[1] In the first part of the paper, we show how to efficiently implement them using the usual single-word LL, SC, and VL primitives. We present two such implementations, one in which LL may return a special value that indicates that a subsequent SC will fail — we call this a *weak*-LL — and another in which LL has the usual semantics. In both implementations, LL and SC on a W-word variable take $O(W)$ time and VL takes constant time. The first of these implementations is simpler than the second because weak-LL does not have to return a consistent multi-word value in the case of interference by a concurrent SC. Also, weak-LL can be used to avoid unnecessary work in universal algorithms (there is no point performing private updates when a subsequent SC is certain to fail). For these reasons, we use weak-LL in our universal constructions.

Our wait-free universal construction is the first such construction to incorporate techniques for implementing large objects. In this construction, we impose an upper bound on the number of private blocks each process may have. This bound is assumed to be large enough to accommodate any single operation. The bound affects the manner in which processes may help one another. Specifically, if a process attempts to help too many other processes simultaneously, then it runs the risk of using more private space than is available. We solve this problem by having each process help as many processes as possible with each operation, and by choosing processes to help in such a way that all processes

---

[1]The multi-word operations considered here access a *single* variable that spans multiple words. Thus, they are not the same as the multi-word operations considered in [1, 2, 5, 6], which access *multiple* variables, each stored in a separate word. The multi-word operations we consider admit simpler and more efficient implementations than those considered in [1, 2, 5, 6].

shared var X: record pid: $0..N-1$; tag: $0..1$ end;
  BUF: array$[0..N-1, 0..1]$ of array$[0..W-1]$ of *wordtype*
initially $X = (0,0)$ ∧ $BUF[0,0] =$ initial value of the implemented variable V

private var $curr$: record pid: $0..N-1$; tag: $0..1$ end; i: $0..W-1$; j: $0..1$
initially $j = 0$

proc $Long\_Weak\_LL$(var r: array$[0..W-1]$ proc $Long\_SC$(*val*: array$[0..W-1]$ of *wordtype*)
    of *wordtype*) returns $0..N$ returns boolean
1: $curr := LL(X)$;   4: $j := 1 - j$;
    for $i := 0$ to $W-1$ do   for $i := 0$ to $W-1$ do
2:      $r[i] := BUF[curr.pid, curr.tag][i]$ 5: $BUF[p,j][i] := val[i]$
    od;   od;
3: if $VL(X)$ then return N 6: return $SC(X,(p,j))$
4: else return $X.pid$ fl

Figure 1: W-word weak-LL and SC using 1-word LL, VL, and SC. W-word VL is implemented by validating X.

are eventually helped. If enough space is available, all processes can be helped by one process at the same time — we call this *parallel* helping. Otherwise, several "rounds" of helping must be performed, possibly by several processes — we call this *serial* helping. The tradeoff between serial and parallel helping is one of time versus space.

The remainder of this paper is organized as follows. In Section 2, we present implementations of the LL, SC, and VL operations for large variables discussed above. We then present our lock-free and wait-free universal constructions and preliminary performance results in Section 3. We end the paper with concluding remarks in Section 4. Due to space limitations, we defer detailed proofs to the full paper.

2 LL and SC on Large Variables

In this section, we implement LL, VL, and SC operations for a W-word variable V, where $W > 1$, using the standard, one-word LL, VL, and SC operations.[2] We first present an implementation that supports only the weak-LL operation described in the previous section. We then present an implementation that supports a LL operation with the usual semantics. In the latter implementation, LL is guaranteed to return a "correct" value of V, even if a subsequent SC operation will fail. Unfortunately, this guarantee comes at the cost of higher space overhead and a more complicated implementation. In many applications, however, the weak-LL operation suffices. In particular, in most lock-free and wait-free universal constructions (including ours), LL and SC are used in pairs in such a way that if a SC fails, then none of the computation since the preceding LL has any effect on the object. By using weak-LL, we can avoid such unnecessary computation.

2.1 Weak-LL, VL, and SC Operations for Large Variables

We begin by describing the implementation of weak-LL, VL, and SC shown in Figure 1.[3] The $Long\_Weak\_LL$ and $Long\_SC$ procedures implement weak-LL and SC operations on a W-word variable V. Values of V are stored in "buffers", and a shared variable X indicates which buffer contains the "current" value of V. The current value is the value written

---
[2]We assume that the SC operation does not fail spuriously. As shown in [1], a SC operation that does not fail spuriously can be efficiently implemented using LL and a SC operation that might fail spuriously.

[3]Private variables in all figures are assumed to retain their values between procedure calls.

to V by the most recent successful SC operation, or the initial value of V if there is no preceding successful SC. The VL operation for V is implemented by simply validating X.

A SC operation on V is achieved by writing the W-word variable to be stored into a buffer, and by then using a one-word SC operation on X to make that buffer current. To ensure that a SC operation does not overwrite the contents of the current buffer, the SC operations of each process p alternate between two buffers, $BUF[p, 0]$ and $BUF[p, 1]$.

A process p performs a weak-LL operation on V in three steps: first, it executes a one-word LL operation on X to determine which buffer contains the current value of V; second, it reads the contents of that buffer; third, it performs a VL on X to check whether that buffer is still current. If the VL succeeds, then the buffer was not modified during p's read, and the value read by p from that buffer can be safely returned. If the VL fails, then the weak-LL rereads X in order to determine the ID of the last process to perform a successful SC; this process ID is then returned. We call the process whose ID is returned a *witness* of the failed weak-LL. As we will see in Section 3.2, the witness of a failed weak-LL can provide useful state information that held "during" the execution of that weak-LL. Note that if the VL of line 3 fails, then the buffer read by p is no longer current, and hence a subsequent SC by p will fail. This implementation yields the following result.

Theorem 1: Weak-LL, VL, and SC operations for a W-word variable can be implemented using LL, VL, and SC operations for a one-word variable with time complexity $O(W)$, $O(1)$, and $O(W)$, respectively, and space complexity $O(NW)$. □

2.2   LL, VL, and SC Operations for Large Variables

We now show how to implement LL and SC with the "usual" semantics. Although the weak-LL operation implemented above is sufficient for our constructions, other uses of "large" LL and SC might require the LL operation to always return a correct value from V. This is complicated by the fact that all W words of V cannot be accessed atomically.

Our implementation of LL, VL, and SC operations for a W-word variable V is shown in Figure 2. Like the previous implementation, this one employs a shared variable X, along with a set of buffers. Also, a shared array A of "tags" is used for buffer management.

Buffer management differs from that described in the previous subsection in several respects. First, each process p now has $4N + 2$ buffers, $BUF[p, 0]$ to $BUF[p, 4N + 1]$, instead of just two. Another difference is that each buffer now contains more information, specifically an old value of V, a new value of V, and two control bits. The control bits are used to detect concurrent read/write conflicts. These bits, together with the tags in array A, are employed to ensure that each LL returns a correct value, despite any interference.

Figure 2 shows two procedures, *Long_LL* and *Long_SC*, which implement LL and SC operations on V, respectively. As before, a VL on V is performed by simply validating X. The *Long_LL* procedure is similar to the *Long_Weak_LL* procedure, except that, in the event that the VL of X fails, more work is required in order to determine a correct return value. The buffer management scheme employed guarantees the following two properties.

(i) A buffer cannot be modified more than once while some process reads that buffer.

(ii) If a process does concurrently read a buffer while it is being written, then that process obtains a correct value either from the *old* field or from the *new* field of that buffer.

In the full paper, we prove both properties formally. We now describe the implementation shown in Figure 2 in more detail, paying particular attention to (i) and (ii).

In describing the *Long_LL* procedure, we focus on the code that is executed in the event that the VL of X fails, because it is this code that distinguishes the *Long_LL* from the *Long_Weak_LL* procedure of the previous subsection. If a process p executes the *Long_LL*

type *buftype* = **record** *b, c*: **boolean**; *new, old*: **array**[0..$W-1$] **of** *wordtype* **end**;
    tagtype = **record** *pid*: 0..$N-1$; *tag*: 0..$4N+1$ **end**

shared var X: *tagtype*; BUF: **array**[0..$N-1$, 0..$4N+1$] **of** *buftype*; A: **array**[0..$N-1$] **of** *tagtype*
initially $X = (0,0) \wedge BUF[0,0].b = BUF[0,0].c \wedge BUF[0,0].new$ = initial value of L

private var *val1, val2*: **array**[0..$W-1$] **of** *wordtype*; *curr, diff*: *tagtype*; i,j: 0..$W-1$; *bit*: **boolean**
initially $j = 1$ and tag 0 is the "last tag sucessfully SC'd"

| **proc** *Long_LL*() **returns array**[0..$W-1$] | **proc** *Long_SC*(*newval*: **array**[0..$W-1$] |
| **of** *wordtype* | **of** *wordtype*) |

```
 1:  curr := LL(X);                              10:  read A[j];
     for i := 0 to W - 1 do                            j := (j + 1) mod N fi;
 2:     val1[i] := BUF[curr.pid, curr.tag].new[i]  11:  select diff : diff ∉ ({last N tags read} ∪
     od;                                                            {last N tags selected} ∪
 3:  if VL(X) then return val1                                      {last tag successfully SC'd});
     else                                         12:  if ¬ VL(X) then return false fi;
 4:     curr := X;                                13:  bit := ¬BUF[p, diff].c;
 5:     A[p] := curr;                             14:  BUF[p, diff].c := bit;
        for i := 0 to W - 1 do                         for i := 0 to W - 1 do
 6:        val1 := BUF[curr.pid, curr.tag].new[i] 15:     BUF[p, diff].old[i] := val1[i]
        od;                                            od;
 7:     bit := BUF[curr.pid, curr.tag].b;         16:  BUF[p, diff].b := bit;
        for i := 0 to W - 1 do                         for i := 0 to W - 1 do
 8:        val2[i] := BUF[curr.pid, curr.tag].old[i] 17:   BUF[p, diff].new[i] := newval[i]
        od;                                            od;
 9:     if BUF[curr.pid, curr.tag].c = bit then   18:  return SC(X, (p, diff))
           return val2 else return val1
     fi fi
```

Figure 2: W-word LL and SC using 1-word LL, VL, and SC. W-word VL is trivially implemented by validating X.

procedure and its VL of X fails, then p might have read a corrupt value from the buffer due to a concurrent write. In order to obtain a correct return value, p reads X again to ascertain the current buffer, and then reads the entire contents of that buffer: *new*, b, *old*, and c. The fields within a buffer are written in the reverse of the order in which they are read in the *Long_LL* procedure. Thus, by property (i), p's read can "cross over" at most one concurrent write by another process. By comparing the values it reads from the b and c fields, p can determine whether the crossing point (if any) occurred while p read the *old* field or the *new* field. Based on this comparison, p can choose a correct return value. This is the essence of the formal proof required to establish property (ii) above.

In describing the *Long_SC* procedure, we focus on the buffer selection mechanism — once a buffer has been selected, this procedure simply updates the *old*, *new*, b, and c fields of that buffer as explained above. The primary purpose of the buffer selection mechanism is to ensure that property (i) holds. Each time a process p executes *Long_SC*, it reads the tag value written to $A[r]$ by some process r (line 10). The tag values are read from the processes in turn, so after N SC operations on V, p has read a tag from each process. Process p selects a buffer for its SC by choosing a new tag (line 11). The new tag is selected to differ from the last N tags read by p from A, to differ from the last N tags selected by p, and to differ from the last tag used in a successful SC by p. The last of these three conditions ensures that p does not overwrite the current buffer, and the first two conditions ensure that property (i) holds. We explain below how tags are selected. First, however, we explain why the selection mechanism ensures property (i).

Observe that, if process q's VL of X (line 3) fails, then before reading from one of p's

```
proc Read_Tag(v)                 proc Store_Tag(v)                  proc Select_Tag()
  if v ∈ Read_Q then               delete(Select_Q, v);                returns 0..4N + 1
    delete(Read_Q, v);             enqueue(Last_Q, v);               y := dequeue(Select_Q);
    enqueue(Read_Q, v)             y := dequeue(Last_Q);             enqueue(Select_Q, y);
  else                             if y ∉ Read_Q then                return y
    enqueue(Read_Q, v);              enqueue(Select_Q, y)
    delete(Select_Q, v);           fi
    y := dequeue(Read_Q);
    if y ∉ Last_Q then
      enqueue(Select_Q, y)
fi fi
```

Figure 3: Pseudo-code implementations of operations on tag queues.

buffers $BUF[p, v]$ (lines 6 to 9), q writes (p, v) to $A[q]$ (line 5). If p selects and modifies $BUF[p, v]$ while process q is reading $BUF[p, v]$, then p does not select $BUF[p, v]$ again for any of its next N SC operations. Thus, before p selects $BUF[p, v]$ again, p reads $A[q]$ (line 10). As long as (p, v) remains in $A[q]$, it will be among the last N tags read by p, and hence p will not select $BUF[p, v]$ to be modified. Therefore, property (i) holds.

We conclude this subsection by describing how the tag selection in line 11 can be efficiently implemented. To accomplished this, each process maintains three local queues — *Read*, *Last*, and *Select*. The *Read* queue records the last N tags read and the *Last* queue records the last tag successfully written (using SC) to X. All other tags reside in the *Select* queue, from which new tags are selected.

The tag queues are maintained by means of the *Read_Tag*, *Store_Tag*, and *Select_Tag* procedures shown in Figure 3. In these procedures, *enqueue* and *dequeue* denote the normal queue operations, $delete(Q, v)$ removes tag v from Q (and does not modify Q if v is not in Q), and $x \in Q$ holds iff tag x is in queue Q.

Process p selects a tag (line 11 of Figure 2) by calling *Select_Tag*. *Select_Tag* moves the front tag in p's *Select* queue to the back, and returns that tag. If that tag is subsequently written to X by a successful SC operation (line 18), then p calls *Store_Tag* to move the tag from the *Select* queue to the *Last* queue. The tag that was previously in the *Last* queue is removed and, if it is not in the *Read* queue, is returned to the *Select* queue.

When process p reads a tag (p, v) (line 10), it calls *Read_Tag* to record that this tag was read. If (p, v) is already in the *Read* queue, then *Read_Tag* simply moves (p, v) to the end of the *Read* queue. If (p, v) is not already in the *Read* queue, then it is enqueued into the *Read* queue and removed from the *Select* queue, if necessary. Finally, the tag at the front of the *Read* queue is removed because it is no longer one of the last N tags read. If that tag is also not the last tag written to X, then it is returned to the *Select* queue.

The *Read* queue always contains the last N tags read, and the *Last* queue always contains the last tag successfully written to X. Thus, the tag selected by *Select_Tag* is certainly not the last tag successfully written to X, nor is it among the last N tags read. In the full paper, we show that maintaining a total of $4N + 2$ tags ensures that the tag selected is also not one of the last N tags selected, as required.

By maintaining a static index table that allows each tag to be located in constant time, and by representing the queues as doubly-linked lists, all of the queue operations described above can be implemented in constant time. Thus, we have the following result.

Theorem 2: LL, VL, and SC operations for a W-word variable can be implemented using LL, VL, and SC operations for a one-word variable with time complexity $O(W)$, $O(1)$, and $O(W)$, respectively, and space complexity $O(N^2W)$. □

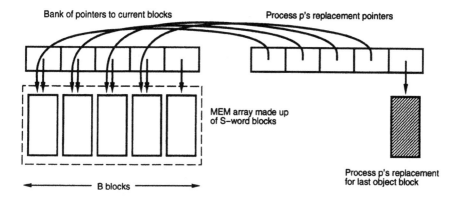

Bank of pointers to current blocks

Process p's replacement pointers

MEM array made up
of S–word blocks

Process p's replacement
for last object block

B blocks

Figure 4: Implementation of the *MEM* array for large object constructions.

3 Large Object Constructions

In this section, we present our lock-free and wait-free universal constructions for large objects. We begin with a brief overview of previous constructions due to Herlihy [4].

Herlihy presented lock-free and wait-free universal constructions for "small" objects as well as a lock-free construction for "large" objects [4]. As described in Section 1, an operation in Herlihy's small-object constructions copies the entire object, which can be a severe disadvantage for large objects. In Herlihy's large-object construction, the implemented object is fragmented into blocks, which are linked by pointers. With this modification, the amount of copying performed by an operation can often be reduced by copying only those blocks that are affected by the operation. However, because of this fragmentation, a significant amount of creative work on the part of the sequential object designer is often required before the advantages of Herlihy's large-object construction can be realized. Also, this approach provides no advantage for common objects such as the queue described in Section 1. Finally, Herlihy did not present a wait-free construction for large objects. Our lock-free and wait-free universal constructions for large objects are designed to overcome all of these problems. These constructions are described next in Sections 3.1 and 3.2, respectively. In Section 3.3, we present performance results comparing our constructions to Herlihy's.

3.1 Lock-Free Universal Construction for Large Objects

Our lock-free construction is shown in Figure 5. In this construction, the implemented object is stored in an array. Unlike Herlihy's small-object constructions, the array is not actually stored in contiguous locations of shared memory. Instead, we provide the illusion of a contiguous array, which is in fact partitioned into blocks. An operation replaces only the blocks it modifies, and thus avoids copying the whole object. Before describing the code in Figure 5, we first explain how the illusion of a contiguous array is provided.

Figure 4 shows an array *MEM*, which is divided into B blocks of S words each. Memory words $MEM[0]$ to $MEM[S-1]$ are stored in the first block, words $MEM[S]$ to $MEM[2S-1]$ are stored in the second block, and so on. A bank of pointers, one to each block of the array, is maintained in order to record which blocks are currently part of the array. In order to change the contents of the array, an operation makes a copy of each block to be changed, and then attempts to update the bank of pointers by installing new

type *blktype* = **array**[0..*S* − 1] **of** *wordtype*

shared var *BANK*: **array**[0..*B* − 1] **of** 0..*B* + *NT* − 1;   /* Bank of pointers to array blocks */
          BLK: **array**[0..*B* + *NT* − 1] **of** *blktype*   /* Array and copy blocks */
initially (∀*k* : 0 ≤ *k* < *B* :: *BANK*[*k*] = *NT* + *k* ∧ *BLK*[*NT* + *k*] = (*k*th block of initial value))

private var *oldlst*, *copy*: **array**[0..*T* − 1] **of** 0..*B* + *NT* − 1; *ptrs*: **array**[0..*B* − 1] **of** 0..*B* + *NT* − 1;
          dirty: **array**[0..*B* − 1] **of boolean**; *dirtycnt*: 0..*T*; *i*, *blkidx*: 0..*B* − 1;
          blk: 0..*B* + *NT* − 1; *ret*: *objrettype*
initially (∀*k* : 0 ≤ *k* < *T* :: *copy*[*k*] = *pT* + *k*)

proc *Read*(*addr*: 0..*BS* − 1) **returns** *wordtype*
   return *BLK*[*ptrs*[*addr* **div** *S*]][*addr* **mod** *S*]

proc *Write*(*addr*: 0..*BS* − 1; *val*: *wordtype*)
   blkidx := *addr* **div** *S*;   /* Compute block index from address */
   if ¬*dirty*[*blkidx*] **then**   /* Haven't changed this block before */
     dirty[*blkidx*] := *true*;   /* Record that block is changed */
     memcpy(*BLK*[*copy*[*dirtycnt*]], *BLK*[*ptrs*[*blkidx*]], *sizeof*(*blktype*)); /* Copy old block to new */
     oldlst[*dirtycnt*], *ptrs*[*blkidx*], *dirtycnt* := *ptrs*[*blkidx*], *copy*[*dirtycnt*], *dirtycnt* + 1
   fi;   /* Install new block, record old block, prepare for next one */
   BLK[*ptrs*[*blkidx*]][*addr* **mod** *S*] := *val*   /* Write new value */

proc *LF_Op*(*op*: *optype*; *pars*: *paramtype*)
   while *true* **do**   /* Loop until operation succeeds */
1:   **if** *Long_Weak_LL*(*BANK*, *ptrs*) = *N* **then**   /* Load object pointer */
      for *i* := 0 **to** *B* − 1 **do** *dirty*[*i*] := *false* **od**; *dirtycnt* := 0;   /* No blocks copied yet */
2:    *ret* := *op*(*pars*);   /* Perform operation on object */
3:    **if** *dirtycnt* = 0 ∧ *Long_VL*(*BANK*) **then return** *ret* **fi**;   /* Avoid unnecessary SC */
4:    **if** *Long_SC*(*BANK*, *ptrs*) **then**   /* Operation is successful, reclaim old blocks */
      for *i* := 0 **to** *dirtycnt* − 1 **do** *copy*[*i*] := *oldlst*[*i*] **od**;
      return *ret*
    fi fi
   od

Figure 5: Lock-free implementation for a large object.

pointers for the changed blocks; the other pointers are left unchanged. This is achieved by using the weak-LL and SC operations for large variables presented in Section 2.1.[4] In Figure 4, process *p* is preparing to modify a word in the last block, but no others. Thus, the bank of pointers to be written by *p* is the same as the current bank, except that the last pointer points to *p*'s new last block.

When an operation by process *p* accesses a word in the array, say *MEM*[*x*], the block that currently contains *MEM*[*x*] must be identified. If *p*'s operation modifies *MEM*[*x*], then *p* must replace that block. In order to hide the details of identifying blocks and of replacing modified blocks, some address translation and record-keeping is necessary. This work is performed by special *Read* and *Write* procedures, which are called by the sequential operation in order to read or write the *MEM* array. As a result, our constructions are not completely transparent to the sequential object designer. For example, instead of writing "*MEM*[1] := *MEM*[10]", the designer would write "*Write*(1, *Read*(10))". However, as discussed in Section 4, a preprocessor could be used to provide complete transparency.

We now turn our attention to the code of Figure 5. In this figure, *BANK* is a *B*-word shared variable, which is treated as an array of *B* pointers (actually indices into the *BLK* array), each of which points to a block of *S* words. Together, the *B* blocks pointed to by *BANK* make up the implemented array *MEM*. We assume an upper bound *T* on the number of blocks modified by any operation. Therefore, in addition to the *B*

---

[4]An extra parameter has been added to the procedures of Section 2.1 to explicitly indicate which shared variable is updated.

blocks required for the object, T "copy blocks" are needed per process, giving a total of $B + NT$ blocks. These blocks are stored in the BLK array. Although blocks $BLK[NT]$ to $BLK[NT + B - 1]$ are the initial array blocks, and $BLK[pT]$ to $BLK[(p + 1)T - 1]$ are process p's initial copy blocks, the roles of these blocks are not fixed. In particular, if p replaces a set of array blocks with some of its copy blocks as the result of a successful SC, then p reclaims the replaced array blocks as copy blocks. Thus, the copy blocks of one process may become blocks of the array, and later become copy blocks of another process.

Process p performs a lock-free operation by calling the LF_Op procedure. The loop in the LF_Op procedure repeats until the SC at line 3 succeeds. In each iteration, process p first reads $BANK$ into a local variable $ptrs$ using a B-word weak-LL. Recall from Section 2.1 that the weak-LL can return a process identifier from $\{0, ..., N - 1\}$ if the following SC is guaranteed to fail. In this case, there is no point in attempting to apply p's operation, so the loop is restarted. Otherwise, p records in its $dirty$ array that no block has yet been modified by its operation, and initializes the $dirtycnt$ counter to zero.

Next, p calls the op procedure provided as a parameter to LF_Op. The op procedure performs the sequential operation by reading and writing the elements of the MEM array. This reading and writing is performed by invoking the $Read$ and $Write$ procedures shown in Figure 5. The $Read$ procedure simply computes which block currently contains the word to be accessed, and returns the value from the appropriate offset within that block. The $Write$ procedure performs a write to a word of MEM by computing the index $blkidx$ of the block containing the word to be written. If it has not already done so, the $Write$ procedure then records that the block is "dirty" (i.e., has been modified) and copies the contents of the old block to one of p's copy blocks. Then, the copy block is linked into p's $ptrs$ array, making that block part of p's version of the MEM array, and the displaced old block is recorded in $oldlst$ for possible reclaiming later. Finally, the appropriate word of the new block is modified to contain the value passed to the $Write$ procedure.

If $BANK$ is not modified by another process after p's weak-LL, then the object contained in p's version of the MEM array (pointed to by p's $ptrs$ array) is the correct result of applying p's operation. Therefore, p's SC successfully installs a copy of the object with p's operation applied to it. After the SC, p reclaims the displaced blocks (recorded in $oldlst$) to replace the copy blocks it used in performing its operation. On the other hand, if another process $does$ modify $BANK$ between p's weak-LL and SC, then p's SC fails. In this case, some other process completes an operation, so the implementation is lock-free.

Before concluding this subsection, one further complication bears mentioning. If the $BANK$ variable is modified by another process while p's sequential operation is being executed, then it is possible for p to read inconsistent values from the MEM array. Observe that this does not result in p installing a corrupt version of the object, because p's subsequent SC fails. However, there is a risk that p's sequential operation might cause an error, such as a division by zero or a range error, because it reads an inconsistent state of the object. This problem can be solved by ensuring that, if $BANK$ is invalidated, control returns directly from the $Read$ procedure to the LF_Op procedure, without returning to the sequential operation. The Unix longjmp command can be used for this purpose. The details are omitted from Figure 5. In the full paper, we prove the following.

Theorem 3: Suppose a sequential object OBJ can be implemented in an array of B S-word blocks such that any operation modifies at most T blocks and has worst-case time complexity C. Then, OBJ can be implemented in a lock-free manner with space overhead[5] $O(NB + NTS)$ and contention-free time complexity $O(B + C + TS)$. □

It is interesting to compare these complexity figures to those of Herlihy's lock-free

---

[5]By *space overhead*, we mean space complexity beyond that required for the sequential object.

construction. Consider the implementation of a queue. By storing head and tail "pointers" (actually, array indices, not pointers) in a designated block, an enqueue or dequeue can be performed in our construction by copying only two blocks: the block containing the head or tail pointer to update, and the block containing the array slot pointed to by that pointer. Space overhead in this case is $O(NB + NS)$, which should be small when compared to $O(BS)$, the size of the queue. Contention-free time complexity is $O(B + C + S)$, which is only $O(B + S)$ greater than the time for a sequential enqueue or dequeue. In contrast, as mentioned in Section 1, each process in Herlihy's construction must actually copy the entire queue, even when using his large-object techniques. Thus, space overhead is at least N times the worst-case queue length, i.e., $\Omega(NBS)$. Also, contention-free time complexity is $\Omega(BS + C)$, since $\Omega(BS)$ time is required to copy the entire queue in the worst case.

When implementing a balanced tree, both constructions require space overhead of $O(N \log(BS))$ for local blocks. However, we pay a logarithmic time cost only when performing an operation whose sequential counterpart modifies a logarithmic number of array slots. In contrast, Herlihy's construction entails a logarithmic time cost for copying for almost every operation — whenever some block is modified, a chain of block pointers must be updated from that block to the block containing the root of the tree.

3.2 Wait-Free Construction for Large Objects

Our wait-free construction for large objects is shown in Figure 6. As in the lock-free construction presented in the previous subsection, this construction uses the *Read* and *Write* procedures in Figure 5 to provide the illusion of a contiguous array. The principal difference between our lock-free and wait-free constructions is that processes in the wait-free construction "help" each other in order to ensure that each operation by each process is eventually completed. To enable each process to perform the operation of at least one other process together with its own, each process p now has $M \geq 2T$ private copy blocks. (Recall that T is the maximum number of blocks modified by a single operation.)

The helping mechanism used in our wait-free, large-object construction is similar to that used in Herlihy's wait-free, small-object construction in several respects. To enable processes to perform each others' operations, each process q begins by "announcing" its operation and parameters in $ANC[q]$ (line 11 in Figure 6). Also, each process stores sufficient information with the object to allow a helped process to detect that its operation was completed and to determine the return value of that operation. This information also ensures that the operation helped is not subsequently reapplied.

There are also several differences between our helping mechanism and Herlihy's. First, in Herlihy's construction, each time a process performs an operation, it also performs the pending operations of all other processes. However, in our construction, the restricted amount of private copy space might prevent a process from simultaneously performing the pending operations of all other processes. Therefore, in our construction, each process helps only as many other processes as it can with each operation. In order to ensure that each process is eventually helped, a *help* counter is added to the shared variable *BANK* used in our lock-free construction. The *help* field indicates which process should be helped next. Each time process p performs an operation, p helps as many processes as possible starting from the process stored in the *help* field. This is achieved by helping processes until too few private copy blocks remain to accommodate another operation (lines 22 to 24). (Recall that the *Write* procedure in Figure 5 increments *dirtycnt* whenever a new block is modified.) Process p updates the *help* field so that the next process to successfully perform an operation starts helping where p stops.

Our helping mechanism also differs from Herlihy's in the way a process detects the completion of its operation. In Herlihy's construction, completion is detected by means

type *anctype* = **record** *op*: *optype*; *pars*: *paramtype*; *bit*: **boolean end**;
   retblktype = **array**[0..N − 1] **of record** *val*: *objrettype*; *applied*, *copied*: **boolean end**
   blktype = **array**[0..S − 1] **of** *wordtype*;
   banktype = **record** *blks*: **array**[0..B − 1] **of** 0..$B + NM$ − 1; *help*: 0..N − 1; *ret*: 0..N **end**

shared var *BANK*: *banktype*; *BLK*: **array**[0..$B + NM$ − 1] **of** *blktype*;
   ANC: **array**[0..N − 1] **of** *anctype*;   /* Announce array */
   RET: **array**[0..N] **of** *retblktype*;   /* Blocks for operation return values */
   LAST: **array**[0..N − 1] **of** 0..N /* Last *RET* block updated by each process */
initially *BANK*.*ret* = N ∧ (∀p :: *ANC*[p].*bit* = *RET*[N][p].*applied* = *RET*[N][p].*copied*) ∧
BANK.*help* = 0 ∧ (∀k : 0 ≤ k < B :: *BANK*.*blks*[k] = $NM + k$ ∧ *BLK*[$NM + k$] = (kth initial block))

private var *oldlst*, *copy*: **array**[0..M − 1] **of** 0..$B + NM$ − 1; *b*, *tmp*, *rb*, *oldrb*: 0..N; *ptrs*: *banktype*;
   match, *done*, *bit*, *a*, *loop*: **boolean**; *applyop*: *optype*; *applypars*: *paramtype*; *j*, *try*: 0..N − 1;
   m: 0..M − 1; *dirty*: **array**[0..B − 1] **of boolean**; *dirtycnt*: 0..M; *i*: 0..B − 1
initially (∀k : 0 ≤ k < M :: *copy*[k] = $pM + k$) ∧ *rb* = p ∧ ¬*bit*

proc *Apply*(q: 0..N − 1)   **proc** *Return_Block*() **returns** 0..N

```
1:  match := ANC[q].bit;                          7:  tmp := Long_Weak_LL(BANK, ptrs);
2:  if RET[rb][q].applied ≠ match then             8:  if tmp ≠ N then
3:      applyop := ANC[q].op;                       9:      return LAST[tmp]
4:      applypars := ANC[q].pars;                       else
5:      RET[rb][q].val := applyop(applypars);      10:     return ptrs.ret
6:      RET[rb][q].applied := match                    fi
    fi
```

proc *WF_Op*(*op*: *optype*; *pars*: *paramtype*)

```
11: ANC[p], bit := (op, pars, ¬bit), ¬bit;                        /* Announce operation */
12: b, done := Return_Block(), false;
13: while ¬done ∧ RET[b][p].copied ≠ bit do /* Loop until update succeeds or operation is helped */
14:     if Long_Weak_LL(BANK, ptrs) = N then                  /* Load object pointers */
15:         for i := 0 to B − 1 do dirty[i] := false od;  dirtycnt := 0;    /* No blocks modified yet */
16:         oldrb, ptrs.ret := ptrs.ret, rb;          /* Record old return block and install new one */
17:         memcpy(RET[rb], RET[oldrb], sizeof(retblktype)); /* Make private copy of return block */
18:         if Long_VL(BANK) then                             /* Check if Long_SC will fail */
                for j := 0 to N − 1 do                         /* Record applied operations */
19:                 a := RET[rb][j].applied;
20:                 RET[rb][j].copied := a
                od;
21:         Apply(p); try, loop := ptrs.help, false;            /* Apply own operation */
22:         while dirtycnt + T ≤ M ∧ ¬loop do /* Help processes while sufficient space remains */
23:             Apply(try);
24:             try := try + 1 mod N;  if try = ptrs.help then loop := true fi
            od;
25:         LAST[p], ptrs.help := rb, try;            /* Relay which return block was modified */
26:         if Long_SC(BANK, ptrs) then           /* Operation is successful, reclaim old blocks */
27:             for m := 0 to dirtycnt − 1 do copy[m] := oldlst[m] od;
28:             RET[rb][p].copied, rb, done := bit, oldrb, true /* Prepare copied bit for next time */
            fi fi
        fi;
29:     b := Return_Block()                          /* Get current or recent return block */
    od;
30: return RET[b][p].val                            /* Get return value of operation */
```

Figure 6: Wait-free implementation for a large object.

of a collection of toggle bits, one for each process, that are stored with the current version of the object. Before attempting to apply its operation, each process p first "announces" a new toggle bit value. When another process helps p, it copies this bit value into the current version of the object. To detect the completion of its operation, p tests whether the bit value stored for it in the current version of the object matches the bit value it previously announced; to access the current version of the object, p first reads the shared object pointer, and then reads the buffer pointed to by that pointer. In order to avoid a race condition that can result in an operation returning an incorrect value, Herlihy's construction requires this sequence of reads to be performed twice. This race condition arises when p attempts to access the current buffer, and during p's access, another process subsequently reclaims that buffer and privately updates it. By dereferencing the object pointer and checking its toggle bit a second time, p can ensure that if the first buffer it accessed has been reclaimed, then p's operation has already been applied. This is because the process that reclaimed the buffer helped all other processes with its operation, and therefore ensured that p's operation was applied. Because our construction does not guarantee that each process helps all other processes at once, p might have to reread the shared object pointer and read its toggle bit many times to ensure that its operation has been applied. We therefore use a different mechanism, explained below, for determining whether an operation has been applied.

To enable a process to detect that its operation has been applied, and to determine the return value of the operation, we use a set of "return" blocks. There are $N+1$ return blocks $RET[0]$ to $RET[N]$; at any time, one of these blocks is "current" (as indicated by a new ret field in the $BANK$ variable) and each process "owns" one of the other return blocks. The current return block contains, for each process q, the return value of q's most recent operation, along with two bits: $applied$ and $copied$. These bits are used by q to detect when its operation has been completed. Roughly speaking, the $applied$ bit indicates that q's operation has been applied to the object and the $copied$ bit indicates that another operation has been completed since q's operation was applied. The interpretation of these bits is determined by $ANC[q].bit$. For example, q's operation has been applied iff q's $applied$ bit in the current return block equals $ANC[q].bit$.

To see why two bits are needed to detect whether q's operation is complete, consider the scenario in Figure 7. In this figure, process p performs two operations. In the first, p's SC is successful, and p replaces $RET[5]$ with $RET[3]$ as the current return block at line 26. During p's first operation, q starts an operation. However, q starts this operation too late to be helped by p. Before p's execution of line 26, q reads $BANK$ in line 7 and determines that $RET[5]$ is the current return block. Now, p starts a second operation. Because p previously replaced $RET[5]$ as the current return block, $RET[5]$ is now p's private copy, so p's second operation uses $RET[5]$ to record the operations it helps. When p executes line 6, it changes q's $applied$ bit to indicate that it has applied q's operation. Note that, at this stage, q's operation has only been applied to p's private object copy, and p has not yet performed its SC. However, if q reads the $applied$ bit of $RET[5]$ (which it previously determined to be the current RET block) at line 13, then q incorrectly concludes that its operation has been applied to the object, and terminates prematurely.

It is similarly possible for q to detect that its $copied$ bit in some return block $RET[b]$ equals $ANC[q].bit$ before the SC (if any) that makes $RET[b]$ current. However, because q's $copied$ bit is updated only $after$ its $applied$ bit has been successfully installed as part of the current return block, it follows that some process must have previously applied q's operation. Thus, q terminates correctly in this case (see line 13).

It remains to describe how process q determines which return block contains the current state of q's operation. It is not sufficient for q to perform a weak-LL on $BANK$ and read the ret field, because the weak-LL is not guaranteed to return a value of $BANK$ if a successful

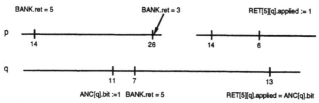

Figure 7: Process q prematurely detects that its *applied* bit equal $ANC[q].bit$.

SC operation interferes. In this case, the weak-LL returns the ID of a "witness" process that performs a successful SC on $BANK$ during the weak-LL operation. In preparation for this possibility, process p records the return block it is using in $LAST[p]$ (line 25) before attempting to make that block current (line 26). When q detects interference from a successful SC, q uses the $LAST$ entry of the witness process to determine which return block to read. The $LAST$ entry contains the index of a return block that was current during q's weak-LL operation. If that block is subsequently written after being current, then it is a copy of a more recent current return block, so its contents are still valid. Our wait-free construction gives rise to the following result.

Theorem 4: Suppose a sequential object OBJ whose return values are at most R words can be implemented in an array of B S-word blocks such that any operation modifies at most T blocks and has worst-case time complexity C. Then, for any $M \geq 2T$, OBJ can be implemented in a wait-free manner with space overhead $O(N(NR + MS + B))$ and worst-case time complexity $O(\lceil N/\min(N, \lfloor M/T \rfloor) \rceil (B + N(R + C) + MS))$.[6] □

3.3 Performance Comparison

In this subsection, we describe the results of preliminary experiments that compare the performance of Herlihy's lock-free construction for large objects to our two constructions on a 32-processor KSR-1 multiprocessor.

The results of one set of experiments are shown in Figure 8. In these experiments, LL and SC primitives were implemented using native KSR locks. Each of 16 processors performed 1000 enqueues and 1000 dequeues on a shared queue. For testing our constructions, we chose B (the number of blocks) and S (the size of each block) to be approximately the square root of the total object size. Also, we chose $T = 2$ because each queue operation accesses only two words. For the wait-free construction, we chose $M = 4$. This is sufficient to guarantee that each process can help at least one other operation. In fact, because two consecutive enqueue (or dequeue) operations usually access the same block, choosing $M = 4$ is sufficient to ensure that a process often helps all other processes each time it performs an operation. These choices for M and T result in very low space overhead compared to that required by Herlihy's construction.

As expected, both our lock-free and wait-free constructions significantly outperform Herlihy's construction as the queue size grows. This is because an operation in Herlihy's construction copies the entire object, while ours copy only small parts of the object.

It is interesting to note that our wait-free construction outperforms our lock-free one. We believe that this is because the cost of recopying blocks in the event that a SC fails

---

[6]It can be shown that each successful operation is guaranteed to advance the help pointer by $\min(N, \lfloor M/T \rfloor)$. Thus, if process p's SC fails $\lceil N/\min(N, \lfloor M/T \rfloor) \rceil$ times, then p's operation is helped. When considering these bounds, note that for many objects, R is a small constant. Also, for queues, C and T are constant, and for balanced trees, C and T are logarithmic in the size of the object.

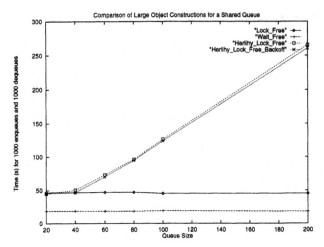

Figure 8: Performance experiments on KSR. $N = 16$, $T = 2$, $M = 4$.

dominates the cost of helping. It is also interesting to note that exponential backoff does not significantly improve the performance of Herlihy's lock-free construction. This stands in contrast to Herlihy's experiments on small objects, where exponential backoff played an important role in improving performance. We believe that this is because the performance of Herlihy's large object construction is dominated by copying and not by contention.

We should point out that we have deliberately chosen the queue to show the advantages of our constructions over Herlihy's. In the full paper, we will also present an implementation of a skew heap — the object considered by Herlihy. We expect that our constructions will still outperform Herlihy's, albeit less dramatically, because ours will copy a logarithmic number of blocks only when the sequential operation does; Herlihy's will do so whenever a block near the bottom of the tree is modified.

4   Concluding Remarks

Our constructions improve the space and time efficiency of lock-free and wait-free implementations of large objects. Also, in contrast to similar previous constructions, ours do not require programmers to determine how an object should be fragmented, or how the object should be copied. However, they do require the programmer to use special *Read* and *Write* functions, instead of the assignment statements used in conventional programming. Nonetheless, as demonstrated by Figure 9, the resulting code is very close to that of an ordinary sequential implementation. Our construction could be made completely seamless by providing a compiler or preprocessor that automatically translates assignments to and from *MEM* into calls to the *Read* and *Write* functions.

The applicability of our construction could be further improved by the addition of a dynamic memory allocation mechanism. This would provide a more convenient interface for objects such as balanced trees, which are naturally represented as nodes that are dynamically allocated and released. There are well-known techniques for implementing dynamic memory management in an array. These techniques could be applied directly by the sequential object programmer, or could be provided as a subroutine library. Several issues arise from the design of such a library. First, the dynamic memory allocation procedures must modify only a small number of array blocks, so that the advantages of our

```
int dequeue()           int enqueue(item)
{                           int item;
  int item;               {
                            int newtail;          /* int newtail;            */
  if (Read(head) == Read(tail))
    return EMPTY;          Write(Read(tail),item);  /* MEM[tail] = item;       */
  item = Read(Read(head));  newtail = (Read(tail)+1)%n; /* newtail = (tail+1) % n; */
  Write(head,(Read(head)+1)%n); if (newtail == Read(head)) /* if (newtail == head)     */
  return item;               return FULL;         /*   return FULL;          */
}                           Write(tail,newtail);   /* tail = newtail;         */
                            return SUCCESS;        /* return SUCCESS;         */
                          }
```

Figure 9: C code used for the queue operations. Comments show "usual" enqueue code.

constructions can be preserved. Second, fragmentation complicates the implementation of *allocate* and *release* procedures. These complications can make the procedures quite inefficient, and can even cause the *allocate* procedure to incorrectly report that insufficient memory is available. Both of these problems are significantly reduced if the size of allocation requests is fixed in advance. For many objects, this restriction is of no consequence. For example, the nodes in a tree are typically all of the same size.

Finally, our constructions do not allow parallel execution of operations, even if the operations access disjoint sets of blocks. We would like to extend our constructions to allow such parallel execution where possible. For example, in our shared queue implementations, an *enqueue* operation might unnecessarily interfere with a *dequeue* operation. In [1], we addressed similar concerns when implementing wait-free operations on multiple objects.

Acknowledgement: We would like to thank Lars Nyland for his help with the performance studies in Section 3.3.

References

[1] J. Anderson and M. Moir, "Universal Constructions for Multi-Object Operations", to appear in the *Proceedings of the 14th Annual ACM Symposium on Principles of Distributed Computing*, 1995.

[2] G. Barnes, "A Method for Implementing Lock-Free Shared Data Structures", *Proceedings of the Fifth Annual ACM Symposium on Parallel Algorithms and Architectures*, 1993, pp. 261-270.

[3] M. Herlihy, "Wait-Free Synchronization", *ACM Transactions on Programming Languages and Systems*, Vol. 13, No. 1, 1991, pp. 124-149.

[4] M. Herlihy, "A Methodology for Implementing Highly Concurrent Data Objects", *ACM Transactions on Programming Languages and Systems*, Vol. 15, No. 5, 1993, pp. 745-770.

[5] A. Israeli and L. Rappoport, "Disjoint-Access-Parallel Implementations of Strong Shared Memory Primitives", *Proceedings of the 13th Annual ACM Symposium on Principles of Distributed Computing*, ACM, New York, August 1994, pp. 151-160.

[6] N. Shavit and D. Touitou, "Software Transactional Memory", to appear in the *Proceedings of the 14th Annual ACM Symposium on Principles of Distributed Computing*, 1995.

Load Balancing :
An Exercise in Constrained Convergence

Anish Arora[1] and Mohamed Gouda[2]

[1] Dept. of Computer & Inf. Science, The Ohio State University, Columbus, OH 43210
[2] Dept. of Computer Sciences, The University of Texas Austin, TX 78712

Abstract. We consider the problem of load balancing to illustrate the design and analysis of distributed control based on a generalized form of stabilization. We call this form of stabilization constrained convergence. Constrained convergence yields novel, fully distributed, global load balancing programs which are (i) adaptive, (ii) fault-tolerant and, most notably, (iii) the first such programs to exhibit stability while interacting with any possible environment.

Keywords: distributed control; stabilization, convergence; stability, freedom from divergence; adaptivity; fault-tolerance

1 Introduction

Whereas distribution enables a system to provide services to its environment with desired availability, reliability, and timeliness characteristics, it also introduces some complex considerations in the design and analysis of the control of the system. These considerations include: *stability of control* so as to avoid divergent or chaotic behavior while interacting with a variety of environment behaviors; *adaptivity of control* so as to maintain desired performance in spite of changes in environment behavior or system parameters [2]; and *robustness of control* so as to tolerate partial system failures and faulty communications [3].

Given the current state of the art in design of distributed control, it seems that traditional approaches are not ideal for reasoning about all of these considerations. Many existing approaches, e.g. queueing-theoretic and flow-theoretic models, are typically suitable for reasoning about steady-state behavior but not about transient-state behavior. Also, many formal approaches, e.g. those based on probabilistic or continuous mathematics, make restrictive assumptions about environment behavior and system parameters and, hence, involve reasoning about only a subset of the behaviors that may be observed in practice. Other less formal approaches, e.g. heuristics and simulations, although suitable for reasoning about larger sets of behaviors, provide little by way of guarantees on the time bounds for performance, adaptation, or resynchronization.

In this paper, we focus our attention on an alternative approach for design and analysis of distributed control. The approach —based on nondeterministic, discrete mathematics— makes use of a generalized form of stabilization [4], namely, constrained convergence, which accommodates reasoning about stability [5], adaptivity [6-7] and fault-tolerance [8-11].

This alternative approach involves two stages of reasoning: In the first stage, the system at hand is considered independently from its environment; it is shown that system computation (i) invariantly preserves certain constraints imposed by the environment, and (ii) upon starting from an arbitrary state (which the system can be in as a result of prior interactions with the environment), converges to specified goal states. In the second stage, the constrained convergence exhibited in the first stage is used to reason about the (stability, adaptivity, and fault-tolerance) behavior of the system when it is executed concurrently with its environment.

We illustrate this approach by a case study. Specifically, we consider the problem of load balancing in distributed systems, for which there exists significant literature based on traditional approaches to compare our work with. Informally, in this problem, the environment produces and consumes load units at multiple nodes and the system moves these load units between the nodes so as to converge to a "balanced" state. We proceed by first formalizing this problem in the next section in terms of constrained convergence. We then show how this formalization enables systematic design of increasingly powerful load balancing programs.

The approach yields novel load balancing programs which have the following desirable properties. The programs are fully distributed: communication is local and point-to-point, and computation does not require access to global state or global time; thus, the programs are scalable. Also, their load balancing actions are specified in a parametric form that allows performance to be tuned to suit the current environment behavior, communication pattern, and processor states; thus, the programs are adaptive. Moreover, our programs are able to converge in spite of arbitrary changes in the network topology; thus, the programs are fault-tolerant. And, perhaps most significantly, they avoid divergent or chaotic behavior when executed concurrently with any environment; thus, the programs exhibit stability and are, to the best of our knowledge, the first such global balancing programs.

The abovementioned properties are especially important for several modern day systems, wherein (i) scale is a pervasive concern, (ii) the system is subject to wide variation in terms of load, (iii) network congestion and failure / repair of processors and channels occur frequently, and (iv) transient states are the norm and not the exception.

The rest of the paper is organized as follows. In Section 2, the problem of load balancing in distributed systems is formalized in terms of constrained convergence. In Section 3, a basic program is derived that balances work loads between adjacent processors. The basic program is augmented, in Section 4, in ring networks; in Section 5, to achieve system-wide load balancing in tree networks; and in Section 6, to achieve system-wide load balancing in directed acyclic networks and, thereby, in any structured or unstructured network. Stability of these programs in the presence of interactions with the environment is discussed in Section 7. Concluding remarks are made in Section 8.

2 Problem Statement

Consider an undirected, connected graph. Associated with each node u in the graph is a variable, integer number $x.u$ of units. Units may be produced and/or consumed —in any number, at any time, and at any node— by an environment. Required is to design a program that satisfies the following four conditions.

- *Distribution* : Each step of program computation accesses the units of at most two adjacent nodes (i.e., nodes in the graph with an edge between them).
- *Constraint* : Each step of program computation can only move units between nodes, but not produce new units nor consume existing units at any node.
- *Convergence* : Starting from any state (i.e., with arbitrary integer numbers assigned to the x's), program computation is guaranteed to terminate in a finite number of steps in a state where
$$(\forall \text{ nodes } u \text{ and } v \text{ in the graph} : |x.u - x.v| \leq 1)$$
- *Stability* : Starting from any state, in all interleavings of productions and consumptions of units by the environment and steps of program computation, no unit is infinitely often moved between nodes.

Load balancing in distributed systems is an important application of designing such a program. In this application, the nodes represent processors, and the edges represent communication channels between processors. The value of each $x.u$ represents the current load of processor u ; this —possibly negative— value may depend on the number of unfinished tasks, the capacity of the processor, completion deadlines of tasks, expected time to completion, arrival rate of tasks, service rate of tasks, etc.

The four conditions mentioned above comprise a simple, minimal specification of the load balancing application: The distribution condition specifies that communication in a distributed system is limited to occur between adjacent processors. The constraint condition specifies that the program computation cannot itself produce or consume load, it can only move load between processors; it follows that program steps preserve the sum of all x's in the graph. The convergence condition specifies that if the environment no longer perturbs (i.e. produces or consumes) the load, the program computation eventually terminates at a state where the load is balanced. The stability condition specifies that, no matter how the environment perturbs the load, no unit of load is moved forever between processors.

We do not specify implementation-level concerns, for example, which node initiates load migration (the sender or the receiver), how (by polling or by interrupts), and when (periodically or demand-driven). This omission is intentional: thus, the program we design is general enough to be implemented in a variety of systems.

For sake of completeness, we define a program computation formally to be a maximal sequence of steps; every noninitial step in the sequence starts execution in the state resulting from the predecessor step and yields a different state upon execution. Maximality of the computation implies that if the sequence is finite then the final step of the computation yields a fixpoint state, i.e. a state that remains unchanged upon execution of any arbitrarily chosen program step. Notice that we allow program computation to be unfair: thus, program steps involving some nodes need may never occur in an infinite program computation.

3 Designing Local Convergence

We now apply the two-stage approach discussed in Section 1 to design load balancing programs. In the first stage, we initially design a program that only balances the work load of adjacent nodes. We then augment the designed program to also balance the work load of non-adjacent nodes. In the second stage, we ensure that the constrained convergence satisfied by the designed program suffices to satisfy the stability condition.

In this section, we conduct the initial design of the first stage. More specifically, we weaken the problem stated in Section 2 by omitting the stability condition and by replacing the convergence condition with the following condition:

> *Local Convergence* : Starting from any state, program computation is guaranteed to terminate in a finite number of steps in a state where
> ($\forall$ *adjacent* nodes u and v in the graph : $|x.u - x.v| \leq 1$).

and derive a program that solves the weakened problem.

From the distribution condition, a step of program computation has the form

> **if** (u and v are adjacent nodes in the graph) $\land$ B
> **then** $x.u$, $x.v := F.(x.u, x.v)$, $G.(x.u, x.v)$ \hfill (1)

It remains to deduce predicate B and functions F and G.

From the local convergence condition, no step can change the fixpoint state where $|x.u - x.v| \leq 1$. This can be accomplished by choosing B as

> $B \equiv |x.u - x.v| > 1$

Without loss of generality, we assume $x.u \geq x.v$ in which case B can be simplified as

> $B \equiv x.u - x.v > 1$ \hfill (2)

From the constraint condition, changing $x.u$ and $x.v$ by F and G should keep their sum fixed. This can be accomplished by choosing F and G as follows.

> F decreases $x.u$ by some, possibly negative, integer Δ, and
> G increases $x.v$ by the same Δ \hfill (3)

From (1), (2), and (3), we can rewrite the step of program computation as

> **if** (u and v are adjacent nodes in the graph) $\land$ $x.u - x.v > 1$
> **then** $x.u$, $x.v := x.u - \Delta$, $x.v + \Delta$
> **where** Δ is any integer satisfying some predicate $C.(\Delta, x.u, x.v)$ \hfill (4)

It remains to deduce the value of Δ (or, equivalently, to deduce predicate C) so that the computation terminates in a finite number of steps. Note that this requirement (of termination) is the only one that we have not yet used in our design of a step of program computation.

Deducing the value of Δ. To guarantee termination, it is sufficient to find a ranking function r that assigns to each state s of the computation a natural number $r.s$ such that if a step leads the computation from state s_1 to s_2, then

$$r.s_1 > r.s_2 \tag{5}$$

One possibility for r is

$$r = (\text{sum } u : u \text{ is a node in the graph} : x.u^2) \tag{6}$$

Now assume that one step is executed changing $x.u$ and $x.v$ into $x.u - \Delta$ and $x.v + \Delta$ while leaving all other $x.w$'s unchanged. (This implies that $x.u - x.v > 1$ from (4).) To ensure that (5) is satisfied, it is sufficient from (6) to show that

$$x.u^2 + x.v^2 > (x.u - \Delta)^2 + (x.v + \Delta)^2$$

We simplify the last expression.

$$
\begin{aligned}
& x.u^2 + x.v^2 > (x.u - \Delta)^2 + (x.v + \Delta)^2 \\
= \ & \{\text{arithmetic}\} \\
& 0 > (-2 \times x.u \times \Delta) + (2 \times x.v \times \Delta) + (2 \times \Delta^2) \\
= \ & \{\text{arithmetic}\} \\
& (x.u - x.v) \times \Delta > \Delta^2 \\
= \ & \{\text{arithmetic}\} \\
& x.u - x.v > \Delta > 0
\end{aligned}
$$

Thus, (5) is satisfied provided

$$C.(\Delta, x.u, x.v) \equiv x.u - x.v > \Delta > 0 \tag{7}$$

The step of program computation. From (4) and (7) the computation step can be written as:

---

if (u and v are adjacent nodes in the graph) $\wedge$ $x.u - x.v > 1$

then $x.u, x.v := x.u - \Delta, x.v + \Delta$

where Δ is any integer satisfying ($x.u - x.v > \Delta > 0$)

Note that the program we have designed allows Δ to be chosen differently in different steps. Moreover, each Δ can be chosen arbitrarily from within a range (cf. (7)) rather than being assigned a pre-determined value (e.g., $(x.u - x.v)/2$). This provides our load balancing scheme with the flexibility to adapt the computation to suit the environment behavior and system parameters.

Note also that this program satisfies the local convergence condition but not necessarily the convergence condition. In the next three sections, we augment the program computation so as remedy this limitation for special classes of distributed systems, respectively ring, tree, hypercube (and other) networks.

4 Designing Global Convergence in Ring Networks

Observe that the convergence condition is equivalent to requiring that program computation terminate at a state where $(max\, u\, :\, x.u) - (min\, u\, :\, x.u) \leq 1$ holds. Hence, one strategy to satisfy the convergence condition, given that the program designed thus far satisfies the local convergence condition, is to augment that program to guarantee termination at a state where some pair of adjacent nodes are assigned maximum and minimum work loads.

This guarantee is easily implemented in a ring network: Distinguish a node TOP on the ring, and require that the work load of all nodes along one direction of the ring, starting from TOP, is nondecreasing. In other words, require that $x.u \geq x.(N.u)$ for each node u such that $N.u \neq TOP$, where $N.u$ denotes the node adjacent to u in the chosen direction. Recalling the distribution and the constraint conditions and that the program designed thus far satisfies local convergence, this requirement is met by augmenting the step of program computation to swap the values of $x.u$ and $x.(N.u)$ when $x.u + 1 = x.(N.u) \wedge N.u \neq TOP$ holds.

The net effect of this requirement is that regardless of the starting values of the x variables, if the computation terminates then in its final state TOP has maximum work load, and the node u such that $N.u = TOP$ has minimum work load.

Formally, the augmented step of program computation is:

---

if	(u and v are adjacent nodes in the graph) $\wedge\ x.u - x.v > 1$
then	$x.u\, ,\, x.v := x.u - \triangle\, ,\, x.v + \triangle$ **where** $\triangle$ satisfies $(x.u - x.v > \triangle > 0)$
elseif	$x.u + 1 = x.(N.u)\ \wedge\ N.u \neq TOP$
then	$x.u\, ,\, x.(N.u) := x.(N.u)\, ,\, x.u$

To prove termination, we note that if executing the step involves executing the first assignment statement, then the value assigned by the function r to the current state decreases, where $r = (\ sum\, u\, :\, u$ is a node in the graph $:\ x.u^2\ )$.

Also, if executing the step involves executing the second assignment statement, then the value assigned by the function r to the current state is unchanged and the value assigned by the function s to the current state decreases, where $s = (\ sum\, u\, :\, (D.u \times x.u)\ )$ and $D.u$ is the distance between TOP and u in the ring along the chosen direction. To check the decrease, it suffices to note that

$$D.u \times x.u + (D.u + 1) \times (x.u + 1) > (D.u + 1) \times x.u + D.u \times (x.u + 1)\ .$$

Therefore, the lexicographic ranking function t, $t = \langle r, s \rangle$, suffices to prove termination.

5 Designing Global Convergence in Tree Networks

An alternative strategy to satisfy the convergence condition, given that the program designed in Section 3 satisfies the local convergence condition, is to augment that program to guarantee termination at a state where the node work load along every simple path starting at a distinguished node TOP is (i) nonincreasing and (ii) decreases at most once.

This guarantee is easily implemented in a tree network: Let TOP be the tree root and let $P.u$ be the parent of each node u in the tree. To achieve (i), require that the work load at every node be the maximum of the work load of all nodes in the subtree rooted at that node. Recalling again the distribution and the constraint conditions and that the program designed thus far satisfies local convergence, this requirement is met by swapping the values of $x.u$ and $x.(P.u)$ when $x.u = x.(P.u)+1$ holds.

To achieve (ii), a means of recognizing that node work load along a path starting at TOP decreases more than once is necessary. Therefore, require that each node u maintains a boolean variable $b.u$ so that as long as the work loads of nodes along a path are identical, the b values at those path nodes are maintained to be *true*; if the work load decreases from a path node to its successor, the b value changes from *true* at that node to *false* at its successor; at subsequent nodes in the path, the b value are maintained to be *false*. This requirement is met by ensuring that $b.u$ is always *true* for $u = TOP$. And, $b.u$ is set to $b.(P.u)$ when $x.u = x.(P.u)$ holds and *false* when $x.u+1 = x.(P.u)$ holds for $u \neq TOP$. (The value of $b.u$ is arbitrary when none of these cases apply.) It now follows that if more than one decrease occurs along a path then —assuming the work load along that path is locally balanced and nonincreasing— there exists a node u such $x.u+1 = x.(P.u)$ and $b.(P.u) = false$ hold. For such u, the values of $x.u$ and $x.(P.u)$ are swapped, so that the smaller work load of u can be subsequently balanced with the larger work load of the parent of $P.u$.

Unfortunately, the program computation designed thus far admits an infinite cycle of swaps, as is illustrated next. Let $x.u = x.(P.u)+1 = x.(P.P.u)-1$ and $b.(P.u) = false$. Now, $x.u$ and $x.(P.u)$ can be first swapped towards achieving (i), and then swapped again towards achieving (ii). This problem is resolved by requiring both swaps to occur *only when* the state of $P.u$ is consistent with its parent, i.e., $x.(P.u) = x.(P.P.u) \wedge b.(P.u) = b.(P.P.u)$ or $x.(P.u)+1 = x.(P.P.u) \wedge \neg b.(P.u) \wedge b.(P.P.u)$. (We abbreviate this consistency criterion as the predicate $ok.(P.u)$.)

The net effect of these requirements is that regardless of the starting values of the x and b variables, if the program computation terminates then in its final state TOP has the maximum work load, the work load along every path starting at TOP decreases at most once, and every node u satisfies $ok.u$.

The augmented step of program computation is stated below. Statement A propagates a larger work load from u to $P.u$. Statement B propagates a smaller work load from u to $P.u$. Statements C and D maintain the variable $b.u$ of u. (For convenience in stating the computation step, we let $P.TOP$ be TOP

itself; hence, $ok.TOP$ is always true. Also, we refer to these statements as the statements of u.)

if	(u and v are adjacent nodes in the graph) $\land$ $x.u - x.v > 1$	
then	$x.u , x.v := x.u - \triangle , x.v + \triangle$ **where** $\triangle$ satisfies $(x.u - x.v > \triangle > 0)$	
elseif	$x.u = x.(P.u) + 1 \ \land \ ok.(P.u)$	
then	$x.u , x.(P.u) , b.(P.u) := x.(P.u) , x.u , true$	(A)
elseif	$x.u + 1 = x.(P.u) \ \land \ \neg b.(P.u) \ \land \ ok.(P.u)$	
then	$x.u , x.(P.u) := x.(P.u) , x.u$	(B)
elseif	$x.u = x.(P.u) \ \land \ b.u \not\equiv b.(P.u)$	
then	$b.u := b.(P.u)$	(C)
elseif	$x.u + 1 = x.(P.u) \ \land \ b.(P.u) \ \land \ b.u$	
then	$b.u := false$	(D)

To prove termination, we note that if executing the step involves executing the first assignment statement, then the value assigned by the function r to the current state decreases, where $r = (\ sum \ u \ : \ u \text{ is a node in the graph} : \ x.u^2 \ )$. Also, executing any other statement does not change the value assigned by r to the current system state.

Hence, it remains to show that every sequence of steps executing only the statements A, B, C, or D is finite. We show this by proving a stronger result: Consider an arbitrary subtree of the given tree. Let S be an arbitrary sequence of steps involving execution of statements A, B, C, and D of nodes that are in the subtree. Then, S is finite.

Our proof is by structural induction on the height of the subtree.

Base Case : Height of the subtree is 0.
In this case, the subtree comprises only one node. By itself, a single node is always balanced; hence, S is the empty sequence.

Induction Step : Height of the subtree exceeds 0.
In this case, let w be the root of the subtree. We claim that there exists a finite prefix of S such that the statements of w are not executed in the corresponding suffix; i.e., there exists a suffix of S that consists of executions of statements of only descendents of w.

To prove the claim, we consider two cases:

- $w = TOP$: in this case, $P.w = w$ and, hence, statements A, B, C and D of w do not execute.

- $w \neq TOP$: in this case, we first show that there exists a finite prefix of S such that in the corresponding suffix the statements A and B of w do not execute; we then show that once the statements A and B of w do not execute, the statements C and D of w together execute at most once.
  Once statement A of w executes, statement B of w is not executed since A establishes $b.(P.w)$. In addition, each time statement A of w updates $x.w$, the value assigned by the function r' to the current state decreases,

where $r' = (\ sum\ u\ :\ x.u) - x.(P.w)$. Other suffix steps do not change the value assigned by r' to the current state. Alternatively, if statement A of w is not executed, then each time statement B of w updates $x.w$, the value assigned by the function r'' to the current state decreases, where $r'' = x.(P.w) - (\ min\ u\ :\ u$ is in the subtree $:\ x.u)$. Other suffix steps do not increase the value assigned by r'' to the current state unchanged. Hence, eventually statements A and B of w do not execute.

Now, consider a suffix of S in which statements A and B of w do not execute. If C or D of w execute in this suffix, the resulting state satisfies the state predicate $ok.w$. As long as this predicate holds, statements C and D are not executed. The only statement executions that can violate $ok.w$ are of statement A of any child of w —in which case $\neg ok.w \land b.w \land x.w > x.(P.w)$ holds— and statement B of any child of w —in which case $\neg ok.w \land \neg b.w \land x.w < x.(P.w)$ holds. In the former case, no statement of w or any child of w may be executed thereafter, thereby preserving the predicate $\neg ok.w \land b.w \land x.w > x.(P.w)$. In the latter case, no statement of w may be executed thereafter, but the statement B (and not A) of a child of w may be executed, which however preserves the predicate $\neg ok.w \land \neg b.w \land x.w < x.(P.w)$. Hence, eventually statements C and D of w do not execute either.

Now, once the statements of w do not execute, the execution of statements A, B, C or D in one subtree of w does not affect the execution of these statements in another subtree of w (note that only the first assignment in the computation step affects the variables of nodes in different subtrees). Hence, based on our claim, we can apply the induction hypothesis for each child of w, to conclude that the suffix is also finite. $\qquad\square$

6 Designing Global Convergence in Hypercube, Mesh, and Omega Networks

In this section, we first show that the load balancing program designed for tree networks is readily adapted for directed acyclic networks. Then, we apply the adapted program in structured networks, such as hypercubes, meshes and omega networks, using constant-time embeddings of directed acyclic graphs in these networks. Finally, we compare the strategies of load balancing that embed a directed acyclic graph (henceforth, dag) with those that embed a ring or a tree, and discuss the fault-tolerance of our load balancing schemes.

To adapt the program for tree networks to acyclic networks, we lift two assumptions that we made earlier when we considered tree networks: we lift the assumption that there is a unique distinguished node TOP to allow multiple distinguished root nodes TOP; and we lift the assumption that there is a unique parent for each node to allow multiple parents for each node.

These allowances notwithstanding, our strategy for achieving convergence remains the same as that for tree networks: guarantee termination at a state where (i) the node work load on every path starting at any TOP node is nonincreasing, and (ii) the node work load along every path starting at any TOP decreases at most once.

This guarantee is easily implemented in an acyclic network, by modifying the computation step for tree networks as follows: (a) Statement A is allowed to propagate larger loads to *any* parent of u, (b) Statement B is allowed to propagate smaller loads to *any* parent of u, (c) Statement C maintains variable $b.u$ according to the values of the variables of u and *all* parents of u, and (d) Statement D maintains variable $b.u$ according to the values of the variables of u and *any* parent of u.

Let $Par.u$ be the set of parents of u in the acyclic graph. And let $ok.v = $
$$((\forall w : w \in Par.v : x.v = x.w) \wedge b.v = (\forall w : w \in Par.v : b.w) \quad \vee$$
$$((\exists w : w \in Par.v : x.v+1 = x.w) \wedge \neg b.v \wedge (\forall w : w \in Par.v : x.v = x.w \vee (x.v+1 = x.w \wedge b.w)))$$

More specifically, the step of program computation for tree networks is modified as follows:

Statement A is replaced by one choice for each $v \in Par.u$:

elseif $x.u = x.v+1 \wedge ok.v$
then $x.u, x.v, b.v := x.v, x.u, true$

Statement B is replaced by one choice for each $v \in Par.u$:

elseif $x.u+1 = x.v \wedge \neg b.v \wedge ok.v$
then $x.u, x.v := x.v, x.u$

Statement C is replaced by the choice:

elseif $(\forall v : v \in Par.u : x.u = x.v) \wedge b.u \not\equiv (\forall v : v \in Par.u : b.v)$
then $b.u := (\forall v : v \in Par.u : b.v)$

Statement D is replaced by one choice for each $v \in Par.u$:

elseif $x.u+1 = x.v \wedge b.v \wedge b.u$
then $b.u := false$

To prove termination of the adapted program computation, we note that if executing the computation step involves executing the first assignment statement, then the value assigned by the function r to the current state decreases, where $r = (sum \; u : u$ is a node in the graph $: x.u^2)$. Also, executing any other statement does not change the value assigned by r to the current system state.

Hence, it remains to show that every sequence of steps executing only the statements $A, B, C,$ or D is finite. We show this by proving a stronger result: Consider an arbitrary subgraph of the given graph. Let S be an arbitrary sequence of steps involving execution of statements $A, B, C,$ and D of nodes that are in the subgraph. Then, S is finite.

Our proof is by structural induction on the depth of nodes in the subgraph (where depth is defined as the maximum distance of a node from one of its descendents in the acyclic subgraph). The proof is essentially identical to the one for subtrees in Section 5, and is hence omitted here.

Application of Load Balancing in Acyclic Networks to Structured Networks. Each edge in a structured network —such as a hypercube, a mesh, or a butterfly network— is readily directed so that the resulting graph becomes acyclic.

Consider, for instance, a hypercube or a mesh network. If each edge in the network is directed from its incident node with smaller coordinate value to its incident node with larger coordinate value, using a lexicographic ordering, the resulting graph is acyclic. Consider, also, an omega or —more generally— a multistage network. If each edge in the network is directed from its incident node with smaller stage number to its incident node with higher stage number, the resulting graph is again acyclic.

Observe that in both instances the direction of each edge depends only on the coordinates of its incidents nodes and, hence, all edges may be directed concurrently. Hence, embedding a dag requires only a constant amount of time, and load balancing is readily achieved using the adapted computation described above.

Of course, an alternative approach would be to embed a ring or a tree and to use the augmented computation step described in Section 4 or 5, respectively, on the virtual graph. Embedding a ring may, however, yield virtual edges that are dilated, i.e., virtual edges that span multiple edges in the underlying network. Consequently, the resulting load balancing computation may not be fully distributed. Moreover, embedding a ring or a tree may reduce the fault-tolerance of load balancing programs. (Recall that fault-tolerance is one of our stated objectives in the design of distributed control programs, such as load balancing programs.) Thus, whereas the failure or repair of any number of nodes or edges preserves the acyclicity of a dag, the failure or repair of even one node or edge may violate a ring or tree. It follows that to achieve fault-tolerance in ring and tree networks, additional programs are needed to reconfigure the virtual graph in the presence of failures and repairs. Several such programs have appeared in the literature; for example, [10, 11] present reconfiguration programs for trees and rings that tolerate any finite number of failures and repairs.

We conclude this section with the remark that similar considerations occur when designing load balancing computations for arbitrary networks. Again, rings, trees, or dags may be embedded, but the specific choice of which embedding is appropriate depends upon the case at hand.

7 Reasoning about Stability

The constrained convergence considered in the first stage of our approach guarantees that no matter how the environment perturbs the state of a program, subsequent computation of the program *in isolation* terminates at a state where the loads are balanced system-wide. In this section, we consider the second stage of our approach, namely reasoning about how our load balancing programs behave when executed *concurrent with* the environment.

Recall that the environment of a load balancing program can both produce new units as well as consume existing units of load. It is convenient to think of the environment steps as perturbations on the x values of the nodes. The environment steps, unlike the program steps, are not constrained: they may perturb the x values arbitrarily.

Of course, constrained convergence guarantees that if the environment perturbs the state at a speed less than that of program convergence, the program is infinitely often at a balanced state. And, if the environment perturbs the state at arbitrarily high speeds but the durations of such perturbations are finite, then the program starts to converge eventually, thereby remaining stable.

For the local and the ring-based global load balancing programs, we are able to show a much stronger result: these programs satisfy the stability condition described in Section 2. In other words, regardless of the speed of environment perturbations, the amount of these perturbations, and the time duration of these perturbations, these programs move each load unit at most a finite number of times. It follows that the system does not diverge (or thrash) when it executes concurrently with any environment.

Theorem 0 *The program for local convergence satisfies stability.*

Proof: Let us organize the load units at each node in a vertical pile. Thus, we can uniquely associate with each load unit its height in its pile. Let us also ensure that when the environment produces load units, they are placed at the tops of these piles; when the environment consumes load units, they are removed anywhere from these piles; and, when local balancing steps move load units, they are moved from the top of the one pile to the top of the other pile.

Using this organization, perturbations by the environment do not increase (and possibly decrease) the height of any existing load unit. Also, local balancing steps decrease the height of the load units that they move and leave the respective heights of the remaining units unchanged. Hence, regardless of how the environment perturbs the state of the local convergence program during program execution, every step of that program leaves the global state "more" balanced. In other words, each load unit moves only finitely often in any interleaving of program steps and environment perturbations. □

Theorem 1 *The program for global convergence in a ring network satisfies stability.*

Proof: Steps in our program for global balancing in ring networks either decrease or leave unchanged the height of the existing load units that they move. Hence, every program step leaves the global state "at least as" balanced. Moreover, in each step where a load unit is moved but its height does not change, its distance from the TOP node (in the chosen direction) decreases and, hence, the unit can be moved at most M times without decreasing its height (where M is the number of nodes). □

In the case of our global-tree and dag global convergence programs, unfortunately, there exist interleavings of program and environment steps where some load units repeatedly do the following: first, these load units move towards TOP nodes as a result of some environment step and, then, they move away from TOP nodes as a result of some other environment step. In all these moves, the height of the load units remains unchanged. Consequently, the constrained convergence of our tree and dag programs is insufficient to satisfy stability for all environments.

Fortunately, however, there exist tree and dag load balancing programs whose constrained convergence is sufficient to satisfy stability for all environments. To exhibit such programs, we exploit the idea that one way to avoid having load units that move both towards TOP nodes and away from TOP nodes – without a decrease in their height – is to choose one direction, say the direction towards TOP nodes, such that if any load unit moves in that direction without a decrease in its height, then that unit cannot subsequently move in the other direction.

Based on this idea, we propose that the x load units at each node be divided into two vertical piles of height y and z, respectively. All y pile load units remain within y piles in program steps, as follows. Local load balancing steps balance the y piles of adjacent nodes; and whenever the y pile of a node has one more unit than the y pile for (one of its) parents then the extra unit is moved to the parent. The net effect of these steps is that when y pile units move either their height decreases, or their height remains the same and their distance from TOP nodes decreases.

In contrast to y pile units, z pile units can move to y piles or remain within z piles in program steps, as follows. Local load balancing steps balance the z piles of adjacent nodes; whenever the z pile of a parent node has one more unit than the z pile of some child then the extra unit is moved to the child; finally, whenever the z pile of a node is taller than its y pile, the extra units are moved from the z pile to the y pile. The net effect of these steps is that when z pile units move their height decreases, or their height remains the same and their distance from leaf nodes decreases, or they move to a y pile.

Thus, effectively, in the new tree/dag programs, local load balancing is performed between adjacent y piles, between adjacent z piles, and from the z pile of each node to the y pile of each node. Moreover, the z piles are maintained to be nondecreasing in the direction from the TOP nodes to the leaf nodes, the z pile of each node is maintained to be at most its y pile, and the y piles are maintained to be nondecreasing from leaf nodes to TOP nodes. (The reader will note the similarity to the load balancing program for ring networks.) The resulting programs satisfies global convergence, as well as stability in all environments.

More formally, the step of program computation in tree networks is:

---

if	(u and v are adjacent nodes in the graph) $\land\ \ y.u - y.v > 1$
then	$y.u,\ y.v := y.u - \triangle,\ y.v + \triangle$ **where** $\triangle$ satisfies $(y.u - y.v > \triangle > 0)$
elseif	(u and v are adjacent nodes in the graph) $\land\ \ z.u - z.v > 1$
then	$z.u,\ z.v := z.u - \nabla,\ z.v + \nabla$ **where** ∇ satisfies $(z.u - z.v > \nabla > 0)$
elseif	$z.u > y.u$
then	$y.u,\ z.u := y.u + \diamond,\ z.y - \diamond$ **where** $\diamond = \lceil (z.u - y.u)/2 \rceil$
elseif	$y.(P.u) + 1 = y.u$
then	$y.u,\ y.(P.u) := y.(P.u),\ y.u$
elseif	$z.u + 1 = z.(P.u)$
then	$z.u,\ z.(P.u) := z.(P.u),\ z.u$

The step for program computation in dag networks is similar.

Theorem 2 *The program described above for global convergence in tree/dag networks satisfies stability.*

It follows from the stability of our programs, that if the environment consumes the load from the bottom of each load pile at a non-zero speed, then every load unit is consumed eventually.

8 Concluding Remarks

In this paper, we have presented novel, fully distributed programs for load balancing. (Preliminary versions of some of these programs were presented in [5, 8].) Our programs make very lax assumptions about the behavior of the environment, the topology of the network, and the states of the nodes. They are distinguished by their stability, adaptivity, fault-tolerance, and scalability.

Related work. Previous work on load balancing in distributed systems has been based on probabilistic models (e.g. [12]), graph-theoretic flow models (e.g. [13]), simulations (e.g. [14]), and heuristics (e.g. [15]). We refer the reader to Shivaratri et al [16] for an overview of the basic issues involved in load balancing.

In contrast to these approaches, we have modeled load balancing in terms of constrained convergence. Constrained convergence is a generalization of earlier (unconstrained) notions of convergence. We find that this generalization has facilitated the systematic design of fully stable load balancing programs, and conclude that the generalization is useful and merits further consideration.

On a related note, Lin and Keller [17] have shown a stabilizing gradient-based local load balancing program; this program is more restrictive than our local load balancing program. Also, Kam and Bastani [18] have shown a stabilizing program that maintains a hierarchical ring in a dynamic network, and partitions a globally known, static set of load units between the processors in the hierarchical ring. More recently, Yen and Bastani [19] have presented inherently fault-tolerant programs for coordinating multi-server systems.

Convergence Span. One way of quantifying the convergence span of stable distributed programs is in terms of rounds [10]. Intuitively, a round consists of a sequence of steps wherein each node makes some minimal progress. More precisely, a round is a minimal, nonempty sequence of steps wherein for each node there exists a step where the node either executes one of its statements or the if-conditions of all its statements are false before or after the step.

Proofs of convergence that exhibit variant functions also yield upper bounds on the convergence span. Thus, from the variant function of the local load balancing program, we can deduce that N^2 rounds is an upper bound on the convergence span, where N is the sum of the x values of all nodes. In this particular case, the bound can be tightened further: Discussions with Ernie Cohen [20] have shown us that the convergence span of our local load balancing program is $\Theta(N^{1.5})$ rounds, in the sense that (i) every local load balancing computation converges within $O(N^{1.5})$ rounds and (ii) there exists a system and a state starting from which a local load balancing computation requires $\Omega(N^{1.5})$ rounds to terminate. Further, we claim that the convergence span of the ring-based program is $O(N^{1.5} \ max \ NM)$, where M is the number of nodes, and that of the tree- and dag-based programs is $O(N^{1.5} \ max \ ND)$ rounds, where D is the depth of the tree or dag at hand.

Future work. Topics that we are studying include: the design of load balancing programs that are (i) specialized for structured systems or (ii) that instead of using a fixed underlying virtual structure, create periodic waves to reach and balance all network nodes. Moreover, we are investigating formal characterizations of the speeds of environment perturbations at which load balancing is better than no load balancing.

Acknowledgements. We thank the anonymous referees for their suggestions.

References

1. J. A. Stankovik: Stability and distributed scheduling algorithms. IEEE Transactions on Software Engineering **SE-11(10)** (1985) 1141-1152
2. D. L. Eager, E.D. Lazowska, J. Zahorjan: Adaptive load sharing in homogeneous distributed systems. IEEE Transactions on Software Engineering **12(5)** (1986) 662-675
3. F. Cristian: Understanding fault-tolerant distributed systems. Communications of the ACM **34(2)** (1991) 56-78
4. E. W. Dijkstra: Self-stabilizing systems in spite of distributed control. Communications of the ACM **17(11)** (1974) 643-644
5. A. Arora, M. G. Gouda: Load balancing: An exercise in constrained convergence. Paper presented to The Austin Tuesday Afternoon Club (1990)
6. M. G. Gouda, T. Herman: Adaptive programming. IEEE Transactions on Software Engineering **17(9)** (1991) 911-921
7. A. Arora, M. G. Gouda, T. Herman: Composite routing protocols. Proceedings of the Second IEEE Symposium on Parallel and Distributed Processing (1990) 70–78
8. A. Arora: A foundation of fault-tolerant computing. PhD Dissertation, The University of Texas at Austin (1992) *ftp://ftp.cis.ohio-state.edu/pub/anish/dissertation/body.ps.Z*
9. A. Arora, M. G. Gouda: Closure and convergence: A foundation of fault-tolerant computing. IEEE Transactions on Software Engineering **19(11)** (1993) 1015-1027
10. A. Arora, M. G. Gouda: Distributed reset. IEEE Transactions on Computers **43(9)** (1994) 1026-1038
11. A. Arora, A. Singhai: Fault-tolerant reconfiguration of trees and rings in networks. Journal of High Integrity Design. to appear
12. C.-Y. H. Hsu, J. W.-S. Liu: Dynamic load balancing algorithms in homogeneous distributed systems. Proceedings of 16th International Conference on Distributed Computer Systems (1986) 216-223
13. H. S. Stone: Multiprocessor scheduling with the aid of network flow algorithms. IEEE Transactions on Computers **4(3)** (1978) 254-258
14. D. L. Eager, E. D. Lazowska, J. Zahorjan: A comparison of receiver-initiated and sender-initiated dynamic load sharing. Performance Evaluation **6(1)** (1986) 53-68
15. J. A. Stankovik: A perspective on distributed computer systems. IEEE Transactions on Computers **33(12)** (1984) 1102-1115
16. N. G. Shivaratri, P. Krueger, M. Singhal: Load distributing for locally distributed systems. IEEE Computer **25(12)** (1994) 33-45
17. F. C. H. Lin, R. Keller: The gradient model load balancing method. IEEE Transactions on Software Engineering **13(1)** (1987) 32-38
18. M. K. Kam, F. B. Bastani: A self-stabilizing ring protocol for load balancing in distributed real-time process control systems. Technical Report #UH-CS-87-9, Department of Computer Science, University of Houston (1987)
19. I.-L. Yen, F. B. Bastani: Robust coordination in distributed multi-server systems. Proceedings of the IEEE Workshop on Advances in Parallel and Distributed Systems (1994) 133-138
20. E. Cohen: On the convergence span of greedy load balancing. Information Processing Letters (1994).

Larchant-RDOSS:
a Distributed Shared Persistent Memory and its Garbage Collector

Marc Shapiro*and Paulo Ferreira**

INRIA Rocquencourt
email: shapiro@sor.inria.fr, Web: http://prof.inria.fr/

Abstract. Larchant-RDOSS is a distributed shared memory that persists on reliable storage across process lifetimes. Memory management is automatic: caching of data and of locks, coherence, collecting objects unreachable from the persistent root, writing reachable objects to disk, and reducing store fragmentation. Memory management is based on a novel garbage collection algorithm, that (i) approximates a global trace by a series of partial traces within dynamically determined subsets of the memory, (ii) causes no extra I/O or locking traffic, and (iii) needs no extra synchronization between the collector and the application processes. This results in a simple programming model, and expected minimal added application latency. The algorithm is designed for the most unfavorable environment (uncontrolled programming language, reference by pointers, non-coherent shared memory) and should work well also in more favorable settings.

1 Introduction

The Reliable Distributed Object Storage System (Larchant-RDOSS) is an execution environment based on the abstraction of a persistent distributed shared memory. Applications see a single memory (a single heap), containing dynamically-allocated data structures (called objects) connected by ordinary pointers. Internally, the memory is divided into granules called *bunches*. An application maps only those bunches that it is currently reading or updating; updates remain local until the application commits.

The system automatically determines which objects are actually shareable by other applications (any object reachable from a persistent object is itself persistent; this is called "persistence by reachability" [3]), by tracing from a persistent root. Such automatic management results in a simple and natural programming model, because the application programmer need not worry about distribution, input-output or deallocation.

---

* Work conducted in part during sabbatical year at Cornell University, supported by funding from Cornell University, Isis Distributed Systems Inc., INRIA, and NATO.
** Student at Université Pierre et Marie Curie, Paris; with support from a JNICT Fellowship of Program *Ciência* (Portugal)

The intended application area is programs sharing a large amount (many gigabytes) of objects on a wide-area network, *e.g.*, across the Internet. Examples include financial databases, design databases, group work applications, or exploratory applications similar to the World-Wide Web.

1.1 Larchant-RDOSS

This setting imposes performance constraints, such as avoiding I/O and synchronization. Furthermore it is not reasonable to expect any strong coherence guarantees.

These performance constraints appear to clash with persistence by reachability. Distributed tracing requires global synchronization. Accessing remote or on-disk portions of the object graph requires costly input-output and network communication. Published concurrent GC typically assume a coherent memory, and require a strong, non-portable synchronization between the application (the "mutator") and the collector.

Our algorithm works around these difficulties. Instead of a global trace, we perform a series of opportunistic local traces that together approximate the global trace. Each local trace scans a dynamically-chosen subset of the memory; each site chooses its subset independently from other sites, in such a way that the trace requires no remote synchronization and no I/O. We avoid mutator-collector synchronization, by relying on the trace itself to discover new pointers. We avoid relying on any particular coherence model by delaying the delete of an object until it has been detected unreachable everywhere. We do however assume that a granule has no more than a single owner at any point in time. For performance we use asynchronous messages, relying on causally-ordered delivery for correctness.

1.2 Outline

This paper briefly describes the overall design of Larchant-RDOSS, in Section 2. Section 3 outlines our garbage collection algorithm, ignoring replicated caching; it can collect an arbitrary subset of the object graph independently; we suggest a locality-based heuristic for choosing the subset that avoids message, I/O and lock traffic. In Section 4, we extend the algorithm to the case where a bunch is replicated into multiple caches, even when the replicas are not known to be coherent. Section 5 presents related work. Section 6 concludes with a summary of our ideas and results.

2 Overall Design

The architecture of Larchant-RDOSS is illustrated in Figure 1. An application program on some site access the shared memory through that site's Cache Server. Stable versions of bunches are stored on disk by Backup Servers. Together, the Cache Servers and the Backup Servers form the Object Storage Service. Auxiliary

Collector Processes perform the garbage collection algorithm on behalf of a Cache or Backup Server. This section describes the applications and the cache and backup servers; garbage collection will be described in more detail in Sections 3 and 4.

2.1 Bunches and Pointers

The distributed shared memory is subdivided into bunches. A bunch is a set of memory segments, containing objects. An application holding a pointer to an object may map the bunch containing it (thus gaining access to the object's data) through the Cache Server of its site. The bunch is the elementary granule of mapping, of locking, of coherence and of garbage collection.

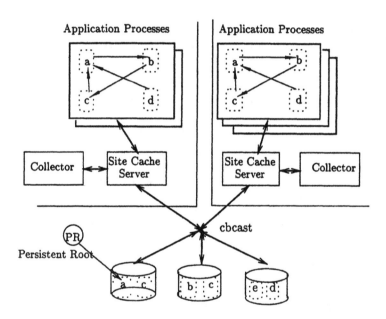

Fig. 1. *General architecture of Larchant-RDOSS*

Multiple applications at multiple sites may map the same bunch, which is said *replicated* into the corresponding site caches. The same bunch may be backed up to multiple disks for availability; it is said replicated on disk.

A process in Larchant-RDOSS starts up with an initial bunch containing a persistent root object, itself containing pointers to other objects. The application follows some arbitrary path of pointers through the object graph. When following a pointer for the first time, the application binds it. The bind primitive ensures that the target object is completely initialized, and sets a lock. Supported lock modes include the both standard consistent locks (read and write), and weak locks (optimistic, no-guarantee).

Binding ensures that, if the target pointer contains a pointer itself, the latter is valid, by reserve-ing a memory location for its own target. The pointer is "swizzled" but the target is not actually bound until it is accessed, as in Texas [22].[3] The primitive reserve sets a special lock ensuring that the address of the corresponding objects will not change.

Allocating a new object in a bunch declares its *layout* to the system, *i.e.*, the location of any pointers it contains. The application freely reads and updates a bound object, including the pointers it contains. This shared memory abstraction is natural, and can be used even from primitive languages such as C or C++.

Updates remain private until the application process commits, at which point all updates are propagated at once. Locking may be pessimistic or optimistic; optimistic locking is useful and efficient in many types of applications; it turns out that the garbage collector uses it also.

We are not assuming the existence of a garbage collector at the application process. The collector described here collects the persistent store, and executes in the Collector Processes.

2.2   Object Storage Service

The Object Storage Service (OSS) is composed of Cache Servers and Backup Servers.

A Backup Server (BS) caches recently-accessed bunches in memory, and stores them on disk. Application and Collector processes access the store through the single Cache Server (CS) running on the local machine. A CS caches bunches recently accessed by local application processes. It caches both bunch data and the associated lock tokens. A cache miss causes a bunch to be copied from disk into the corresponding BS cache, sent to a CS and copied into its cache, and from there copied into the requesting application or collector. When an application commits, it propagates any changed bunches to its cache server, which multicasts the changes to all other copies.

At some point in time, any single bunch can be replicated in any number of Cache Servers, of Backup Servers, of disks, of application processes, and of Collector processes. The server that, either holds the exclusive (write) token for a bunch, or was the last to hold it, is the *owner* of that bunch. An update may commit updates only at the owner site. Updates flow from an application or a collector process, to the local (owner) CS, which propagates it to the other servers. A BS stores updates on disk. Since an update or a token flows only from the owner to other processes, it can be sent using causal broadcast [5].

---

[3] On storage and in a cache manager, a reference has a location-independent representation. In memory, a reference is a pointer to the memory location of the target. The location of a same object may differ between in different application processes. Swizzling a reference means to compute the address of its target and to fill the corresponding pointer with that address. The application code only observes swizzled pointers and can dereference them with no overhead.

2.3 Data Structures

The contents of a bunch is described by some special data structures. These contain all the information needed for garbage collection and swizzling.

An *Object Map* describes the location and *class* of objects inside the bunch. An *In-List* indicates which of these objects might be pointed at from another bunches. Each in-list element, called a *scion*, identifies a different potential {source bunch, target object} pair. A special form of scion indicates a persistent root.

An object's class describes its layout and type. A class is an object itself, named by a pointer. The layout gives the location and type of pointers inside objects of that class.

A *Reference Map* indicates the location and type of pointers inside the bunch. Each pointer is described in location-independent form, *i.e.*, the Reference Map identifies the target bunch, and object within that bunch, of each pointer. An *Out-List* indicates which of those references cross out of the bunch's boundaries; elements of the out-list are called *stubs*.

All the above data structures are normally stored within the bunch itself, making the bunch a self-contained unit of I/O, storage, and collection. The exception is a class, which is identified by a pointer, and hence may be stored in another bunch. Classes and types are not used by the language-independent layers of RDOSS, and will be ignored in the remainder of this document.

To allocate an object, a program calls a typed version of malloc which allocates both the memory for the new object, and the corresponding map entries. Layout information is extracted automatically from the binary files by our programming environment. Some unsafe contructs are forbidden (specifically, the union of a pointer and a non-pointer, and casts from non-pointer to pointer) but otherwise the language and the compiler remain unchanged.

3 Garbage Collection of the Persistent Shared Memory

We now focus on the Garbage Collection of the persistent shared memory.

3.1 Requirements and Limitations of Existing Algorithms

A garbage collection algorithm must be correct and have good performance. It is correct if it is both safe and live, *i.e.*, if it never collects a reachable object, and never deadlocks or livelocks.

Ideally, it would also be *complete*, *i.e.*, would eventually collect all garbage. However, completeness is at odds with performance and scalability. To be complete, a GC would have to globally trace the whole graph of objects reachable from the persistent root set (called *live* objects). But, in a large-scale persistent shared memory, this is not feasible, for a number of reasons.

First, all known tracing algorithms require a global synchronization, which is not realistic in a large-scale system.

Second, at any point in time, the major part of the object graph is swapped out to disk, and cannot be accessed economically.

Third, object copying and pointer patching appear to require write-locks that compete with the applications'.

Fourth, existing concurrent GC algorithms require instrumenting *every* mutator pointer instruction with a "barrier" in order to inform the collector of the value read or written. This slows down the applications considerably and is not portable.

3.2 Main Ideas of our Algorithm

Apparently, the problem is hopeless. But we will now show a solution that gives an excellent approximation of the global concurrent trace and does not have the same drawbacks.

Instead of a global synchronized trace, of the whole object graph on the whole network, it approximates the same result with a series of replicated, opportunistic, non-synchronized, piecewise, local traces. Each bunch is traced at each site where it is cached, and the results summarized at the bunch owner (this will be explained in Section 4.2). Groups of multiple bunches mapped at some site are scanned at once, thus collecting cycles of garbage that span bunches.

In order to not compete with the application, the GC works on a separate data set; namely, any datum write-locked by an application is ignored by the collector (*i.e.*, is conservatively considered live). To avoid input/output, the collector also ignores data that is swapped to disk.

The collector does not cause any lock traffic, because it locks an object only at a cache server where the lock is already cached. Its locks do not compete with application locks, because the collector runs as an optimistic transaction.

The collector makes no assumptions about the mutual consistency of the many replicas of some bunch, apart from the assumption that only the owner of a bunch can commit a write into that bunch. Thus, data can be incoherent. The GC compensates for incoherence by being more conservative. Any object that has been reachable continues to be considered reachable as long as the collector does not positively determine, at all copies and independently of the coherence protocol, that it is not.

There is no barrier; the algorithm discovers pointer assignments the next scan of the collector itself, effectively batching pointer assignments.

For clarity, we will explain the algorithm in three steps: (i) collecting a single replica of a single bunch on a single site, (ii) collecting a group of bunches on a single site, (iii) collecting the multiple, possibly incoherent, replicas of a single bunch at all its sites. We will show each step and argue their correctness, while also justifying the design decisions listed above. The first two steps are quite simple and will be detailed next. The last one will be explained in Section 4.

Our algorithm is a hybrid of tracing and counting: (i) It *traces* bunches within groups limited by what is economically feasible. Specifically, the trace stops when it would require input-output or network or lock traffic. (ii) The algorithm uses *reference counting* (via the scions, at the group boundary) when tracing would be too expensive. (iii) A tracing group changes dynamically, seamlessly, and at each site independently from other sites.

The group-formation heuristics must trade off performance and scalability on the one hand against completeness; our current heuristics favor the former.

Our algorithm (following the example of some centralized GC algorithms, such as reference counting [21] and conservative GC [8]) is not provably complete. The trade-off between completeness and performance can be tuned by the choice of the grouping heuristic. Our current heuristic, based on locality (see Section 3.5) has a good chance of collecting cycles of garbage in all real-life situations.

3.3 Scanning a Single Replica at a Single Site

A particular replica of a bunch can be scanned on its site, independently of other bunches and independently of remote versions of the same bunch.

The in-list presented in Section 2.3 identifies all the pointers that reach into a bunch. Ignoring for a short while concurrent updates, it is safe to scan, by considering the in-list as its root set. This is illustrated in Figure 2. Such a collection is complete with respect to the bunch, *i.e.,* it will deallocate any cycle of garbage that is entirely within the bunch. However it is conservative with respect to other bunches, since it can not deallocate a cycle of garbage that crosses the bunch boundary; thus, the in-list serves as a reference counter for inter-bunch references.

Here is how a trace proceeds. Any object pointed from the in-list is marked reachable. An object inside the bunch, pointed from a reachable object, is itself marked reachable. If a reachable object points outside the bunch, a corresponding stub is allocated in the out-list. The result of the walk is a reachable-set and a new out-list. Any objects not in the reachable-set can be deallocated locally; the bunch owner may safely reallocate a deallocated object.

The new out-list is compared with the one resulting from the previous scan. Stubs that didn't previously exist indicate that a new inter-bunch reference has been created; the collector sends a **create** message to the (owner of the) target bunch so that it can create the corresponding scion.

Pointer updates are not noticed until the bunch is scanned (in contrast to concurrent garbage collectors where the mutator must immediately inform the collector of pointer updates, by using a read or write barrier), and in an arbitrary order. To ensure safety, all **create** messages are sent before any deletes.

To see why this is important, consider a pointer x pointing to an object A, and a pointer y; the program assigns the value of x to y, then modifies x, *e.g.,*

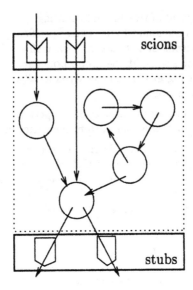

Fig. 2. *Collecting a single replica of a single bunch*

$$y := x; \; x := \text{NULL}$$

The scan could discover the second assignment earlier than the first. Ordering the create before the delete ensures that the target A is not deallocated prematurely, even if x contained the last pointer to A. We will see in Section 4 that deletes may be further delayed in the case of multiple copies.

A create message is sent asynchronously. Since a new pointer value can only, either point to a locally-created object, or be a copy of an existing, reachable pointer, it follows that the target object will not be collected prematurely.

Stubs that have disappeared since the latest scan indicate that an inter-bunch reference no longer exists. A delete message is sent, asynchronously, in order to remove the corresponding scion in the target bunch. To avoid race conditions, no delete message is sent until all the create messages have been. Furthermore, in the case of a replicated bunch, a delete message may need to be delayed even further (see Section 4).

The collector runs as an optimistic transaction: if the collector has started scanning a bunch, and an application later takes a write lock and modifies it, then the collector aborts and its effects are undone. (A liveness assumption is that the GC transaction eventually commits.) Thus, the collector does not compete for data locks with the application, but it is still safe to ignore concurrent mutator updates. The collector is trivially safe and live; it is complete with respect to cycles of garbage enclosed within the bunch, but conservative with respect to possible garbage referenced from another bunch.

When an object has been moved, any pointers that reference it must be patched. This would entail finding the bunches containing these pointers, and taking a write

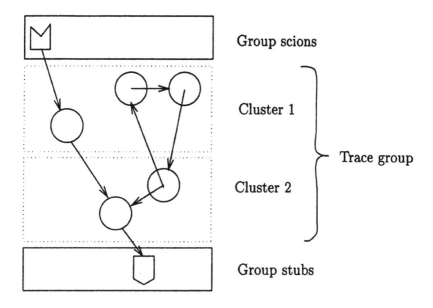

Fig. 3. *Collecting a group of bunches at a single site*

lock on them. In fact, pointer patching can be delayed until such source bunches are next mapped and swizzled.

Consistency is not a problem because the collector will move an object only if the source bunch is not protected by a reserve lock.

3.4 Group Scanning of Multiple Bunches at a Single Site

Just as the collector can scan a single bunch replica at a single site, it can scan any group of bunches at a single site. The algorithm is exactly the same as above, except that scions for pointers internal to the group are not considered roots (this is easy to check because a scion identifies its predecessor bunch), and that scanning continues across bunch boundaries, as long as the group is not exited. Figure 3 shows an example group of two bunches.

A group will contain only bunches that are not write-locked by an application. (A liveness assumption is that no bunch will remain locked indefinitely.) As above, a collection aborts if the application modifies a bunch that has already been scanned. This ensures that the collector does not compete with the application for

locks. For the same reasons as the single-group case, the algorithm is trivially correct. Group collection is complete with respect to bunches in the group, *i.e.*, a cycle of garbage, possibly crossing bunch boundaries, but remaining within the group, will be collected. It is conservative with respect to bunches not in the group.

3.5 Group Heuristics

The significance of group scanning is that *any arbitrary subset of the persistent memory can be scanned,* on a single site, independently of the rest of the memory. The choice of a group can only be heuristic, and should maximize the amount of garbage collected while minimizing the cost.

We will use the locality-based heuristics of a group of all the bunches that are cached on the site at the time the collector happens to run, except those currently being written by an application. This heuristics avoids all input-output costs, and minimizes aborts. Furthermore there is no lock traffic cost since any locks are taken only if cached locally.

This policy favors performance and scalability over completeness. We believe it has a high probability of collecting garbage in all real-life situations, for the following two reasons. First, empirical results from centralized GCs show that cycles are rare and usually small. Second, our intuition is that since a bunch swapped to disk has not been accessed recently, it has a low probability of containing new garbage. However at this point, we do not yet have experimental results confirming this intuition.

We are aware of the limitations of our current policy. For instance, it does not collect cycles of garbage that reside partially on disk or on another server. Collecting such a cycle involves I/O costs, which must be balanced against the expected gain. An I/O is very costly, but in the general case there is no way of knowing how much garbage a bunch contains short of loading it into memory and scanning it.[4]

We are implementing the locality-based heuristic as a first shot. If experimental results show that an excessive amount of garbage is retained, we will explore others. To improve completeness it is necessary to cache more aggressively, for instance by following pointers from already-cached bunches, or by loading random bunches into a cache. Such an aggressive policy might compete in the cache with the applications' working set.

4 Collecting the Multiple Copies of a Cached Bunch

4.1 Garbage Collection and Incoherent Replicas

The simple technique of avoiding concurrent mutator updates, by running the collector as an optimistic transaction, does not work well if replicas of a bunch are present at multiple storage servers.

Since we do not assume coherent copies, the collector could observe some pointer value on one site, while the mutator has assigned a different value on another site.

---

[4] This is in contrast to the Sprite Log File System [19], where the semantics allow the collector to quantify the amount of garbage in a "segment" (their equivalent of a bunch) without actually reading it. Note also that Cook *et al.* [9] propose some heuristics for estimating the relative amount of garbage in partitions (*i.e.*, in bunches) without reading them; this work does not take their ideas into account.

Let us illustrate this problem with an example (see Figure 4). Imagine that pointer x in bunch C1 points to object A in bunch C3. An application program at site S1 assigns NULL to x. Then the collector of site S1 runs. Site S1 is the owner of C1.

Concurrently, another application program assigns pointer y (within bunch C2) with the value of x, as such: y := x. Then the collector runs at sites S2 and S3 (the owner sites of C2 and C3, respectively). To make the example interesting, we suppose that the assignment to y is ordered before the assignment to x, *i.e.*, y now points to object A.

When the collector runs at each site, site S1 sends a delete (C1, A) message to S3, and site S2 sends create (C2, A), also to S3. However, in an asynchronous system, a message can be delayed indefinitely, so the delete could be received before the create, with catastrophic results. (We will call this a "fast delete message".) Furthermore,

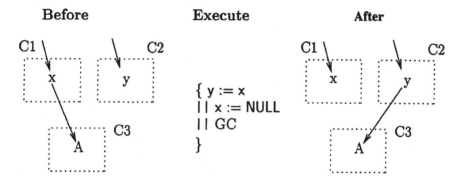

Fig. 4. *Possible race conditions with concurrent read-write-scans of a replicated bunch.*

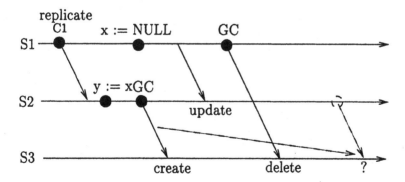

Fig. 5. *Timeline for the execution of Figure 4, showing the effect of a late create or a slow create message.*

since the collectors run at unpredictable times, the delete could actually be sent before the create, with equally catastrophic results. (This will be called an "early delete".) These conditions are illustrated by Figure 5.

4.2 An Asynchronous Solution to the Problem

One possible solution would be to impose coherence between mutators and add synchronization between mutators and collectors; this is essentially what is found in existing concurrent GCs. This solution is undesirable for performance reasons. Instead, we propose an asynchronous solution that avoids both early deletes and fast delete messages. We will look at these two elements in turn; our solution, the "Union of Partial Out-Lists" (UPOL) is illustrated by Figures 6 and 7.

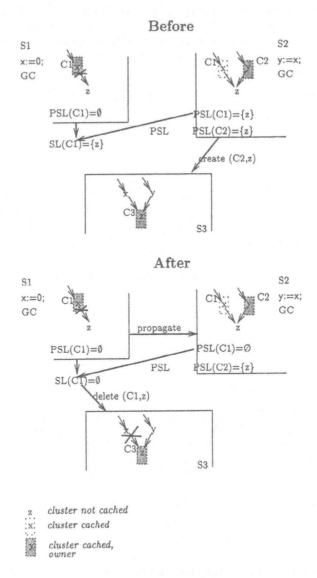

Fig. 6. Union of Partial Out-Lists solution, before and after application of a pointer update.

Avoiding Early Deletes We delay the sending of a delete message until all logically-preceding creates have been sent. To do this: (i) we delay sending deletes until the corresponding update has been applied at all the copies of the bunch, and (ii) we force any creates from some site to be sent before applying any update at that site.

To get (ii), we scan any modified bunches before accepting updates on the same bunch (this may cause an extra delay at commit time).

Property (i) could be achieved by getting an acknowlegment from the coherence layer; but this is not necessary, since the necessary information already is available from the collector. We stated earlier that each copy of a bunch is collected at its site, and the results are summarized at the bunch owner. We can now explain precisely what that means.

Each bunch copy is collected according to the algorithm in Section 3.3 or Section 3.4, creating a new out-list, the *Partial Out-List* (POL) for that copy. It is partial because it only lists the stubs reachable at that site. After the collection, each Partial Out-List is sent to the owner of the bunch in a POL message.

The owner collects all Partial Out-Lists; the complete out-list for the bunch is just the union of the most recent Partial Out-List of each copy. The owner sends a delete message only when a stub disappears from the complete out-list, and a non-owner never sends a delete.

This works because of three properties of stubs: (i) a reachable stub can become unreachable at any site; (ii) a stub that is unreachable at all sites will never become reachable; and (iii) only the owner of a bunch can make a new stub appear in that bunch.

Property (i) is a consequence of the transitivity of the reachability property. For instance, suppose that the variable x in the previous example is reachable from the persistent root only through pointer z located in another bunch, say C4. The application running at the owner of C4 can modify z, making x unreachable, hence the stub from x to A is also unreachable, even though the bunch C1 containing x has not been modified at that site.

Property (ii) is by the stability property of garbage.

Property (iii) is because we assume that only the owner of a bunch can write into that bunch.

Because of these properties, and assuming (possibly unreliable) FIFO communication, it is safe for the owner consider only the most recently-received version of each site's Partial Out-List. It doesn't matter how old it is: it can only err on the side of conservativeness, *i.e.*, of considering as live an object that is not reachable any more.

A limitation of the UPOL algorithm is that collection is sensitive to the way cycles of garbage are replicated. Suppose a cycle of garbage involves objects located in bunches A and B. If A and B are both cached at site 1, the cycle can be collected locally. If A and B are both replicated at sites 1 and 2, both sites can also collect the cycle. But if A is replicated at 1 and 2, and B is only cached at 1, then site 2

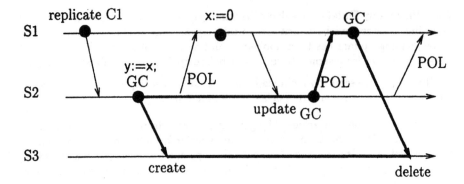

Fig. 7. *Timeline for the Union of Partial Out-Lists solution, illustrating asynchronous messages and causal ordering.*

cannot collect the cycle, and by the UPOL algorithm it cannot be collected at all. If this turns out to be a problem in practice, a possible approach would be to bias the caching policy to avoid the above situation.

Avoiding Fast Delete A careful examination of Figure 7 shows that the POL message creates a causal dependency between the create message and the delete message (the thick arrows in the figure). Any of the well-known techniques for causal delivery of messages [4] will therefore ensure that the create message will not be overcome by the corresponding delete. Larchant-RDOSS sends the create, POL, and delete messages using the Isis cbcast primitive.

5   Related Work

Multiprocessor and concurrent GC algorithms [2, 10] are not directly applicable, because they typically are based on strong consistency and scale assumptions. Even Le Sergent and Berthommieu [15] consider a small-scale, strongly-consistent DSM.

Much previous work in distributed garbage collection [6, 20] considers processes communicating by messages (without shared memory), using a hybrid of tracing and counting. Each process traces its internal pointers; references across process boundaries are reference-counted as they are sent in messages. Some object-oriented databases use a similar approach [1, 23, 16].

In order to collect cycles of garbage, Lang, Queinnec and Piquer [14] augment a hybrid algorithm with a scan of dynamically-changing groups of processes. Their groups are remote and entail a complex joining/disbanding protocol and complex synchronization inside a group. Our grouping algorithm is a simplification of the Lang-Queinnec-Piquer proposal since our groups are local. Furthermore our groups are not determined *a priori* but opportunistically.

The concept of PBR was first proposed by Atkinson and Morrison [3, 17] in the early 1980's. PBR-related collection is considered for instance in O'Toole and Nettles [18], where the collector scans a possibly old copy of the data. We have found two distributed shared memories with PBR in the literature. The specification of the Casper collector [13] is sketchy and seems incapable of collecting a persistent object that has become garbage. EOS [12] has a tracing and copying GC that takes into account user placement hints to improve locality. However, their GC is quite complex and has not been implemented.

Larchant-RDOSS is a simplified version of our own work on Larchant-BMX [11]. Whereas in Larchant-RDOSS the collector may abort in case of conflicts with the mutator, the Larchant-BMX collector is fully concurrent. It uses the O'Toole and Nettles algorithm. RDOSS allows non-coherent memory whereas Larchant-BMX is based upon entry consistency, and therefore does not need the UPOL technique. In Larchant-BMX the granule of consistency and locking is different from the GC granule: the former is the object and the latter is the bunch.

Many hybrid GCs have been published (e.g., Bishop [7]). Ours has the following novel features. The tracing is replicated. Collectors are unsynchronized. Replicas need not be consistent. The counting boundaries change dynamically and are different at each site. Our collector discovers changed pointers at collection time and orders safely the corresponding events. The collector runs as an optimistic transaction.

6 Conclusion

The problem of tracing a large-scale shared distributed store seems intractable at first glance. We have shown an algorithm that gives an approximation of the global trace, with none of the drawbacks. This algorithm causes no input-output nor lock traffic. It opportunistically scans groups of bunches, according to a locality-based heuristics. The algorithm is independent of any particular coherence management (it does not assume coherent memory) but does assume a single owner per bunch. There is no coordination or synchronization between the application programs (mutators) and the collector. It works even with primitive programming languages, with no language or compiler changes (but small programming restrictions are necessary). Collector messages are asynchronous but require a causally-ordered communication layer.

We explained our algorithm in the context of a shared persistent virtual memory containing ordinary memory pointers. Since this is the worst-case scenario, the same algorithm should be applicable to many other cases, such as persistent object stores and shared-memory multiprocessors.

Larchant-RDOSS is currently being implemented, as well as a similar (but slightly different) design, Larchant-BMX [11]. When stable, the code will be made publicly available.

References

1. Laurent Amsaleg, Michael Franklin, and Olivier Gruber. Efficient incremental garbage collection for workstation/server database systems. Rapport de Recherche RR-2409, Institut National de la Recherche en Informatique et Automatique, Rocquencourt (France), November 1994.
2. Andrew W. Appel, John R. Ellis, and Kai Li. Real-time concurrent garbage collection on stock multiprocessors. In *Proc. Prog. Lang. Design and Implementation*, pages 11–20, 1988.
3. M. P. Atkinson, P. J. Bailey, K. J. Chisholm, P. W. Cockshott, and R. Morrison. An approach to persistent programming. *The Computer Journal*, 26(4):360–365, 1983.
4. Özalp Babaoğlu and Keith Marzullo. *Consistent Global States of Distributed Systems: Fundamental Concepts and Mechanisms*, chapter 4, pages 55–93. Addison-Wesley, ACM Press, second edition edition, 1993.
5. Kenneth Birman, Andre Schiper, and Pat Stephenson. Lightweight causal and atomic group multicast. *ACM Transactions on Computer Systems*, 9(3):272–314, August 1991.
6. Andrew Birrell, Greg Nelson, Susan Owicki, and Edward Wobber. Network objects. In *Proceedings of the 14th ACM Symposium on Operating Systems Principles*, pages 217–230, Asheville, NC (USA), December 1993.
7. Peter B. Bishop. *Computer Systems with a Very Large Address Space and Garbage Collection*. PhD thesis, Massachusetts Institute of Technology Laboratory for Computer Science, Cambridge, Mass. (USA), May 1977. Technical report MIT/LCS/TR-178.
8. Hans-Juergen Boehm and Mark Weiser. Garbage collection in an uncooperative environment. *Software — Practice and Experience*, 18(9):807–820, September 1988.
9. Jonathan E. Cook, Alexander L. Wolf, and Benjamin G. Zorn. Partition selection policies in object database garbage collection. In *Proc. Int. Conf. on Management of Data (SIGMOD)*, pages 371–382, Minneapolis MN (USA), May 1994. ACM SIGMOD.
10. Damien Doligez and Xavier Leroy. A concurrent, generational garbage collector for a multithreaded implementation of ML. In *Proc. of the 20th Annual ACM SIGPLAN-SIGACT Symp. on Principles of Programming Lang.*, pages 113–123, Charleston SC (USA), January 1993.
11. Paulo Ferreira and Marc Shapiro. Garbage collection and DSM consistency. In *Proc. of the First Symposium on Operating Systems Design and Implementation (OSDI)*, pages 229–241, Monterey CA (USA), November 1994. ACM.
12. Olivier Gruber and Laurent Amsaleg. Object grouping in Eos. In *Proc. Int. Workshop on Distributed Object Management*, pages 184–201, Edmonton (Canada), August 1992.
13. Bett Koch, Tracy Schunke, Alan Dearle, Francis Vaughan, Chris Marlin, Ruth Fazakerley, and Chris Barter. Cache coherency and storage management in a persistent object system. In *Proceedings of the Fourth International Workshop on Persistent Object Systems*, pages 99–109, Martha's Vineyard, MA (USA), September 1990.
14. Bernard Lang, Christian Queinnec, and José Piquer. Garbage collecting the world. In *Proc. of the 19th Annual ACM SIGPLAN-SIGACT Symp. on Principles of Programming Lang.*, Albuquerque, New Mexico (USA), January 1992.
15. T. Le Sergent and B. Berthomieu. Incremental multi-threaded garbage collection on virtually shared memory architectures. In *Proc. Int. Workshop on Memory Management*, number 637 in Lecture Notes in Computer Science, pages 179–199, Saint-Malo (France), September 1992. Springer-Verlag.
16. Umesh Maheshwari. Distributed garbage collection in a client-server, transactional, persistent object system. Technical Report MIT/LCS/TM-574, Mass. Inst. of Technology, Lab. for Comp. Sc., Cambridge, MA (USA), October 1993.

17. R. Morrison, M. P. Atkinson, A. L. Brown, and A. Dearle. Bindings in persistent programming languages. *SIGPLAN Notices*, 23(4):27–34, April 1988.

18. James O'Toole, Scott Nettles, and David Gifford. Concurrent compacting garbage collection of a persistent heap. In *Proceedings of the 14th ACM Symposium on Operating Systems Principles*, pages 161–174, Asheville, NC (USA), December 1993.

19. Mendel Rosenblum and John K. Ousterhout. The design and implementation of a log-structured file system. *ACM Transactions on Computer Systems*, 10(1):26–52, February 1992.

20. Marc Shapiro, Peter Dickman, and David Plainfossé. SSP chains: Robust, distributed references supporting acyclic garbage collection. Rapport de Recherche 1799, Institut National de la Recherche en Informatique et Automatique, Rocquencourt (France), nov 1992. Also available as Broadcast Technical Report #1.

21. Paul R. Wilson. Uniprocessor garbage collection techniques. In *Proc. Int. Workshop on Memory Management*, number 637 in Lecture Notes in Computer Science, Saint-Malo (France), September 1992. Springer-Verlag.

22. Paul R. Wilson and Sheetal V. Kakkad. Pointer swizzling at page fault time: Efficiently and compatibly supporting huge address spaces on standard hardware. In *1992 Int. Workshop on Object Orientation and Operating Systems*, pages 364–377, Dourdan (France), October 1992. IEEE Comp. Society, IEEE Comp. Society Press.

23. V. Yong, J. Naughton, and J. Yu. Storage reclamation and reorganization in client-server persistent object stores. In *Proc. of the Data Engineering Int. Conf.*, pages 120–133, Houston TX (USA), February 1994.

Broadcasting in Hypercubes with Randomly Distributed Byzantine Faults

Feng Bao , Yoshihide Igarashi , Keiko Katano

Department of Computer Science
Gunma University, Kiryu, 376 Japan
Email: igarashi@comp.cs.gunma-u.ac.jp

Abstract. We study all-to-all broadcasting in hypercubes with randomly distributed Byzantine faults. We construct an efficient broadcasting scheme $BC1\text{-}n\text{-}cube$ running on the n-dimensional hypercube (n-cube for short) in $2n$ rounds, where for communication by each node of the n-cube, only one of its links is used in each round. The scheme $BC1\text{-}n\text{-}cube$ can tolerate $\lfloor (n-1)/2 \rfloor$ Byzantine node and/or link faults in the worst case. If there are at most f Byzantine faulty nodes randomly distributed in the n-cube, $BC1\text{-}n\text{-}cube$ succeeds with a probability higher than $1 - (64nf/2^n)^{\lceil n/2 \rceil}$. In other words, if $1/(64nk)$ of all the nodes (i.e., $2^n/(64nk)$ nodes) fail in Byzantine manner randomly in the n-cube, then the scheme succeeds with a probability higher than $1 - k^{-\lceil n/2 \rceil}$. We also consider the case where all nodes are faultless but links may fail randomly in the n-cube. Scheme $BC1\text{-}n\text{-}cube$ succeeds with a probability higher than $1 - k^{-\lceil n/2 \rceil}$ provided that not more than $1/(64(n+1)k)$ of all the links in the n-cube fail in Byzantine manner randomly. For the case where only links may fail, we give another broadcasting scheme $BC2\text{-}n\text{-}cube$ which runs in $2n^2$ rounds. Broadcasting by $BC2\text{-}n\text{-}cube$ is successful with a high probability if the number of Byzantine faulty links randomly distributed in the n-cube is not more than a constant fraction of the total number of links. That is, it succeeds with a probability higher than $1 - n \cdot k^{-\lceil n/2 \rceil}$ if $1/(48k)$ of all the links in the n-cube fail in Byzantine manner randomly.

1 Introduction

Broadcasting is the process of information dissemination in a communication network by which messages originated from the source nodes are transmitted to all the nodes in the network. The broadcasting has wide applications to the control of distributed systems and to parallel computing. In this paper we consider all-to-all broadcasting.

Recently a lot of attentions have been given to broadcasting in the presence of faulty nodes and faulty links [*see for example*, 1, 2, 8, 12] . Two alternative assumptions about faults are usually made; either an upper bound k on the total number of faults is supposed [5, 9, 10, 13, 15], or it is assumed that links and/or nodes fail independently with a fixed probability [3, 4, 6, 7, 11, 14]. If an upper bound on the number of faults is imposed, and if we consider the worst case of the fault tolerance, the maximum number of faults that can be tolerated should be smaller than the connectivity of the network. Thus, for large networks, the probabilistic approach seems to be more realistic. There are two kinds of assumptions with regard to types of faults. The one assumption is that any fault is the fail-stop type (i.e., any faulty node or link does not transmit any message), such as considered in [6,7,9,10,13]. The other assumption is so-called Byzantine type (i.e., a faulty node or link may alter arbitrarily the messages that pass through it or even fabricate a false message) [4,14]. In this paper we consider the faults of Byzantine type.

In [4], only complete graphs, *core* graphs and *fat ring* graphs are studied in the presence of Byzantine faulty nodes. Hypercubes with Byzantine faulty links are studied in [14] for all-port broadcasting(each node is allowed to communicate with all its adjacent nodes in the same time). So far, broadcasting for hypercubes with Byzantine faulty nodes has not been much studied. In this paper we study one-port broadcasting(each node is allowed to communicate with only one of its adjacent nodes each time) in the hypercubes with Byzantine faulty nodes and/or links. We assume that exact f faulty nodes (or links) are distributed randomly in a network. In other words, we assume that all the configurations of f faulty nodes (or links) are equally probable. We give two broadcasting schemes for the hypercubes. Our broadcasting schemes are reliable in the hypercubes with randomly distributed faults. The time period for forwarding a message from a node to one of its adjacent nodes is called a round. We assume that each node can forward messages and can receive messages in the same round. The two schemes need $2n$ and $2n^2$ rounds, respectively, and in each round, only one of the links of each node is exploited. A broadcasting scheme works in a way that the same procedure is executed by every node concurrently. Hence, the network is required to be synchronized with a global clock so that the round of broadcasting at every node always coincides. All faultless nodes finally obtain the correct messages from all the other faultless nodes by majority voting.

The paper is organized as follows. In Section 2, we present our first broadcasting scheme $BC1$-n-$cube$ and analyze its performance for tolerating Byzantine node and/or link faults in the worst case. In Section 3, we calculate a lower bound on the probability that broadcasting by $BC1$-n-$cube$ succeeds in the presence of randomly distributed f faulty nodes of Byzantine type. From the lower bound on the probability we say that $BC1$-n-$cube$ is a reliable broadcasting scheme. The lower bound we give in Section 3 is good for large values for n since we want to analyze it in an asymptotical manner. For small values for n, $BC1$-n-$cube$ also behaves very well. For each of small values for n, it is not difficult to estimate individually the probability of successful broadcasting. We therefor will not care the case of small values for n in this paper. In Section 4, we give $BC1$-n-$cube$-$neighbor$ which is a variation of $BC1$-n-$cube$. Then we construct the second broadcasting scheme, $BC2$-n-$cube$ by using $BC1$-n-$cube$-$neighbor$. We show that broadcasting by $BC2$-n-$cube$ succeeds with a high probability even if the number of randomly distributed faulty links is a constant fraction of the total number of links in the hypercube. Concluding remarks are given in Section 5.

2 A Reliable Broadcasting Scheme

The n-dimensional hypercube (n-cube for short) is defined to be the graph with $N = 2^n$ nodes labeled by 2^n binary numbers from 0 to $2^n - 1$, where there exists an edge between any two nodes if and only if the binary representations of their labels differ by exactly one bit. For convenience, we will number the bit positions of each node (i.e., the bit positions of each node label) of the n-cube from right to left as 0 to $n - 1$. The Hamming weight of node u is denoted by $\mathbf{w}(u)$. For node u ($0 \leq u \leq 2^n - 1$) and bit position i ($0 \leq i \leq n - 1$), u^i denotes the adjacent node of u such that u and u^i differ at just the ith bit (also called the ith dimension). For example, $10011^2 = 10111$ and $10011^4 = 00011$. More generally, we will use the notation $u^{\{i_1, i_2, \cdots i_k\}}$ to denote the node which differs from u at the i_1th, i_2th, $\cdots$, i_kth bits. For example, $10011^{\{1,2,4\}} = 00101$ and $10011^{\{0,3,4\}} = 01010$. The link between u and u^i is denoted by $\mathbf{e}_i(u)$. Note that $\mathbf{e}_i(u) = \mathbf{e}_i(u^i)$. We assume that each node in the n-cube is a processor and that each edge is a communication link connecting two processors located on its extremes.

In this section, we present an all-to-all broadcasting scheme for hypercubes. The scheme can tolerate randomly distributed Byzantine faults with a high probability. Our goal is to let every faultless node know the values of all the other faultless nodes when the broadcasting by the scheme is completed. More formally speaking, we say that each node u of the n-cube has initially a value $val(u)$. Each node u obtains information about the value of every other node v through the broadcasting process. Let $\bar{V}^u[v]$ denote the value of v obtained by u through the process. We say that the broadcasting succeeds if the following condition $C1$ is finally satisfied:

$C1 : \bar{V}^u[v] = val(v)$ for every pair of faultless nodes u and v of the n-cube.

To tolerate Byzantine faults, we send the message copies through disjoint paths and we make the majority voting after these message copies are received.. For example, when a node u receives 5 "yes"'s and 4 "no"'s as another node v's value, u makes a decision that v's value is "yes". The all-to-all broadcasting presented in this paper exploits n disjoint paths between any pair of nodes in the n-cube. Although it is a well known fact that there exist n disjoint paths between any pair of nodes in the n-cube, we need the paths used in the broadcasting process satisfying some properties so that our one-port broadcasting is efficient.

Example: Consider the 4-cube. There are many choices of 4 disjoint paths from node 1001 to node 1110. If we chose (1001, 1000, 1010, 1110) as one of the 4 paths for broadcasting, we hope that (1001, 1000, 1010) is one of the 4 paths from 1001 to 1010 used for broadcasting. And also we hope that (1000, 1010, 1110) is one of the 4 paths from 1000 to 1110 used for broadcasting and that (1000, 1010, 1110) is the prefix-path of one of the 4 paths from 1000 to some other nodes.

The broadcasting scheme is processed in many rounds of communication. A round is actually a concurrent step of transmission. Typically, it starts with round 0, then, round 1, round 2, $\cdots$, round n, round $n+1$, $\cdots$. We regard the number of rounds needed for broadcasting as the time complexity of the broadcasting. The broadcasting by BC1-n-cube takes $2n$ rounds. In round r of the broadcasting process by the scheme, each node u sends and receives messages to and from its neighbor $u^{[r]_n}$, where $[r]_n$ denotes $r \bmod n$. When node u transmits the value of another node v to $u^{[r]_n}$ through $e_{[r]_n}(u)$, u must inform $u^{[r]_n}$ that the value being transmitted is the value of v. Hence, the message being transmitted should be in the form like "the value of node v is X"

Our scheme demands that each node u $(0 \le u \le 2^n - 1)$ should have $n+1$ registers. Each register consists of 2^n cells. The vth cell of the ith register $(0 \le i \le n-1)$ and the vth cell of the last register of node u are denoted by $V_i^u[v]$ and $V^u[v]$, respectively. The cell $V_i^u[v]$ is used by node u to store the value of v received through $e_i(u)$. The values of $V_i^u[v]$ and $V^u[v]$ are denoted by $\bar{V}_i^u[v]$ and $\bar{V}^u[v]$, respectively. Due to the possible existence of Byzantine faults, $\bar{V}_i^u[v]$ may not be equal to $val(v)$. At the end of the broadcasting process we let $V^u[v] :=$ the majority voting of $\{\bar{V}_0^u[v], \bar{V}_1^u[v], ..., \bar{V}_{n-1}^u[v]\}$ (see Fig. 1). Each node u has to

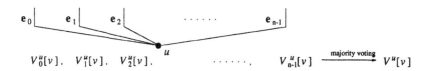

Fig. 1. The value of v transmitted to u via $e_i(u)$ is kept in $V_i^u[v]$.

decide to transmit which of the $\bar{V}_0^u[v], \bar{V}_1^u[v], \cdots, \bar{V}_{n-1}^u[v]$ to $u^{[r]_n}$ in each round r (note: some $V_i^u[v]$'s may be empty at this time). We next define a function $R(r, w)$ which will be used for each node u to decide which of $\bar{V}_0^u[v], \bar{V}_1^u[v], \cdots, \bar{V}_{n-1}^u[v]$ for every v should be transmitted to $u^{[r]_n}$ in round r. More precisely, in round r node u transmits only values of those nonempty $V_i^u[v]$'s to $u^{[r]_n}$ such that $i = R(r, v \oplus u)$, where $v \oplus u$ is the bitwise EXCLUSIVE OR of v and u. The function $R(r, w)$ is formally defined as follows:

Let r be an integer such that $0 \le r \le 2n - 1$, and let w be an integer such that $0 \le w \le 2^n - 1$. We treat w as a binary string of length n. Denote the bits of w from right to left as $b_0(w), b_1(w), b_2(w), \cdots, b_{n-1}(w)$ (i.e., $w = b_{n-1}(w) \cdots b_1(w) b_0(w)$).

(1) For $0 \le r \le n - 1$,

$$R(r, w) = \begin{cases} r & \text{if } w = 0, \\ \max\{k \mid b_k(w) = 1\} & \text{if } 0 < w < 2^r, \\ undefined & \text{if } w \ge 2^r. \end{cases}$$

(2) For $n \le r \le 2n - 1$,

$$R(r,w) = \begin{cases} \max\{k \mid b_k(w) = 1\} & \text{if } w \equiv 0 \bmod 2^{[r]_n} \text{ and } w > 2^{[r]_n}, \\ \max\{k \mid b_k(w) = 1 \text{ and } k < [r]_n\} & \text{if } w \not\equiv 0 \bmod 2^{[r]_n}, \\ undefined & \text{if } w = 0 \text{ or } w = 2^{[r]_n}. \end{cases}$$

We show some examples of function values of $R(r,w)$ for $n = 8$ in Fig. 2.

$[r]_n$	$[r]_n$	$[r]_n$	$[r]_n$
w 00100101	w 00100101	w 00001010	w 01011000
bit position 76543210	bit position 76543210	bit position 76543210	bit position 76543210
$R(3,w)$ undefined	$R(11, w)=2$	$R(5, w)=3$	$R(11, w)=6$

Fig. 2. Some examples for function $R(r,w)$.

By "u sends $(v, \bar{V}_j^u[v])$ to u^i", we mean that in round i or round $i + n$ (i.e., round r such that $[r]_n = i$), u informs u^i that $\bar{V}_j^u[v]$ is the value of v kept in the vth cell in the jth register of u. If u receives a message from $u^{[r]_n}$ in round r, the message should be in the form (v, X), and otherwise u would refuse to accept it. However, it is possible that $u^{[r]_n}$ sends (v', X') to u in round r, while in round r, u receives (v, X) which may be different from (v', X') due to the corruption of the message during the communication through $\mathbf{e}_{[r]_n}(u)$. We use a description "u receives (v, X) from u^i" to express an operation that u receives a message from u^i about $val(v)$ which might be kept in the the vth cell in the jth register of u^i.

The following is our broadcasting scheme $BC1$-n-$cube$. It is executed at every node u of the n-$cube$ concurrently.

$BC1$-n-$cube$ /* a description of the execution at node u */
begin
    /* the value of u is initially set into the uth cell in each register of u */
    for every v ($0 \leq v \leq 2^n - 1$) and every i ($0 \leq i \leq n - 1$)

$$V_i^u[v] := \begin{cases} val(u) & \text{if } u = v \\ default & \text{if } u \neq v; \end{cases}$$

    for $round := 0$ **to** $2n - 1$ **do**
        begin
            for every pair of v and i ($0 \leq v \leq 2^n - 1, 0 \leq i \leq n - 1$) satisfying
            $\bar{V}_i^u[v] \neq default$ and $i = R(round, v \oplus u)$
                send $(v, \bar{V}_i^u[v])$ to $u^{[round]_n}$;   /* delivery from u */
            for every (v, X) ($0 \leq v \leq 2^n - 1$) from $u^{[round]_n}$
                if $\bar{V}_{[round]_n}^u[v] = default$ **then** $V_{[round]_n}^u[v] := X$ /* reception */
        end;

for every v $(0 \leq v \leq 2^n - 1)$

$V^u[v] :=$ the majority voting of $\{\bar{V}_0^u[v], \bar{V}_1^u[v], ..., \bar{V}_{n-1}^u[v]\}$

end.

The scheme $BC1\text{-}n\text{-}cube$ is used for all-to-all broadcasting. However, if only one node or some nodes have messages (values) to broadcast, $BC1\text{-}n\text{-}cube$ can be naturally changed to one-to-all or part-to-all broadcasting. No matter what the broadcasting mode is (e.g., one-to-all, part-to-all or all-to-all), if any node v holds a message $val(v)$, $val(v)$ is disseminated to every node u through n node disjoint paths. The following example (Fig. 3) shows how $val(v)$ reaches u through n node disjoint paths.

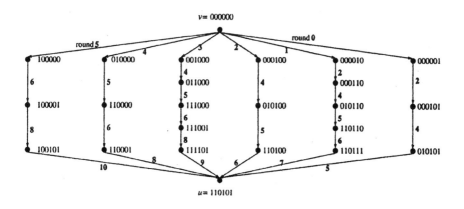

Fig. 3. $val(v)$ reaches u through n node disjoint paths.

Lemma 1. *For every pair of distinct nodes, u and v $(0 \leq u, v \leq 2^n - 1, u \neq v)$, $val(v)$ reaches $V_i^u[v]$'s $(0 \leq i \leq n - 1)$ through n disjoint paths by $BC1\text{-}n\text{-}cube$ if there are no faults in the n-cube.*

Proof. Assume $u = v^{\{i_k, i_{k-1}, \cdots, i_1\}}$, where $0 \leq i_1 < i_2, \cdots, < i_k \leq n - 1$ and $1 \leq k \leq n$. Now we consider every $V_j^u[v]$ $(0 \leq j \leq n - 1)$.

Case 1: $j = i_k$. By $BC1\text{-}n\text{-}cube$ the final value of $V_j^u[v]$ comes from v to u through the following path:

$$v \to v^{i_1} \to v^{\{i_2, i_1\}} \to \cdots \to v^{\{i_{k-1}, \cdots, i_2, i_1\}} \to v^{\{i_k, i_{k-1}, \cdots, i_2, i_1\}} = u.$$

Case 2: $j = i_t$ for some $t < k$. By $BC1\text{-}n\text{-}cube$ the final value of $V_j^u[v]$ comes from v to u through the following path:

$$v \to v^{i_{t+1}} \to v^{\{i_{t+2}, i_{t+1}\}} \to \cdots \to v^{\{i_k, \cdots, i_{t+2}, i_{t+1}\}} \to v^{\{i_k, \cdots, i_{t+2}, i_{t+1}, i_1\}}$$
$$\to v^{\{i_k, \cdots, i_{t+2}, i_{t+1}, i_2, i_1\}} \to \cdots \to v^{\{i_k, \cdots, i_{t+2}, i_{t+1}, i_{t-1}, \cdots, i_2, i_1\}}$$
$$\to v^{\{i_k, \cdots, i_{t+2}, i_{t+1}, i_t, i_{t-1}, \cdots, i_2, i_1\}} = u.$$

Case 3: $i_t < j < i_{t+1}$ for some t.　By $BC1$-n-cube the final value of $V_j^u[v]$ comes from v to u through the following path:

$$v \to v^j \to v^{\{i_{t+1},j\}} \to v^{\{i_{t+2},i_{t+1},j\}} \to \cdots \to v^{\{i_k,\cdots,i_{t+2},i_{t+1},j\}}$$
$$\to v^{\{i_k,\cdots,i_{t+2},i_{t+1},j,i_1\}} \to v^{\{i_k,\cdots,i_{t+2},i_{t+1},j,i_2,i_1\}} \to \cdots$$
$$\to v^{\{i_k,\cdots,i_{t+2},i_{t+1},j,i_{t-1},\cdots,i_2,i_1\}} \to v^{\{i_k,\cdots,i_{t+2},i_{t+1},j,i_t,i_{t-1},\cdots,i_2,i_1\}}$$
$$\to v^{\{i_k,\cdots,i_{t+2},i_{t+1},i_t,i_{t-1},\cdots,i_2,i_1\}} = u.$$

Case 4: $j > i_k$ or $j < i_1$.　By $BC1$-n-cube the final value of $V_j^u[v]$ comes from v to u through the following path:

$$v \to v^j \to v^{\{j,i_1\}} \to v^{\{j,i_2,i_1\}} \to \cdots \to v^{\{j,i_k,i_{k-1},\cdots,i_2,i_1\}} \to v^{\{i_k,\cdots,i_2,i_1\}}$$
$$= u.$$

Let $P_i(v,u)$ be the path through which the final value of $V_i^u[v]$ is sent from v to u. For $i = 0, 1, 2, ..., n-1$, the paths $P_i(v,u)$'s are node disjoint (we do not count v and u in the nodes on $P_i(v,u)$). Let j is not in $\{i_1, i_2, \cdots, i_k\}$. The jth bit of every node on $P_j(v,u)$ is 1 while the jth bit of every node on $P_i(v,u)$ is 0 for $i \neq j$. Hence, we only need to prove that $P_i(v,u)$ and $P_j(v,u)$ are node disjoint for any pair of different i and j in $\{i_1, i_2, \cdots, i_k\}$. Without loss of generality, we let $i = i_t$, $j = i_s$ and $t > s$. From Case 1 and Case 2, the ith bit of every node on $P_i(v,u)$ is 1 while the i_{t-1}th bit of every node on $P_i(v,u)$ is 0. Let w be a node on $P_j(v,u)$. Either the ith bit of w is 0, or if the ith bit of w is 1 then the i_{t-1}th bit of w must be 1. Hence, $P_i(v,u)$ and $P_j(v,u)$ are node disjoint.　□

Observation: Suppose that the sequence of the moving directions (i.e., dimensions) on $P_i(v,u)$ is $(e_{j_1}, e_{j_2}, \cdots, e_{j_k})$, where $i = j_k$. For any node $v^{\{j_1,j_2,\cdots,j_s\}}$ on $P_i(v,u)$ such that $s < k$, $P_{j_s}(v, v^{\{j_1,j_2,\cdots,j_s\}})$ is a prefix-path of $P_i(v,u)$. If there are no faults on $P_i(v,u)$, about the broadcasting process by $BC1$-n-cube the following equalities hold true:

$$val(v) = \bar{V}_{j_1}^{v^{j_1}}[v] = \bar{V}_{j_2}^{v^{\{j_1,j_2\}}}[v] = \cdots = \bar{V}_{j_k}^{v^{\{j_1,j_2,\cdots,j_k\}}}[v] = \bar{V}_i^u[v].$$

From this observation and Lemma 1 we have the following theorem.

Theorem 2. *If u and v are faultless nodes in the n-cube and at most $\lfloor \frac{n-1}{2} \rfloor$ paths among $P_0(v,u), P_1(v,u), ..., P_{n-1}(v,u)$ have node and/or link Byzantine faults, then $\bar{V}^u[v] = val(v)$ when the broadcasting by $BC1$-n-cube is completed.*

Proof. There are at least $\lceil \frac{n+1}{2} \rceil$ faultless paths among $P_0(v,u), P_1(v,u), ..., P_{n-1}(v,u)$. If $P_i(v,u)$ is faultless, then $\bar{V}_i^u[v] = val(v)$. Hence, $\bar{V}^u[v] =$ the majority voting of $\{\bar{V}_0^u[v], \bar{V}_1^u[v], \cdots, \bar{V}_{n-1}^u[v]\} = val(v)$.　□

Corollary 3. *Broadcasting by $BC1$-n-cube can tolerate up to $\lfloor \frac{n-1}{2} \rfloor$ node and/or link Byzantine faults.*

Broadcasting scheme $BC1$-n-cube is efficient in the following sense. When a node u sends the message $(v, \bar{V}_j^u[v])$ to its neighbor u^i, the node u^i keeps this message by $V_i^{u^i}[v] := \bar{V}_j^u[v]$. Then $\bar{V}_i^{u^i}[v]$ finally takes part in the majority voting on deciding $\bar{V}^{u^i}[v]$. Every transmission in the broadcasting process by $BC1$-n-cube is useful to tolerate at most $\lfloor \frac{n-1}{2} \rfloor$ Byzantine faults. In other words, for any pair of distinct nodes u and v, n copies of $val(u)$ are sent from u to v through n node disjoint paths. No surplus transmissions are made by $BC1$-n-$cube$ for this purpose, and there are no broadcasting schemes that can tolerate $\lfloor \frac{n-1}{2} \rfloor + 1$ Byzantine faults in the n-$cube$ in the worst case. From this observation we can say that $BC1$-n-$cube$ is optimal for tolerating Byzantine faults as many as possible in the worst case. If the size of the initial value at any node is $O(1)$, the communication complexity of $BC1$-n-$cube$ is $O(2^{2n}n^2)$.

3 Randomly Distributed Faulty Nodes

In this section we consider the situation where faulty nodes of Byzantine type are randomly distributed in the n-$cube$ and all links are faultless. This assumption is somewhat different from the assumption used in [4] and [5]. We assume that f faulty nodes are randomly distributed (i.e., all configurations with f faulty nodes are equally probable), whereas in [4] and [5] it is assumed that each node fails with a fixed probability. However, these two assumptions are closely related. Suppose that a scheme is successful with probability P_N^f in broadcasting on a network with N nodes including f faulty nodes randomly distributed. Then the same scheme is successful with probability $\sum_{i=0}^{N} \binom{N}{i} p^i (1-p)^{N-i} P_N^i$ when each node fails independently with probability p. Hence, the former is a rather primary assumption.

We denote a configuration of the n-$cube$ with f faulty nodes by d_n^f. The following notations are introduced.

$D_n^f = \{d_n^f \mid d_n^f$ is a configuration of the n cube with f faulty nodes$\}$,

$D_n^f(u,v) = \{d_n^f \mid u$ and v $(u \neq v)$ are faultless, and at least $\lceil \frac{n}{2} \rceil$ paths among $P_0(u,v), P_1(u,v), \cdots, P_{n-1}(u,v)$ are faulty in $d_n^f\}$,

$D_n^f(fail) = \{d_n^f \mid$ there are a pair of faultless nodes u and v $(u \neq v)$ such that at least $\lceil \frac{n}{2} \rceil$ paths among $P_0(u,v), P_1(u,v), \cdots, P_{n-1}(u,v)$ are faulty in $d_n^f\}$.

It is immediate that $|D_n^f| = \binom{2^n}{f}$ and $D_n^f(fail) \subseteq \cup_{u,v} D_n^f(u,v)$. Hence, $|D_n^f(fail)| \leq \sum_{u,v} |D_n^f(u,v)|$.

Lemma 4. *For any pair of distinct nodes u and v of the n-cube, the following inequality holds true:*

$$|D_n^f(u,v)| < \binom{n}{\lceil n/2 \rceil} \binom{2^n - \lceil n/2 \rceil}{f - \lceil n/2 \rceil} n^{\lceil n/2 \rceil}.$$

Proof. For any pair of nodes u and v of the n-cube, there are at most n intermediate nodes on each path $P_i(u,v)$ $(0 \leq i \leq n-1)$. Hence, by simply counting, we have

$$|D_n^f(u,v)| < \binom{n}{\lceil n/2 \rceil} \binom{2^n - \lceil n/2 \rceil}{f - \lceil n/2 \rceil} n^{\lceil n/2 \rceil}. \qquad \square$$

Theorem 5. *If there are at most f faulty nodes of Byzantine type randomly distributed in the n-cube, then broadcasting by BC1-n-cube succeeds with a probability higher than $1 - \left(\frac{64nf}{2^n}\right)^{\lceil n/2 \rceil}$*

Proof. Suppose that there are at most f faulty nodes of Byzantine type randomly distributed in the n-cube. By a counting argument and Lemma 4 we have the following inequalities:

$$
\frac{|D_n^f(fail)|}{|D_n^f|} \leq \frac{\sum_{u \neq v} |D_n^f(u, v)|}{|D_n^f|}
$$

$$
< \frac{2^n(2^n - 1)n^{\lceil n/2 \rceil} \binom{n}{\lceil n/2 \rceil} \binom{2^n - \lceil n/2 \rceil}{f - \lceil n/2 \rceil}}{\binom{2^n}{f}}
$$

$$
= 2^n(2^n - 1)n^{\lceil n/2 \rceil} \binom{n}{\lceil n/2 \rceil} \cdot \frac{f!}{2^n(2^n - 1)\cdots(2^n + 1 - f)}
$$

$$
\cdot \frac{(2^n - \lceil n/2 \rceil)(2^n - \lceil n/2 \rceil - 1)\cdots(2^n + 1 - f)}{(f - \lceil n/2 \rceil)!}
$$

$$
= 2^n(2^n - 1)n^{\lceil n/2 \rceil} \binom{n}{\lceil n/2 \rceil} \cdot \frac{f(f - 1)\cdots(f + 1 - \lceil n/2 \rceil)}{2^n(2^n - 1)\cdots(2^n + 1 - \lceil n/2 \rceil)}
$$

$$
< 2^n(2^n - 1)n^{\lceil n/2 \rceil} \binom{n}{\lceil n/2 \rceil} \left(\frac{f}{2^n}\right)^{\lceil n/2 \rceil}
$$

$$
< 2^{2n} \cdot 4^{\lceil n/2 \rceil} n^{\lceil n/2 \rceil} \left(\frac{f}{2^n}\right)^{\lceil n/2 \rceil} \leq \left(\frac{64nf}{2^n}\right)^{\lceil n/2 \rceil}
$$

Hence, $BC1$-n-cube succeeds with a probability higher than $1 - \left(\frac{64nf}{2^n}\right)^{\lceil n/2 \rceil}$. □

Corollary 6. *If at most $\frac{2^n}{64nk}$ faulty nodes of Byzantine type are randomly distributed in the n-cube, $BC1$-n-cube succeeds in broadcasting with a probability higher than $1 - k^{-\lceil n/2 \rceil}$.*

4 Randomly Distributed Faulty Links

In this section we assume that all the nodes are faultless and that some faulty links are randomly distributed. Our assumption about randomness in this section is similar to the assumption in the preceding section. We assume that f faulty links of Byzantine type are randomly distributed in the n-cube. We give a broadcasting scheme called $BC2$-n-cube. This scheme can tolerate a situation such that the number of randomly distributed faulty links is not more than a constant fraction of the total number of links in the n-cube. However, broadcasting process by $BC2$-n-cube contains some redundant transmissions, and it runs in n time as much as $BC1$-n-cube runs (i.e., it runs in $2n^2$ rounds).

We first analyze the reliability of $BC1$-n-$cube$ in the case where there are only faulty links randomly distributed in the n-$cube$. The number of links of the n-$cube$ is $2^{n-1}n$. For any pair of distinct nodes u and v the length of each path used to transmit messages from u to v is at most $n+1$. From these facts the next theorem can be proved in a similar way to the proof of Theorem 5. We omit the proof here.

Theorem 7. *If there are at most f faulty links of Byzantine type randomly distributed in the n-$cube$, then broadcasting by $BC1$-n-$cube$ succeeds with a probability higher than $1 - \left(\frac{64(n+1)f}{2^{n-1}n} \right)^{\lceil n/2 \rceil}$*

Corollary 8. *If at most $\frac{2^{n-1}n}{64(n+1)k}$ faulty links of Byzantine type are randomly distributed in the n-$cube$, then broadcasting by $BC1$-n-$cube$ succeeds with a probability higher than $1 - k^{-\lceil n/2 \rceil}$.*

We next modify $BC1$-n-$cube$ by adding some restrictions on the delivery control and the reception control. This modified one is called $BC1$-n-$cube$-$neighbor$. It is executed at every node u of the n-$cube$ concurrently.

$BC1$-n-$cube$-$neighbor(val^u)$ /* a description of the execution at node u */
begin
    for every pair of v and i $(0 \leq v \leq 2^n - 1, 0 \leq i \leq n - 1)$

$$V_i^u[v] := \begin{cases} val^u & \text{if } u = v \\ default & \text{if } u \neq v; \end{cases}$$

    for $round := 0$ **to** $2n - 1$ **do**
        begin
            for every pair of v and i $(0 \leq v \leq 2^n - 1, 0 \leq i \leq n - 1)$ satisfying
            $i = R(round, u \oplus v)$, $\bar{V}_i^u[v] \neq default$, and $\mathbf{w}(u^{[round]_n} \oplus v) \leq 2$
                send $(v, \bar{V}_i^u[v])$ to $u^{[round]_n}$;   /* delivery */
            for every (v, X) $(0 \leq v \leq 2^n - 1)$ from $u^{[round]_n}$
                if $\bar{V}_{[round]_n}^u[v] = default$ **then** $V_{[round]_n}^u[v] := X$ /* reception */
        end;
    for every v such that $\mathbf{w}(v \oplus u) = 1$ (i.e., every neighbor of u)
        $V^u[v] :=$ majority voting of $\{\bar{V}_0^u[v], \bar{V}_1^u[v], ..., \bar{V}_{n-1}^u[v]\}$
end.

We cannot complete broadcasting by just $BC1$-n-$cube$-$neighbor$. The purpose of the scheme is to make each node collect messages hold in its adjacent nodes through n disjoint paths. It is used in scheme $BC2$-n-$cube$. The scheme $BC1$-n-$cube$-$neighbor$ is not as efficient as $BC1$-n-$cube$, since some transmissions through a node do not contribute to the majority voting at the node but they contribute indirectly to the majority voting of its adjacent nodes. For example, in the 4-$cube$, node $u = 0000$ sends its value to node $v = 1000$ by $BC1$-4-$cube$-$neighbor$ through 4 disjoint paths; (1) $0000 \rightarrow 0001 \rightarrow 1001 \rightarrow 1000$, (2) $0000 \rightarrow 0010 \rightarrow 1010 \rightarrow 1000$, (3) $0000 \rightarrow 0100 \rightarrow 1100 \rightarrow 1000$, (4)

$0000 \to 1000$. In the process nodes 1100, 1010 and 1001 receive the messages from u, but the messages are not used for the majority voting at these nodes. The messages sent through these 4 paths are used for the majority voting at v. However, in the process of broadcasting by $BC1$-n-$cube$ all the messages transmitted to a node contribute finally to the majority voting at the node.

We are now ready to describe our second broadcasting scheme called $BC2$-n-$cube$. It is executed at every node u of the n-$cube$ concurrently.

$BC2$-n-$cube$ /* a description of the execution at node u */
begin
  /* the set consisting of $(u, val(u))$ is initially set into val^u */
  $val^u := \{(u, val(u))\}$;
  for $r := 0$ **to** $n - 1$ **do**
    begin
      $val_r^u := \{(v, X) \mid (v, X) \in val^u$ and $\mathbf{w}(u \oplus v) = r\}$;
      $BC1$-n-$cube$-$neighbor(val_r^u)$;
      $val^u := val^u \bigcup \left(\bigcup_{i=0}^{n-1} V^u[u^i] \right)$
    end
end.

The key point of difference between $BC1$-n-$cube$ and $BC2$-n-$cube$ is that for $BC1$-n-$cube$ the majority voting is made at the end of the broadcasting while for $BC2$-n-$cube$ the majority voting is made whenever a message is disseminated one step away (see Fig. 4). When all nodes are healthy, the advantage is exploited by $BC2$-n-$cube$.

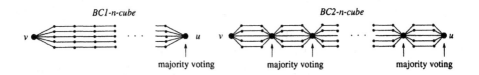

Fig. 4. The principles of $BC1$-n-$cube$ and $BC2$-n-$cube$ are different.

Theorem 9. *If for every pair of adjacent nodes u and v, at most $\lfloor \frac{n-1}{2} \rfloor$ paths among $P_0(u, v), P_1(u, v), ..., P_{n-1}(u, v)$ are faulty, then for every node w the final value of val^w is $\{(y, val(y)) \mid 0 \le y \le 2^n - 1\}$ when $BC2$-n-$cube$ is executed at every node concurrently.*

Proof. By $BC1$-n-$cube$-$neighbor$, for every adjacent pair of nodes u and v, the value at u is sent to v through paths $P_0(u, v), \cdots, P_{n-1}(u, v)$. For every i and y $(0 \le i \le n-1, 0 \le y \le 2^n - 1)$, in the ith loop of the **for** statement of $BC2$-n-$cube$, by calling $BC1$-n-$cube$-$neighbor$ the value $(y, val(y))$ can reach every node

w within Hamming distance $i + 1$ from y. Hence, if for every pair of adjacent nodes u and v, at most $\lfloor \frac{n-1}{2} \rfloor$ paths among $P_0(u, v), P_1(u, v), ..., P_{n-1}(u, v)$ are faulty, then the final value of val^w is $\{(y, val(y)) \mid 0 \leq y \leq 2^n - 1\}$. □

Theorem 10. *If there are at most f faulty links of Byzantine type randomly distributed in the n-cube, then broadcasting by BC2-n-cube succeeds with probability higher than $1 - n \left(\frac{48f}{2^{n-1}n} \right)^{\lceil n/2 \rceil}$*

Proof. We denote a configuration of the n-cube with f-faulty links by $\bar{d}_n^f$. We use the following notations:

$\bar{D}_n^f = \{\bar{d}_n^f \mid \bar{d}_n^f$ is a configuration of the n-cube with f faulty links $\}$,

$\bar{D}_n^f(u, v) = \{\bar{d}_n^f \mid u$ and v are a pair of adjacent nodes, and there are at least $\lceil n/2 \rceil$ faulty paths among $P_0(u, v), P_1(u, v), ..., P_{n-1}(u, v)$ in $\bar{d}_n^f\}$,

$\bar{D}_n^f(fail) = \{\bar{d}_n^f \mid$ there are a pair of faultless adjacent nodes u and v such that at least $\lceil n/2 \rceil$ paths among $P_0(u, v), P_1(u, v), ..., P_{n-1}(u, v)$ are faulty in $\bar{d}_n^f\}$.

Apparently $|\bar{D}_n^f| = \binom{2^{n-1}n}{f}$ and $\bar{D}_n^f(\text{fail}) \subseteq \cup_{\mathbf{W}(u \oplus v)=1} \bar{D}_n^f(u, v)$. Thus,

$$|\bar{D}_n^f(fail)| \leq \sum_{\mathbf{W}(u \oplus v)=1} |\bar{D}_n^f(u, v)|.$$

For any pair of adjacent nodes u and v, there are at most 3 links on each path $P_i(u, v)$ $(0 \leq i \leq n - 1)$. Hence, by simply counting, we have $|\bar{D}_n^f(u, v)| < 3^{\lceil n/2 \rceil} \binom{n}{\lceil n/2 \rceil} \binom{2^{n-1}n - \lceil n/2 \rceil}{f - \lceil n/2 \rceil}$.

Suppose that there are at most f faulty links randomly distributed in the n-cube. Then we have the following inequalities:

$$\frac{|\bar{D}_n^f(fail)|}{|\bar{D}_n^f|} \leq \frac{\sum_{\mathbf{W}(u \oplus v)=1} |\bar{D}_n^f(u, v)|}{|\bar{D}_n^f|} < \frac{2^n \cdot 3^{\lceil n/2 \rceil} n \binom{n}{\lceil n/2 \rceil} \binom{2^{n-1}n - \lceil n/2 \rceil}{f - \lceil n/2 \rceil}}{\binom{2^{n-1}n}{f}}$$

$$= 2^n \cdot 3^{\lceil n/2 \rceil} n \binom{n}{\lceil n/2 \rceil} \cdot \frac{f!}{2^{n-1}n(2^{n-1}n - 1) \cdots (2^{n-1}n + 1 - f)} \cdot$$
$$\frac{(2^{n-1}n - \lceil n/2 \rceil)(2^{n-1}n - \lceil n/2 \rceil - 1) \cdots (2^{n-1}n + 1 - f)}{(f - \lceil n/2 \rceil)!}$$

$$= 2^n \cdot 3^{\lceil n/2 \rceil} n \binom{n}{\lceil n/2 \rceil} \cdot \frac{f(f - 1) \cdots (f + 1 - \lceil n/2 \rceil)}{2^{n-1}n(2^{n-1}n - 1) \cdots (2^{n-1}n + 1 - \lceil n/2 \rceil)}$$

$$< 2^n \cdot 3^{\lceil n/2 \rceil} n \binom{n}{\lceil n/2 \rceil} \left(\frac{f}{2^{n-1}n} \right)^{\lceil n/2 \rceil}$$

$$< 2^n \cdot 3^{\lceil n/2 \rceil} \cdot 4^{\lceil n/2 \rceil} n \cdot \left(\frac{f}{2^{n-1}n} \right)^{\lceil n/2 \rceil} \leq n \left(\frac{48f}{2^{n-1}n} \right)^{\lceil n/2 \rceil}$$

Hence, broadcasting by $BC2\text{-}n\text{-}cube$ succeeds with a probability higher than $1 - n\left(\frac{48f}{2^{n-1}n}\right)^{\lceil n/2 \rceil}$. □

The next corollary is immediate from Theorem 10.

Corollary 11. *If at most $\frac{2^{n-1}n}{48k}$ faulty links of Byzantine type are randomly distributed in the n-cube, then broadcasting by $BC2\text{-}n\text{-}cube$ succeeds with a probability higher than $1 - k^{-\lceil n/2 \rceil}n$.*

Broadcasting by $BC2\text{-}n\text{-}cube$ succeeds with a high probability if the number of faulty links is not more than a fixed fraction of the total number of links in the n-cube. However, $BC2\text{-}n\text{-}cube$ is not as efficient as $BC1\text{-}n\text{-}cube$. It needs $2n^2$ rounds to complete broadcasting, and its broadcasting process contains excessive message transmissions. If the size of the initial value at any node is $O(1)$, the communication complexity of $BC2\text{-}n\text{-}cube$ is $O(2^{2n}n^3)$. For every node u, at the beginning of the rth loop of the **for** statement in the main procedure, val_r^u is set to be $\{(v, X) \mid (v, X) \in val^u \text{ and } \mathbf{w}(u \oplus v) = r\}$. Then every node u obtains messages from its neighbors by calling $BC1\text{-}n\text{-}cube\text{-}neighbor(val_r^u)$. Hence, during the rth loop of the main procedure, each node u obtains $val_r^{u^0}, val_r^{u^1}, \cdots, val_r^{u^{n-1}}$. Since $val_r^{u^i}$ is set to be $\{(v, val(v)) \mid \mathbf{w}(u^i \oplus v) = r\}$ in the rth loop, each $val_r^{u^i}$ contains $\binom{n}{r}$ items in the form $(v, val(v))$. Among them only $\binom{n-1}{r}$ items contain values of nodes at distance $r + 1$ from u, and other $\binom{n}{r} - \binom{n-1}{r}$ items contain values of nodes at distance $r - 1$ from u. Hence, during the rth loop of the main procedure, only $(n - r)/n$ of all messages $(v, val(v))$'s in $val_r^{u^i}$ $(0 \le i \le n - 1)$ are useful in u. The other messages have already arrived at u in an earlier loop (i.e., in the $r - 2$th loop).

We can eliminate this type of inefficiency by additional control on the message delivery mechanism in $BC1\text{-}n\text{-}cube\text{-}neighbor$. By the additional control we can avoid excessive message transmissions in the broadcasting process. For $V \subseteq \{(v, val(v)) \mid v \in n\text{-}cube\}$, we denote $\{(v, val(v)) \in V \mid \mathbf{w}(u \oplus v) = r + 1\}$ by $\langle r, u \rangle \cdot V$. The following is an improved version from $BC1\text{-}n\text{-}cube\text{-}neighbor$.

$BC2\text{-}n\text{-}cube\text{-}neighbor(val^u)$ /* a description of the execution at node u */
begin
    for every pair of v and i $(0 \le v \le 2^n - 1, 0 \le i \le n - 1)$

$$V_i^u[v] := \begin{cases} val^u & \text{if } u = v \\ default & \text{if } u \ne v; \end{cases}$$

    for $round := 0$ **to** $2n - 1$ **do**
        begin
            for every pair of v and i $(0 \le v \le 2^n - 1, 0 \le i \le n - 1)$ satisfying
            $i = R(round, u \oplus v)$ and $\bar{V}_i^u[v] \ne default$ **do begin** /*delivery */
                if $\mathbf{w}(u^{[round]_n} \oplus v) = 1$ **then**
                    send $(v, \bar{V}_i^u[v])$ to $u^{[round]_n}$;
                if $\mathbf{w}(u^{[round]_n} \oplus v) = 2$ **then**
                    send $(v, \langle r, v^{[round]_n} \rangle \cdot \bar{V}_i^u[v])$ to $u^{[round]_n}$ **end**;

for every (v, X) $(0 \leq v \leq 2^n - 1)$ from $u^{[round]_n}$

    if $\bar{V}^u_{[round]_n}[v] = default$ **then** $V^u_{[round]_n}[v] := X$ /* reception */

end;

for every v such that $\mathbf{w}(u \oplus v) = 1$ (i.e., every neighbor of u)

    $V^u[v] :=$ majority voting of $\{\bar{V}^u_0[v], \bar{V}^u_1[v], \cdots, \bar{V}^u_{n-1}[v]\}$

end.

If we replace $BC1$-n-$cube$-$neighbor$ by $BC2$-n-$cube$-$neighbor$ in $BC2$-n-$cube$, then we obtain an improved version of $BC2$-n-$cube$. The fault tolerance of the improved $BC2$-n-$cube$ is exactly the same as the original $BC2$-n-$cube$, but the broadcasting process by the improved one contains less excessive transmissions than the original one. There is another factor of inefficiency of $BC2$-n-$cube$. In the rth loop of the main procedure of $BC2$-n-$cube$, $(v, val(v))$ reaches u if $\mathbf{w}(u \oplus v) = r + 1$. In other words, at the beginning of the rth loop $(v, val(v))$ is contained in $r + 1$ packages among $val_r^{u^0}, val_r^{u^1}, \cdots, val_r^{u^{n-1}}$, and these packages are sent to u in the rth loop. These overlapped messages are a burden of communication cost in the broadcasting process by $BC2$-n-$cube$. This type of excessive messages can also be reduced by adding further delivery control in $BC2$-n-$cube$-$neighbor$ so that for each pair of distinct i and j, $\bar{V}^u[u^i]$ and $\bar{V}^u[u^j]$ do not have common information. Such modification on $BC2$-n-$cube$-$neighbor$ reduces the communication complexity of $BC2$-n-$cube$ to the same order of the communication complexity of $BC1$-n-$cube$, but its control mechanism becomes more complicated.

5 Concluding Remarks

We presented two broadcasting schemes on the n-cube, $BC1$-n-$cube$ and $BC2$-n-$cube$. The former scheme can tolerate Byzantine faults with a high probability if the number of faulty nodes is not more than a constant fraction of $2^n/n$. The latter scheme can tolerate Byzantine faults at only links with a high probability if the number of faulty links is not more than a constant fraction of $2^{n-1}n$. We cannot find so far any efficient broadcasting scheme that can tolerate $c \cdot 2^n$ randomly distributed faulty nodes of Byzantine type with a high probability for some nonzero constant c independent of n. Finding such a scheme is an interesting problem for further study. It is not difficult to see that both the lower bounds given in Theorem 5 and Theorem 10 on the reliability of the schemes are not tight. We conjecture that the coefficients 64 and 48 of $1 - \left(\frac{64nf}{2^{n-1}}\right)^{\lceil n/2 \rceil}$ and $1 - n\left(\frac{48f}{2^{n-1}n}\right)^{\lceil n/2 \rceil}$ in these theorems, respectively can be largely reduced. This problem is also interesting for further investigation.

References

1. Alam, M. S. and Melhem, R. G., " How to use an incomplete hypercube for fault tolerance," *Proc. of the 1st European Workshop on Hypercubes and Distributed*

Computers, pp.329-341, 1989.

2. Alon, N., Barak, A. and Mauber, U., "On disseminating information reliably without broadcasting," *the 7th International Conference on Distributed Computing Systems*, pp.74-81, 1987.

3. Bienstock, D., "Broadcasting with random faults," *Discret Applied Mathematics*, Vol. 20, pp.1-7, 1988.

4. Blough, D. B. and Pelc, A., "Optimal communication in networks with randomly distributed faults" *Networks*, vol. 23, pp.691-701, 1993.

5. Carlsson, S., Igarashi, Y., Kanai, K., Lingas, A., Miura, K. and Petersson, O., "Information disseminating schemes for fault tolerance in hypercubes," *IEICE Trans. on Fundamentals of Electronics, Communications and Computer Sciences*, E75-A, pp.255-260, 1992.

6. Chlebus, B. S., Diks, K. and Pelc, A., "Optimal broadcasting in faulty hypercubes," *Proc. of the 21st International Symposium on Fault-Tolerant Computing*, pp.266-273, 1991.

7. Chlebus, B. S., Diks, K and Pelc, A., "Sparse networks supporting efficient reliable broadcasting," *Proc. of ICALP'93*, LNCS, Vol. 710, Springer-Verlag, pp.388-397, 1993.

8. Fraigniaud, P. and Peyrat, C., "Broadcasting in a hypercubes when some calls fail," *Information Processing Letters*, Vol.39, pp.115-119, 1991.

9. Gargano, L. and Vaccaro, U., "Minimum time broadcasting network tolerating a logarithmic number of faults," *SIAM J. of Discrete Math.*, Vol.5, pp.178-198, 1992.

10. Gargano, L., Rescigno, A. and Vaccaro, U., "Fault tolerant hypercubes broadcasting via information dispersal," *Networks*, Vol.23, pp.271-282, 1993.

11. Hastad, J., Leighton, T. and Newman, M., "Fast computation using faulty hypercubes," *Proc. of the 21st ACM Symposium on Theory of Computing*, pp.251-263, 1989.

12. Hedetniemi, S. M., Hedetniemi, S. T. and Liestman, A. L., "A survey of gossiping and broadcasting in communication networks," *Networks*, Vol.18, pp.1249-1268, 1988.

13. Igarashi, Y., Kanai, K, Miura, K. and Osawa, S., "Optimal schemes for disseminating information and their fault tolerance," *IEICE Trans. on Information and Systems*, pp.22-29, 1992.

14. Pelc, A., "Reliable communication in networks with Byzantine link failures," *Networks*, pp.441-459, 1992.

15. Ramanathan, P. and Shin, K. G., "Reliable broadcasting in hypercube multiprocessors," *IEEE Trans. on Computers*, Vol.37, pp.1654-1657, 1988.

On the Number of Authenticated Rounds in Byzantine Agreement

Malte Borcherding

Institute of Computer Design and Fault Tolerance
University of Karlsruhe
76128 Karlsruhe
malte.borcherding@informatik.uni-karlsruhe.de

Abstract. Byzantine Agreement requires a set of nodes in a distributed system to agree on the message of a sender despite the presence of arbitrarily faulty nodes. Solutions for this problem are generally divided into two classes: authenticated protocols and non-authenticated protocols. In the former class, all messages are (digitally) signed and can be assigned to their respective signers, while in the latter no messages are signed. Authenticated protocols can tolerate an arbitrary number of faults, while non-authenticated protocols require more than two thirds of the nodes to be correct.

In this paper, we investigate the fault tolerance of protocols that require signatures in a certain number of communication rounds only. We show that a protocol that is to tolerate one half of the nodes as faulty needs only few authenticated rounds (logarithmic in the number of nodes), while tolerating more faults requires about two authenticated rounds per additional faulty node.

Keywords: Byzantine Agreement, fault tolerance, distributed systems, authentication

1 Introduction

The problem of Byzantine Agreement (introduced in [LSP82]) arises when a set of nodes in a distributed system need to have a consistent view of messages uttered by one of them, despite the presence of arbitrarily faulty nodes. The problem is defined as follows: One of the nodes is distinguished as *sender* who attempts to transmit a value to the rest of the nodes. A protocol solving Byzantine Agreement must fulfill the following conditions:

- Each correct node eventually decides for a value.
- All correct nodes decide for the same value.
- If the sender is correct, all nodes decide for the value of the sender.

Protocols solving Byzantine Agreement are generally divided into two classes: authenticated protocols and non-authenticated protocols. In authenticated protocols, all messages are signed digitally in a way that the signatures cannot be forged and a signed message can be unambiguously assigned to its signer. This mechanism allows a node to prove to others that it has received a certain message from a certain node. Authenticated protocols can tolerate an arbitrary number of faulty nodes. In non-authenticated protocols, no messages are signed. These protocols require more than two thirds of the participating nodes to be correct ([LSP82]).

While signatures allow for very fault-tolerant protocols, signing messages is a time-consuming action; typical durations for an RSA signature with a 512 bit key are 50 to 100 ms. Hence, it is useful to investigate the fault tolerance properties of authenticated protocols which require as few signatures as possible.

In this paper, we have a closer look at protocols where the nodes have to sign messages in certain communication rounds only. One implication of our results is that tolerating one half of the nodes as faulty requires a number of authenticated rounds logarithmic in the number of nodes, while tolerating more faults needs about two authenticated rounds per additional faulty node.

2 Preliminaries

2.1 System Model

Our world consists of n nodes connected by a complete network. We assume that t of the nodes may behave in an arbitrary manner, while $c = n - t$ behave correctly. The nodes operate at a known minimal speed, and messages are transmitted reliably in bounded time. The receiver of a message can identify its immediate sender, and we assume the existence of an authentic signature scheme such that a signature cannot be forged and each node knows whom a signature on a message belongs to.

During a protocol execution, the nodes communicate in successive *rounds*. In each round, a node may send messages to other nodes, receive the messages sent to it in the current round and perform some local computation. m of the rounds $(s_1, \ldots, s_m)$ are distinguished as *authenticated rounds*. In these rounds, all messages are to be signed.

2.2 The *EIG* Protocol

Our examinations are based on the Exponential Information Gathering *(EIG)* protocol which was introduced by Bar-Noy *et al.* [BNDDS87], based on the protocol in [LSP82]. In this protocol, the sender starts by sending its value to all other nodes. In the following t rounds, each node forwards all messages it received in the previous round to the other nodes[1].

During protocol execution, each node maintains an *EIG* tree which contains the received information in a structured manner. Such a tree has $t + 1$ levels, one level per communication round. The root has $n - 1$ children, and in each of the

---

[1] In [FL82, DS83] it is shown that $t + 1$ rounds are necessary and sufficient to reach agreement with or without authentication.

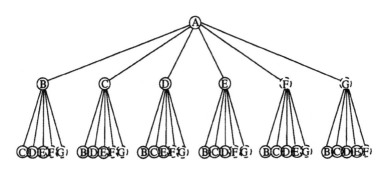

Fig. 1. An *EIG* tree

following levels, the vertices have one child less than those of the previous level. Hence, on level t, each vertex has $n - t$ children which constitute the leaves of the tree (we consider the root level as level 1).

The vertices have labels which are assigned in the following manner: The root is labeled with the sender's name. In the following levels, the children of a vertex are labeled with the names of the nodes not yet on the path from the root. We identify a vertex in the tree by the labels of the vertices from the root to the vertex in question. Figure 1 depicts such a tree for $n = 7$. In this example, we assume that F and G are faulty; we have marked the respective vertices with dashed circles.

In the first round of the protocol, each node stores the value received from the sender in the root of its *EIG* tree. In the following rounds, each correct node broadcasts the contents of the level of its tree most recently filled in, and fills the next level with the messages it receives. If a node X receives a message from Y claiming that it has stored v in vertex $ABCDE$, X stores v in vertex $ABCDEY$ of its *EIG* tree. Hence, a value in vertex $ABCDEY$ is interpreted as "Y said E said ... B said A said v". If a node failed to send a value, a default value is stored. A level that corresponds to an authenticated round will be called *authenticated level*.

After a node has completed its tree (after round $t+1$), it applies the following *resolve function* to the vertices: The resolved value for a vertex its stored value iff it is a leaf, and the majority of the resolved values of its children otherwise. If there is no such majority, a default value is used. The value a node eventually uses as decision value is the resolved value of the root.

We require that a vertex on an authenticated level is to be resolved using values signed by the node corresponding to the label of the vertex. Messages without these signatures are not considered in the resolve function (they are not even assigned a default value). If all children of a vertex are removed due to missing correct signatures, it is treated as a leaf and resolved to its own value. A vertex is called *common*, if its resolved value is the same in the trees of all correct nodes for all possible executions of the protocol.

2.3 Compact *EIG* trees

For our purposes, we use *binary* trees as a more compact representation of the original *EIG* trees. These binary trees only contain information about *numbers* of correct and faulty children of a vertex, rather than actually listing all children.

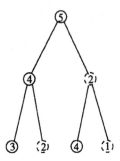

Fig. 2. Compact representation of an *EIG* tree

Figure 2 depicts the compact representation of the tree of Figure 1. It is interpreted as follows: We assume that five nodes, including the sender, are correct, and two nodes are faulty. Hence, the message of the sender is echoed by four correct nodes and two faulty nodes. The echoes of the correct nodes are echoed by three correct and two faulty nodes, those of the faulty nodes are echoed by four correct and one faulty node(s). So a vertex in the compact tree represents a class of vertices of the original *EIG* tree. Each class comprises vertices with the same sequence of faulty/correct vertices on the path to the root. We call a vertex in the compact tree *common*, if all the represented vertices of the *EIG* tree are common; a vertex in the compact tree is said to be *resolved to its stored value* if this is true for all represented vertices of the original *EIG* tree. A vertex is called *correct*, if it represents messages of correct nodes, and *faulty* otherwise. When referring to the levels of such a tree, we will start with level 1 for the root level. Levels corresponding to authenticated rounds will be called *authenticated levels*.

Each vertex in a tree is identified by a binary string. It represents the (unique) path from the root to the vertex, including both ends: If we pass a correct vertex, we append a "1" to the string, and a "0" otherwise. So, in our example, the vertex with the value 2 on the third level is identified by the string "110". We will write x^k for a succession of k equal characters x. As variables for strings, we will use σ and τ.

On these strings, we define functions $|\sigma|_0$, $|\sigma|_1$, and $|\sigma|$, giving the numbers of 0s and 1s in the string, and its length, respectively. Furthermore, we have a function $v(\sigma)$ which gives the label of the vertex. It is defined as follows:

$$v(\sigma 0) = \max(0, t - |\sigma|_0)$$
$$v(\sigma 1) = \max(0, c - |\sigma|_1).$$

Lemma 1. *The vertices of a binary EIG tree have the following properties:*

(a) $v(\sigma 0) = 0 \Leftrightarrow \sigma = 0^t$
(b) $v(\sigma 1^k 1) > v(\sigma 1^k 0) \Rightarrow \forall \tau, |\tau| \le k : v(\sigma \tau 1) > v(\sigma \tau 0)$

Proof. Immediate from the definition of $v(\cdot)$. □

3 Correctness Requirements

If we express the conditions for Byzantine agreement in terms of resolving vertices of the *EIG* trees, we have the following requirements: The *EIG* protocol is correct iff

- In every execution of the protocol, the root is common and
- if the sender is correct, every node resolves the root of its tree to the value it received in the first round.

The condition that the nodes eventually decide for a value is fulfilled trivially by the limited height of the trees and the bounded time for the execution of a round.

3.1 General Vertices

In order to find out the exact requirements for a correct protocol execution, we first look at the requirements for a general vertex to be common. We have to distinguish the cases of a correct and a faulty vertex:

Lemma 2. *A correct vertex σ is common and resolved to its stored value iff at least one of the following conditions is true:*

(a) $v(\sigma) = 0$
(b) $|\sigma| = t + 1$
(c) σ *is on an authenticated level*
(d) $v(\sigma 1) > v(\sigma 0)$ *and $\sigma 1$ is common and resolved to its stored value*

Proof. "$\Rightarrow$": by inspection of a vertex σ for which (a)–(d) do not hold. "$\Leftarrow$": (a), (b) and (d) are trivial. (c): A correct node will only utter consistent messages with the correct signature. Hence, all nodes store the same signed value in their trees and resolve this vertex to the stored value. □

Recursive application of Lemma 2, making use of Lemma 1 (b), yields

Corollary 3. *Let σ be a correct vertex on a non-authenticated level $l < t+1$, and let s be the next authenticated level after l or, if that does not exist, $t + 1$. Then σ is common and resolved to its stored value iff $v(\sigma 1^{s-l-1} 1) > v(\sigma 1^{s-l-1} 0)$.*

We state the requirements for faulty vertices to be common only for the special case 0^l, because this will be the only case we need.

Lemma 4. *A faulty vertex 0^l is common iff at least one of the following conditions is true:*

(a) 0^l0 and 0^l1 are common, and if l is an authenticated level, then $v(0^l1) > 0$
(b) $v(0^l) = 0$

Proof. "$\Rightarrow$": Suppose 0^l0 or 0^l1 is not common, and $v(0^l) > 0$. Then the resolved values for 0^l can differ, since the resolved values for the common children can be chosen by the faulty nodes in a way that the non-common vertex is crucial for the majority. If l is an authenticated level and $v(0^l1) = 0$, then 0^l0 could be resolved to unsigned values. Hence, 0^l would be resolved to its stored value, which is not common. If $v(0^l1) > 0$ and a correct node has stored a signed value, all other nodes will consider this signed value when resolving 0^l. "$\Leftarrow$": simple.$\square$

Taking into account Lemma 1 (a), we get the following

Corollary 5. 0^{t+1} *is common.*

The next lemma shows that the requirements for a correct vertex to be common are the same as for that vertex to be common *and* to be resolved to its stored value.

Lemma 6. *A correct common vertex σ is resolved to its stored value.*

Proof. Suppose it is resolved to a different value. Then σ has to be on a non-authenticated level $l \neq t + 1$ (Lemma 2). Let s be as in Corollary 3. From Corollary 3 follows that $v(\sigma 1^{s-l-1}1) \leq v(\sigma 1^{s-l-1}0)$ and $\sigma 1^{s-l-1}0$ is common. With an argument similar to the proof of Lemma 4, the latter condition would require that $v(\sigma 1^{s-l-1}0^{t+1-|\sigma|-(s-l-1)}) > 0$ which contradicts Lemma 1 (a). $\square$

This Lemma allows us to use Corollary 3 on Lemma 4 (a). Taking into account Lemma 1 (b) and Lemma 2, we can transcribe Lemma 4 as follows:

Corollary 7. *Let 0^l be a faulty vertex on level $l < t + 1$, and let s be the next authenticated level after l or, if that does not exist, $t + 1$. Then 0^l is common iff one of the following conditions is true:*

(a) $s > l + 1$ and $v(0^l1^{s-l-1}1) > v(0^l1^{l-s-1}0)$ and 0^s is common.
(b) $s = l + 1$ and 0^s is common.

Note that the condition $v(0^l1^{s-l-1}1) > v(0^l1^{l-s-1}0)$ in Corollary 7 (a) is equivalent to $c \geq t - 2l + s$ (from the definition of $v(\cdot)$). We will use this observation in the next section.

3.2 Requirements for a Common Root

Having stated the requirements for general vertices, we can easily deduce the requirements for a common root. We use Lemma 2 and Corollary 3 for a correct sender, and Corollary 5 and Corollary 7 for a faulty sender.

Figure 3 gives an overview of the requirements in the two cases of a correct and a faulty sender. We have sketched two binary *EIG* trees; the ">"-sign under two vertices means that the label of the left vertex must be greater than that of the right vertex. The horizontal lines denote authenticated levels.

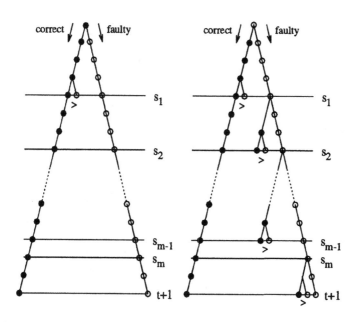

Fig. 3. Requirements for a correct protocol execution. Left: sender correct, right: sender faulty

Sender correct: Requirement RC distinguishes whether or not the root is on an authenticated level:

$$RC = \begin{cases} c \geq 1 & \text{if } s_1 = 1 \\ (c \geq t + s_1) & \text{else} \end{cases}$$

Sender faulty: Here, we present the requirements in a recursive manner. A requirement RF_i deals with the tree above and including level s_i. For the root to be common with a faulty sender, RF_0 must hold:

$$RF_0 = \begin{cases} RF_1 & \text{if } s_1 \leq 2 \\ (c \geq t + s_1 - 2) \wedge RF_1 & \text{else} \end{cases}$$

$$RF_i \ (i = 1, \ldots, m-1) = \begin{cases} RF_{i+1} & \text{if } s_{i+1} = s_i + 1 \\ (c \geq t - 2s_i + s_{i+1}) \wedge RF_{i+1} & \text{else} \end{cases}$$

$$RF_m = \begin{cases} c \geq 1 & \text{if } s_m = t \\ (c \geq 2t - 2s_m + 1) & \text{else} \end{cases}$$

Since the requirement $(c \geq t + s_1 - 2)$ from RF_0 is subsumed by $(c \geq t + s_1)$ from RC, it will not show up in the following considerations.

Our aim is to determine authenticated rounds s_i $(i = 1, \ldots, m)$ such that RC and RF_0 are fulfilled for a minimal c. We will call these s_i an *optimal distribution of authenticated rounds*. It will be convenient to consider only distributions which have no successive authenticated rounds except at the beginning of the protocol. The next theorem shows that there is an optimal distribution with this property.

Theorem 8. *There is an optimal distribution of authenticated rounds for which the following holds: If there is a succession of more than one authenticated rounds, it starts at round 1.*

Proof. We show that a distribution with a succession of authenticated rounds not starting at 1 can be optimized. From the assumption, there is a k such that $s_k > 1$, $s_{k+1} = s_k + 1$, and $s_{k-1} < s_k - 1$ (for convenience, we define s_0 to be 0). From RF_{k-1} (or RC, if $k = 1$), we require $c \geq t - 2s_{k-1} + s_k$. Now consider another distribution with the same authenticated rounds s_i', except that $s_k' = s_k - 1$. Now RF_{k-1} becomes $c \geq t - 2s_{k-1}' + s_k' = t - 2s_{k-1} + s_k - 1$. Furthermore, RF_k changes from no requirement to $c \geq t - 2s_k' + s_{k+1}' = t - s_k + 3$. Both requirements allow for a smaller c than the original RF_{k-1} (note that $s_{k-1} \leq s_k - 2$). $\square$

So, for a distribution with a block of b successive rounds at the beginning, we have the following inequations (note that we defined s_0 to be 0):

$$\begin{aligned} c \geq t - 2s_{i-1} + s_i &\Leftrightarrow 2s_{i-1} - s_i + c \geq t \ (i = b+1, \ldots, m) \\ c \geq 2t - 2s_m + 1 &\Leftrightarrow 2s_m + c \geq 2t + 1 \end{aligned} \tag{1}$$

Since we are interested in a minimal c, we replace the "$\geq$"s by "$=$"s and solve the resulting system of equations, including the information that the first b rounds are authenticated (hence $s_i = i$ for $i = 1, \ldots, b$). These $m + 1$ linear equations can be written as an $(m + 1) \times (m + 2)$-matrix. Columns 1 to m represent the coefficients of s_1 to s_m, the $m+1$st column represents the coefficient of c, and the last column represents the constants on the right hand side of the equations:

$$
\begin{pmatrix}
1 & 0 & \cdots\cdots\cdots\cdots\cdots & 0 & 1 \\
0 & 1 & 0 \cdots\cdots\cdots\cdots 0 & & 2 \\
\vdots & \ddots & \ddots & \vdots & \vdots \\
0 & \cdots & 0\ 1\ 0\cdots\cdots\cdots 0 & & b \\
0 & \cdots & 0\ 2-1\ 0\ \cdots\ 0\,1 & & t \\
\vdots & & \ddots\ \ddots\ \ddots\ \ddots & \vdots & \vdots \\
0 & \cdots\cdots\cdots & 0\ 2-1\ \ 0\,1 & & t \\
0 & \cdots\cdots\cdots & 0\ 2-1\,1 & & t \\
0 & \cdots\cdots\cdots\cdots & 0\ \ 2\,1\,2t+1 & &
\end{pmatrix}
\tag{2}
$$

Eliminating the elements below the diagonal yields matrix (3):

$$
\begin{pmatrix}
1 & 0 \cdots\cdots\cdots\cdots\cdots & 0 & 1 \\
0 & 1\ 0\cdots\cdots\cdots\cdots\cdots & 0 & 2 \\
\vdots & \ddots\ \ddots\ \ddots & \vdots & \vdots \\
0 & \cdots\ 0\ 1\ 0\cdots\cdots\cdots & 0 & b \\
0 & \cdots\cdots 0-1\ 0\cdots\cdots\ 0 & 1 & t-2b \\
0 & \cdots\cdots\cdots 0-1\ 0\cdots\ 0 & 3 & 3t-4b \\
\vdots & \ddots\ \ddots\ \ddots\ \vdots & \vdots & \vdots \\
0 & \cdots\cdots\cdots\cdots 0-1\ 0 & 2^{m-b-1}-1 & (2^{m-b-1}-1)t-2^{m-b-1}b \\
0 & \cdots\cdots\cdots\cdots 0-1\ 2^{m-b}-1 & & (2^{m-b}-1)t-2^{m-b}b \\
0 & \cdots\cdots\cdots\cdots\cdots 0\ 2^{m-b+1}-1 & & 2^{m-b+1}(t-b)+1
\end{pmatrix}
\tag{3}
$$

Finally, we multiply rows $b+1$ to $m+1$ by -1 and eliminate the elements above the diagonal:

$$
\begin{pmatrix}
1 & 0 \cdots\cdots\cdots\cdots 0 & 1 \\
0 & 1\ 0\cdots\cdots\cdots 0 & 2 \\
\vdots & \ddots\ \ddots\ \ddots & \vdots \\
\vdots & 0\ 1\ 0\cdots\cdots 0 & b \\
\vdots & 0\ 1\ 0\cdots\cdots 0 & 1\cdot\frac{t+1-2^{m-b+1}b}{2^{m-b+1}-1}+2b \\
\vdots & 0\ 1\ 0\cdots 0 & 3\cdot\frac{t+1-2^{m-b+1}b}{2^{m-b+1}-1}+4b \\
\vdots & \ddots\ \ddots\ \ddots\ \vdots & \vdots \\
0 & \cdots\cdots\cdots 0\ \ 1\,0\ (2^{m-b}-1)\cdot\frac{t+1-2^{m-b+1}b}{2^{m-b+1}-1}+2^{m-b}b \\
0 & \cdots\cdots\cdots\cdots 0\,1\ \frac{2^{m-b+1}(t-b)+1}{2^{m-b+1}-1}
\end{pmatrix}
\tag{4}
$$

From matrix (4), we can deduce the following (real-valued) solutions for the s_i and c:

$$
s_i = \begin{cases}
i & ,\ 1 \le i \le b \ \text{(only for } b > 0) \\
2^{i-b}b + (2^{i-b}-1)\cdot\frac{t+1-2^{m-b+1}b}{2^{m-b+1}-1} & ,\ b < i \le m
\end{cases}
$$

$$c \geq \frac{2^{m-b+1}(t-b)+1}{2^{m-b+1}-1} \tag{5}$$

Replacing c by $n-t$ and solving (5) for m yields (note that (5) can only be fulfilled for $n+b-2t > 0$):

$$m \geq log_2(n+1-t) - log_2(n+b-2t) + b - 1. \tag{6}$$

Since we are interested in as few authenticated rounds as possible, we try to minimize m. To find a b such that m is minimal, we solve $m'(b) = 0$ which leads to:

$$1 - \frac{1}{(n+b-2t) \cdot \ln(2)} = 0.$$

Since $m''(b) = \frac{1}{(n+b-2t)^2 \cdot \ln(2)} > 0$ and $b \geq 0$, we have the minimal m at:

$$b = \max(0, 2t - n + \underbrace{\frac{1}{\ln(2)}}_{\approx 1.44}).$$

Together with (6), this yields:

$$m \geq \begin{cases} log_2(\frac{n+1-t}{n-2t}) - 1 & \text{if } 2t \leq n - \frac{1}{\ln(2)} \\ log_2(n+1-t) + 2t - n + \underbrace{\frac{1}{\ln(2)} + log_2(\ln(2)) - 1}_{\approx -0.08} & \text{else} \end{cases}$$

To summarize these results and to show how they are cast into integer values, we state the following main theorem:

Theorem 9. *Let n be a number of nodes with at most t of them being faulty. Then there is a protocol solving Byzantine Agreement with m authenticated rounds, where*

$$m = \begin{cases} \lceil log_2(\frac{n+1-t}{n-2t}) - 1 \rceil & \text{if } 2t \leq n - 2 \\ \lceil log_2(n+1-t) + 2t - n \rceil & \text{else} \end{cases}$$

With $b = \max(0, 2t - n + 2)$, the authenticated rounds s_i $(i = 1, \ldots, m)$ are:

$$s_i = \begin{cases} i & \text{for } 1 \leq i \leq b \text{ (only if } b > 0) \\ \lceil 2^{i-b}b + (2^{i-b} - 1) \cdot \frac{t+1-2^{m-b+1}b}{2^{m-b+1}-1} \rceil & \text{for } b < i \leq m \end{cases}$$

Proof. We have to show that the constraints remain satisfied if we use rounded m and s_i. To round up m is valid, since that lowers the right hand side of (5) and hence allows for even lower c. That rounding up the s_i is valid follows from c and t being integer values: The constraints in (1) are of the form $c \geq t - 2s_{i-1} + s_i$. It follows that $c \geq t - 2\lceil s_{i-1} \rceil + s_i$. Since all summands except s_i are integers, we can safely deduce that $c \geq t - 2\lceil s_{i-1} \rceil + \lceil s_i \rceil$.

Finally, we show that the selected b is an optimal integer: Since there is only one optimal real-valued b, the optimal integer-valued b must be one of $\max(0, 2t - n + 1.5 \pm 0.5)$. Since both bs yield the same values for m, we can choose the higher one. $\square$

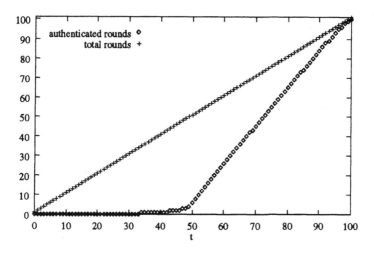

Fig. 4. Minimal authenticated rounds for a given t with $n = 100$.

Example. Figure 4 depicts the required number of authenticated rounds with respect to the number of tolerated faults for $n = 100$. As expected, a maximum of $(n-1)/3 = 33$ faulty nodes can be tolerated without authentication. To tolerate $n/2 = 50$ faulty nodes, only $\lceil \log_2(n/2 + 1) \rceil = \lceil \log_2(51) \rceil = 6$ authenticated rounds are necessary, namely rounds $1, 2, 4, 7, 14,$ and 26.

4 Conclusion

We have investigated the fault-tolerance properties of Byzantine Agreement protocols when messages are signed in certain rounds only. We have shown how to determine the authenticated rounds, depending on the number of faulty nodes to be tolerated. One implication of the results is that $n/2$ faulty nodes can be tolerated with as few as $\lceil \log_2(n/2 + 1) \rceil$ authenticated rounds, while each additional faulty node requires about two more authenticated rounds.

Further work in this area is necessary. We have not yet shown that the results in this paper are optimal, since other, maybe better-suited, resolve functions in the EIG protocol are possible. Furthermore, the EIG protocol is far from efficient with respect to the number of messages, and does not employ early-stopping mechanisms in case less than t of the nodes actually behave faulty.

References

[BNDDS87] Amotz Bar-Noy, Danny Dolev, Cynthia Dwork, and H. Raymond Strong. Shifting gears: Changing algorithms on the fly to expedite Byzantine Agreement. In *Proceedings of the 6th ACM Symposium on Principles of Distributed Computing (PODC)*, pages 42–51, Vancouver, 1987.

[DS83]   Danny Dolev and Raymond Strong. Authenticated algorithms for Byzantine Agreement. *SIAM Journal of Computing*, 12(5):656–666, November 1983.

[FL82]   Michael J. Fischer and Nancy A. Lynch. A lower bound for the time to assure interactive consistency. *Information Processing Letters*, 14(4):183–186, 1982.

[LSP82]   Leslie Lamport, Robert Shostak, and Marshall Pease. The Byzantine Generals problem. *ACM Transactions on Programming Languages and Systems*, 4(3):382–401, 1982.

Total Ordering Algorithms for Asynchronous Byzantine Systems *

Louise E. Moser and P. M. Melliar-Smith

Department of Electrical and Computer Engineering
University of California, Santa Barbara, CA 93106

Abstract. The Total algorithms are used within asynchronous fault-tolerant distributed systems to derive a total order on messages from a causal order provided by an underlying multicast communication protocol. We present several Total algorithms that represent varying compromises between latency to message ordering and resilience to crash and Byzantine faults. The algorithms use a multi-stage voting strategy to achieve agreement on the total order, and depend on the random structure of the causal order to achieve probabilistic termination.

1 Introduction

Within asynchronous fault-tolerant distributed systems, the Total algorithms are used to derive a total order on messages from a causal order provided by an underlying multicast communication protocol. A causal order on messages is valuable because it precludes anomalies in the processing of messages. A total order is even more valuable because it simplifies the programming of the application. In particular, when data are replicated to provide fault tolerance, a total order on messages ensures that updates are processed in the same order at every replica within the system.

The objective of the Total algorithms is to place a total order on messages in such a way that non-faulty processes construct identical total orders and non-Byzantine processes construct consistent total orders. The algorithms are executed independently and concurrently by each of the processes. They derive the total order on messages directly from the causal order without the need to communicate additional messages.

An important aspect of the Total algorithms is that they are truly fault tolerant in that they continue to order messages even though some processes are faulty, provided that the resilience requirements are met. Most other ordered multicast protocols become blocked temporarily if even one process fails, and depend on a low-level failure detector [7, 8] to unblock the protocol by detecting a failed process and reconfiguring the system to exclude it. During such reconfiguration, no new messages can be ordered. The Total algorithms do not incur this hiatus following a failure.

---

* This work was supported by the Advanced Research Project Agency, Grant No. N00174-93-K-0097.

In [14] we presented two Total algorithms for deriving a total order on messages from a causal order that tolerate crash faults. The simpler of those two algorithms tolerates k crash faults in an n-process system, where $n > 3k$, while a slightly more complex version tolerates k crash faults in an n-process system, where $n > 2k$.

Here we extend those Total algorithms to handle Byzantine faults and, thus, obtain mixed failure mode algorithms that share resilience between crash and Byzantine faults. These Total algorithms depend on digital signatures to confirm the source of a message and to detect messages that purport to be the same message but that have different contents and/or acknowledgments. Digital signatures are computationally expensive, but are not as expensive as alternative authentication protocols that require additional rounds of message exchange.

The first Total algorithm presented here tolerates k_f crash faults and k_b Byzantine faults in an n-process system, where $n > 3k_f + 5k_b$. The second algorithm, which is slightly more complex, requires n processes, where $n > 2k_f + 5k_b$, to tolerate k_f crash faults and k_b Byzantine faults. We also present two algorithms that effectively convert Byzantine faults into crash faults and allow the non-Byzantine Total algorithms to be used. For these algorithms, the coefficient of k_b in the above resilience constraints is reduced from 5 to 3, the known lower bound. Thus, the third algorithm requires n processes, where $n > 3k_f + 3k_b$, while the fourth algorithm requires n processes, where $n > 2k_f + 3k_b$.

The primary application for these algorithms is not, as might be expected, safety-critical systems; such systems invariably use synchronous Byzantine algorithms. Rather, these algorithms are valuable for secure asynchronous distributed systems, where they protect the fault-tolerant group communication protocol against Trojan horse attacks.

2 Related Work

The problem of maintaining a consistent total order on messages in an asynchronous fault-tolerant distributed system is related to the problem of maintaining consensus in such systems. In [9] Fischer, Lynch and Paterson demonstrated that consensus is impossible to achieve in an asynchronous distributed system, even for crash faults and just one faulty process.

Pease, Shostak and Lamport [15] introduced a model for the Byzantine Generals and Consensus problems in which the behavior of a faulty process can be Byzantine, *i.e.* completely arbitrary even to the extent of being malicious. For this Byzantine model, they showed that, in a synchronous system, these problems admit solutions if and only if $n > 3k$, where n is the number of processes and k is the number of Byzantine processes in the system.

Consensus decisions are sometimes required in isolation, but are often used in sequence as for total ordering of messages. Bar-Noy, Deng, Garay, and Kameda [1] investigated algorithms that yield a sequence of consensus decisions for synchronous systems with Byzantine processes. Bar-Noy and Dolev [2] gave an algorithm for solving many instances of the consensus problem in a pipeline fashion using single-bit messages. Gopal and Toueg [11] presented an algorithm for the sequence agreement problem for both synchronous and asynchronous systems, with Byzantine faults in the synchronous case, but restricted to omission faults in the asynchronous case.

To address consensus in asynchronous systems, several researchers [4, 16] developed randomized protocols in which processes take random steps by tossing coins and which terminate with probability 1. Using a different approach, Bracha [6] developed probabilistic consensus protocols for asynchronous systems that depend on the communication medium for randomization. Our algorithms fall within this latter category.

The Total algorithms presented in this paper are multiple failure mode algorithms that can withstand combinations of crash and Byzantine faults. Multiple failure mode algorithms have previously been considered by other researchers for synchronous systems [10, 13, 18]. Two of the Total algorithms essentially convert Byzantine faults into crash faults. This technique has also been employed by other researchers [3, 5, 17, 19].

Efficient algorithms for sequences of consensus decisions, or for total ordering, in asynchronous Byzantine distributed systems have yet to appear in the literature.

3 The Model

We consider an asynchronous fault-tolerant distributed system with n processes, where $n \geq 2$, in which processes communicate by broadcasting messages. The system is asynchronous in that no bound can be placed on the time required for a computation or for communication of a message. The system is subject to process and communication faults. Messages may be lost or arbitrarily delayed.

A *faulty* process may either have crashed or be Byzantine. A *crashed* process makes no further broadcasts after a certain point in its execution of the algorithm. A *Byzantine* process cannot be relied upon to execute the algorithms correctly, and may exhibit arbitrary behavior.

The causal order used by the Total algorithms can be derived from the acknowledgments of messages typically used in broadcast communication. In the presence of Byzantine faults, this causal order need not comply with the usual requirements for a partial order but, when restricted to the messages from non-Byzantine processes, is the causal order defined by Lamport [12]. We define a *Byzantine causal order* in terms of the follows relation on messages:

- Each message m_1 follows itself.
- If m_2 follows m_1 and m_3 follows m_2, then m_3 follows m_1.
- If m_1 and m_2 are both originated by the same non-Byzantine process, then either m_1 follows m_2 or m_2 follows m_1.
- If m_1 and m_2 are distinct messages, m_2 follows m_1, and m_2 is originated by a non-Byzantine process, then m_1 does not follow m_2.
- If m_1 and m_2 are distinct messages, m_1 follows m_2, m_2 follows m_1, and m_3 is originated by a non-Byzantine process, then m_3 does not follow m_1 or m_2.

- If m_1 does not follow m_2, m_2 does not follow m_1, and m_1, m_2 and m_3 are all originated by the same Byzantine process, then (1) m_3 follows m_1 if and only if m_3 follows m_2, and (2) m_1 follows m_3 if and only if m_2 follows m_3.

These properties place constraints on the senders of the messages regarding the messages they can acknowledge. Note that the third and fourth properties above guarantee that messages originated by a non-Byzantine process are totally ordered. Sequence numbers in messages can be used to implement this.

We assume that a digital signature mechanism in the underlying multicast communication protocol prevents a Byzantine process from originating a message purporting its origin to be some other process. Furthermore, we assume that, if a Byzantine process sends different messages to different destinations, purporting that they are the same message, then the digital signature mechanism enables the destinations to recognize the messages as distinct and to process them as distinct messages.

A Byzantine process can disrupt the causal order in one of two ways. First, it can originate a message that occurs within a (non-trivial) cycle. A non-Byzantine process cannot originate such a message, because a message m from a non-Byzantine process cannot acknowledge a message that acknowledges m. A non-Byzantine process executing one of the Total algorithms does not advance a message to the total order unless it has already advanced all of the messages that precede that message in the causal order. Thus, it does not advance to the total order any message that occurs within a cycle, or any message that follows a message within a cycle. If a Byzantine process ever creates a cycle, then none of its subsequent messages will be ordered. When a cycle is detected, the Byzantine processes whose messages occur in the cycle are removed from the configuration. The non-faulty processes execute a cycle detection algorithm in their processing of messages and acknowledgments.

A Byzantine process can disrupt the causal order in a second way. It can originate two or more concurrent messages with the same process identifier and sequence number, but different contents and/or acknowledgments, neither of which follows the other and possibly each of which purports to follow different messages. We call such messages *mutants* of each other. Although mutant messages are allowed to occur, the voting strategy of the first and second Total algorithms is resilient to them, and the voting strategy of the third and fourth Total algorithms allows only one of the messages that are mutants to vote. For all four Total algorithms, only the first of the messages that are mutants is ordered. When a second mutant message is about to be ordered, the Byzantine process that originated that message is removed from the configuration.

We assume that the underlying multicast communication protocol satisfies the following liveness and fairness properties. The liveness requirement is that, if a non-faulty process originates a message, then it constructs a causal order containing that message. The fairness assumption is that there is no bias in the selection of processes to broadcast or in the choice of processes to receive messages. Of course, the fairness assumption restricts the class of asynchronous behaviors being considered and, thus, the causal orders input to the Total algorithms.

4 The Total Algorithms

The Total algorithms operate within the context of a distributed system in which processes communicate by broadcasting messages. The objective of the algorithms is to place a total order on messages in such a way that non-faulty processes construct identical total orders and non-Byzantine processes construct consistent total orders. The algorithms are executed independently and concurrently by each process.

The input to the Total algorithms is a Byzantine causal order of messages; the output of the algorithms is a total order of messages. The algorithms accept the causal order, and extend the total order, incrementally. Only information derived from the causal order is used to construct the total order; no other communication between processes is necessary. As each process receives messages, it constructs the causal order and executes one of the Total algorithms, which results in its total order being extended by zero or more messages. The algorithms ensure that non-faulty processes determine identical total orders on messages even though they have different prefixes of the Byzantine causal order, due to delayed or lost messages.

A *candidate message* is a message in the Byzantine causal order that is not yet in the total order and that only follows messages already in the total order. A set of candidate messages is called a *candidate set*. As a process advances a candidate set from the causal order to the total order, the candidate set for the next extension is automatically determined. Even though two different processes have different candidate sets to consider for a given extension of the total order, the algorithms ensure that the two processes decide to extend the total order with the same candidate set.

A decision by a process to advance a candidate set to the total order is determined by the votes of the messages in the causal order. These votes are not contained explicitly in the messages, but are deduced from the causal relationships between messages. Each process makes its own decisions independently of the other processes.

Messages in the causal order provide votes on the candidate sets. Each candidate set is voted on separately and independently. Voting on a candidate set takes place in a sequence of stages, and each candidate set has its own sequence of stages. Voting proceeds sequentially through the stages for a particular candidate set, but concurrently on all of the candidate sets, since it cannot be predetermined which message is able to vote for which candidate set at which stage.

At stage 0, the vote of a message on a candidate set depends on which candidate messages that message follows. At stage i, $i > 0$, the vote of a message on a candidate set depends on whether that message follows "enough" (defined below) messages that vote at stage $i - 1$. A message may not vote at a stage at which a previous message from its source votes. A message may be unable to vote at any stage on a candidate set if the Voting Criteria (given below) are not satisfied. Conversely, a message may be able to vote at several stages if the Voting Criteria are satisfied for each of those stages and no previous message from its source has voted at those stages. Since each message follows itself in the causal order, a message can include itself in the number of messages required to vote.

5 The $3k_f + 5k_b$ Algorithm

For this algorithm, we assume that the resiliency constraint between the number n of processes, the maximum number k_f of crashed processes, and the maximum number k_b of Byzantine processes is $3k_f + 5k_b < n$. The algorithm is defined by the Eligibility, Voting, and Decision Criteria given below; these criteria determine whether the candidate set S is chosen for inclusion in the total order at the lth extension. The number of votes required for a further vote and the number of votes required for a decision are at least N_v and N_d, where

$$N_v = (n - k_f - k_b)/2 \quad \text{and} \quad N_d = (n + k_f + 3k_b + 1)/2$$

The Eligibility Criteria

At stage i, where $i \geq 0$,

- A non-Byzantine process determines that a message m is eligible to vote on S if
  - The process has obtained a prefix of the causal order that contains m.
  - No previous message in that prefix from the source of m can vote on S for the lth extension of the total order at stage i.

The Voting Criteria

At stage 0,

- A message votes for S if that message follows every message in S and it follows no other candidate message. (A candidate message votes for the set containing only itself.)
- A message votes against S if that message follows any candidate message other than those in S. (A candidate message votes against all sets of which it is not a member.)

At stage i, where $i > 0$,

- A message votes for S if
  - It follows at least two messages that vote on S at stage $i - 1$,
  - It follows at least N_v messages that vote for S at stage $i - 1$, and
  - It follows fewer messages that vote against S than vote for S at stage $i - 1$.

- A message votes against S if
  - It follows at least two messages that vote on S at stage $i - 1$,
  - It follows at least N_v messages that vote against S at stage $i - 1$, and
  - It does not vote for S at stage i.

The Decision Criteria

At stage i, where $i \geq 0$,

- A non-Byzantine process decides for S if
  - It determines that at least N_d messages vote for S at stage i, and
  - For each proper subset of S, it decides against that proper subset.
- A non-Byzantine process decides against S if
  - It determines that at least N_d messages vote against S at stage i, or
  - It decides for a proper subset of S.

6 The $2k_f + 5k_b$ Algorithm

For this algorithm, we assume that the relationship between the number n of processes, the maximum number k_f of crashed processes, and the maximum number k_b of Byzantine processes is $2k_f + 5k_b < n$. The algorithm is defined by the Eligibility, Voting, Proposing, and Deciding Criteria given below; these criteria determine whether the candidate set S is chosen for inclusion in the total order. The Proposing Criteria provide a tentative decision, which becomes the actual decision when enough processes are aware of the proposal. The Decision Criteria ensure that, after a process failure, the remaining processes cannot be unaware of the decision. The number of messages related to an indifferent proposal, the number of votes required for a proposal, and the number of proposals required for a decision must be at least N_v, N_p, and N_d, respectively, where

$$N_v = n - k_f - k_b, \quad N_p = (n + k_b + 1)/2, \quad \text{and} \quad N_d = k_f + 2k_b + 1$$

The Eligibility Criteria

At stage i, where $i \geq 0$,

- A non-Byzantine process determines that a message m is eligible to vote on S if
  - The process has obtained a prefix of the causal order that contains m.
  - No previous message in that prefix from the source of m has voted on S for the lth extension of the total order at stage i.
- A non-Byzantine process determines that a message m is eligible to propose on S for the lth extension of the total order if
  - The process has obtained a prefix of the causal order that contains m.
  - No previous message in that prefix from the source of m has proposed on S for the lth extension of the total order at stage i.

The Voting Criteria

At stage 0,

- A message votes for S if it follows every message in S and it follows no other candidate message. (A candidate message votes for the set containing only itself.)

- A message votes against S if it follows a candidate message not in S. (A candidate message votes against all sets of which it is not a member.)

At stage i, where $i > 0$,

- A message votes for S if

  • It follows a message that proposes for S at stage $i - 1$.

- A message votes against S if

  • It follows a message that proposes against S at stage $i - 1$,

  or

  • It follows no message that proposes for or against S at stage $i - 1$, and
  • It follows at least N_v messages that propose indifferent to S at stage $i - 1$.

The Proposing Criteria

At stage i, where $i \geq 0$,

- A message proposes for S if

  • It follows at least N_p messages that vote for S at stage i.

- A message proposes against S if

  • It follows at least N_p messages that vote against S at stage i.

- A message proposes indifferent to S if

  • It does not propose for or against S at stage i, and
  • It follows at least N_v messages that vote on S at stage i.

The Decision Criteria

At stage i, where $i \geq 0$,

- A non-Byzantine process decides for S if

  • It determines that at least N_d messages propose for S at stage i, and
  • For each proper subset of S, it decides against that proper subset.

- A non-Byzantine process decides against S if

  • It determines that at least N_d messages propose against S at stage i, or
  • It decides for a proper subset of S.

7 The $3k_f + 3k_b$ Algorithm

For this algorithm, we assume that the relationship between the number n of processes, the maximum number k_f of crashed processes, and the maximum number k_b of Byzantine processes is $3k_f + 3k_b < n$. The Eligibility Criteria now contain a third requirement. This requirement essentially converts the messages from Byzantine processes into messages from crashed processes. With this requirement, mutants that are not followed by N_e messages never become eligible to vote. The number of messages required for eligibility to vote, the number of votes required for a further vote, and the number of votes required for a decision, are at least N_e, N_v, and N_d, where

$$N_e = (n + k_b + 1)/2, \quad N_v = (n - k_f - k_b)/2, \quad \text{and} \quad N_d = (n + k_f + k_b + 1)/2$$

The Eligibility Criteria

At stage i, where $i \geq 0$,

- A non-Byzantine process determines that a message m is eligible to vote on S if
  - The process has obtained a prefix of the causal order that contains m.
  - No previous message in that prefix from the source of m can vote on S for the lth extension of the total order at stage i.
  - The prefix contains at least N_e messages from distinct processes, each of which follows m and does not follow a mutant of m.

The rest of the algorithm is the same as the $3k_f + 5k_b$ algorithm with k_b set to 0 and k_f set to $k_f + k_b$ and by removing the qualifier non-Byzantine.

8 The $2k_f + 3k_b$ Algorithm

For this algorithm, we assume that the relationship between the number n of processes, the maximum number k_f of crashed processes, and the maximum number k_b of Byzantine processes is $2k_f + 3k_b < n$. The Eligibility Criteria for voting are the same as those for the $3k_f + 3k_b$ algorithm. In addition, we have Eligibility Criteria for proposing that are identical to those for voting. The number of messages required for eligibility to vote, the number of messages related to an indifferent proposal, the number of votes required for a proposal, and the number of proposals required for a decision are at least N_e, N_v, N_p, and N_d, where

$$N_e = (n + k_b + 1)/2, \quad N_v = n - k_f - k_b, \quad N_p = (n+1)/2, \quad \text{and} \quad N_d = k_f + k_b + 1$$

The Eligibility Criteria

At stage i, where $i \geq 0$,

- A non-Byzantine process determines that a message m is eligible to vote (propose) on S if
  - The process has obtained a prefix of the causal order that contains m.
  - No previous message in that prefix from the source of m can vote (propose) on S for the lth extension of the total order at stage i.
  - The prefix contains at least N_e messages from distinct processes, each of which follows m and does not follow a mutant of m.

The rest of the algorithm is the same as the $2k_f + 5k_b$ algorithm with k_b set to 0 and k_f set to $k_f + k_b$ and by removing the qualifier non-Byzantine.

9 Correctness of the Algorithms

The correctness of the algorithms depends on demonstrating the following theorems. The first and second theorems establish the partial correctness of the algorithms. The first theorem requires that no two non-Byzantine processes disagree on the lth message to be placed in the total order. The Byzantine processes are not required, and cannot be required, to reach such agreement. The second theorem requires that the total order is consistent with the Byzantine causal order.

Theorem 1. If m and m' are distinct messages and a non-Byzantine process p determines that m is the lth message of the total order, then no non-Byzantine process q determines that m' is the lth message.

Theorem 2. If m and m' are distinct messages and a non-Byzantine process determines that m' follows m in the total order, then m does not follow m' in the causal order

The third and fourth theorems establish probabilistic termination. The third theorem requires that the non-faulty processes reach agreement on the lth message in the total order eventually with probability 1. In an asynchronous fault-tolerant distributed system, termination is precluded by the impossibility result [9]. The fourth theorem requires that, for each message from a non-faulty process, the non-faulty processes place that message in the total order eventually with probability 1.

Theorem 3. The probability that a non-faulty process p places an lth message in the total order increases asymptotically to unity as the number of steps taken by p tends to infinity.

Theorem 4. For each message m broadcast by a non-faulty process q, the probability that a non-faulty process p places m in the total order increases asymptotically to unity as the number of steps taken by p tends to infinity.

The proofs of these four theorems depend on a number of intermediate lemmas, which are omitted due to lack of space. The inequalities used in proving these lemmas and theorems are summarized below.

The proofs for the $3k_f + 5k_b$ algorithm, where $N_v = (n - k_f - k_b)/2$ and $N_d = (n + k_f + 3k_b + 1)/2$, depend on the following properties and inequalities:

- Votes and decisions do not conflict: $N_v + N_d > n + k_b$
- Decisions do not conflict: $N_d + N_d > n + k_b$
- Stages of voting advance: $N_v + N_v - 1 \leq n - k_f - k_b$
- Decisions are feasible: $N_d \leq n - k_f - k_b$.

Similarly, the proofs for the $2k_f + 5k_b$ algorithm, where $N_v = n - k_f - k_b$, $N_p = (n + k_b + 1)/2$, and $N_d = k_f + 2k_b + 1$, depend on the following properties and inequalities:

- Votes and decisions do not conflict: $N_v + N_d > n + k_b$
- Proposals do not conflict: $N_p + N_p > n + k_b$
- Decisions do not conflict: $N_d > k_f + k_b$
- Stages of voting and proposing advance: $N_v \leq n - k_f - k_b$
- Proposals for or against are feasible: $N_p \leq n - k_f - k_b$ and $N_p \leq N_v - k_b$
- Decisions are feasible: $N_d \leq n - k_f - k_b$.

The proofs for the $3k_f + 3k_b$ algorithm, where $N_e = (n + k_b + 1)/2$, $N_v = (n - k_f - k_b)/2$, and $N_d = (n + k_f + k_b + 1)/2$, and for the $2k_f + 3k_b$ algorithm, where $N_e = (n + k_b + 1)/2$, $N_v = n - k_f - k_b$, $N_p = (n+1)/2$, and $N_d = k_f + k_b + 1$, depend in addition on the following properties and inequalities:

- Noneligibility of a mutant of an eligible message to vote (propose): $N_e + N_e - k_b > n$
- Eligibility of a message with no mutant to vote (propose): $N_e \leq n - k_f - k_b$.

Probabilistic termination depends on showing that, as a non-faulty process continues to take steps, the probability that its causal order prefix contains a pattern, which enables it to decide, asymptotically approaches unity. The details of the proof are omitted due to lack of space.

10 Performance Trade-Offs of the Algorithms

To evaluate the performance of the Total algorithms, we determine the mean latency from transmission to delivery into the total order, defined here as the number of messages that must be transmitted to obtain the required number of messages from distinct processes to order the message.

In this analysis, we assume that the causal order is such that each of the processes has an equal opportunity to transmit, that each message is received by all processes, and that there are no faulty processes.

In a system of n processes, the mean number of messages required to obtain messages from m distinct processes is

$$L(n, m) = \sum_{i=0}^{m-1} \sum_{j=0}^{\infty} \left(\frac{i}{n}\right)^j = \sum_{i=0}^{m-1} \frac{n}{n - i}$$

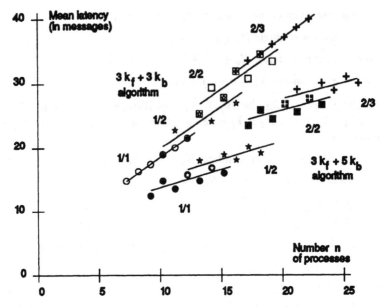

Fig. 1.: The mean latency, measured in messages, from transmission to delivery into the total order for various numbers of processes and for various levels of resilience. The black symbols show the latency for the $3k_f + 5k_b$ algorithm, and the open symbols show the latency for the $3k_f + 3k_b$ algorithm. The resilience is indicated as the number of Byzantine faults followed by the number of crash faults.

The latency for the $3k_f + 5k_b$ algorithm is $L(n, N_d)$, while the latency for the $2k_f + 5k_b$ algorithm is $L(n, N_p) + L(n, N_d) - 1$, since a message counts as both the last required message to vote and also as the first message to propose. Similarly, the latency for the $3k_f + 3k_b$ algorithm is $L(n, N_e) + L(n, N_d) - 1$ and for the $2k_f + 3k_b$ algorithm is $L(n, N_e) + L(n, N_p) + L(n, N_d) - 2$.

Figure 1 shows the mean latency for both the $3k_f + 5k_b$ algorithm and the $3k_f + 3k_b$ algorithm. The improved resilience to Byzantine faults provided by the $3k_f + 3k_b$ algorithm, compared to the $3k_f + 5k_b$ algorithm, has a price. The extra eligibility requirement of the $3k_f + 5k_b$ algorithm increases the latency. In the figure, the solid symbols present the latency for the $3k_f + 5k_b$ algorithm without the extra eligibility requirement and the open symbols present the latency for the $3k_f + 5k_b$ algorithm with the extra requirement. The latencies are shown for various numbers of processes and for various levels of resilience. In representing the resilience, the number of Byzantine faults is indicated before the number of crash faults; thus, 2/3 represents a system resilient to two Byzantine faults and three crash faults. Note that in some cases the latencies are the same for two different resiliencies and the symbols are overlaid. An odd-even effect is clearly visible in the results.

In general, the mean latency is lower without the extra eligibility requirement, but the extra requirement may allow a higher level of resilience for the

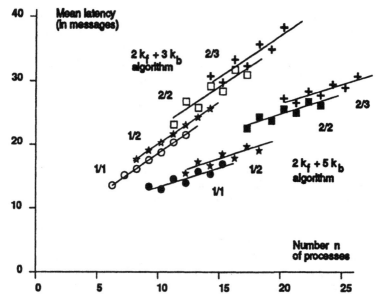

Fig. 2.: The mean latency, measured in messages, from transmission to delivery into the total order for various number of processes and for various levels of resilience. The black symbols show the latency for the $2k_f+5k_b$ algorithm, and the open symbols show the latency for the $2k_f+3k_b$ algorithm. The resilience is indicated as the number of Byzantine faults followed by the number of crash faults.

same number of processes. For example, in a 12-process system resilient to one Byzantine and two crash faults, the mean latency is 15.24 messages without the extra eligibility requirement and 21.08 messages with it. In a 10-process system, however, resilience to one Byzantine and two crash faults is impossible without the extra eligibility requirement, but can be achieved with it.

Figure 2 shows the corresponding mean latencies for the $2k_f+5k_b$ algorithm and for the $2k_f+3k_b$ algorithm, with a similar difference between the algorithms. When comparing Figure 1 with Figure 2, however, it is much less clear whether the $3k_f+5k_b$ algorithm has a lower latency than the $2k_f+5k_b$ algorithm, or whether the $3k_f+3k_b$ has a lower latency than the $2k_f+3k_b$ algorithm. For some numbers of processes and levels of resilience one has a lower latency, and for other numbers of processes and levels of resilience the other has a lower latency.

11 Conclusion

We have described four algorithms for deriving a total order from a causal order on messages in the presence of Byzantine faults. These algorithms employ a multi-stage voting strategy. Two of the algorithms include messages from Byzantine processes in the voting. These two algorithms exhibit excellent latency, but do not achieve the maximum possible resilience. The other two algorithms use an extra eligibility requirement for voting that essentially converts Byzantine faults into crash faults and increases the resilience of the algorithms. However, converting Byzantine faults into crash faults seldom yields the most efficient algorithms. We continue to seek a voting strategy that tolerates the theoretical maximum number of Byzantine faults and that matches the lower latency of our most efficient algorithms.

References

1. A. Bar-Noy, X. Deng, J. A. Garay and T. Kameda, "Optimal amortized distributed consensus," *Proceedings of the 5th International Workshop on Distributed Algorithms*, Delphi, Greece, October 1991, Lecture Notes in Computer Science 579, Springer Verlag, pp. 95-107.
2. A. Bar-Noy and D. Dolev, "Consensus algorithms with one-bit messages," *Distributed Computing*, vol. 4, 1991, pp. 105-110.
3. R. Bazzi and G. Neiger, "Simulating crash failures with many faulty processors," *Proceedings of the 6th International Workshop on Distributed Algorithms*, Haifa, Israel, November 1992, Lecture Notes in Computer Science 647, Springer Verlag, pp. 166-184.
4. M. Ben-Or, "Another advantage of free choice: Completely asynchronous agreement protocols," *Proceedings of the 2nd Annual ACM Symposium on Principles of Distributed Computing*, Montreal, Quebec, Cananda, August 1983, pp. 27-30.
5. G. Bracha, "Asynchronous Byzantine agreement protocols," *Information and Computation*, vol. 75, no. 2, November 1987, pp. 130-143.
6. G. Bracha and S. Toueg, "Asynchronous consensus and broadcast protocols," *Journal of the ACM*, vol. 31, no. 4, October 1985, pp. 824-840.
7. T. D. Chandra and S. Toueg, "Unreliable failure detectors for asynchronous systems," *Proceedings of the Tenth ACM Symposium on Principles of Distributed Computing*, Montreal, Quebec, Canada, August 1991, pp. 325-340.
8. T. D. Chandra, V. Hadzilacos and S. Toueg, "The weakest failure detector for solving consensus," *Proceedings of the Eleventh ACM Symposium on Principles of Distributed Computing*, Vancouver, British Columbia, Canada, August 1992, pp. 147-158.
9. M. J. Fischer, N. A. Lynch and M. S. Paterson, "Impossibility of distributed consensus with one faulty process," *Journal of the ACM*, vol. 32, no. 2, April 1985, pp. 374-382.
10. J. A. Garay and K. J. Perry, "A continuum of failure models for distributed computing," *Proceedings of the 6th International Workshop on Distributed Algorithms*, Haifa, Israel, November 1992, Lecture Notes in Computer Science 647, Springer Verlag, pp. 153-165.
11. A. Gopal and S. Toueg, "Reliable broadcast in synchronous and asynchronous environments," *Proceedings of the 3rd International Workshop on Distributed Algorithms*, Nice, France, September 1989, Lecture Notes in Computer Science 392, Springer Verlag, pp. 110-23.
12. L. Lamport, "Time, clocks, and the ordering of events in a distributed system," *Communications of the ACM*, vol. 21, no. 7, July 1978, pp. 558-565.
13. F. J. Meyer and D. K. Pradhan, "Consensus with dual failure modes," *IEEE Transactions on Parallel and Distributed Systems*, vol. 2, no. 2, April 1991, pp. 214-222.

14. L. E. Moser, P. M. Melliar-Smith and V. Agrawala, "Asynchronous fault-tolerant total ordering algorithms," *SIAM Journal of Computing*, vol. 22, no. 4, August 1993, pp. 727-750.

15. M. Pease, R. E. Shostak and L. Lamport, "Reaching agreement in the presence of faults," *Journal of the ACM*, vol. 27, no. 2, 1980, pp. 228-234.

16. M. O. Rabin, "Randomized Byzantine generals," *Proceedings of the 24th Annual Symposium on Foundations of Computer Science*, Tucson, AZ, November 1983, pp. 403-409.

17. F. B. Schneider, "Byzantine generals in action: Implementing fail-stop processors," *ACM Transactions on Computer Systems*, vol. 2, no. 2, May 1984, pp. 145-154.

18. P. Thambidurai and Y. K. Park, "Interactive consistency with multiple failure modes," *Proceedings of the 7th IEEE Symposium on Reliable Distributed Systems*, Columbus, OH, October 1988, pp. 93-100.

19. S. Toueg, K. J. Perry and T. K. Srikanth, "Fast distributed agreement," *SIAM Journal of Computing*, vol. 16, no. 3, June 1987, pp. 445-457.

A Uniform Self-Stabilizing Minimum Diameter Spanning Tree Algorithm

(Extended Abstract)

Franck Butelle[1], Christian Lavault[2] and Marc Bui[1]

[1] Université de Paris 10 – 200, Avenue de la République 92000 Nanterre. France.
[2] LIPN, CNRS URA 1507 (Institut *Galilée*),
Université Paris-Nord, Avenue J-B. Clément 93430 Villetaneuse. France.

Abstract. We present a uniform self-stabilizing algorithm, which solves the problem of distributively finding a minimum diameter spanning tree of an arbitrary positively real-weighted graph. Our algorithm consists in two stages of stabilizing protocols. The first stage is a uniform randomized stabilizing *unique naming* protocol, and the second stage is a stabilizing *MDST* protocol, designed as a *fair composition* of Merlin–Segall's stabilizing protocol and a distributed deterministic stabilizing protocol solving the (MDST) problem. The resulting randomized distributed algorithm presented herein is a composition of the two stages; it stabilizes in $O(n\Delta + \mathcal{D}^2 + n\log\log n)$ expected time, and uses $O(n^2 \log n + n\log W)$ memory bits (where n is the order of the graph, Δ is the maximum degree of the network, $\mathcal{D}$ is the diameter in terms of hops, and W is the largest edge weight). To our knowledge, our protocol is the very first distributed algorithm for the (MDST) problem. Moreover, it is fault-tolerant and works for any anonymous arbitrary network.

1 Introduction

Many computer communication networks require nodes to broadcast information to other nodes for network control purposes, which is done efficiently by sending messages over a spanning tree of the network. Now optimizing the worst-case message propagation delays over a spanning tree is naturally achieved by reducing the diameter to a minimum (see Sect. 1.2); especially in high-speed networks (where the message delay is essentially equal to the propagation delay). However, when communication links fail or come up, and when processors crash or recover, the spanning tree may have to be rebuilt. When the network's topology changes, one option is to perform anew the entire computation of a spanning tree with a minimum diameter from scratch. We thus examine the question of designing an efficient fault-tolerant algorithm, which constructs and dynamically maintains a minimum diameter spanning tree of any anonymous network. The type of fault-tolerance we require is so-called *"self-stabilization"*, which means, informally, that an algorithm must be able to "recover" from any arbitrary transient fault. In this setting, we exhibit a self-stabilizing minimum diameter spanning tree. Our algorithm is asynchronous, it works for arbitrary anonymous network topologies (unique processes ID's are not required), it is uniform (i.e., every process executes the same code; processes are identical), symmetry is broken by randomization, and it stabilizes in efficient time complexity.

1.1 Self-Stabilizing Protocols

We consider distributed networks where processes and links from time to time can crash and recover (i.e., dynamic networks), where additionally, when processes recover, their memory may be recovered within an arbitrary inconsistent state (to model arbitrary memory corruption). Despite these faults, we wish the network to be able to maintain and/or to be able to rebuilt certain information about itself (e.g., in this particular case, maintaining a minimum diameter spanning tree). When the intermediate period between one recovery and the next failure is long enough, the system stabilizes.

The theoretical formulation of this model was put forth in the seminal paper of Dijkstra [11], who, roughly, defined the network to be "self-stabilizing" if starting from an *arbitrary* initial state (i.e., after any sequence of faults), the network after some bounded period of time (denoted as *stabilization time*) exhibits a behaviour as if it was started from a good initial state (i.e, stabilizes to a "good" behaviour, or "legitimate state"). Notice that such a formulation does not allow any faults during computation, but allows an arbitrary initial state. Thus, if new faults occur during computation, it is modelled in a self-stabilizing formulation as if it were a *new initial state* from which the network again must recover. In summary, self-stabilization is a very strong fault-tolerance property which covers many types of faults and provides a uniform approach to the design of a variety of fault-tolerant algorithms.

1.2 The Minimum Diameter Spanning Tree (MDST) Problem

The use of a control structure spanning the entire network is a fundamental issue in distributed systems and interconnection networks. Since *all* distributed total algorithms have a time complexity $\Omega(D)$, where D is the network diameter, a spanning tree of minimum diameter makes it possible to design a wide variety of time efficient distributed algorithms.

Let $G = (V(G), E(G))$ be a connected, undirected, positively real-weighted graph. The (MDST) problem is to find a spanning tree of G of minimum diameter.

In the remainder of the paper, we denote the problem (MDST), *MDST* denotes the protocol and MDST abbreviates the "Minimum Diameter Spanning Tree".

1.3 Related Works and Results

The few literature related to the (MDST) problem mostly deals either with graph problems in the Euclidian plane (Geometric Minimum Diameter Spanning

Tree), or with the Steiner spanning tree construction (see [19, 20]). The (MDST) problem is clearly a generalization of the (GMDST) problem. Note that when edge weights are real numbers (possibly negative), The (MDST) problem is NP-complete.

Surprisingly, although the importance of having a MDST is well-known, only few papers have addressed the question of how to design algorithms which construct such spanning trees. While the problem of finding and dynamically maintaining a minimum spanning tree has been extensively studied in the literature (e.g., [3, 18] and [4, 17]), there exist no algorithms that construct and maintain dynamically information about the diameter, despite the great importance of this issue in the applications. (Very recently, the distributed (MDST) problem was addressed in [7, 22]). In this paper, we present an algorithm which is robust to transient failures, and dynamically maintains a minimum diameter spanning tree of any anonymous network: a much more efficient (computationally cheaper) solution indeed than recomputing from scratch over and over again.

As opposed to the (quasi-) absence of investigations dealing with the (MDST) problem, and although self-stabilization is quite a new strand of research in distributed computing, a large number of self-stabilizing algorithms and theoretical related results were proposed during the past few years (e.g., [1, 2, 5, 6, 12, 13, 14, 15, 21, 25, 26]). Due to their features, self-stabilizing protocols were first used in the design of many existing systems (e.g., DECNET protocols [24]).

Our distributed self-stabilizing algorithm is composed of a first uniform stabilizing randomized stage protocol *UN* of *"unique naming"* for arbitrary anonymous networks and of a second stabilizing stage protocol *MDST*, which constructs a MDST. The second stage performs a MDST protocol for *named* networks which results after the first stage stabilizes. This second stage is itself constructed as the *fair composition* [14, 15, 25] of Merlin–Segall's stabilizing distributed routing protocol and a new deterministic protocol for the (MDST) problem. The resulting algorithm $\mathcal{A}$ is thus a composition of the two stages (see Sect. 4.2) to obtain a randomized, uniform, self-stabilizing MDST algorithm $\mathcal{A}$ for general anonymous graph systems.

The complexity of protocols is analyzed by the following complexity measures. The **Time Complexity** of a self-stabilizing algorithm is mainly defined as the time required for stabilization (or *"round complexity"*). More formally, the *stabilization time* of a self-stabilizing deterministic (resp. randomized) algorithm is the maximal (resp. maximal expected) number of rounds that takes the system to reach a legitimate configuration, where the maximum is taken over all possible executions (see the model $\mathcal{M}$ in Sect. 2). The **Space Complexity** of a self-stabilizing algorithm can be expressed as the number of bits required to store the state of each process; i.e., in the message passing model, the maximal size of local memory used by a process. The **Communication Complexity** is measured in terms of the number of bits of the registers; i.e., in the message passing model, the maximal number of bits exchanged by the processes until an execution of the algorithm stabilizes. The time, space and communication

Main contributions of the present paper:

- A first stage consisting of a uniform stabilizing randomized *UN* protocol for any arbitrary network G, which is an adapted variant of the UN protocol designed in [2]. In model $\mathcal{M}$, our randomized *UN* protocol stabilizes in $O(n \log \log n)$ expected time, with a space complexity $O(n^2 \log n)$.
- An original second stage stabilizing protocol *MDST*, which is designed as the fair composition of Merlin–Segall's stabilizing routing protocol and a new deterministic protocol for the (MDST) problem. The second stage thus constructs a MDST of the named network G. In the model $\mathcal{M}$, the protocol *MDST* stabilizes in $O(n\Delta + \mathcal{D}^2)$ time, and its space complexity is $O(n \log n + n \log W)$ bits (where Δ is the maximum degree of G, $\mathcal{D}$ is the diameter in terms of hops and W is the largest edge weight).
- In model $\mathcal{M}$, the resulting randomized composed algorithm $\mathcal{A}$ stabilizes in $O(n\Delta + \mathcal{D}^2 + n \log \log n)$ expected time and uses $O(n^2 \log n + n \log W)$ memory bits. To our knowledge, it appears to be the very first algorithm to *distributively* solve the (MDST) problem. Moreover, our randomized distributed algorithm $\mathcal{A}$ is fault-tolerant and works for any anonymous arbitrary network.

The remainder of the paper is organized as follows: in Sect. 2, we define the formal model $\mathcal{M}$ and requirements for uniform, self-stabilizing protocols, and in Sect. 3 we present the stages of the composed uniform self-stabilizing MDST algorithm $\mathcal{A}$. Section 4.2 and Sect. 5 are devoted to the correctness proof, and to the complexity analysis of stabilizing protocols (*UN*, *MDST*, and algorithm $\mathcal{A}$), respectively. The paper ends with concluding remarks in Sect. 6.

2 Model $\mathcal{M}$ (Message Passing)

Formal definitions regarding Input/Output Automata are omitted from this abstract [6, 26].

IO Automata, Stabilization, Time Complexity – An Input/Output Automaton (IOA) is a state machine with state transitions which are given labels called *actions*. There are three kinds of actions. The environment affects the automaton through *input actions* which must be responded to in any state. The automaton affects the environment through *output actions*; these actions are controlled by the automaton to only occur in certain states. *Internal actions* only change the state of the automaton without affecting the environment.

Formally, an IOA is defined by a *state* set S, an *action* set L, a *signature* Z (which classifies L into input, output, and internal actions), a *transition relation* $T \subseteq S \times L \times S$, and a non-empty set of *initial states* $I \subseteq S$. We mostly deal with *uninitialized IOA*, for which $I = S$ (S finite). An action a is said to be *enabled* in state s if there exist $s' \in S$ such that $(s, a, s') \in T$; input actions are always enabled. When an IOA "runs", it produces an execution. An *execution fragment* is an alternating sequence of states and actions $(s_0, a_1, s_1 \ldots)$, such that $(s_i, a_i, s_{i+1}) \in T$ for all $i \geq 0$. An execution fragment is *fair* if any internal or output action which is continuously enabled eventually occurs. An *execution* is an execution fragment which starts with an initial state and is fair. A *schedule* is a subsequence of an execution consisting only of the actions. A *behaviour* is a subsequence of a schedule consisting only of its input and output actions. Each IOA generates a set of behaviours. Finally, let A and B denote two IOA, we say that A *stabilizes* to B if every behaviour of A has a suffix which is also a behaviour of B.

For time complexity, we assume that every internal or output action which is continuously enabled occurs in one unit of time. We say that A stabilizes to B in time t if A stabilizes to B and every behaviour of A has a suffix which occurs within time t. The *stabilization time* from A to B is the smallest t such that A stabilizes to B in time t.

Network Model – The model $\mathcal{M}$ is for message passing protocols. The system is a standard point-to-point asynchronous distributed network consisting of n communicating processes connected by m bidirectional links. As usual, the network topology is described by a connected undirected graph $G = (V, E)$, devoid of multiple edges and loop-free. G is defined on a set V of vertices representing the processes and E is a set of edges representing the bidirectional communication links operating between neighbouring vertices: in the sequel, $|V| = n$, and $|E| = m$. We view communication interconnection networks as undirected graphs. Henceforth, we use the terms *graph* (resp. *nodes/edges*) and *network* (resp. *processes/links*) interchangeably.

Each node and link is modelled by an IOA [6, 26]. A protocol is *uniform* if all processes perform the same protocol and are indistinguishable; i.e., in our model, we do not assume that processes have unique identities (ID's). We drop the adjective "uniform" from now on. The model $\mathcal{M}$ assumes that the messages are transferred on links in FIFO order, and in a finite but unbounded delay. It is also assumed that any non-empty set of processes may start the algorithm (such starting processes are "initiators"), while each non-initiator remains quiescent until reached by some message. In model $\mathcal{M}$, processes have no global knowledge about the system (no structural information is assumed), but only know their neighbours in the network (through the mere knowledge of their ports). In particular, the model $\mathcal{M}$ assumes that nothing is known about the network size n or the diameter $D(G)$ (no upper bound on n or on $D(G)$ is either known). Regarding the use of memory, $\mathcal{M}$ is such that the amount of memory used by the protocols remains bounded, i.e., only a bounded number of messages are stored on each link at any instant. The justification for this assumption is twofold: first, not much can be done with unbounded links in a stabilizing setting [6, 12, 26], and secondly, real channels are inherently bounded anyway. In other words, we model bounded links as unit capacity data links which can store at any given instant at most one circulating message. A link uv from node u to node v is modelled as a queue Q_{uv}, which can store at most one message from some message alphabet Σ at any instant time. The external interface to the link uv includes an input action $\text{SEND}_{uv}(m)$ ("send message m from u"), an output action $\text{RECEIVE}_{uv}(m)$ ("deliver message m at v"), and an output action FREE_{uv} ("the link uv is currently free"). If a $\text{SEND}_{uv}(m)$ occurs when $Q_{uv} = \emptyset$, the effect is that $Q_{uv} = \{m\}$; when $Q_{uv} = \emptyset$, FREE_{uv} is enabled. If a $\text{SEND}_{uv}(m)$ occurs when $Q_{uv} \neq \emptyset$, there is no change of state. Note that by the above timing assumptions, a message stored in a link will be delivered in one unit of time.

We refer to [6] for detailed and formal definitions of the notions of *queued node automaton, network automaton for a graph* G, and similarly for the notions of *internal reset* and *stabilization by local checking and global reset*. (See Sect. 4.2 for the definition of local checkability and the statement of the two main theorems used in the correctness proof of the algorithm).

3   The Algorithm

Let $G = (V(G), E(G))$ be a connected, undirected, positively real-weighted graph, where the weight of an edge $e = uv \in E(G)$ is given by ω_{uv}. In the remainder of the paper, we use the graph theoretical terminology and notation. The weight of a path $[u_0, \ldots, u_k]$ of G ($u_i \in V(G)$) is defined as $\sum_{i=0}^{k-1} \omega_{u_i u_{i+1}}$. For all nodes u and v, the *distance* from u to v, denoted $d_G(u, v)$, is the lowest weight of any path length from u to v in G (∞ if no such path exists). The distance $d_G(u, v)$ represents the *shortest path* from u to v, and the largest (maximal) distance from node v to all other nodes in $V(G)$, denoted $s_G(v)$, is the *separation* of node v: viz. $s_G(v) = \max_{u \in V(G)} d_G(u, v)$ [10]. $D(G)$ denotes the diameter of G, defined as $D(G) = \max_{v \in V(G)} s_G(v)$, and $\mathcal{D}(G)$ the diameter in terms of hops. $R(G)$ denotes the radius of G, defined as $R(G) = \min_{v \in V} s_G(v)$. $\Psi_{G}(u)$ represents a shortest-paths tree (SPT) rooted at node u: ($\forall v \in V(G)$) $d_{\Psi_{G}(u)}(u, v) = d_G(u, v)$. The set of all SPT's of G is then denoted $\Psi(G)$. The name of the graph will be omitted when it is clear from the context.

3.1   A High-Level Description

3.1.1 Unique Naming Protocol   The *unique naming* protocol solves the (UN) problem, where each process u must select one ID distinct from all other processes'. The protocol executes propagation of information (propagation of the ID of process u) and feedback (u collects the ID's of all other processes): i.e., a "PIF" protocol. Our randomized stabilizing protocol UN is a variant of the memory adaptive UN PIF protocol presented in [2] and slightly differs in the following respects. First, our results hold for the message passing model $\mathcal{M}$, even though they can easily be transposed in the link register model (and *vice versa*: the results in [2] can easily be extended to the message passing model). Next, we do not use the ranking phase designed in the original protocol, but a simple ID's conflict checking phase. Besides, our maximum estimate for the size of the network is arbitrarily chosen to be $\leq \lg n$ (see the proof of Theorem 12 in [8]), instead of $n^{1/2} - n^{1/3}$ in [2]. Note that the model $\mathcal{M}$ assumes that nothing is

known about n or $D(G)$ (not even an upper bound), therefore, the UN Monte-Carlo protocol in [2] *cannot* be turned into a randomized Las Vegas protocol (e.g., a protocol solving the (UN) problem with probability 1).

Due to the lack of space, we do not give a detailed description of our protocol *UN* herein. A full description of the three phases executed in the protocol can be found in [2] (for the original version) and in [8] (for our own variant). However, for better understanding of self-stabilization (showed in Sect. 4.2), let us just point out the behaviour of protocol *UN* in phase 3. Each process in phase 3 repeatedly broadcasts a message with its ID. At the end of each broadcast, if u detects a conflict, it initiates a Reset. In addition, u collects the ID's of all other processes (provided by feedback) and checks that all processes have unique ID's. The variable *IDList* contains the list of ID's of the visited processes. At the beginning of each broadcast, it is set to the initiator's ID; each visited process attaches its own ID to the list before forwarding it to its neighbours. After stabilization, every process remains forever in phase 3.

3.1.2 Construction of a MDST The definition of separation must be generalized to *"dummy nodes"* (so-called in contrast to actual vertices of V). Such a fictitious node may possibly be inserted on any edge $e \in E$. Thus, let $e = uv$ be an edge of weight ω_{uv}, a dummy node γ inserted on e is defined by specifying the weight α of the segment $u\gamma$. According to the definition, the separation $s(\gamma)$ of a *general node* γ, whether it is an actual vertex in V or a dummy node, is clearly given by: $s(\gamma) = \max_{z \in V} d(\gamma, z)$. A node γ^* such that $s(\gamma^*) = \min_\gamma s(\gamma)$ is called an *absolute center* of the graph. Recall that γ^* always exists in a connected graph, and that is not unique in general.

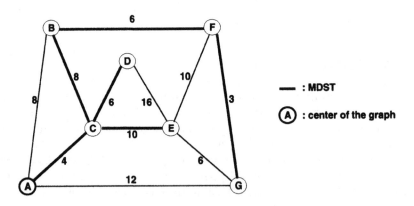

Fig. 1. Example of a MDST T^* ($D(G) = 22$ and $D(T^*) = 27$)

Similarly, the definition of $\Psi(u)$ is also generalized so as to take these dummy nodes into account. Finding a MDST actually amounts to search for an absolute center γ^* of G, and the SPT rooted at γ^* is then a MDST of G. Such is the purpose of the following Lemma:

Lemma 1. [9] *The (MDST) problem for a given graph G is (polynomially) reducible to the problem of finding an absolute center of G.*

a) Computation of an absolute center of a graph
According to the results in [10], we use the following Lemma to find an absolute center of G.

Lemma 2. *Let $G = (V, E)$ be a weighted graph. An absolute center γ^* of G is constructed as follows:*
(i) On each edge $e \in E$, find a general node γ_e of minimum separation.
(ii) Among all the above γ_e's, γ^* is a node achieving the smallest separation.

Proof. (the proof is constructive)
(i) This first step is performed as follows: for each edge $e = uv$, let $\alpha = d(u, \gamma)$. Since the distance $d(\gamma, z)$ is the length of either a path $[\gamma, u, \ldots, z]$, or a path $[\gamma, v, \ldots, z]$,

$$s(\gamma) = \max_{z \in V} d(\gamma, z) = \max_{z \in V} \min\{\alpha + d(u, z), \omega_{uv} - \alpha + d(v, z)\}. \qquad (1)$$

If we plot $f_z^+(\alpha) = \alpha + d(u, z)$ and $f_z^-(\alpha) = -\alpha + \omega_{uv} + d(v, z)$ in Cartesian coordinates for fixed $z = z_0$, the real-valued functions $f_{z_0}^+(\alpha)$ and $f_{z_0}^-(\alpha)$ (separately depending on α in the range $[0, \omega_e]$) are represented by two line segments $(S_1)_{z_0}$ and $(S_{-1})_{z_0}$, with slope $+1$ and -1, respectively. For a given $z = z_0$, the smallest of the two terms $f_{z_0}^+(\alpha)$ and $f_{z_0}^-(\alpha)$ (in (1)) is thus found by taking the *convex cone* of $(S_1)_{z_0}$ and $(S_{-1})_{z_0}$. By repeating the above process for each node $z \in V$, all convex cones of segments $(S_1)_{z \in V}$ and $(S_{-1})_{z \in V}$ are clearly obtained (see Fig. 2).

Now we can draw the *upper boundary* $B_e(\alpha)$ ($\alpha \in [0, \omega_e]$) of all the above convex cones of segments $(S_1)_{z \in V}$ and $(S_{-1})_{z \in V}$. $B_e(\alpha)$ is thus a curve made up of piecewise linear segments, which passes through several local minima (see Fig. 2). The point γ achieving the smallest minimum value (i.e., the global minimum) of $B_e(\alpha)$ represents the absolute center γ_e^* of the edge e.

(ii) By definition of the γ_e^*'s, $\min_\gamma s(\gamma) = \min_{\gamma_e^*} s(\gamma_e^*)$, and γ^* achieves the smallest separation. Therefore, an absolute center of the graph is found at any point where the minimum of all $s(\gamma_e^*)$'s is attained. □

By Lemma 2, we may consider this method from an algorithmic viewpoint. For each $e = uv$, let C_e be the set of pairs $\{(d_1, d_2) \mid (\forall z \in V) \; d_1 = d(u, z), d_2 = d(v, z)\}$ Now, a pair (d_1', d_2') is said to *dominate* a pair (d_1, d_2) iff $d_1 \leq d_1'$, and $d_2 \leq d_2'$ (viz. the convex cone of (d_1', d_2') is over the convex cone of (d_1, d_2)). Any such pair (d_1, d_2) will be ignored when it is dominated by another pair (d_1', d_2').

Notice that the local minima of the upper boundary $B_e(\alpha)$ (numbered from 1 to 3 in Fig. 2) are located at the intersection of segments $f_i^-(\alpha)$ and $f_{i+1}^+(\alpha)$,

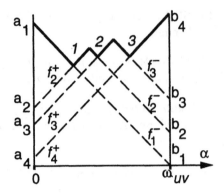

Fig. 2. Example of an upper boundary $B_e(\alpha)$

when all dominated pairs are removed. If we sort the set C_e in descending order with respect to the first term of each remaining pair (d_1, d_2), we thus obtain the list $L_e = ((a_1, b_1), \ldots, (a_{|L_e|}, b_{|L_e|}))$ consisting in all such remaining ordered pairs. Hence, the smallest minimum of $B_e(\alpha)$ for a given edge e clearly provides an absolute center γ_e^*. (See Procedure Gamma_star(e) in Sect. 3.2). By Lemma 2, once all the γ_e^*'s are computed, an absolute center γ^* of the graph is obtained. By Lemma 1, finding a MDST of the graph reduces to the problem of computing γ^*.

b) All-Pairs Shortest-Paths Protocol (APSP)

In the previous paragraph, we consider distances $d(u, z)$ and $d(v, z)$, for all $z \in V$ and each edge $e = uv$. Such distances must be computed by a failsafe distributed routing protocol, e.g., Merlin–Segall's APSP protocol designed in [23].

The justification for this choice is threefold. First, shortest paths to each destination v are computed by executing the protocol independently for each v. Thus, an essential property of Merlin–Segall's algorithm is that the routing tables are cycle-free at any time (Property (a) in [23]). Next, the protocol is also adapted to any change in the topology and the weight of edges (Property (b)). Finally, the protocol converges in dynamic networks and is indeed self-stabilizing (Property (c)). (See Lemma 5).

3.2   A Formal Description

Assume the list L_e defined above (in Paragraph 3.1) to be already constructed (for example with a heap, whenever the routing tables are computed), the following procedure computes the value of γ_e^* for any fixed edge e.

Procedure Gamma_star(e) _____

    var min, α : real   **Init** $min \leftarrow +\infty$; $\alpha \leftarrow 0$;

    For i=1 to $|L_e|$ **do**

        compute the intersection (x, y) *of segments* f_i^- *and* f_{i+1}^+ :

        $x = \frac{1}{2}(\omega_e - a_i + b_{i+1})$; $y = \frac{1}{2}(\omega_e + b_{i+1} + a_i)$

        if $y < min$ **then** $min \leftarrow y$; $\alpha \leftarrow x$;

    Return(α, min)

_____

The distributed protocol *MDST* finds a MDST of an input graph $G = (V, E)$ by computing the diameter of the SPT's for all nodes. Initially, an edge weight ω_{uv} is only known by its two endpoints u and v. In the first stage, the randomized, stabilizing protocol *UN* provides each process u with its unique ID, denoted ID_u (see Sect. 3.1).

Protocol MDST (for process u) _____

    Type elt : **record** *alpha_best, upbound* : real ; ID_1, ID_2: **integer end** ;

    Var Λ : set of elt ; φ, φ_u^* : elt ; D, R, α, *localmin* : real ;

        d_u : array of weights ;   *(* $d_u[v]$ estimates $d(u,v)$ *)*

1. **For all** $v \in V$

    Compute $d_u[v]$, D and R ;   *(* by Merlin–Segall's protocol *)*

2. $\varphi.upbound \leftarrow R$;

3. **While** $\varphi.upbound > D/2$ **do for** any edge uv s.t. $ID_v > ID_u$

    (a) $(\alpha, localmin) \leftarrow$ Gamma_star(uv) ;

    (b) **If** $localmin < \varphi.upbound$ **then** $\varphi \leftarrow (\alpha, localmin, ID_u, ID_v)$;

4. $\Lambda \leftarrow \{\varphi\}$;

5. **Receive** $\langle \varphi \rangle$ from all sons of u in $\Psi(r)$

    (r is s.t. $ID_r = \min_{v \in V} \{ID_v\}$) ; $\Lambda \leftarrow \Lambda \cup \{\varphi\}$;

6. Minimum finding:

    (a) Compute φ_u^* s.t. $\varphi_u^*.upbound = \min_{\varphi \in \Lambda} \varphi.upbbound$;

        Send $\langle \varphi_u^* \rangle$ to father in $\Psi(r)$;

    (b) **If** $ID_u = ID_r$ **then** upon reception of $\langle \varphi \rangle$ from all sons of r, r forwards $\langle \varphi_u^* \rangle$ to all other nodes.

_____

Remark. In order to complete self-stabilization, the deterministic protocol *MDST* must be repeatedly executed .

A *sequential* algorithm for the (MDST) problem may also be derived from the above protocol, since $\Psi(\gamma)$ is then a MDST of G, where γ is the general node s.t. $s(\gamma) = upbound$.

Improvements: In practice, some improvements in protocol *MDST* can easily be carried out. Indeed, reducing the enumeration of dummy nodes may be done by discarding several edges of G from the exploration. To be able to discard an edge, we only need to know bounds on the minimum diameter D^* of all spanning trees of G. Note that the lower bound on D^* is obviously $D(G)$, and that D^*

is also bounded from above by the minimum diameter taken over all SPT's, viz. $D^* \leq \min_{T \in \Psi(G)} D(T)$. In the example of Fig. 1, such improvements lead to discard from the exploration the edges EF, AB, AC, BF, CD, DE, EG, FG. (See [8]).

4 Correctness

4.1 Self-Stabilization

Fix a network automaton $\mathcal{N}$ for a given graph G, the definition of local checkability is stated as follows [6].

Definition 3. Let $\mathcal{L} = \{LP_{uv}\}$ be a set of local predicates, and let ψ be any predicate of $\mathcal{N}$. A network automaton $\mathcal{N}$ is locally checkable for ψ using $\mathcal{L}$ if the following conditions hold.

(i) For all states $s \in S(\mathcal{N})$, if s satisfies LP_{uv} for all $LP_{uv} \in \mathcal{L}$, then $s \in \psi$.

(ii) There exists $s \in S(\mathcal{N})$ such that s satisfies LP_{uv} for all $LP_{uv} \in \mathcal{L}$.

(iii) Each $LP_{uv} \in \mathcal{L}$ is stable: for all transitions (s, a, s') of $\mathcal{N}$, if s satisfies LP_{uv} then so does s'.

The main theorem in [6] is about self-stabilization by local checking and global reset. Roughly, it shows that any protocol which is locally checkable for some global property can be transformed into an equivalent protocol, which stabilizes to a variant of the protocol in which the global property holds in its initial state. This transformation increases the time complexity by an overhead given in [6, Theorem 10].

Also recall the fundamental Theorem 4 which states the fair composition of two stabilizing protocols P_1 and P_2 [14].

Theorem 4. *If the four conditions hold,*

(i) protocol P_1 stabilizes to ψ_1;

(ii) protocol P_2 stabilizes to ψ_2 if ψ_1 holds;

(iii) protocol P_1 does not change variables used by P_2 once ψ_1 holds; and,

(iv) all executions are fair w.r.t. both P_1 and P_2,

then the fair composition of P_1 and P_2 stabilizes to ψ_2.

4.2 Correctness Proof

Let ψ be a predicate over the variables of protocol UN, and ψ' a predicate over the variables of protocol $MDST$ (see Sect. 2). Now, protocol $MDST$ is the fair combination of two subprotocols. The first protocol uses Merlin–Segall's APSP routing algorithm (see Sect. 3.1), while the second subprotocol deterministically computes the value γ^* (see Sect. 3.1). Hence, the local predicates LP_{uv} and LP'_{uv} corresponding to the predicates ψ and ψ', respectively, are defined by

$$LP_{uv} \equiv \{(\forall ID_i, ID_j \in IDList_u)\ i \neq j \implies ID_i \neq ID_j\}$$
$$\wedge\ \{(\forall ID_i, ID_j \in IDList_v)\ i \neq j \implies ID_i \neq ID_j\}$$
$$\wedge\ (u \text{ and } v \text{ are both in phase 3}) \text{ for predicate } \psi \equiv (\forall uv \in E)\ LP_{uv},$$

where the variable *IDList* is defined in Sect. 3.1. And, similarly,

$$LP'_{uv} \equiv (d_u[v] < +\infty) \wedge (d_v[u] < +\infty), \text{ for predicate } \psi' \equiv (\forall uv \in E) \ LP'_{uv}.$$

Note that this does not mean that the estimate values $d_u[v]$ are exact, but that they are not too bad. Of course, if some distances $d_u[v]$ are wrong, it may cause the construction of a MDST to fail. However, the routing protocol is self-stabilizing, and after a while the estimate distances shall be correct and a MDST will be found.

Lemma 5. *Let* $\mathcal{L} = \{LP_{uv}\}$ *be the set of local predicates over the variables of the randomized protocol UN. A network automaton* $\mathcal{N}$ *is locally checkable for* ψ *using* $\mathcal{L}$.

Proof. (By Definition 3). Condition *(i)* clearly holds by the definition of ψ. Condition *(ii)* holds for a state $s \in S(\mathcal{N})$ such that processes ID's are all distinct in phase 3.

Now suppose $s \in S(\mathcal{N})$ satisfies LP_{uv}. In the case when no failures occur, u and v obviously remain in phase 3 by construction of protocol *UN*. In the case when nodes recoveries occur (with arbitrary ID's), u and v are able to detect conflicts and if necessary they initiate a Reset. After a while, each process (and especially u and v) returns to phase 3 with one unique ID. Therefore, condition *(iii)* holds. □

Lemma 6. *Let* $\mathcal{L}' = \{LP'_{uv}\}$ *be the set of local predicates over the variables of Merlin–Segall's APSP protocol. A network automaton* $\mathcal{N}$ *is locally checkable for* ψ' *using* $\mathcal{L}'$.

Proof. (By Definition 3). Condition *(i)* clearly holds by the definition of ψ'. Since G is connected, there exists a path $[u, \dots, v]$ such that the distance $d_G(u,v)$ is finite. Hence, condition *(ii)* holds for the corresponding state $s \in S(\mathcal{N})$. Finally, condition *(iii)* clearly holds by convergence of Merlin–Segall's routing protocol. (See [23, Property (c)], and Sect. 3.1). □

Recall that $\varphi_u^*.upbound$ denotes the best value of $s(\gamma^*)$ computed so far at node u. We show now that both protocols *MDST* and $\mathcal{A}$ stabilize to the desired postcondition θ defined by:

$$\theta \equiv (\forall u \in V) \ \varphi_u^*.upbound = s(\gamma^*).$$

The local predicate LP''_{uv} corresponding to θ is defined by:

$$LP''_{uv} \equiv \varphi_u^*.upbound = s(\gamma^*) \wedge \varphi_v^*.upbound = s(\gamma^*).$$

Lemma 7. *Assume processes ID's are all distinct, the protocol MDST stabilizes to* θ.

Proof. (Sketch) First, protocol *MDST* is locally checkable for θ using the set $\mathcal{L}'' = \{LP''_{uv}\}$. By Definition 3, conditions *(i)* and *(ii)* clearly hold. Condition *(iii)* derives from the fact that Merlin–Segall's protocol stabilizes to ψ', while the computation of γ^* is deterministic. Consequently, protocol *MDST* is locally checkable and stabilizes to θ by [6, Theorem 10]. □

Theorem 8. *The randomized algorithm $\mathcal{A}$ stabilizes to θ with probability 1.*

Proof. The following conditions hold.

(i) By Lemma 5 and [6, Theorem 10], protocol *UN* stabilizes to ψ with probability 1.

(ii) By Lemma 7, protocol *MDST* stabilizes to θ if ψ holds.

(iii) By construction, protocol *UN* does not change variables used by *MDST* once ψ holds.

(iv) Since protocol *MDST* terminates, there are only finitely many executions of *MDST* between two executions of *UN*. The protocol *UN* stabilizes to θ with probability 1 and since θ is true, each ID remains unchanged, and so does the computation of γ^*. Therefore, all executions are fair w.r.t. to both *UN* and *MDST*.

By Theorem 4, algorithm $\mathcal{A}$ which is the fair composition of *UN* and *MDST* stabilizes to θ with probability 1. □

5 Analysis

5.1 Protocol *UN*

The three phases executed in protocol *UN* are described in [2, 8]. (See Sect. 3.1).

Lemma 9. *Each Reset lasts at most $2D + n$ rounds. If two processes have the same ID, then within at most $O(n)$ rounds some process in the network will order a Reset. After a Reset, it takes the system $4n$ rounds either to perform global memory adaptation, or to complete another Reset.*

Note that the maximum number of rounds needed for the completion of phases 1 and 2 is exactly $4n$.

Lemma 10. *If n processes choose random ID's from the set $[N] = \{1, \ldots, N\}$, where $N \geq n^2/\epsilon$, all ID's will be unique with probability $p > 1 - \epsilon$, for all $0 < \epsilon < 1$.*

Proof. The probability p that all processes randomly choose distinct ID's is

$$p = \frac{N(N-1)\cdots(N-n+1)}{N^n} = \prod_{i=1}^{n-1}(1 - i/N).$$

Assuming that $n/N \leq 1/2$, or $N \geq 2n$ yields

$$p > \prod_{i=1}^{n-1} e^{-2i/N} > e^{-n^2/N}.$$

Since $(\forall 0 < \epsilon < 1)\, e^{-\epsilon} > 1 - \epsilon$, we have that $p > 1 - \epsilon$ when $N \geq n^2/\epsilon$. Hence, it is sufficient to randomly select the n identities from the set $[N]$, with $N \geq n^2/\epsilon$, in which case the identities are all distinct with probability $> 1 - \epsilon$, for fixed $0 < \epsilon < 1$. □

Lemma 11. *If after a Reset there exist $n' < n$ distinct ID's in the network, then a Reset is initiated by the end of phase 2 with probability $\geq 1 - 2^{n'-n}$.*

Theorem 12. *Let Δ be the maximum degree of the network. Starting from any state, the probability that the system will stabilize in $O(n(1 + \log\log n - \log\log(\Delta + 1)))$ rounds is $\geq 1 - \delta$, for some constant $0 < \delta < 1$ which does not depend on the network. The expected number of rounds until protocol UN stabilizes is $O(n\log\log n)$. The maximal memory size used by each process in any execution of protocol UN is at most $O(n^2 \log n)$ bits.*

5.2 Protocol $MDST$

Lemma 13. *The time complexity of protocol MDST is at most $O(n\Delta + \mathcal{D}^2)$, and its space complexity is $O(n\log n + n\log W)$ bits, where W is the largest edge weight.*

Proof. It is shown in [23] that after i update rounds, all shortest paths of at most i hops have been correctly computed, so that after at most $\mathcal{D}$ rounds, all shortest paths to node u are computed. Shortest paths to each destination are computed by executing the protocol independently for each destination. Since a round costs $O(\mathcal{D})$ time, the stabilization time of Merlin–Segall's protocol is $O(\mathcal{D}^2)$. Now, the computation of γ^* requires a minimum finding over a tree (viz., $O(n)$) and local computations on each adjacent edge of G (viz., $O(\Delta)$, where Δ is the maximum degree). Hence, the stabilization time of the protocol $MDST$ is $O(n\Delta + \mathcal{D}^2)$.

Finally, $O(n\log n + n\log W)$ space complexity is needed to maintain global routing tables. □

Note that since $\mathcal{D} \leq D \leq W\mathcal{D}$, the "hop time complexity" used above is more accurate.

5.3 Complexity Measures of Algorithm $\mathcal{A}$

The following theorem summarizes our main result, and its proof follows from the previous Lemma.

Theorem 14. *Starting from any state, the probability that algorithm $\mathcal{A}$ will stabilize is $\geq 1 - \delta$, for some constant $0 < \delta < 1$ which does not depend on the network. Recall $\mathcal{D}$ be the diameter of G in terms of hops, Δ the maximum degree, and W the largest edge weight. The expected time complexity of $\mathcal{A}$ is $O(n\Delta + \mathcal{D}^2 + n\log\log n)$, and its space complexity is at most $O(n^2 \log n + n\log W)$ bits.*

Since the number of messages required in Merlin–Segall's protocol is at most $O(n^2 m)$, the communication complexity of $\mathcal{A}$ is $O(n^2 m K)$ bits (where $K = O(\log n + \log W)$ bits is the largest message size).

6 Concluding Remarks

We proposed a uniform self-stabilizing algorithm for distributively finding a MDST of a positively weighted graph. Our algorithm is new. It works for arbitrary anonymous networks topologies, symmetry is broken by randomization; it stabilizes in $O(n\Delta + \mathcal{D}^2 + n \log \log n)$ expected time, and requires at most $O(n^2 \log n + n \log W)$ memory bits. The assumptions of our model $\mathcal{M}$ are quite general, and in some sense, the algorithm might be considered reasonably efficient in such a setting (even though the communication complexity appears to be the weak point of such algorithms). Whatsoever, the stabilization complexities can be improved in terms of time and space efficiency by restricting the model's assumptions and using the very recent results proposed in [16] and [5]. First, the randomized uniform self-stabilizing protocol presented in [16] provides each (anonymous) process of a uniform system with a distinct identity. This protocol for unique naming uses a predefined fixed amount of memory and stabilizes within $\Theta(D)$ expected time (where D is the diameter of the network). Secondly, following [5], we may restrict our model and assume that a pre-specified bound $B(D)$ on the diameter D is known. In $O(D)$ time units, the stabilizing protocol in [5] produces a shortest paths tree rooted at the minimal ID node of the network; in addition, the complexity of the space requirement and messages size is $O(\log B(D))$. In this restricted model (i.e., assuming the knowledge of an upper bound on D), the fair composition of the two protocols yields a randomized uniform self-stabilizing algorithm which finds a MDST with stabilization time (at most) $O(n)$ and space complexity $O(\log B(D))$. In this setting, the fact that the space complexity does *not* depend on n makes the solution more adequate for dynamic networks.

References

1. Y. Afek and G. Brown. Self-stabilization of the alternating-bit protocol. In *Proc. Symp. Reliable Distr. Syst.*, pages 80–83, 1989.
2. E. Anagnostou, R. El-Yaniv, and V. Hadzilacos. Memory adaptive self-stabilizing protocols. In *Proc. WDAG*, pages 203–220, 1992.
3. B. Awerbuch. Optimal distributed algorithms for minimum weight spanning tree, counting, leader election and related problems. In *Proc. ACM STOC*, pages 230–240, 1987.
4. B. Awerbuch, I. Cidon, and S. Kutten. Communication-optimal maintenance of replicated information. In *Proc. IEEE FOCS*, pages 492–502, 1990.
5. B. Awerbuch, S. Kutten, Y. Mansour, B. Patt-Shamir, and G. Varghese. Time optimal self-stabilizing synchronization. In *Proc. ACM STOC*, 1993.
6. B. Awerbuch, B. Patt-Shamir, G. Varghese, and S. Dolev. Self-stabilization by local checking and global reset. In *Proc. WDAG*, pages 326–339, 1994.
7. M. Bui and F. Butelle. Minimum diameter spanning tree. In *OPOPAC Proc., Int. Workshop on Principles of Parallel Computing*, pages 37–46. Hermès & Inria, Nov. 1993.
8. F. Butelle, C. Lavault, and M. Bui. A uniform self-stabilizing minimum diameter spanning tree algorithm. RR 95-07, LIPN, University of Paris-Nord, May 1995.

9. P. M. Camerini, G. Galbiati, and F. Maffioli. Complexity of spanning tree problems: Part I. *Europ. J. Oper. Research*, 5:346–352, 1980.

10. N. Christophides. *Graph Theory: An algorithmic approach*. Computer Science and Applied Mathematics. Academic press, 1975.

11. E. W. Dijkstra. Self-stabilizing systems in spite of distributed control. *CACM*, 17(11):643–644, 1974.

12. S. Dolev, A. Israeli, and S. Moran. Resource bounds on self-stabilizing message driven protocols. In *Proc. ACM PODC*, 1991.

13. S. Dolev, A. Israeli, and S. Moran. Uniform dynamic self-stabilizing leader election Part 1: Complete graph protocols. In *Proc. WDAG*, 1991.

14. S. Dolev, A. Israeli, and S. Moran. Self-stabilization of dynamic systems assuming read/write atomicity. *Distributed Computing*, 7(1):3–16, 1993.

15. S. Dolev, A. Israeli, and S. Moran. Uniform self-stabilizing leader election Part 2: General graph protocol. Technical report, Technion – Israel, Mar. 1995.

16. S. Dolev. Optimal Time Self-Stabilization in Uniform Dynamic Systems. In *Proc. 6th IASTED Int. Conf. on Parallel and Distributed Computing and Systems*, 1994.

17. D. Eppstein, G. F. Italiano, R. Tamassia, R. E. Tarjan, J. Westbrook, and M. Yung. Maintenance of a minimum spanning forest in a dynamic plane graph. *J. Algo.*, 13:33–54, 1992.

18. R. G. Gallager, P. A. Humblet, and P. M. Spira. A distributed algorithm for minimum weight spanning trees. *TOPLAS*, 5(1):66–77, 1983.

19. J.-M. Ho, D. T. Lee, C.-H. Chang, and C. K. Wong. Minimum diameter spanning trees and related problems. *SIAM J. Comput.*, 20(5):987–997, Oct. 1991.

20. E. Ihler, G. Reich, and P. Wildmayer. On shortest networks for classes of points in the plane. In *Int. Workshop on Comp. Geometry – Meth., Algo. and Applic.*, LNCS, pages 103–111, Mar. 1991.

21. S. Katz and K. J. Perry. Self-stabilizing extensions for message-passing systems. *Distributed Computing*, 7(17–26), 1993.

22. C. Lavault. *Évaluation des algorithmes distribués: analyse, complexité, méthode*. Hermès, 1995.

23. P. M. Merlin and A. Segall. A failsafe distributed routing protocol. *IEEE Trans. Comm.*, COM-27(9):1280–1287, Sept. 1979.

24. R. Perlman. Fault-tolerant broadcast of routing information. *Computer Networks*, 7:395–405, 1983.

25. S. K. Shukla, D. Rosenkrantz, and S. S. Ravi. Observations on self-stabilizing graph algorithm for anonymous networks. Technical report, University of Albany, NY, 1995.

26. G. Varghese. Self-stabilization by counter flushing. In *Proc. ACM PODC*, pages 244–253, 1994.

Self-Stabilization of Wait-Free Shared Memory Objects*

Jaap-Henk Hoepman[1], Marina Papatriantafilou[2,3], and Philippas Tsigas[3]

[1] CWI, P.O. Box 94079, 1090 SB Amsterdam, The Netherlands.
[2] CTI & CE and Informatics Dept., Patras University, Greece.
[3] MPI für Informatik, Im Stadtwald, 66123 Saarbrücken, Germany.
Email: jhh@cwi.nl, {ptrianta,tsigas}@mpi-sb.mpg.de

Abstract. It is an interesting question whether one can device highly fault tolerant distributed protocols that tolerate both processor failures as well as transient memory errors. To answer this question we consider self-stabilizing wait-free shared memory objects. In this paper we propose a general definition of a self-stabilizing wait-free shared memory object that expresses safety guarantees even in the face of processor failures. We prove that within this framework one cannot construct a self-stabilizing single-reader single-writer regular bit from single-reader single-writer safe bits. This impossibility result leads us to postulate a self-stabilizing *dual-reader single-writer* safe bit as the minimal object needed to achieve self-stabilizing wait-free interprocess communication and synchronization. Based on this model, adaptations of well known wait-free constructions of regular and atomic shared registers are proven to be self-stabilizing.

1 Introduction

The importance of reliable distributed systems can hardly be exaggerated. In the past, research on fault tolerant distributed systems has focused either on system models in which processors fail, or on system models in which the memory is faulty. In the first model a distributed system must remain operational while a certain fraction of the processors is malfunctioning. When constructing shared memory objects like, for instance, atomic registers, this issue is addressed by considering *wait-free* constructions which guarantee that any operation executed by a single processor is able to complete even if all other processors crash in the meantime. Originally, research in this area focussed on the construction of atomic registers from weaker (safe or regular) ones [VA86, Lam86, PB87, LTV89, IS92]. Later attention shifted to stronger objects (cf. [AH90, Her91] and many others).

In the second model a distributed system is required to overcome arbitrary changes to its state within a bounded amount of time. If the system is able to do so, it is called *self-stabilizing*. Self-stabilizing protocols have been extensively

---

* Research partially supported by the Dutch foundation for scientific research (NWO) through NFI Proj. ALADDIN (contr. # NF 62-376) and a NUFFIC Fellowship, and by the EC ESPRIT II BRA Proj. ALCOM II (contr. # 7141).

studied in the past. Originating from the work of Dijkstra on self-stabilizing mutual exclusion on rings [Dij74], several other self-stabilizing protocols have been proposed for particular problems, like mutual exclusion on other topologies [BGW89, BP89, DIM93], the construction of a spanning-tree [AKY90], orienting a ring [IJ93, Hoe94], and network synchronization [AKM+93]. Another approach focuses on the construction of a 'compiler' to automatically transform a protocol belonging to a certain class to a similar, self-stabilizing, one [KP90, AKM+93]. For a general introduction to self-stabilization see [Sch93, Tel94].

To develop truly reliable systems both failure models must be considered together. We briefly summarize recent theoretical research that addresses this issue. Anagnostou and Hadzilacos [AH93] show that no self-stabilizing, fault-tolerant, protocol exists to determine, even approximately, the size of a ring. Gopal and Perry [GP93] present a 'compiler' to turn a fault-tolerant protocol for the synchronous rounds message-passing model into a protocol for the same model which is both fault-tolerant and self-stabilizing. A combination of self-stabilization and wait-freedom in the construction of clock-synchronization protocols is presented in [DW93, PT94]. Another approach to combining processor and memory failures is put forward by Afek et al. [AGMT92, AMT93] and Jayanti et al. [JCT92]. They analyze whether shared objects do or do not have wait-free (self-)implementations from other objects of which at most t are assumed to fail. Objects may fail by giving responses which are incorrect, or by responding with a special error value, or even by not responding at all. In so-called gracefully degrading constructions, operations during which more than t objects fail are required to fail in the same manner.

We are interested in exploring the relation between self-stabilization and wait-freedom in shared memory objects. A shared memory object is a data structure stored in shared memory which may be accessed concurrently by several processors through the invocation of operations defined for it. Self-stabilizing wait-free objects occur naturally in distributed systems in which both processors and memory may be faulty. We give a general definition of self-stabilizing wait-free shared memory objects, and focus on studying the self-stabilizing properties of wait-free shared registers. Single-writer single-reader safe bits—traditionally used as the elementary memory units to build these registers with—are shown to be too weak for our purposes. Focusing on registers, being the weakest type of shared memory objects, allows us to determine the minimal object properties needed for a system to be able to converge to legal behaviors after transient memory faults, as well as to remain operative in the presence of processor crashes.

Shared registers are shared objects reminiscent of ordinary variables, that can be read or written by different processors concurrently. They are distinguished by the level of consistency guaranteed in the presence of concurrent operations ([Lam86]). A register is *safe* if a read returns the most recently written value, unless the read is concurrent with a write in which case it may return an arbitrary value. A register is *regular* if a read returns the value written by a concurrent or an immediately preceding write. A register is *atomic* if all operations on the register appear to take effect instantaneously and act consistent with a sequential execution. Shared registers are also distinguished by the number of processors that may invoke a read or a write operation, and by the number of values they may assume. These dimensions imply a hierarchy with single-writer single-reader $(1W1R)$ binary safe registers (a.k.a. bits) on the lowest level, and multi-writer multi-reader $(nWnR)$ l-ary atomic registers on the highest level. A *construction* or *implementation* of a register is comprised of i) a data structure consisting of memory cells called *sub-registers* and ii) a set of read and write procedures which provide the means to access it.

Li and Vitányi [LV91] and Israeli and Shaham [IS92] were the first to consider self-stabilization in the context of shared memory constructions. Both papers implicitly call a shared memory construction self-stabilizing if for every *fair* run started in an arbitrary state, the object behaves according to its specification except for a finite prefix of the run. Moreover, they do not seem to consider the possibility of pending operations. We feel, however, that this notion of a self-stabilizing object does not agree well with the additional requirement that the object is wait-free, since self-stabilization of the object now only guarantees recovery from transient errors in fair runs (in which no processors crash), while an object should be wait-free to ensure that a single processor can make progress even if all other processors have crashed.

Our contribution in this paper is threefold. First, in Sect. 2, we propose a general definition of a self-stabilizing wait-free shared memory object, that ensures that all operations after a transient error will eventually behave according to their specification even in the face of processor failures. Second, in Sect. 3, we prove that within this framework one cannot construct a self-stabilizing single-reader single-writer regular bit from single-reader single-writer safe bits—which have traditionally been used as the basic building blocks in wait-free shared register implementations. This impossibility result leads us to postulate a self-stabilizing *dual*-reader single-writer safe bit, which models a flip-flop with its output wire split in two (cf. Sect. 4). Using this bit as a basic building block, we formally prove, as a third contribution, that adaptations of well known wait-free implementations of regular and atomic shared registers are self-stabilizing (cf. Sects. 4.1, 4.2, and 4.3). This shows that our definition of self-stabilizing wait-free shared objects is viable—in the sense that it is neither trivial nor impractical. Section 5 concludes this paper with directions for further research.

2 Defining Self-Stabilizing Wait-Free Objects

In the definition of shared memory objects we follow the concept of *linearizability* (cf. [Her91]), which we, for the sake of self containment, briefly paraphrase here. Consider a distributed system of n sequential processors. A shared memory object is a data-structure stored in shared memory that may be accessed by several processors concurrently. Such an object defines a set of *operations* $\mathcal{O}$ which provide the only means for a processor to modify or inquire the state of the object. The set of processors that can invoke a certain operation may be restricted. Each operation $O \in \mathcal{O}$ takes zero or more parameters p on its invocation and returns a value r as its response $(r = O(p))$. Each such operation execution is called an *action* and is a sequential execution of a procedure's steps; each step may be either a *sub-operation* on the cells of the data structure, or local computations of the procedure. We denote by $t_i(A) \geq 0$ the invocation time of an action A and by $t_r(A) > t_i(A)$ its response time (on the real time axis). Processors are sequential and, therefore, cannot invoke an action if their previously invoked action has not responded yet. To model processor crash failures we introduce for each processor p a *crash action* ψ_p. No invocation or response of an action at processor p, nor another crash action ψ_p may occur later than the time $t(\psi_p)$ processor p crashes. In terms of the implementation of an object, no sub-operations may be executed by p after the crash action ψ_p either.

The desired behavior of an object is described by its *sequential specification* S. This specifies the state of the object, and for each operation its effect on the state and its (optional) response. We write $(s, r = O(p), s') \in S$ if invoking O with parameters p in state s changes the state of the object to s' and returns r as its response. A *run* over the object is a tuple $\langle \mathcal{A}, \rightarrow \rangle$ with actions $\mathcal{A}$ and partial order $\rightarrow$ such that for $A, B \in \mathcal{A}$, $A \rightarrow B$ iff $t_r(A) < t_i(B)$. Similarly, $\psi_p \rightarrow A$ iff $t(\psi_p) < t_i(A)$. If two actions are incomparable under $\rightarrow$, they are said to *overlap*. Runs have infinite length, and capture the real time ordering between actions invoked by the processors. An implementation of a shared object is *wait-free* if in all runs each invocation of an action A is followed by a matching response after finite time (i.e. $t_r(A) - t_i(A) < \infty$), unless the processor p invoking A crashed at time $t(\psi_p)$ such that $0 < t(\psi_p) - t_i(A) < \infty$. A *sequential execution* $\langle \mathcal{A}, \Rightarrow \rangle$ over the object is an infinite sequence $s_1 A_1 s_2 A_2 \ldots$, where $\bigcup_i A_i = \mathcal{A}$, s_i a state of the object as in its sequential specification, and $\Rightarrow$ a total order over $\mathcal{A}$ defined by $A_i \Rightarrow A_j$ iff $i < j$. A run $\langle \mathcal{A}, \rightarrow \rangle$ *corresponds* with a sequential execution $\langle \mathcal{A}, \Rightarrow \rangle$ if the set of actions $\mathcal{A}$ is the same in both runs, and if $\Rightarrow$ is a total extension of $\rightarrow$ (i.e. $A \rightarrow B$ implies $A \Rightarrow B$). Stated differently, the sequential execution corresponding to a run is a run in which no two actions are concurrent but in which the 'observable' order of actions in the run is preserved.

Definition 1. A run $\langle \mathcal{A}, \rightarrow \rangle$ over an object is *linearizable w.r.t. sequential specification* S, if there exists a corresponding sequential execution $\langle \mathcal{A}, \Rightarrow \rangle$, such that $(s_i, A_i, s_{i+1}) \in S$ for all i.

An object is linearizable w.r.t. its sequential specification S if all possible runs over the object are linearizable w.r.t. S. Informally speaking, an object is linearizable w.r.t.to specification S if all actions appear to take effect instantaneously and act according to S.

2.1 Adding Self-Stabilization

Li and Vitányi [LV91] and Israeli and Shaham [IS92] were the first to consider self-stabilizing wait-free constructions. Both papers implicitly use the following straightforward definition of a self-stabilizing wait-free object.

Definition 2. A shared wait-free object is self-stabilizing if an arbitrary *fair* execution (in which all operations on all processors are executed infinitely often) started in an arbitrary state, is linearizable except for a finite prefix.

A moment of reflection shows that assuming fairness may not be very reasonable for wait-free shared objects. The above definition requires that after a transient error *all* processors cooperate to repair the fault. On the other hand, wait-freedom should imply that processors can make sensible progress even if other processors have crashed. This observation leads us to the following stronger, still informal, definition of a self-stabilizing wait-free shared object.

Definition 3. A shared wait-free object is self-stabilizing, if an arbitrary execution started in an arbitrary state is linearizable except for a bounded finite prefix.

Let us develop a formal version of this definition. To model self-stabilization we need to allow runs that start in an arbitrary state; in particular we have to allow runs in which a subset of the processors start executing an action at an arbitrary point within its implementation. Such runs model the case in which transient memory errors occurs during an action, or, rather, the case where alteration of the program counter by the transient error forces the processor to jump to an arbitrary point within the procedure implementing the operation. For such so called *pending* actions A, and for such actions alone, we set $t_i(A) = 0$. Slow pending actions can carry the effects of a transient error arbitrarily far into the future[4]. Hence we can only say something meaningful about that part of a run after the time that all pending actions have finished, or the processors on which these pending actions run have crashed.

An action A *overlaps a pending action* iff there exists a pending action B on some processor p with $t_i(B) = 0$ such that $t_r(B) \not< t_i(A)$ and $t(\psi_p) \not< t_i(A)$. Define count(A) equal 0 for all actions A overlapping a pending action, and define count(A) equal to i if A is executed as the i-th action of a certain processor not overlapping a pending action. As a special case—to be used later—for all actions A with count$(A) = 0$ for which there exists a B with count$(B) = 1$ and $A \| B$ set count$(A) = \oplus$ instead. Actions A with count$(A) = \oplus$ overlap both with pending actions and with actions not overlapping any pending actions. As each processor executes sequentially, and actions are unique, count is well-defined.

Definition 4. A run $\langle \mathcal{A}, \rightarrow \rangle$ is *linearizable w.r.t. sequential specification S after k processor actions*, if there exists a corresponding sequential execution $\langle \mathcal{A}, \Rightarrow \rangle$, such that for all i, if count$(A_i) > k$ then $(s_i, A_i, s_{i+1}) \in S$.

---

[4] A pending action may carry something "malicious" in its local state that might disorder the system at any time after it is used to modify a sub-register. Consider for instance the Vitányi-Awerbuch register (cf. [VA86] and Sect. 4.3). If a pending action writes a huge tag only to the last register S_{in} in the row, no later action except one executed by processor n will see this tag. If writes after the pending action use a lower tag, they will be ignored by actions of processor n, even if these writes occur strictly before the actions of processor n.

Note that the definition allows the first k actions of a processor to behave arbitrarily (even so far as to allow e.g. a read action to behave as a write action or vice versa), but the effect of such an arbitrary action should be globally consistent. Thus this definition gives the strong guarantee that all actions following such arbitrarily behaving actions will agree on how that action actually behaved. In particular, for $k = 0$ and in the absence of pending actions, the definition implies that all actions agree on the effect of the transient error on the state of the object; for example, for a shared register all reads that occur immediately after a transient error should return the same value.

Definition 5. An implementation of a shared object with sequential specification S is *k-stabilizing wait-free* if all its runs are wait-free and linearizable w.r.t. S after k processor actions.

In the above definition the stabilization delay k is taken to be independent of the type of operations performed by a processor, while one might very well feel that the difficulty of stabilizing different types of operations on the same object may vary. Indeed, preliminary versions of this definition were more fine-grained and included separate delays for different types of operations (e.g. allowing the first k_w writes and the first k_r reads performed by a processor on a read/write register to be arbitrary). It turns out that this amount of detail is really unnecessary, essentially because different types of operations on a shared object already need to reach some form of agreement on the state of the object.

The above definition is general and considers all objects whose behavior is described by a sequential specification. Since our goal is to study, from the lowest level, the requirements needed to support shared objects that are both wait-free and self-stabilizing, we need to define safe and regular self-stabilizing registers. A register is a shared object on which read operations R and write operations $W(v)$ are defined. For a run $\langle \mathcal{A}, \rightarrow \rangle$ over such a register, define the set $\mathcal{R}$ of read actions that do not act as writes, and define the set $\mathcal{W}$ of write actions plus read actions that act as writes. For $R \in \mathcal{R}$ define val(R) as the value returned by read action R and for $W \in \mathcal{W}$ define val(W) as the value 'actually' written by action W. Also for $W \in \mathcal{W}$ and $R \in \mathcal{R}$ define W *directly precedes* R, $W \rightleftarrows R$, if $W \rightarrow R$ and if there is no $W' \in \mathcal{W}$ such that $W \rightarrow W' \rightarrow R$. If no such write exists, we take the imaginary initial write $W_\perp$ responsible for writing the arbitrary initial value val($W_\perp$). Let us write $A \| B$ if neither $A \rightarrow B$ nor $B \rightarrow A$. Define the *feasible* writes of a read R as all $W \in \mathcal{W}$ such that $W \rightleftarrows R$ or $W \| R$.

A write $W(v)$ on a register behaves correctly if val($W(v)$) $= v$. A read R on a *safe* register behaves correctly if $R \in \mathcal{R}$ and there is a write W such that $W \| R$, or val(R) $=$ val(W) for a write W with $W \rightleftarrows R$. A read on a *regular* register behaves correctly if $R \in \mathcal{R}$ and val(R) $=$ val(W) for some feasible write of R.

Definition 6. A safe or regular register is *k-stabilizing wait-free* if all its runs are wait-free and for all its runs only actions A with count(A) $\leq k$ behave arbitrarily. Such a register is simply *stabilizing wait-free* if all its runs are wait-free and for all its runs only pending write actions W and read actions R overlapping pending writes behave arbitrarily *without* behaving as a write (i.e. $R \in \mathcal{R}$).

3 Stabilizing $1W1R$ Safe Bits Are Not Strong Enough.

In this section we prove that $1W1R$ safe bits are not strong enough to give self-stabilizing wait-free shared registers; this is shown by proving that there exists no implementation of a $1W1R$ wait-free k-stabilizing regular binary register using stabilizing $1W1R$ binary safe sub-registers.

It is a common convention to view the scheduling of processor steps as being chosen by an *adversary*, who seeks to force the protocol to behave incorrectly. The adversary is in control of (i) choosing the configuration of the system after a transient error and (ii) scheduling the processes' steps in a run.

The heart of the problem of such an implementation can be described as follows. Since the writer (the reader) cannot read the sub-registers which it can write, in order to know their contents and converge into correct stabilized behaviors, it has to rely on information that either is local or is passed to it through shared sub-registers that can be written only by the reader (the writer, respectively). The adversary can set the system in a state in which this information is inconsistent; subsequently, by scheduling the processes' sub-actions on the same sub-register to be concurrent, it can destroy the information propagation because of the weak consistency that safeness guarantees.

If an implementation of a $1W1R$ binary regular register from stabilizing $1W1R$ safe binary sub-registers exists, it must use two sets of sub-registers (that can be considered as two "big" sub-registers): one (S_W) that can be written by the writer and read by the reader and one (S_R) that can be written by the reader and read by the writer. A system configuration C is a tuple (L_R, L_W, S_R, S_W) that describes a system state, where L_R, L_W denote the reader's and writer's local states, respectively. Since there is a single reader, we assume that the value of the register depends only on the state of its implementation, i.e. for any configuration, the value of the register in that configuration is the value that would be returned by the $k+1$-th read of a sequence of reads taking place in a time interval during which no write action is executed. Similarly, we assume that the behaviour of an operation solely depends on the state in which it is executed and not in its position in the run, i.e. if a read behaves as a write in some state, it must behave as a write in that state wherever that state occurs in the run.

A read action on the regular register may involve several sub-reads of S_W; however, in the course for a contradiction, attention may be restricted to runs in which all those sub-reads observe the same value of S_W, say sw. Then, we can consider that the value returned by each read is determined by a *reader's function* $f_R(lr, sw)$; let also $f_R^x(lr, sw)$ denote the value returned by the x-th read of a sequence of reads that start from a configuration where $L_R = lr$ and all find $S_W = sw$.

Theorem 7. *There exists no deterministic implementation of a wait-free k-stabilizing $1W1R$ binary regular register using $1W1R$ binary stabilizing safe sub-registers.*

Proof. Suppose that such an implementation exists. Since we look for a contradiction we may safely restrict attention to runs with no pending actions.

Consider an arbitrary initial configuration C and a run starting from C, in which the following actions are sequentially scheduled: k reads, k writes (writing arbitrary values), a $Write(0)$ action W_0 and a $Write(1)$ action W_1. The system configuration after W_0 is $C_0 = (lr, lw_0, sr, sw_0)$. Since the register is k-stabilizing by assumption the last of $k + 1$ reads starting in C_0 must return 0, so $f_R^{k+1}(lr, sw_0) = 0$. Similarly, the last of $k + 1$ reads starting after W_1 must return 1, Therefore, during the W_1 action the writer performs some sub-writes $s_1, \ldots, s_m$ on bits of S_W in that order. We write $sw \setminus s_1..s_i$ to denote the value of S_W after sub-writes $s_1, \ldots, s_i$ have been applied, while S_W held sw initially. Then $f_R^{k+1}(lr, sw_0 \setminus s_1..s_m) = 1$. Hence there will be an s_i $(1 \le i \le m)$, such that

$$f_R^{k+1}(lr, sw_0' = sw_0 \setminus s_1..s_{i-1}) = 0 \text{ and } f_R^{k+1}(lr, sw_1 = sw_0 \setminus s_1..s_i) = 1 \quad (1)$$

The former value for S_W could be observed by reads scheduled after s_{i-1} and before any other sub-operation of W_1, the latter by reads scheduled after s_i and before any other sub-operation of W_1. If $k + 1$ reads are scheduled to take place overlapping s_i and they all observe sw_0' they will return 0 (Eq. 1); moreover, since the register is k-stabilizing by assumption, none of those reads should perform as write. Now let lr' be the local state of the reader after those reads and sw_1' the contents of S_W after completion of W_1 in that schedule. Again because the register is k-stabilizing,

$$f_R^{k+1}(lr', sw_1') = 1 \quad (2)$$

Now let the adversary set the system in $C_{01} = (lr, lw_0, sr, sw_1)$, i.e., differing from C_0 only in the contents of S_W, and schedule again a $Write(1)$ action. By our assumption and Eq. 1, the value of the register in C_{01} equals 1, while the writer observes the same state as before and, hence, it again performs the same sequence of subwrites. The adversary can again schedule $k + 1$ reads overlapping s_i, as before; although the value of the corresponding bit does not change now during this subwrite, all these $k + 1$ reads may observe sw_0' instead of sw_1', because of the safeness of the corresponding bit. From the previous paragraph and our initial assumption it is known that none of these reads performs as a write, while the $k+1$-th read returns 0 (Eq. 1). But the only feasible writes are a write of 1 (recall Eq. 2) and the write of the initial value, which is 1. This is a contradiction, as the $k + 1$-th read must return the value of a feasible write.

4 Self-Stabilizing Constructions of Shared Registers

If we assume the existence of stabilizing dual-reader single-writer safe bits, the reasoning of the previous section does not apply: to know the value of its own shared bits the writer can simply read them. This assumption is legitimate, because assuming a $1W2R$ safe bit exists is not much stronger than assuming a $1W1R$ safe bit exists. After all, the latter models a flip-flop with a single output wire, whereas the first models a flip-flop with its output wire split in two. We will formally prove in the next sections that if these $1W2R$ safe bits are used as basic building blocks in some well-known wait-free constructions of shared registers, the resulting constructions become, after minor modifications, self-stabilizing.

S: stabilizing $1W2R$ safe bit

operation $Read() : \{0,1\}$
   return $(Read(S))$;

operation $Write(v : \{0,1\})$
$l : \{0,1\}$
   $l := Read(S)$;
   if $l \neq v$ then $Write(S,v)$;

Protocol 1. A stabilizing $1W1R$ regular bit

4.1 A Stabilizing 1W1R Regular Bit

Protocol 1 presents the adaptation of Lamport's [Lam86] construction of a $1W1R$ regular bit from a $1W1R$ safe bit, into a stabilizing wait-free one using a wait-free stabilizing $1W2R$ safe bit. We proceed by proving its correctness.

Theorem 8. *Protocol 1 implements a wait-free stabilizing $1W1R$ regular binary register using one wait-free stabilizing $1W2R$ safe binary register.*

Proof. Let $\langle \mathcal{A}, \rightarrow \rangle$ be an arbitrary run of reads R and writes W over the regular bit. Write $R(S)$ $(W(S))$ for the read from (write to) the safe bit S performed by read R (write W). Let $w_\perp$ be the initializing write of S, and set $\text{val}(W_\perp) = \text{val}(w_\perp)$ for the initializing write of the regular bit. If $\langle \mathcal{A}, \rightarrow \rangle$ has a pending write W, set $\text{val}(W)$ to the value of S just after W; this is the value an interference free read starting after W will read. For all other, non-pending, writes set $\text{val}(W(v)) = v$. According to Def. 6 it remains to show that in $\langle \mathcal{A}, \rightarrow \rangle$ all reads R not overlapping a pending write return the value written by a feasible write. Due to space constraints, we state the following claim without a proof.

Claim 9. *If R does not overlap a pending write and $R(S)$ is interference free and $W \rightleftarrows R(S)$ then $\text{val}(W) = \text{val}(R(S))$.*

Consider a read R not overlapping a pending write. Then $\text{val}(R) = \text{val}(R(S))$. If $R(S)$ is interference-free, then by Claim 9, for a write W with $W \rightleftarrows R(S)$ we have $\text{val}(W) = \text{val}(R(S)) = \text{val}(R)$ and W is feasible for R. If $R(S)$ is interfered, there is a write $W(x)$ with $W\|R$ writing S and W cannot be pending by assumption. Then W read S by $R'(S)$ and $\text{val}(R'(S)) = \neg x$. By Claim 9 and the fact that now $R'(S)$ is executed by a write so it cannot overlap another write, for W' with $W' \rightleftarrows W$ we must have $\text{val}(W') = \neg x$. As $W\|R$, then $W' \rightleftarrows R$ or $W'\|R$, so both W and W' are feasible for R and $\text{val}(R)$ equals one of these.

4.2 A Stabilizing 1W1R *l*-ary Regular Register

Protocol 2 presents the adaptation of Lamport's [Lam86] construction of a $1W1R$ l-ary regular register from l $1W1R$ regular bits, into a wait-free stabilizing one using l $1W1R$ wait-free stabilizing regular bits. We prove its correctness below.

Let $\langle \mathcal{A}, \rightarrow \rangle$ be an arbitrary run over the regular l-ary register. Number the writes consecutively, writing W^i for the write with index i. Let W^0 be the pending write if it exists, and $W_\perp$ otherwise. Let us write $R(S_v)$ for the read of

---

$S_0 \ldots S_{l-1}$: stabilizing   operation $Read() : \{0, \ldots, l-1\}$
    $1W1R$ regular bit $w : \{0, \ldots, l\}$
                                          $w := 0$;

operation $Write(v : \{0, \ldots, l-1\})$ while $Read(S_w) = 0 \wedge w < l$
    $Write(S_v, 1)$;   do $w := w + 1$;
    while $v \neq 0$ if $w = l$ then return $(l-1)$;
    do $v := v - 1$; $Write(S_v, 0)$;   else return (w) ;

Protocol 2. A stabilizing $1W1R$ l-ary regular register

S_v by read R, and let us write $W(S_v)$ for the write to S_v by a write W. The index of $W(S_v)$ equals the index of W (and the index of $w_{v,\perp}$ always equals 0). For reads R not overlapping a pending write, define $\pi(R)$ to be the largest index i such that W^i is feasible for R and $val(W^i) = val(R)$.

Consider the values of all S_v just after W^0 (i.e. the value read by an non-interfered read starting after W^0). Set $val(W^0)$ to the minimal v such that $S_v = 1$, setting $val(W^0) = l - 1$ if no such v exists. For all other writes $W(v)$ set $val(W(v)) = v$. Due to space constraints, we state the following claim without proof.

Claim 10. *Let R be a read not overlapping a pending write. If $W^i(u) \to R$ then $\pi(R(S_v)) \geq i$ for all $v \leq u$. If R reads S_{w+1} then $\pi(R(S_w)) \leq \pi(R(S_{w+1}))$.*

Theorem 11. *Protocol 2 implements a stabilizing $1W1R$ l-ary regular register using l stabilizing $1W1R$ regular binary registers.*

Proof. According to Def. 6 we have to show that in $\langle \mathcal{A}, \to \rangle$ all reads not overlapping a pending write return the value written by a feasible write. First consider a read R with $val(R(S_v)) = 1$ for some v. Let $\pi(R(S_v)) = i$. Then $val(R) = v$, $val(W^i) = v$ and $W^i \not\to R$. W^i is not a feasible write for R only if there exists a $W^j(w)$ such that $W^i \to W^j(w) \to R$ (and so $i < j$). If $w \geq v$, then by Claim 10 $\pi(R(S_v)) \geq j > i$, and if $w < v$, then using Claim 10 inductively $i < j \leq \pi(R(S_w)) \leq \pi(R(S_v))$. This contradicts the assumption that $\pi(R(S_v)) = i$. Now consider a read R where, for all v, $val(R(S_v)) = 0$. Then $val(R) = l - 1$. Because all writes write 1, if anything, to S_{l-1}, and $val(R(S_{l-1})) = 0$, we have $\pi(R(S_{l-1})) = 0$. Then, using Claim 10 inductively, $\pi(R(S_v)) = 0$ for all v, and so, for all v, the value of S_v just after W^0 equals 0. Hence, $val(W^0) = l - 1$ by definition. By a similar argument as before, W^0 is feasible for R.

4.3 A 1-Stabilizing $nWnR$ l-ary Atomic Register

Protocol 3 presents the adaptation of the Vitányi-Awerbuch [VA86, AKKV88] multi-reader multi-writer atomic register construction from $1W1R$ multi-valued regular registers, into a wait-free 1-stabilizing $nWnR$ l-ary atomic register using n^2 wait-free stabilizing $1W1R$ ∞-ary regular registers. We prove its correctness

$S_{11} \ldots S_{nn}$: stabilizing $1W1R$ regular: $\mathbb{N} \times \{1, \ldots, n\} \times \mathcal{V}$
(with fields *tag*, *id*, and *val*)

operation $Write_i(v : \mathcal{V})$
$max : \mathbb{N} \times \{1, \ldots, n\} \times \mathcal{V}$
    $max := \max_{1 \leq j \leq n} Read(S_{ji})$;
    for $j := 1$ **to** n
    do $Write(S_{ij}, \langle max.tag + 1, i, v \rangle)$;

operation $Read_i() : \mathcal{V}$
$max : \mathbb{N} \times \{1, \ldots, n\} \times \mathcal{V}$
    $max := \max_{1 \leq j \leq n} Read(S_{ji})$;
    for $j := 1$ **to** n
    do $Write(S_{ij}, max)$;
    return $(max.val)$;

Protocol 3. A 1-stabilizing $nWnR$ *l*-ary atomic register

below. In the protocol, $\mathcal{V}$ is the domain of values written and read by the multi-writer register. The construction uses n^2 regular stabilizing regular registers S_{ij} written by processor i and read by processor j. These registers store a *label* consisting of an unbounded *tag*, a processor *id* with values in the domain $\{1, \ldots, n\}$, and a *value* in $\mathcal{V}$. Labels are lexicographically ordered by $\leq$.

The sequential specification of an atomic register simply states that a write updates the state to be the value written, whereas a read returns the state of the register. Let $\langle \mathcal{A}, \rightarrow \rangle$ be a run of the above protocol. In the remainder of the proof, $\langle \mathcal{A}, \rightarrow \rangle$ is the above run with actions A with $\text{count}(A) = 0$ (thus $\text{count}(A) \neq \oplus$) removed. We will show that for this "sub-run" there exists a corresponding sequential execution $\langle \mathcal{A}, \Rightarrow \rangle$ such that $\Rightarrow$ is an extension of $\rightarrow$ and for all reads R with $\text{count}(R) > 1$, R returns the current state of the register. As for actions A, B with $\text{count}(A) = 0$ and $\text{count}(B) \neq 0$ in the original run either $A \rightarrow B$ or $A \| B$, we can prepend all these A to $\langle \mathcal{A}, \Rightarrow \rangle$ such that the resulting sequential execution $\langle \mathcal{A}, \Rightarrow \rangle$ corresponds to the original run $\langle \mathcal{A}, \rightarrow \rangle$ and satisfies Def. 4.

We are going to partition $\mathcal{A}$ into a set $\mathcal{R}$ of actions that behave as reads and a set $\mathcal{W}$ of actions that behave as writes. To this end, define

$$\mathcal{F} = \{A \in \mathcal{A} \mid \text{count}(A) = \oplus \vee \text{count}(A) = 1\}$$
$$\mathcal{R}^- = \{A \in \mathcal{A} \mid \text{count}(A) > 1 \text{ and } A \text{ is a read}\}$$
$$\mathcal{W}^- = \{A \in \mathcal{A} \mid \text{count}(A) > 1 \text{ and } A \text{ is a write}\}$$

Then $\mathcal{F}$ corresponds to the set of actions that, according to Def. 4, may behave arbitrary. We further subdivide $\mathcal{F}$ into actions $\mathcal{F}_W$ that seem to behave as a write and actions $\mathcal{F}_R$ that seem to behave as a read, making sure that no two apparent writes write the same label. Define for $A \in \mathcal{A}$, $\text{label}(A)$ as the label written by A, and for a set of actions $\mathcal{F}$, $\text{label}(\mathcal{F}) = \{\text{label}(F) \mid F \in \mathcal{F}\}$. Set $\mathcal{L} = \text{label}(\mathcal{F}) \setminus \text{label}(\mathcal{W}^-)$ and let $\mathcal{F}_W$ be an arbitrary subset of $\mathcal{F}$ such that

$(F1)$ $\text{label}(\mathcal{F}_W) = \mathcal{L}$, and
$(F2)$ For all $A, B \in \mathcal{F}_W$, if $\text{label}(A) = \text{label}(B)$ then $A = B$, and
$(F3)$ For all $A \in \mathcal{F}_W$ and $B \in \mathcal{F}$, if $\text{label}(A) = \text{label}(B)$ then $t_i(A) < t_i(B)$.

Now set $\mathcal{F}_R = \mathcal{F} \setminus \mathcal{F}_W$ and define $\mathcal{W} = \mathcal{W}^- \cup \mathcal{F}_W$ and $\mathcal{R} = \mathcal{R}^- \cup \mathcal{F}_R$.

Lemma 12. *If $A \to B$ then* $\mathrm{label}(A) \leq \mathrm{label}(B)$. *If $B \in \mathcal{W}^-$ this inequality is strict.*

Proof. Let A be performed by processor i and B be performed by processor j. If $A \to B$, then the write to S_{ij} by A precedes the read of S_{ij} by B. Because we only consider actions with count $\neq 0$, the write to S_{ij} is not pending, and by $A \to B$ the read of S_{ij} does not overlap a pending write. Then the write of A to S_{ij} or a later write action C of i to S_{ij} is a feasible write to the read of S_{ij} of B—hence this read returns the value written to S_{ij} by processor i during action A or the later action C. Since processor i both reads and writes from S_{ii}, and count$(A) \neq 0$, $\mathrm{label}(A) \leq \mathrm{label}(C)$. Therefore the read of S_{ij} by B returns a label greater than or equal to $\mathrm{label}(A)$. B picks the maximum of all labels read, so if B is a read, $\mathrm{label}(A) \leq \mathrm{label}(B)$ and if B is a write, then $\mathrm{label}(A) < \mathrm{label}(B)$.

Lemma 13. *For all $R \in \mathcal{R}$ there exists a $W \in \mathcal{W}$ such that* $\mathrm{label}(W) = \mathrm{label}(R)$ *and $R \not\to W$.*

Proof. Define $A \rightsquigarrow B$ iff $\mathrm{label}(A) = \mathrm{label}(B)$ and $B \not\to A$. Then $A \rightsquigarrow A$. Let $R \in \mathcal{R}$ be arbitrary, and pick a $B \in \mathcal{A}$ such that $B \rightsquigarrow R$ and for no $A \in \mathcal{A}$, $A \neq B$, $A \rightsquigarrow B$. If $B \in \mathcal{W}$ we are done, so assume $B \in \mathcal{R}$. Suppose count$(B) > 1$. Then there is an operation C on the same processor with count$(C) = 1$ and $C \to B$. If $\mathrm{label}(C) = \mathrm{label}(B)$ then $C \rightsquigarrow B$, while if $\mathrm{label}(C) < \mathrm{label}(B)$ (the only other possible case according to Lemma 12) then the contents of the register from which B obtains $\mathrm{label}(B)$ has changed after C read that same register. This register then is written by an operation D with $\mathrm{label}(D) = \mathrm{label}(B)$ before B reads it. Then $D \not\to C$, which, as count$(C) = 1$, implies count$(D) \neq 0$ and hence $D \rightsquigarrow B$. This contradicts the assumption that there is no A such that $A \rightsquigarrow B$.

We conclude that count$(B) \leq 1$ and hence $B \in \mathcal{F}$, so $\mathrm{label}(B) \in \mathrm{label}(\mathcal{F})$. So either there exists a $W \in \mathcal{W}^-$ such that $\mathrm{label}(W) = \mathrm{label}(B) = \mathrm{label}(R)$, or $\mathrm{label}(B) \in \mathcal{L}$ and by $(F1)$ there exists a $W' \in \mathcal{F}_W$ with $\mathrm{label}(W') = \mathrm{label}(B) = \mathrm{label}(R)$. In the first case, by Lemma 12, $R \not\to W$ as required. In the second case, since $B \in \mathcal{F}$ we must have by $(F3)$, $t_i(W') < t_i(B)$. Then as $B \rightsquigarrow R$ implies $R \not\to B$, this in turn implies $R \not\to W'$.

Lemma 14. *For all $W, W' \in \mathcal{W}$ if* $\mathrm{label}(W) = \mathrm{label}(W')$ *then $W = W'$.*

Proof. There are three cases

$W, W' \in \mathcal{W}^-$: By the protocol then W and W' must be executed by the same processor (or else their id-fields differ). But then either $W \to W'$ or $W' \to W$. By Lemma 12 then $\mathrm{label}(W) \neq \mathrm{label}(W')$, a contradiction.

$W \in \mathcal{W}^-, W' \in \mathcal{F}_W$: If $W \in \mathcal{W}^-$ then $\mathrm{label}(W) \notin \mathcal{L}$, and if $W' \in \mathcal{F}_W$ then $\mathrm{label}(W') \in \mathcal{L}$ by $(F1)$. Therefore $\mathrm{label}(W) \neq \mathrm{label}(W')$, a contradiction.

$W, W' \in \mathcal{F}_W$: If $\mathrm{label}(W) = \mathrm{label}(W')$, then by $(F2)$ we have $W = W'$.

Now we can define a reading mapping $\pi : \mathcal{R} \mapsto \mathcal{W}$ for a particular run $\langle \mathcal{A}, \to \rangle$ by $\pi(R) = W$ if $\mathrm{label}(R) = \mathrm{label}(W)$ and $W \in \mathcal{W}$.

Lemma 15. *For all $R \in \mathcal{R}$, $\pi(R)$ is defined and unique, $R \not\to \pi(R)$, and R returns the value written by $\pi(R)$.*

Proof. That $\pi(R)$ is defined and $R \not\to \pi(R)$ follows from Lemma 13. That it is unique follows from Lemma 14. If $\pi(R) \in \mathcal{W}^-$, then $\mathsf{label}(\pi(R)).val$ equals the value written by $\pi(R)$. If $\pi(R) \in \mathcal{F}_W$ we define the (arbitrary) value written by $\pi(R)$ to equal $\mathsf{label}(\pi(R)).val$

We now show that every run $\langle \mathcal{A}, \to \rangle$ with the above reading function π is atomic. Define for $W \in \mathcal{W}$ its clan $[W]$ by $[W] = \{W\} \cup \{R \in \mathcal{R} \mid \pi(R) = W\}$, and let $\Gamma = \{[W] \mid W \in \mathcal{W}\}$ be the set of all clans. Define $\to'$ over Γ by

$$[W] \to' [W'] \iff (\exists A \in [W], B \in [W'] :: A \to B)$$

Lemma 16. *For all $W \in \mathcal{W}$ and $A, B \in [W]$ we have $\mathsf{label}(A) = \mathsf{label}(B)$. Also if $W \neq W'$, then for all $A \in [W], B \in [W']$ we have $\mathsf{label}(A) \neq \mathsf{label}(B)$.*

Proof. It follows from the definition of $[W]$ and $\pi(R)$ and from Lemma 14.

Lemma 17. *$\to'$ is an acyclic partial order over Γ.*

Proof. Suppose not. Then there exists a chain

$$[W_1] \to' [W_2] \to' \cdots \to' [W_m] \to' [W_1]$$

with $m > 1$, and $W_i \neq W_j$ if $i \neq j$. This implies that for all i with $1 \leq i \leq m$ there exist actions $A_i, B_i \in [W_i]$ such that $A_i \to B_{i+1}$ (addition modulo $m+1$ from now). By Lemma 12 and 16 $\mathsf{label}(A_i) \leq \mathsf{label}(B_{i+1}) = \mathsf{label}(A_{i+1})$. Then $\mathsf{label}(A_1) = \mathsf{label}(A_2)$, contrary to Lemma 16.

Applying these lemmas and the results of [AKKV88] we get the result.

Theorem 18. *Protocol 3 implements a 1-stabilizing $nWnR$ l-ary atomic register using n^2 stabilizing $1W1R$ ∞-ary regular registers.*

Proof. Define a total order $\Rightarrow$ over $\mathcal{A}$ extending $\to$ as follows. First extend $\to'$ over Γ to a total order $\Rightarrow'$ (according to Lemma 17, this is possible). Now for $A \in [W]$ and $B \in [W']$ let $A \Rightarrow B$ if $[W] \Rightarrow' [W']$ (a). This extends $\to$ because if $A \to B$, then by the definition of $\to'$, $[W] \to' [W']$ and thus $[W] \Rightarrow' [W']$. For $A, B \in [W]$ fix an arbitrary extension $\Rightarrow$ of $\to$ such that for the only writer $W \in [W]$ we have for all other $C \in [W]$ that $W \Rightarrow C$ (b). This is an extension of $\to$ because by Lemma 15, $C \not\to W$. Now $\Rightarrow$ is a total order over $\mathcal{A}$ such that for all $R \in \mathcal{R}$ $\pi(R) \Rightarrow R$ by Lemma 15 and (b). Also there does not exists a $W \in \mathcal{W}$ such that $\pi(R) \Rightarrow W \Rightarrow R$, because by (a) and the fact that $R \notin [W]$ by Lemma 16, either $W \Rightarrow [\pi(R)]$ or $R \Rightarrow [W]$. Hence $W \Rightarrow \pi(R)$ or $R \Rightarrow W$.

5 Further Research

Our results are a first step towards exploring the relation between self-stabilization and wait-freedom in the construction of shared objects. There are still a lot of interesting questions in this new area that remain unanswered. First of all, this paper describes a first attempt to propose a reasonable and general definition of a self-stabilizing wait-free shared object. Although we believe our approach is viable, further research is necessary to demonstrate this, or to decide that other definitions may be more appropriate. Second, our construction of the 1-stabilizing $nWnR$ atomic register uses unbounded time-stamps to invalidate old values. We would like to know whether this necessarily so, or if the space requirements of a k-stabilizing atomic register can be bounded. Finally, following the work of Aspnes and Herlihy [AH90], it is an interesting venture to classify, based on their sequential specification, all k-stabilizing shared memory objects that can be constructed from k'-stabilizing atomic registers, and to provide a general method to do so.

Acknowledgements

It's a pleasure to thank Moti Yung for his encouragement in this work. We are grateful to the anonymous referees for their accurate and insightful comments, and to the MPI and the CWI for their hospitality during mutual visits.

References

[AGMT92] AFEK, Y., GREENBERG, D., MERRITT, M., AND TAUBENFELD, G. Computing with faulty shared memory. In *11th PODC* (Vancouver, BC, Canada, 1992), ACM Press, pp. 47–58.

[AKY90] AFEK, Y., KUTTEN, S., AND YUNG, M. Memory-efficient self stabilizing protocols for general graphs. In *4th WDAG* (Bari, Italy, 1990), LNCS 486, Springer Verlag, pp. 15–28.

[AMT93] AFEK, Y., MERRITT, M., AND TAUBENFELD, G. Benign failure models for shared memory. In *7th WDAG* (Lausanne, Switzerland, 1993), LNCS 725, Springer Verlag, pp. 69–83.

[AH93] ANAGNOSTOU, E., AND HADZILACOS, V. Tolerating transient and permanent failures. In *7th WDAG* (Lausanne, Switzerland, 1993), LNCS 725, Springer Verlag, pp. 174–188.

[AH90] ASPNES, J., AND HERLIHY, M. P. Wait-free data structures in the asynchronous PRAM model. In *2nd SPAA* (Crete, Greece, 1990), ACM Press, pp. 340–349.

[AKKV88] AWERBUCH, B., KIROUSIS, L. M., KRANAKIS, E., AND VITÁNYI, P. M. B. A proof technique for register atomicity. In *8th FST&TCS* (Pune, India, 1988), LNCS 338, Springer Verlag, pp. 286–303.

[AKM+93] AWERBUCH, B., KUTTEN, S., MANSOUR, Y., PATT-SHAMIR, B., AND VARGHESE, G. Time optimal self-stabilizing synchronization. In *25th STOC* (San Diego, CA, USA, 1993), ACM Press, pp. 652–661.

[BGW89] BROWN, G. M., GOUDA, M. G., AND WU, C. L. Token systems that self-stabilize. *IEEE Trans. on Comput.* **38**, 6 (1989), 845–852.

[BP89] BURNS, J. E., AND PACHL, J. Uniform self-stabilizing rings. *ACM Trans. Prog. Lang. & Syst.* 11, 2 (1989), 330–344.

[Dij74] DIJKSTRA, E. W. Self-stabilizing systems in spite of distributed control. *Comm. ACM* 17, 11 (1974), 643–644.

[DIM93] DOLEV, S., ISRAELI, A., AND MORAN, S. Self-stabilization of dynamic systems assuming only read/write atomicity. *Distr. Comput.* **7**, 1 (1993), 3–16.

[DW93] DOLEV, S., AND WELCH, J. L. Wait-free clock synchronization. In *12th PODC* (Ithaca, NY, USA, 1993), ACM Press, pp. 97–108.

[GP93] GOPAL, A. S., AND PERRY, K. J. Unifying self-stabilization and fault-tolerance. In *12th PODC* (Ithaca, NY, USA, 1993), pp. 195–206.

[Her91] HERLIHY, M. P. Wait-free synchronization. *ACM Trans. Prog. Lang. & Syst.* **13**, 1 (1991), 124–149.

[Hoe94] HOEPMAN, J.-H. Uniform deterministic self-stabilizing ring-orientation on odd-length rings. In *8th WDAG* (Terschelling, The Netherlands, 1994), LNCS 857, Springer Verlag, pp. 265–279.

[IJ93] ISRAELI, A., AND JALFON, M. Uniform self-stabilizing ring orientation. *Inf. & Comput.* **104**, 2 (1993), 175–196.

[IS92] ISRAELI, A., AND SHAHAM, A. Optimal multi-writer multi-reader atomic register. In *11th PODC* (Vancouver, BC, Canada, 1992), ACM Press, pp. 71–82.

[JCT92] JAYANTI, P., CHANDRA, T., AND TOUEG, S. Fault-tolerant wait-free shared objects. In *33rd FOCS* (Pittsburgh, Penn., USA, 1992), IEEE Comp. Soc. Press, pp. 157–166.

[KP90] KATZ, S., AND PERRY, K. J. Self-stabilizing extensions for message-passing systems. In *9th PODC* (Quebec City, Quebec, Canada, 1990), ACM, ACM Press, pp. 91–101.

[Lam86] LAMPORT, L. On interprocess communication. Part I: Basic formalism, part II: Algorithms. *Distr. Comput.* 1, 2 (1986), 77–101.

[LTV89] LI, M., TROMP, J., AND VITÁNYI, P. M. B. How to share concurrent wait-free variables. Tech. Rep. CS-R8916, CWI, Amsterdam, 1989.

[LV91] LI, M., AND VITÁNYI, P. M. B. Optimality of wait-free atomic multiwriter variables. Tech. Rep. CS-R9128, CWI, Amsterdam, The Netherlands, 1991.

[PT94] PAPATRIANTAFILOU, M., AND TSIGAS, P. Wait-free self-stabilizing clock synchronization. In *4th SWAT* (Århus, Denmark, 1994), LNCS 824, Springer Verlag, pp. 267–277.

[PB87] PETERSON, G. L., AND BURNS, J. E. Concurrent reading while writing ii: The multi-writer case. In *28th FOCS* (Los Angeles, CA, USA, 1987), IEEE Comp. Soc. Press, pp. 383–392.

[Sch93] SCHNEIDER, M. Self-stabilization. *ACM Comput. Surv.* **25**, 1 (1993), 45–67.

[Tel94] TEL, G. *Introduction to Distributed Algorithms.* Cambridge University Press, 1994.

[VA86] VITÁNYI, P. M. B., AND AWERBUCH, B. Atomic shared register access by asynchronous hardware. In *27th FOCS* (Toronto, Ont., Canada, 1986), IEEE Comp. Soc. Press, pp. 233–243.

Deterministic, Constant Space, Self-Stabilizing Leader Election on Uniform Rings

Gene Itkis[1] *, Chengdian Lin[2] **, Janos Simon[2] ***

[1] Computer Science Dept., Technion, Haifa, Israel 32000
[2] Computer Science Dept., University of Chicago, Chicago IL 60637, USA

Abstract. Self-stabilizing leader election protocols elect a single processor, leader, even when initiated from an arbitrary (e.g. faulty) configuration. Deterministic self-stabilizing leader election is impossible even on rings, if the number of processors is composite, no matter what computational resources are available to the processors. Moreover, it remains impossible even if the number of processors is prime, but each processor has less than $\log(n-1)$ bits of memory and the ring is unidirectional (i.e. each processor sees only itself and its clockwise neighbor). We show, however, that the deterministic self-stabilizing leader election is possible even if the processors are of constant size if the rings are bi-directional. More precisely, we present a deterministic uniform and constant space leader election protocol for prime sized rings under a central demon.

Key Words: Fault Tolerant, Finite Automata, Leader Election, Ring, Se lf-Stabilization

1 Introduction

Self-stabilization is an abstraction of fault-tolerance for transient faults. It guarantees that the system will eventually reach a *legal* configuration when started from an arbitrary initial configuration; and after reaching a legal configuration, the system configurations remain legal forever. For the *leader election*, in any legal configuration exactly one processor, *leader*, has a special *LEADER* flag set, and this processor remains a leader in any subsequent configurations.

Deriving self-stabilizing protocols is a notoriously difficult task. Protocols for leader election are among the best studied in the literature. The pioneering paper of Dijkstra [3] showed that round-robin token management (which is essentially equivalent to leader election) is impossible on a ring of unknown size if processors are uniform and deterministic. The proof is a formalization of the intuition that there is no way to break the symmetry in a ring of composite size. Israeli and Jalfon [6] proposed the first randomized token management scheme in the

---

* Partially supported by Israeli Council for Higher Education.
  Email: itkis@csa.cs.Technion.AC.IL
** Email: lin@cs.uchicago.edu
*** Email: simon@cs.uchicago.edu

shared memory (processors can see the state of their neighbors) model. They also showed that any (randomized) protocol requires $\Omega(\sqrt{\log n})$ states to represent a token. A beautifully simple probabilistic synchronous protocol for odd size unidirectional rings of constant size processors was presented by Herman [4]. Under assumption of no deadlock, [12] gave a randomized constant space leader election protocol for bi-directional rings in the message passing model, but this is a very strong assumption. Recently, Awerbuch, Itkis and Ostrovsky [7] obtained sublogarithmic space randomized self-stabilizing protocol for leader election (as well as spanning tree and other tasks) for networks with arbitrary topology. It was subsequently improved to constant space per node by Itkis, and Itkis and Levin [7, 8] (these results were detailed in [9]). These constructions were later modified in [1] to extend the scope of tasks solvable deterministically in $O(\log^* n)$ space per edge (beyond forest construction, for which algorithms of Itkis and Levin were already deterministic).

Although deterministic symmetry breaking is impossible for rings of composite size, for prime sized rings the symmetry can be broken by the central demon. Because all processors must be in the same state if a prime sized ring can be shifted into itself by a nontrivial rotation. Indeed, Burns and Pachl [2] give a deterministic uniform token management protocol for unidirectional rings of prime size. Their protocol uses $O(n^2/\ln n)$ states per processor. This was subsequently improved by to $O(n\sqrt{n/\ln n \ln \ln n})$ states per processor by Lin and Simon [11]. Any deterministic unidirectional protocol requires at least $n-1$ states for a ring of size n (see e.g. [10]). For bi-directional rings, Huang [5] gave a deterministic protocol with $O(n)$ states per processor.[3]

So, on one hand, there are constant space but probabilistic protocols for leader election, on the other, $n-1$ states are necessary for deterministic leader election on unidirectional rings. The question of whether there is a deterministic uniform self-stabilizing protocol for leader election on bi-directional rings, that uses sublogarithmic space per processor had remained open until now since at least 1989 [2].

In this paper, we settle this question by presenting such a protocol using $O(1)$ space (and stabilizing in $O(n^2)$ time). Our result helps to delimit more precisely the boundary between what is achievable and what is not, and thus gives a better insight to the nature of self-stabilization. Of course, in practice reliance on the primality of the network size may not be desirable.

We informally describe our protocol in Sect. 2. In Sect. 3, we give the formal model and the definition of the protocol. The proof of correctness is in Sect. 4.

2 Protocol Description

We consider a bi-directional ring of a prime number of identical nameless processors (finite automata). Processors use shared memory to communicate with their neighbors. A central demon (scheduler) picks a processor to make a move.

---

[3] If the size of the transition table is used as a measure of its complexity, then the complexity of the protocol in [5] is $\Theta(n^3)$, while that of [11] is $\Theta(n^3/(\ln n \ln \ln n)^2)$.

In an atomic move, the processor changes to a new state which is a function of its current state and the states of its two neighbors. The goal is to elect a unique leader deterministically. We describe our protocol in the following two sub-sections. We first present the basic idea for an error-free environment, then we make it self-stabilizing.

2.1 Basic Protocol

The first field of the state of each processor is a binary $Label \in \{0, 1\}$. A *segment* is a maximal contiguous sequence of alternating labels. The end processors of a segment are called *border processors*; the first processor reading clockwise) is the *head*, and the last processor is the *tail*. A processor P flips its label if the label is the same as those of both of its neighbors, thus eliminating unit size segments.

At the boundary of two segments, two border processors (the tail of left segment and the head of right segment) agree to measure their lengths asynchronously. The measurement protocol works as follows: each border processor first marks itself as the *FARTHEST* processor in its segment reached so far in the measurement process. Segments take turns: the right segment moves first. In a turn, a segment sends a *measurement token* from the border processor to the *FARTHEST* processor in the direction currently being measured. When the farthest processor receives the token, it gives the *FARTHEST* status to its neighbor in the current direction. The token then changes directions and returns to the border processor. When a border processor receives the returning token, it gives it to the border processor of the adjacent segment, signaling that it is its turn do the measurement.

The measurement protocol runs until one segment finishes its measurement: the token detects that the *FARTHEST* processor is a border. The segment then declares itself the loser (not longer in length), and enters the *switch mode*, to merge with the other segment. In switch mode the losing segment is shrunk by switched its labels, starting at a border. Thus, the borders can only move or disappear, so the number of segments cannot increase. Since the number of processors is a prime, all segments are unit size or there are segments of different sizes. In either case, some shortest segment will disappear. Thus, the number of segments is reduced until only one is left.

When the ring has only one segment, the unique head is the leader.

2.2 Self-Stabilizing Protocol

In order to obtain self-stabilization, we need to make few changes to the basic protocol. We sketch these changes, as well as the motivation for them below. We use an imprecise, anthropomorphic language that we hope is easy to understand: formal descriptions and proof of correctness are given later.

If the measurement token gets lost, the border processor will never get informed. As the result, a deadlock could happen. Secondly, the adversary (demon) can intentionally set the states in a way that the right end of every segment believes to be the winner, and left end of every segment believes to be the loser.

Thus every segment will switch its labels to merge into the preceding segment. The adversary can make this into an infinite loop.

To prevent the deadlock caused by lost tokens, we stipulate that the head (of the right segment) sends out a measurement token every time it is chosen by the demon and there is no token in its neighborhood. (There is a symmetric rule for the tail processor.) This rule introduces many tokens. We impose a discipline on them that will ensure that the useless tokens do not interfere with the basic measuring algorithm. We do not allow a token to pass other tokens in front of it. This may produce multiple processors with *FARTHEST* status: the *FARTHEST* processor closest to the tail processor is the genuine one. To ensure that the correct farthest processor is used in the protocol, we make sure that the measurement token always travels to the end of the segment and returns. When the returning token sees the first *FARTHEST* status on its way back, it knows that this is the genuine *FARTHEST* processor. Therefore the returning token copies the *Status* field from the neighbor processor to update the *FARTHEST* status. Also, a returning measurement token will kill all other existing measurement tokens that it encounters.

To avoid the infinite loop of switching labels, we add a field (a *switchable flag*) to the state of a processor. When a processor receives a switch token, it switches its label, turns off the switchable flag and passes the switch token on. The switchable flag will be turned on by measurement tokens in the measurement phase. A switch token will be killed by its holding processor if either the receiver's switchable flag is off or the receiver's label is already different. In its life, a switch token also reinitializes processors' states and prepares for the next round of measurement. This strategy makes sure that a switch phase will be followed by a measurement phase.

A processor P will check and update the *LEADER* flag when it holds a measurement token. If P is a head then it elects itself the leader, otherwise it clears the *LEADER* flag. This guarantees that only one processor will be elected as the leader when there is only one segment in the ring. Because, after a switch phase, the new head is the same as the old head.

3   Formal Definition of the Model and of the Protocol

Let Σ be a set of states, $\delta : \Sigma \times \Sigma \times \Sigma \to \Sigma$ be a transition function. Let δ be defined only when the state changes, so $\delta(s^l, s, s^r) \neq s$. Let (n, Σ, δ) denote a ring of n identical processors P_i, $0 \leq i \leq n-1$, such that each processor P_i is connected to P_{i-1} on the left and to P_{i+1} on the right (we omit mod n as in the subscripts above), and has a state set Σ. Let $\gamma = (a_0, a_1, \cdots, a_{n-1}) \in \Sigma^n$ be a configuration of the ring (n, Σ, δ), with a_i being the state of P_i for $0 \leq i \leq n-1$. Then $\delta_i(\gamma) \stackrel{def}{=} \gamma'$ if $\gamma' = (a_0, a_1, \cdots, a_{i-1}, x, a_{i+1}, \cdots, a_{n-1})$ such that $x = \delta(a_{i-1}, a_i, a_{i+1})$, $\delta_i(\gamma)$ is undefined if $\delta(a_{i-1}, a_i, a_{i+1})$ is. A processor P_i is *enabled* in configuration γ if $\delta_i(\gamma)$ is not undefined. Write $\gamma \to \gamma'$ if $\delta_i(\gamma) = \gamma'$

for some i, and say P_i makes a *step*. [4]

A computation of the ring (n, Σ, δ) is a (finite or infinite) sequence $\gamma_0 \gamma_1 \cdots$ such that $\gamma_{j-1} \to \gamma_j$ for all j (we also write $\gamma_j > \gamma_i$ if $j > i$).

Thus, only one processor takes a step at a time, each step in the computation depends on the configuration resulting from the previous step in the sequence and the ring is bi-directional. If more than one processor is enabled at a configuration γ, then the central demon (scheduler) will select one of the enabled processors to take a step. Note that there is an implicit symmetry-breaking in this assumption: it is easy to see that there is no fully symmetric deterministic leader election algorithm for the fully parallel synchronous rings of any length.

For *Leader Election*, we let the state set Σ have a leader field with value $\{0, 1\}$. A processor is called a *leader* if its leader field is 1.

Definition Ring (n, Σ, δ) *elects a leader* in k steps if for any (infinite) computation $\gamma_0 \gamma_1 \cdots$, there is exactly one leader P at γ_i for any $i \geq k$.

We give Σ, δ such that for any prime $n > 2$ (case $n = 2$ is trivial), the ring (n, Σ, δ) elects a leader in $O(n^2)$ steps. The state set Σ has the following 9 fields:

1. Label: $\{0, 1\}$
2. Turn Flag: $\{0, 1\}$
3. Right Switchable Flag (Up or Down): $\{\overrightarrow{U}, \overrightarrow{D}\}$
4. Left Measurement Status: $\{\overleftarrow{F}, N\}$
5. Left Measurement States: $\{\overleftarrow{M}, \overleftarrow{RM}, \overrightarrow{S}, \overleftarrow{C}, \overleftarrow{GRM}, \overrightarrow{GS}, N\}$
6. Left Switchable Flag (Up or Down): $\{\overleftarrow{U}, \overleftarrow{D}\}$
7. Right Measurement Status: $\{\overrightarrow{F}, N\}$
8. Right Measurement States: $\{\overrightarrow{M}, \overleftarrow{RM}, \overleftarrow{S}, \overrightarrow{C}, \overrightarrow{GRM}, \overleftarrow{GS}, N\}$
9. Leader $\{0, 1\}$

In the state definition above, N indicates a normal (quiescent) status for the corresponding field of the state. The *Turn Flag* will be used by two border processors at a boundary to determine whose turn it is to do the measurement. The third to fifth fields are for the measurement protocol originated and monitored by a tail (*left-measurement*). If the *Right Switchable Flag* is up, then the current *Label* is right switchable by token $\overrightarrow{S}$. The *Left Measurement Status* field indicates whether the processor has the *FARTHEST* status $\overleftarrow{F}$ in the *left-measurement*. The fifth field defines the movement of *left-measurement* tokens. We have four kinds of tokens in this field: *Measurement Token* $\overleftarrow{M}$, *Returning Measurement Token* $\overrightarrow{RM}$, *Switch Token* $\overrightarrow{S}$ and *Clean-up Token* $\overleftarrow{C}$. We use the concatenation of a G and a token to represent a temporary token getting (receiving) mode.

---

[4] Notice, that other popular definitions of a step (i.e. a period such that any P enabled at the beginning of a step makes at least one transition in that step) are more lenient: many our steps can occur in one their step.

For example, the right neighbor uses $\overrightarrow{GS}$ to get the *Switch Token* $\overrightarrow{S}$. The sixth to eighth fields are for the *right-measurement* protocol originated and monitored by a head. They are symmetric to those of the *left-measurement*.

If two tokens of opposite directions collide, in the same field, we use the following guidelines to eliminate one token. A *Switch Token* (**S-token**) always survives; a *Returning Measurement Token* (***RM-token***) kills a *Measurement Token* (**M-token**); a *Clean-up Token* (**C-token**) kills an ***RM-token***.

We use P_i to denote the value in the i-th field of processor P, and parentheses $(a, b, c, d, e, f, g, h)_P$ to denote the whole state. We often denote P's left neighbor by P^l, and P's right neighbor by P^r. We also use $[P_i^l, P_i, P_i^r]$ to denote P's view of i-th field in the three processors of its neighborhood The following are the state transition rules:

General Rule for Passing Tokens:

Normally, it takes three steps to transmit a token to the right. For example, for an **S-token**, the right neighbor processor P^r first enters the getting (receiving) mode $\overrightarrow{GS}$. Processor P then releases the token by entering released (normal) mode N. Finally, P^r receives the token by changing form $\overrightarrow{GS}$ to $\overrightarrow{S}$. Similar rules must be given for each token, both for left and right movement.

Note that the movement of a token cannot be guaranteed to be completed in three consecutive steps: the demon could pick other enabled processors to make moves. It should be clear that the token will be eventually passed to the next neighbor if the relevant processors are chosen by the demon.

We list the rules, followed by short explanations. These rules are to be applied in order. That is, **R1** should be applied before **R2**, **R2** should be applied before **R3**, and so on. We only deal with the first eight fields in the following rules except in the last rule **R9** for leader election. The symbol $*$ means that the value in the field does not change. Due to space constraints, we omit some obvious pseudo codes, but leave the explanations.

R1 (<u>Auto Switch Rule</u>):

If three labels are the same in a neighborhood, then the middle processor P switches its label and resets the other fields.

R2 (S-token Passing Rule):

The *S-token* has the highest priority, it is passed to the next neighbor according to the general passing rule. An *S-token* survives until it detects that the receiver is either non-switchable or has a different label. The receiver also initializes all its other fields.

R2A01:   if $[P_1^l, P_1, P_1^r] = [a, b, c]$ then
R2A02:   if $(P_8^r = \overleftarrow{S})$ and $(P_8 \neq \overleftarrow{S})$ and $(P_6 = \overleftarrow{U})$ and $(b = c)$ then
R2A03: $(b, *, *, *, *, *, N, \overleftarrow{GS})_P$ {enter receiving mode}
R2A04:   endif;
R2A05:   if $([P_8, P_8^r] = [\overleftarrow{GS}, N])$ and $(P_6 = \overleftarrow{U})$ and $(b = c)$ then
R2A06: $(\bar{c}, 0, \overrightarrow{D}, N, \overleftarrow{C}, \overrightarrow{D}, N, \overleftarrow{S})_P$ {receive S-token, switch label}
R2A07:   elseif $[P_8, P_8^r] = [\overleftarrow{GS}, N]$ then
R2A08: $(b, *, *, *, *, \overleftarrow{D}, N, \overrightarrow{C})_P$ {clean up}
R2A09:   endif;
R2A10:   if $P_8 = \overleftarrow{S}$ then
R2A11:   if $P_8^l = \overleftarrow{GS}$ then
R2A12: $(b, *, *, *, *, \overleftarrow{D}, N, N)_P$ {release S-token}
R2A13:   elseif $(P_6^l = \overleftarrow{D})$ or $(a \neq b)$ then
R2A14: $(b, *, *, *, *, \overleftarrow{D}, N, \overrightarrow{C})_P$ {kill S-token}
R2A15:   endif;
R2A16:   endif;
R2A17: endif;

When a processor kills an $\overrightarrow{S}$, it also updates its turn flag (**R2B08, R2B15, R2B17**) to force the right neighbor P^r to do a reset when P^r is selected to do the right-measurement as a head.

R2B01:   if $[P_1^l, P_1, P_1^r] = [a, b, c]$ then
R2B02:   if $(P_5^l = \overrightarrow{S})$ and $(P_5 \neq \overrightarrow{S})$ and $(P_3 = \overrightarrow{U})$ and $(a = b)$ then
R2B03: $(b, *, *, N, \overrightarrow{GS}, *, *, *)_P$ {enter receiving mode}
R2B04:   endif;
R2B05:   if $([P_5^l, P_5] = [N, \overrightarrow{GS}])$ and $(P_3 = \overrightarrow{U})$ and $(a = b)$ then
R2B06: $(\bar{a}, 0, \overrightarrow{D}, N, \overrightarrow{S}, \overleftarrow{D}, N, \overrightarrow{C})_P$ {receive S-token, switch label}
R2B07:   elseif $([P_5^l, P_5] = [N, \overrightarrow{GS}])$ then
R2B08: $(b, P_2^r, \overrightarrow{D}, N, \overleftarrow{C}, *, *, *)_P$ {clean up}
R2B09:   endif;
R2B10:   if $P_5 = \overrightarrow{S}$ then
R2B11:   if $P_5^r = \overrightarrow{GS}$ then
R2B12: $(b, *, \overrightarrow{D}, N, N, *, *, *)_P$ {release S-token}
R2B13:   elseif $(P_3^r = \overrightarrow{D})$ or $(b \neq c)$ then {kill S-token}
R2B14:   if $P_8^r = \overleftarrow{RM}$ then
R2B15: $(b, P_2^r, \overrightarrow{D}, N, \overleftarrow{C}, *, *, *)_P$ {copy turn flag, see **R6A12**}
R2B16:   else
R2B17: $(b, \bar{P}_2^r, \overrightarrow{D}, N, \overleftarrow{C}, *, *, *)_P$ {update turn flag, see **R6A06**}
R2B18:   endif;
R2B19:   endif;
R2B20:   endif;
R2B21: endif;

R3 (C-token Passing Rule):

The **C-token** has the second highest priority. Since a **C-token** will be overridden by an **M-token** if the **C-token** has been received by the intended receiver (see **Rule R8**), the passing of a **C-token** is very simple. The neighbor receiver simply clears the *FARTHEST* status and copies the token without asking the sender to release it. We omit the symmetric codes for passing the $\overleftarrow{C}$ token.

R3A01: if $([P_1^l, P_1] = [\bar{a}, a])$ and $(P_8^l = \overrightarrow{C})$ then

R3A02: $P_8 = \overrightarrow{C};\ P_7 = N;$

R3A03: endif;

R4 (Error Correction Rule):

If a processor is in the receiving mode (e.g. $\overleftarrow{GS}$), but the sender does not hold the token $(\overleftarrow{S})$ nor is in the release mode (N), then something is wrong. So the processor will reset its state. We omit the codes for the *left-measurement*.

R4A01: if $[P_1, P_1^r] = [a, b]$ then

R4A02:   if $(P_8 = \overleftarrow{GS})$ and $((P_8^r \neq \overleftarrow{S})$ and $(P_8^r \neq N))$ then

R4A03: $(a, *, *, *, *, \overrightarrow{D}, N, \overrightarrow{C})_P$

R4A04:   endif;

R4A05:   if $(P_8 = \overleftarrow{GRM})$ and $((P_8^r \neq \overleftarrow{RM})$ and $(P_8^r \neq N))$ then

R4A06: $(a, *, *, *, *, \overrightarrow{D}, N, \overrightarrow{C})_P$

R4A07:   endif;

R4A08: endif;

R5 (S-token and RM-token Creation Rule):

This rule applies to a border processor when it holds an M token. For a head processor P, if it has *FARTHEST* status in the *left-measurement*, then it concludes that the segment has lost to the *right-measurement* of right segment. Therefore P switches its label and starts to broadcast the **S-token** $\overrightarrow{S}$ to the right. Otherwise P sends the returning measurement token $\overrightarrow{RM}$. We only give the codes for a head processor. A tail processor has the symmetric responsibility.

R5A01: if $([P_1^l, P_1, P_1^r] = [a, a, \bar{a}])$ and $(P_5 = \overleftarrow{M})$ then

R5A02:   if $P_4^l = \overleftarrow{F}$ then

R5A03: $(\bar{a}, 0, \overrightarrow{D}, N, \overrightarrow{S}, \overrightarrow{D}, N, \overrightarrow{C})_P$ {enter switch phase}

R5A04:   else

R5A05: $(a, *, *, N, \overrightarrow{RM}, *, *, *)_P$ {M-token returns }

R5A06:   endif;

R5A07: endif;

R6 (M-token and C-token Creation Rule):

The two neighbor border processors at the boundary of two segments use their second field to determine whose turn it is to do the measurement. If the sum of two values $(P_2^l + P_2)$ is odd and $P_8 = \overleftarrow{RM}$ then it is P^l's turn to do the measurement. Otherwise it is P's turn. The turn flag will be updated when the border processor receives the returning RM token (see **Rule R7**).

A head processor P at its turn will always try to run a new copy or a new phase of *Measurement Protocol*. Before running a new copy of *Measurement Protocol*, it always does a reset by first sending a clean-up token $\overrightarrow{C}$.

The following code blocks are for a head processor and a tail processor respectively. They are not symmetric.

R6A01: if $[P_1^l, P_1, P_1^r] = [a, a, \bar{a}]$ then

R6A02:   if $(P_8 = \overleftarrow{RM})$ and $(P_2^l + P_2$ is odd) then

R6A03:   Exit $\{P^l$'s turn$\}$

R6A04:   endif;

R6A05:   if $(P_2^l + P_2)$ is odd then

R6A06: $P_8 = \overrightarrow{C}$ $\{$reset r-measurement$\}$

R6A07:   endif;

R6A08:   Change P_2 such that $(P_2^l + P_2)$ is even;

R6A09:   if $(([P_8, P_8^r] = [\overrightarrow{C}, \overrightarrow{C}])$ and $(P_5^l = \overrightarrow{C}))$ or $((P_5^l = \overrightarrow{RM})$ and $(P_8 = \overrightarrow{RM}))$ then

R6A10: $(a, *, *, *, *, \overrightarrow{U}, \overleftarrow{F}, \overrightarrow{M})_P$ $\{$run Measurement Protocol$\}$

R6A11:   elseif $(P_8 \neq \overrightarrow{M})$ then

R6A12: $(a, *, *, *, *, \overleftarrow{D}, N, \overrightarrow{C})_P$ $\{$error, need clean up $\}$

R6A13:   endif;

R6A14: endif;

R6B01: if $[P_1^l, P_1, P_1^r] = [\bar{a}, a, a]$ then

R6B02:   if not $((P_8^r = \overleftarrow{RM})$ and $(P_2 + P_2^r$ is odd)) then

R6B03:   if $P_8^r = \overrightarrow{C}$ then

R6B04: $P_5 = \overleftarrow{C}$ $\{$also do clean up$\}$

R6B05:   endif;

R6B06:   Exit $\{$not my turn$\}$

R6B07:   endif;

R6B08:   if $([P_5^l, P_5] = [\overleftarrow{C}, \overleftarrow{C}])$ or $(P_5 = \overrightarrow{RM})$ then

R6B09: $(a, *, \overrightarrow{U}, \overleftarrow{F}, \overrightarrow{M}, *, *, *)_P$ $\{$run Measurement Protocol$\}$

R6B10:   elseif $(P_5 \neq \overrightarrow{M})$ then

R6B11: $(a, *, \overleftarrow{D}, N, \overrightarrow{C}, *, *, *)_P$ $\{$error, need clean up$\}$

R6B12:   endif;

R6B13: endif;

R7 (RM-token Passing Rule):

The RM token will kill the forward M tokens. Before releasing the RM, a processor copies the status field from its neighbor as a way of moving the *FAR-*

THEST flag one processor farther away. When a processor receives a returning token, it also flips the turn flag to yield the turn for measurement to the other segment. We omit the similar codes for $[P_1^l, P_1, P_1^r] = [\bar{a}, a, b]$.

R7A01: if $[P_1^l, P_1, P_1^r] = [b, a, \bar{a}]$ then

R7A02:   if $P_8^r = \overleftarrow{RM}$ then

R7A03: $(a, *, *, *, *, *, *, \overleftarrow{GRM})_P$ {enter receiving mode}

R7A04:   endif;

R7A05:   if $[P_8, P_8^r] = [\overleftarrow{GRM}, N]$ then

R7A06: $(a, \bar{P}_2, *, *, *, *, *, \overleftarrow{RM})_P$ {receive RM-token, flip turn flag}

R7A07:   endif;

R7A08:   if $[P_5, P_5^r] = [\overrightarrow{RM}, \overrightarrow{GRM}]$ then

R7A09: $(a, *, *, P_4^r, N, *, *, *)_P$ {copy status, release RM-token}

R7A10:   endif;

R7A11: endif;

R8 (M-token Passing Rule):

The passing of an **M-token** is similar to that of a **C**-token. A qualified receiver simply copies the **M-token** without asking the sender to release it. The receiver of an $\overleftarrow{M}$ ($\overrightarrow{M}$) token turns on the left (right) switchable flag by setting $P_3 = \overrightarrow{U}$ ($P_6 = \overleftarrow{U}$). Again, we omit the symmetric codes for passing the $\overleftarrow{M}$ token.

R8A01: if $([P_1^l, P_1, P_1^r] = [\bar{a}, a, b])$ and $(P_8^l = \overrightarrow{M})$ then

R8A02:   if $(P_8 \neq \overrightarrow{C})$ or $(P_8^r = \overrightarrow{C})$ or $(a = b)$ then

R8A03: $(a, *, *, *, *, \overrightarrow{U}, *, \overrightarrow{M})_P$

R8A04:   endif;

R8A05: endif;

R9 (Leader Election Rule):

Suppose that processor P changes from some other state to hold an $\overrightarrow{M}$ after applying rules **R1** to **R8**. P then elects itself the leader by setting $P_9 = 1$ if it is a head. Otherwise, P clears the leader flag by setting $P_9 = 0$.

4 Proof of Correctness

A rule is *enabled* at a processor P, if P changes its state after applying the rule. Let $P_1, P_2, \cdots, P_n$ be all processors in the ring. We use $P_{i,c}$ to denote the value of P_i's c-th field. Recall that a segment is a maximal contiguous sequence of alternating labels. Let $\Phi(\gamma)$ be the number of segments at configuration γ.

Lemma 1. *(No Deadlock) For any configuration γ in Γ, some processor is enabled at γ.*

Proof. Suppose that no processor is enabled at γ. There are no S tokens and RM tokens in the ring. Otherwise rule **R2**, **R4** or **R7** applies. Because **R1**, **R3**,

R6 and **R8** do not apply, every processor must have $\overleftarrow{M}$ and $\overrightarrow{M}$ tokens. But this means an RM token will be created at some boundary by rule **R5**. ∎

Lemma 2. *Let γ be any configuration, and let γ' be any configuration which can be reached in a finite number of steps from γ. Then $\Phi(\gamma') \leq \Phi(\gamma)$.*

Proof. The only possibility of increasing Φ is that some processor switches its label. **R1** decreases Φ. **R2** and **R5** switch labels only if two neighbor labels are the same, so they do not create new segments. ∎

By lemma 2, any infinite computation reaches a point after which Φ is constant. Let γ_0 be a configuration with this property. Therefore, from γ_0 on Φ is a constant. We want to show that $\Phi = 1$. Suppose not; then $\Phi > 1$.

To help us with the proof of correctness, we add a new field (a TAG with value 0 or 1) to each state. The purpose of this TAG and the additional rule we impose on it is to force some fairness on the demon, so as to eventually select each enabled processor. The TAG field will not affect the actual protocol. We add to our transition rules the following:

1. A processor P_i is only enabled if $TAG_i \neq TAG_{i-1} + 1$
2. If processor P_i takes a step, it also sets its $TAG_i = TAG_{i-1} + 1$

Lemma 3. *In an infinite computation, every processor will be selected by the demon infinitely many times.*

Proof. If some processor P_i is only selected by the demon finitely many times, eventually processor P_i never changes its TAG. But then processor P_{i+1} eventually takes no steps. Because after changing its TAG, P_{i+1} will not be able to take a further step until P_i does. Eventually no processor takes a step. But because 2 does not divide n, there always is an enabled processor. Contradiction. ∎

Lemma 4. *Every S-token has a finite life.*

Proof. If the left switchable flag of P is turned down by an $\overleftarrow{S}$, the flag can be up again only by receiving an $\overrightarrow{M}$. Since $\overleftarrow{S}$ token kills $\overrightarrow{M}$ tokens, P is left non-switchable as long as this $\overleftarrow{S}$ is alive. If P ever receives this $\overleftarrow{S}$ back, P will kill it since the left switchable flag is still down. Same argument applies to $\overrightarrow{S}$. ∎

Definition. A segment $Seg\ P_i, \cdots, P_j$ is said to be **Right-Ordered** at γ, if the right measurement field of Seg has form $(\overrightarrow{M})^a (\overleftarrow{GRM})^b (\overleftarrow{RM})^c (N)^d (\overrightarrow{C})^e$ and Seg has an $\overrightarrow{F}$, where $a \geq 0, b \leq 1, c \leq 1, d \geq 0, e \geq 0$ and $a+b+c+d+e = j-i+1$. The right-order of Seg, $RightOrder(Seg, \gamma)$, is defined as $l - i + 1$. where P_l is the rightmost processor in Seg which has an $\overrightarrow{F}$. If Seg is not **Right-Ordered** at γ, then $RightOrder(Seg, \gamma)$ is undefined.

In a symmetric way, Seg is said to be **Left-Ordered**, if its left measurement field has form $(\overleftarrow{C})^e (N)^d (\overrightarrow{RM})^c (\overrightarrow{GRM})^b (\overleftarrow{M})^a$ and it has an $\overleftarrow{F}$, where $a \geq 0$,

$b \leq 1$, $c \leq 1$, $d \geq 0$, $e \geq 0$ and $a + b + c + d + e = j - i + 1$. $LeftOrder(Seg, \gamma)$ is defined as $j - l + 1$ where P_l is the leftmost processor in Seg with an $\overleftarrow{F}$. $LeftOrder(Seg, \gamma)$ is undefined, if Seg is not **Left-Ordered** at γ.

It follows from the transition rules, that the **Right-Ordered** (**Left-Ordered**) property will be maintained as long as there is no **S-token** in the segment.

Lemma 5. *Let Seg_1 $(P_l, \cdots, P_n)$, Seg_2 $(P_1, \cdots, P_m)$ be two neighbor segments and suppose there is no **S-token** in Seg_1 and Seg_2. If Seg_1 is **Left-Ordered** and Seg_2 is **Right-Ordered** at γ, then there is some γ' such that*

$$LeftOrder(Seg_1, \gamma') = LeftOrder(Seg_1, \gamma) + 1 \text{ and}$$

$$RightOrder(Seg_2, \gamma') = RightOrder(Seg_2, \gamma) + 1$$

Proof. Let $LeftOrder(Seg_1, \gamma) = x$ and $RightOrder(Seg_2, \gamma) = y$. WLOG, assume it is P_1's turn at the boundary of Seg_1 and Seg_2, that is, $(P_{n,2} + P_{1,2})$ is even or $(P_{1,8} \neq \overleftarrow{RM})$. By following the rules, it is not difficult to see that at some γ_1, P_1 will get an $\overleftarrow{RM}$ back and flip the turn flag. Now it is P_n's turn, P_n will first make an $\overleftarrow{M}$. This $\overleftarrow{M}$ will travel to P_l and change to an $\overrightarrow{RM}$. Because an $\overrightarrow{RM}$ will copy status values from right to left by rule **R7**, we have $LeftOrder(Seg_1, \gamma_2) = x + 1$ when P_n receives the $\overrightarrow{RM}$ at γ_2. If $RightOrder(Seg_2, \gamma_2) = y + 1$, then we are done. Otherwise, by a similar argument, we will have $RightOrder(Seg_2, \gamma_3) = y + 1$ when P_1 finishes another turn (by receiving an $\overleftarrow{RM}$) at some γ_3. ∎

Lemma 6. *New S-tokens will be created.*

Proof. Consider a segment Seg_1 and let its processors be $P_1, \cdots, P_m$, where $m > 1$. If there is any $\overrightarrow{C}$ in Seg_1, by rule **R3**, it will eventually travel to P_m. If there is any $\overleftarrow{RM}$ between P_2 and P_m, by rule **R7**, it will eventually travel to P_1. Therefore we may assume that at some γ_1, there is no $\overleftarrow{RM}$ between P_2 and P_m, and all $\overrightarrow{C}$ tokens have been sent towards the right. If there is some $\overrightarrow{M}$ in Seg_1, then this $\overrightarrow{M}$ will travel to P_m and create an $\overleftarrow{RM}$ at P_m. Thus, segment Seg_1 will have form $\overleftarrow{RM}$ $(N)^d (\overrightarrow{C})^e$ when this $\overleftarrow{RM}$ returns to P_1. Now only P_1 can take a move in the right measurement field.

Let Seg_0 be Seg_1's left segment, and have processors $P_l, \cdots, P_n$. If it is P_n's turn, then Seg_0 will have an $\overleftarrow{M}$ token (see line **R6B07**) which will generate a returning $\overrightarrow{RM}$ token by rule **R5**. It will be P_1's turn when P_n receives the $\overrightarrow{RM}$ token (see line **R7B06**). When P_1 is selected by the demon next time, by rule **R6**, P_1 will create an $\overrightarrow{F}$ in Seg_1. So Seg_1 will be **Right-Ordered**.

Similarly, Seg_0 will be **Left-Ordered** at some γ_3. We may now use Lemma 5. An $\overleftarrow{S}$ token will be created when the $RightOrder$ of Seg_1 is $Length(Seg_1)$, or an $\overrightarrow{S}$ token will be created when the $LeftOrder$ of Seg_0 is $Length(Seg_0)$. ∎

Definition. The travel set of token $\overleftarrow{S}$ denoted by $Travel(\overleftarrow{S})$ consists all processors visited by $\overleftarrow{S}$ during its lifetime. $Travel(\overrightarrow{S})$ is defined similarly.

Remark The labels of a travel set form an alternating sequence of 0s and 1s. This sequence can be considered as a sub-segment.

Lemma 7. Let $T_1 = Travel(\overleftarrow{S}_1)$, and $T_2 = Travel(S_2)$ (either $\overleftarrow{S}_2$ or $\overrightarrow{S}_2$). If $P \in T_1$ and P was visited by S_1 and later by S_2, then $T_1 \subseteq T_2$.

Proof. We give the proof for $T_2 = Travel(\overleftarrow{S}_2)$. Suppose that the processors in T_1 are $P_1, P_2, \cdots, P_m$. When a processor receives an *S-token* , it turns off both its left-switchable and right-switchable flags. In order for P to receive $\overleftarrow{S}_2$, P_m must have $\overleftarrow{S}_2$ first. But only an $\overrightarrow{M}$ can turn on P_m's left-switchable flag. This $\overrightarrow{M}$ must come from P_1. So all processors in T_1 must have turned on their left-switchable flags before P receives $\overleftarrow{S}_2$. If $\overleftarrow{S}_2$ can not visit P_1, then there must be some $\overrightarrow{S}_3$ visiting T_1 from the left. When two S-tokens visit T_1 like this, rule **R.1** will eventually be applied and cause Φ to decrease. ∎

It should be clear that the lemma above also holds if $T_1 = Travel(\overrightarrow{S}_1)$. At γ_0, we define a group of travel sets $T_{11}, T_{12}, \cdots, T_{1n}$, where $T_{1i} = \{P_i\}$. When an *S-token* becomes dead at $\gamma > \gamma_0$, we have a new group of travel sets. One travel set in the new group is the union of some travel sets in the old group. This continues, until members in the group are all fixed. Suppose that now the computation is at γ_1, and that the fixed travel sets are $T_1, T_2, \cdots, T_k$. It is easy to see that every T_i has size at least two, otherwise rule **R.1** will decrease Φ.

Definition. A travel set is *active* if it is visited by an *S-token* infinitely many times.

Lemma 8. For each $1 \leq i \leq k$, T_i is active.

Proof. By Lemma 6, we may assume that T_k is active and that $\overleftarrow{S}$ visits T_k infinitely many times. If T_{k-1} is not active, then eventually the last processor of T_{k-1} will not switch its label (assume it is 1). The first processor (P) of T_k will change to 0, at some γ, because T_k is active. Then T_{k-1} and T_k will merge. ∎

Lemma 9. For any travel set T, an S token is always killed at the boundary. That is, the neighbor in the S token's direction has the same label.

Proof. Let T be $P_1, \cdots, P_m$, and suppose the *S-token* is an $\overleftarrow{S}$. If P_n, P_1 have different labels after P_1's label switch, then P_n, P_1, P_2 all have the same label when P_1 is about to receive the $\overleftarrow{S}$ from P_2. But P_1 will apply rule **R.1** instead of receiving the $\overleftarrow{S}$, and this results in a decrease in Φ. ∎

Let $l_i = Size(T_i)$. Since n is prime, k travel sets can not have the same size. WLOG, assume that $l_1 < l_2 \geq l_3$.

Lemma 10. *Eventually, Φ decreases.*

Proof. T_2 is active, it is visited by an **S-token** of same direction at least twice. Suppose they are $\overleftarrow{S}_1, \overleftarrow{S}_2$ (the case of $\overrightarrow{S}_1, \overrightarrow{S}_2$ will be the same). Let T_1 be $P_{n-l_1+1}, \cdots, P_n$, and T_2 be $P_1, \cdots, P_{l_2}$. Suppose $\overleftarrow{S}_1$ was killed at γ_1 and $\overleftarrow{S}_2$ was created at γ_2. There is no $\overrightarrow{F}$ in T_2 at γ_1, in order to create an **S-token** there must exist some $\gamma_3 < \gamma_2$ such that P_{l_2} has $\overrightarrow{F}$ at γ_3.

P_1 has a $\overrightarrow{C}$ token at γ_1. We want show that P_1 has a $\overrightarrow{C}$ token just before it starts the right measurement to create $\overleftarrow{S}_2$. A processor P sends a $\overrightarrow{C}$ token when it receives an S token; and, by (rules **R2B** and **R6**), this will force P's right neighbor P^r to reset P^r's right measurement protocol.

We may assume that there is no other S token visiting T_1 and T_2 between γ_1 and γ_3. Otherwise, either P_n or P_1 will receive the S token, P_1 will be forced to reset its right measurement protocol.

Thus, at some γ', P_1 has a $\overrightarrow{C}$ token to start the right measurement to create $\overleftarrow{S}_2$. And P_n also has a $\overleftarrow{C}$ token to begin with (**R6B04**). T_2 has the form $(\overrightarrow{C})^a(*)^b$ at γ. T_2 is **Right-Ordered** when it has the form $(\overrightarrow{M})^a(\overrightarrow{C})^b$. When T_2 receives the first $\overleftarrow{RM}$, at some γ'' after γ, it has right order 2. Now it is P_n's turn and T_2 will be waiting for T_1 to do the left measurement. When T_2 gets another turn again, T_2 is **Right-Ordered**, T_1 is **Left-Ordered**, and both have order 2. By Lemma 5, P_{n-l_1+1} will get an $\overleftarrow{F}$ before P_{l_2} gets an $\overrightarrow{F}$. Thus P_{n-l_1+1} will create an $\overrightarrow{S}$ before P_1 gets another turn. P_{n-1}, P_n, P_1 will have the same labels when $\overrightarrow{S}$ arrives at P_{n-1}. By rule **R1**, Φ will decrease when P_n takes another step. ■

Theorem 11. *The protocol is a self-stabilizing leader election protocol.*

Proof. We may assume that the ring has only one segment. After a switch phase, the new head is the same as the old head. Eventually, by rule **R9**, only this head is the leader. ■

5 Self-Stabilizing Time

A time bound of $O(n^3)$ steps can be easily obtained, because Φ will decrease after $O(n^2)$ steps. We now show that the system stabilizes in $O(n^2)$ steps.

Theorem 12. *The protocol elects a leader in $O(n^2)$ steps.*

Proof. The total number of moves caused by all initial switch tokens on the ring is $O(n)$. Therefore, after the initial tokens are gone, the length of a segment can only increase (unless the segment disappears). Note that the sum of length increases on all segments is bounded by n.

Let us fix a processor P. Suppose it is in one of two adjacent segments of length x and y (assume $x \le y$) respectively. After the measurement, every processor of these two segments was activated $O(x)$ times, because the measurement protocol stops when the shorter segment finishes. At least one of these two segments will switch after the measurement. If only the shorter segment switches, the longer segment increases its length by x. If the longer segment also switches, the propagation will cause some segment to increase the length by at least x. Thus, some segment will increase its length by x after P was activated $O(x)$ times. Therefore, there will be only one segment when P is activated for $O(n)$ times. This gives the $O(n^2)$ time bound. ∎

References

1. B. Awerbuch and R. Ostrovsky. Memory-efficient and self-stabilizing network reset. *PODC'94*, pp. 254-263
2. J.E. Burns and J. Pachl. Uniform Self-Stabilizing Rings. *ACM Transactions on Programming Languages and Systems. (April 1989)*, pp. 330-344.
3. E.W. Dijkstra. Self-stabilizing systems in spite of distributed control. *Commum. ACM 17, 11 (Nov. 1974)*, pp. 643-644.
4. T. Herman. Probabilistic Self-Stabilization. *IPL 35 (1990)*, pp.63-67.
5. S. T. Huang. Leader Election in Uniform Rings. *ACM Transactions on Programming Languages and Systems. (July 1993)*, pp. 563-573.
6. A. Israeli and M. Jalfon. Token management schemes and random walks yield self stabilizing mutual exclusion. *PODC'90*, pp. 119-130.
7. G. Itkis. Self-stabilizing distributed computation with constant space per edge. Presented at colloquia at MIT, IBM, Bellcore, CMU, ICSI Berkeley, Stanford, SRI, UC Davis. 1992. Includes joint results with B. Awerbuch and R. Ostrovsky, and with L. Levin.
8. G. Itkis and L. Levin. Self-stabilization with constant space. Manuscript, Nov. 1992 (submitted to *STOC'93*; Also reported by L. Levin in ICALP Tutorial Lecture, July 1994. Later version: Fast and lean self-stabilizing asynchronous protocols. TR#829, Technion, Israel, July 1994.
9. G. Itkis and L. Levin. Fast and Lean Self-Stabilizing Asynchronous Protocols, *STOC'94*, pp. 226–239.
10. C. Lin. Resource efficient self-stabilizing systems, Ph.D. Dissertation, University of Chicago, 1995
11. C. Lin and J. Simon. Observing Self-Stabilization, *PODC'92*, pp. 113-123.
12. A. Mayer, Y. Ofek, R. Ostrovsky and M. Yung. Self-Stabilizing Symmetry Breaking in Constant-Space, *STOC'92*, pp. 667-678.

Efficient Detection of Restricted Classes of Global Predicates *

Craig M. Chase and Vijay K. Garg

Parallel and Distributed Systems Laboratory
Electrical and Computer Engineering Department
The University of Texas at Austin
http://maple.ece.utexas.edu/

Abstract. We show that the problem of predicate detection in distributed systems is NP-complete. We introduce a class of predicates, *linear predicates*, such that for any linear predicate B there exists an efficient detection of the least cut satisfying B. The dual of linearity is *post-linearity*. These properties generalize several known properties of distributed systems, such as the set of consistent cuts forms a lattice, and the WCP and GCP predicate detection results given in earlier work. We define a more general class of predicates, *semi-linear predicates*, for which efficient algorithms are known to detect whether a predicate has occurred during an execution of a distributed program. However, these methods may not identify the least such cut. Any stable predicate is an example of a semi-linear predicate. In addition, we show that certain unstable predicates can also be semi-linear, such as mutual exclusion violation.

Finally, we show application of max-flow to the predicate detection problem. This result solves a previously open problem in predicate detection, establishing the existence of an efficient algorithm to detect predicates of the form $x_1 + x_2 \cdots + x_n < k$ where x_i are variables on different processes, k is some constant, and n is larger than 2.

1 Introduction

Detection of a global predicate is a fundamental problem in distributed computing. This problem arises in many contexts such as designing, testing and debugging of distributed programs. For example, the detection of global predicate arises in implementing the most basic command of a debugging system:"stop the program when the predicate q is true." To stop the program, it is necessary to detect the predicate q; a non-trivial task if q requires access to the global state.

There have been three approaches in solving the detection of global predicates. The first approach is based on the global snapshot algorithm by Chandy and Lamport [CL85, Bou87, SK86]. Their approach requires repeated computation of consistent global snapshots of the computation until the desired predicate becomes true. This approach works only for stable predicates, that is, predicates which do not turn false once they become

---

* This work has been supported in part by the Texas Instruments/Jack Kilby Faculty Fellowship, by NSF grants CCR-9409736 and CCR-9110605, by a TRW faculty assistantship award, a General Motors Faculty Fellowship, and an IBM grant

true. If the desired predicate q were not stable then their approach would fail because q may turn true only between two successive snapshots. Further, their approach does not provide any indication as to when the snapshot needs to be taken. Thus, it may either result in excessive overhead when the snapshots are taken too often, or in significant delay between the occurrence and the detection of the predicate q.

The second approach to global predicate detection is based on the construction of the lattice of global states. This approach, first presented by Cooper and Marzullo [CM91], allows user to detect *definitely*: q and *possibly*: q where q is any predicate defined on a single global state. The predicate *possibly*: q is true if in the lattice of global states there is a path from the initial global state to the final global state in which q is true in some intermediate state. The predicate *definitely*: q is true if q becomes true in all paths from the initial state to the final state. This approach works even for unstable predicates. However, given n processes each with m "relevant" local states, their approach requires exploring $O(m^n)$ possible global states in the worst case.

The third approach is based on exploiting the structure of the predicate q. This approach, instead of building the lattice, directly uses the computation to deduce if q became true. For example, [GW94, GW92] present algorithms to detect *possibly*: q and *definitely*: q of complexity $O(n^2m)$ when q is a conjunction of local predicates. Similarly, [TG93] presents an efficient algorithm to detect $x_1 + x_2 < k$ where x_1 and x_2 are variables on different processes. In a recent paper [SS95], Stoller and Schneider propose combining this approach with that of Cooper and Marzullo [2]. This hybrid technique permits low-order polynomial detection of many predicates.

In this paper, we study techniques and limits of the third approach. This paper makes the following contributions.

- We show that a detection algorithm for conjunctive predicates cannot be generalized to any arbitrary boolean expression of local predicates. In particular, the problem of detecting whether a boolean expression became true in a distributed computation is an NP-complete problem. The problem stays NP-complete even when processes do not communicate with each other and each process executes a single instruction.
- We define a property on the space of boolean predicates that we call *linearity*. We show that there exists a polynomial algorithm to detect the least global cut that satisfies a given linear boolean predicate. We also show that the set of global cuts satisfying a boolean predicate B is an inf-lattice if and only if B is a linear boolean predicate. Thus, linearity captures the class of predicates for which efficient detection of the *least* satisfying cut is possible. For example, the monotonicity condition on channel predicates [GCKM95] is a special case of linearity.
- By considering the dual property of linearity, we get a necessary and sufficient condition for a given set of global cuts to be a lattice. This generalizes many earlier results. For example, the fact that the set of all recoverable cuts form a lattice [JZ90] is an easy consequence of our result.
- When the linearity property does not hold for a predicate B, we show that a weaker property, called *semi-linearity*, is sufficient to permit detection of B with a polynomial algorithm. However, it is not, in general, possible to detect the *least* satisfying

---

[2] Stoller and Schneider's method is exponential in the size of the *fixed set*. The cardinality of the fixed set is at most $n - 1$.

cut when B is only semi-linear. The class of semi-linear predicates subsumes stable predicates [CL85].

- Finally, we give an efficient algorithm to detect predicates of the form $x_1 + x_2 + ... + x_N < C$. This solves an open problem in [TG93] where the problem was solved for $N = 2$. Also see [BR94] where it is remarked that the technique in [TG93] does not appear to be generalizable to more than two processes.

The techniques presented in this paper can be used in distributed debugging systems for implementing breakpoints, in distributed fault monitoring systems for detecting an erroneous state reached by a distributed program, and in the design of distributed algorithms by optimizing the general predicate detection algorithm.

We have restricted ourselves to the global predicates defined on a *single* cut of the distributed computation. Other researchers have also considered predicates that involve multiple cuts. For example, [MC88, GW92] discuss linked predicates, [HPR93, BR94] discuss atomic sequences, and [FRGT94] discuss regular patterns. We refer the reader to [BM93, SM94] for surveys of stable and unstable predicate detection.

This paper is organized as follows. Section 2 describes our model of execution of a distributed program. We use the notion of a *deposet* to model an execution. Section 3 proves the intractability of the general problem. Section 4 describes the linearity property and its applications. Section 5 describes the semi-linearity property. Section 6 describes use of max-flow algorithms for detecting "Bounded Sum" predicates. Finally, Sect. 7 presents the concluding remarks.

2 Our Model of the Execution of a Distributed Program

We model the execution of a sequential process as a sequence of distinct states. For each state, s, the program prescribes what action will be taken to transition to next state. A distributed system consists of a set of n processes $P \stackrel{\text{def}}{=} \{P_1, \ldots, P_n\}$. Processes do not share any clock or memory; they communicate and synchronize with each other by messages over a set of channels. We assume that messages are not lost, altered, or spuriously introduced into a channel. We do not assume that channels are FIFO.

We limit the type of actions any process P_i may take to:

1. Compute new values for some subset of the program variables. — We denote the set of program variables for process P_i as X_i.
2. Send a message on channel C_{ij} for some $j : 1 \leq j \leq N$ — The contents of the message can be any tuple of values of variables in X_i.
3. Receive a message from channel C_{ji} for some $j : 1 \leq j \leq n$ — we assume that receives are blocking.

We permit the value of program variables to change only during the transitions between states. Thus, any state s from process P_i defines a unique value for all variables in X_i. We use S_i to denote the set of states generated by P_i in one execution of the program. Similarly, we permit the contents of a channel C_{ij} to change only during transitions between states on P_i or P_j. Thus, any two states $s \in S_i$ and $t \in S_j$ uniquely define the set of tuples (messages) in channel C_{ij}. We say that for two states s and t, $s \prec_{im} t$ if and only if s *immediately* precedes t in some process P_i. If $s \prec_{im} t$ then exactly one of the actions, A1, A2 or A3 occurs between s and t. We define the initial and final states on each process as: $Init(i) \stackrel{\text{def}}{=} \min S_i$ and $Final(i) \stackrel{\text{def}}{=} \max S_i$. We use $s \prec t$ to denote that s precedes t (not necessarily immediately).

We say that $s \rightsquigarrow t$ (for states $s \in S_i$ and $t \in S_j$) if and only if process P_i transitions from s to some other state by sending a message to P_j and process P_j transitions from some state to t by receiving that message. Following Lamport, we define the causally-precedes relation, $\rightarrow$, (also known as "happened before") as the transitive closure of $\{\prec_{im}\} \cup \{\rightsquigarrow\}$.

The set of states $S \stackrel{\text{def}}{=} \cup_i S_i$ and the relation $\rightarrow$ form an irreflexive partial order. More specifically, $(S, \rightarrow)$ is a deposet (decomposed partially ordered set) [Gar92, TG93]. The execution rules governing transitions between states lead to the following definition:

Definition 1 *A deposet is a tuple* $(S_1, \ldots S_n, \rightsquigarrow)$ *such that* $(S, \rightarrow)$ *is an irreflexive partial order that satisfies:*

1. $\forall u, \forall i : u \in S, 1 \le i \le n : u \not\rightarrow Init(i)$
2. $\forall u, \forall i : u \in S, 1 \le i \le n : Final(i) \not\rightarrow u$
3. $\forall s, t \in S : s \prec_{im} t \Rightarrow |\{u \mid s \rightsquigarrow u \lor u \rightsquigarrow t\}| \le 1$

(D1) says that no state happens before the initial state of any process. Similarly, (D2) says that any final state does not happen before any state. (D3) says that there is at most one message either sent or received between any two consecutive states.

An important concept for deposets is that of a consistent cut. A *cut* is a subset of S containing exactly one state from each sequence S_i. Given two states $x, y \in S$, we say that $x || y$ iff $(x \not\rightarrow y) \land (y \not\rightarrow x)$. These two states are then called *concurrent*. A subset $G \subset S$ is *consistent* (denoted by consistent(G)) iff $\forall x, y \in G : x || y$. Since each sequence S_i is totally ordered, it is clear that if $|G| = N$ and consistent(G) then G must include exactly one state from each S_i, *i.e.*, G is a consistent cut.

A consequence of the Definition 1 is the following.

Lemma 2 *For any state s and any process P_i, there exists a non-empty sequence of consecutive states called the "interval concurrent to s on P_i" and denoted by $I_i(s)$) such that:*

1. $I_i(s) \subseteq S_i$ — *i.e., the interval consists of only states from process P_i, and*
2. $\forall t \in I_i(s) : t || s$ — *i.e., all states in the interval are concurrent with s.*

Proof. If $s \in S_i$, then the lemma is trivially true. The interval consists of exactly the set $\{s\}$ (which is concurrent with itself). So we assume that $s \notin S_i$. Define $I_i(s).lo = \min\{t | t \in S_i \land t \not\rightarrow s\}$. This is well-defined since $Final(i) \not\rightarrow s$ due to (D2). Similarly, on account of (D1), we can define $I_i(s).hi = \max\{t | t \in S_i \land s \not\rightarrow t\}$.

We show that $I_i(s).lo \preceq I_i(s).hi$. If not, we do a case analysis.
Case 1: There exists $t : I_i(s).hi \prec t \prec I_i(s).lo$. Since $t \prec I_i(s).lo$ implies $t \rightarrow s$ and $I_i(s).hi \prec t$ implies $s \rightarrow t$, we get a contradiction ($t \rightarrow t$).
Case 2: $I_i(s).hi \prec_{im} I_i(s).lo$. From the definition of $I_i(s).lo$, it is easy to see that there must be a message sent from the state previous to $I_i(s).lo$. Similarly, from the definition

of $I_i(s).hi$, there exists a message received just after $I_i(s).hi$. However, (D3) prohibit:
more than one send or receive event between two successive states. Thus, this case i:
also not possible.

From the above discussion it follows that $I_i(s).lo \preceq I_i(s).hi$. Further, for any state
t such that $I_i(s).lo \preceq t \preceq I_i(s).hi$, $t \not\rightarrow s$ and $s \not\rightarrow t$ holds.

Given: a deposet S of n sequences, a set of variables X partitioned into n subsets $X_1, \ldots, X_n$, and a predicate B defined on X.
Determine if there exists a consistent cut $G \in S$ such that $B(G)$ has the value true.

We now show that the predicate detection problem is NP-Complete.

Theorem 1. *GLOB is NP-complete.*

Proof. First note that the problem is in NP. A verifier for the problem takes as input a cut G and then determines if that cut is consistent and if the predicate is true. The verification that the cut is consistent can easily be done in polynomial time (for example, using vector clocks [Mat89, Fid89] and examining all pairs of states from the cut). Therefore, if the predicate itself can be evaluated in polynomial time, then the detection of that predicate belongs to the set NP.

We show NP-completeness of the simplified predicate detection problem where all program variables are restricted to taking the values "true" or "false", and at most one variable from each X_i can appear in B. We reduce the satisfiability problem (SAT) of a boolean expression to GLOB by constructing an appropriate deposet.

Given an expression, B, defined over a set of n variables, $\{ u_1, \ldots, u_n \}$, construct a deposet as follows. For each variable u_i, define a process P_i which hosts variable u_i (*i.e.*,$X_i = \{u_i\}$). Let the sequence S_i consist of exactly two states. In the first state, u_i has the value false. In the second state, u_i has the value true. There are no messages exchanged during the computation (*i.e.*,$\forall s \in S_i, \forall t \in S_j : i \neq j : s||t$).

It is easily verified that the predicate B is true for some cut in S if and only if B is satisfiable.

■

The above result shows that detection of a general global predicate is intractable even for simple distributed computation. This implies that the class of predicates must be restricted to allow for efficient detection. The remaining sections discuss three such restricted classes.

4 Linear Predicates

In this section, we describe a class of global predicates for which efficient detection algorithms can be derived. We first define the relation $\leq$ for cuts. Let $\mathcal{G}_S$ (or, simply $\mathcal{G}$) be the set of all cuts for deposet S. For two cuts $G, H \in \mathcal{G}$, we say that $G \leq H$ iff $\forall i : G[i] \preceq H[i]$ where $G[i] \in S_i$ and $H[i] \in S_i$ are the states from process P_i in cuts G and H respectively. It is clear that for any deposet S, $(\mathcal{G}, \leq)$ is a lattice.

A key concept in deriving an efficient algorithm is that of a *forbidden* state. Given a deposet S, a predicate B, and a cut $G \subset S$, a state $G[i]$ is called forbidden if its inclusion in any cut H, where $G \leq H$, implies that B is false for H. Formally,

Definition 4 *Given any boolean expression B, we define*

$$forbidden(G, i) \stackrel{\text{def}}{=} \forall H : G \leq H : (G[i] \neq H[i]) \vee \neg B(H)$$

Based on the concept of a forbidden state, we define a predicate B to be linear with respect to deposet S if for any cut G in the deposet, the fact that B is false in G implies that G contains a forbidden state. Formally,

Definition 5 *A boolean predicate B is* linear *with respect to a deposet S iff:*

$$\forall G \in \mathcal{G} : \neg B(G) \Rightarrow \exists i : forbidden(G, i)$$

Observe that the linearity of a boolean predicate also depends on the set $\mathcal{G}$ and, therefore, on the deposet S. We would typically be interested in predicates which are linear for all deposets consistent with a program.

The following is an easy consequence of the definition of linearity.

Lemma 6 *The following are properties of linear predicates:*

1. *If B_1 and B_2 are linear, then so is $B_1 \wedge B_2$.*
2. *If B is defined using variables of a single process, then B is linear.*
3. *The predicate that a cut is consistent is linear. That is, Let $B(G) \equiv \forall i, j : G[i] \| G[j]$. Then, B is a linear predicate.*

Proof. We just show the third part. $\neg B(G)$ implies $\exists i, j : G[i] \to G[j]$. This implies that for all $H \geq G, G[i] \to H[j]$. Thus, $\forall H : G \leq H : \neg(G[i] = H[i]) \vee \neg B(H)$. That is, B is a linear predicate.

∎

Observe that as a consequence of Lemma 6, weak conjunctive predicates [GW92] are linear.

4.1 The Least Satisfying Cut Exists for Linear Predicates

Note that any global predicate, B, defines a (possibly empty) subset of cuts $\mathcal{G}_B \subseteq \mathcal{G}$ where B holds for all cuts in $\mathcal{G}_B$. We now show that if B is linear then $\mathcal{G}_B$ is an inf-semilattice. An implication of this result is that the *least* cut satisfying B is well-defined.

Lemma 7 *Let $\mathcal{G}_B \subseteq \mathcal{G}$.*
$\mathcal{G}_B$ is an inf-semilattice iff B is linear with respect to $\mathcal{G}$.

Proof. ($\Leftarrow$) We prove the contrapositive. Assume that B is not linear. This implies that there exists a cut G such that $\neg B(G)$, and $\forall i : \exists H_i \geq G : (G[i] = H_i[i])$ and $B(H_i)$. Consider $Y = \cup_i \{H_i\}$. Note that all elements of $Y \in \mathcal{G}_B$. However, $inf Y$ which is G is not an element of $\mathcal{G}_B$. This implies that $\mathcal{G}_B$ is not an inf-semilattice.

($\Rightarrow$) We again show the contrapositive. Let $Y = \{H_1, H_2, ..H_k\}$ be any subset of $\mathcal{G}_B$ such that its infimum, G, does not belong to $\mathcal{G}_B$. By the definition of $\leq$ for cuts, $G = inf Y$ implies that $\forall i$, there exists $j \in 1..k$ such that $G[i] = H_j[i]$. Since $B(H_j)$ is true for all j, it follows that G is a counter example proving that B is not linear.

∎

Some earlier results can be shown to be special cases of Lemma 7. For example, consider channel predicates as described in [GCKM95]. Let C denote the state of any channel and M denote any set of messages.

Definition 8 *A channel predicate, $c(C)$, is said to be* monotonic *iff:*

$$\forall C : \neg c(C) \Rightarrow (\forall M : \neg c(C \cup M)) \vee (\forall M : \neg c(C - M))$$

That is, given any channel state, C, in which the predicate is false, then either sending more messages is guaranteed to leave the predicate false, or receiving more messages is guaranteed to leave the predicate false. An example of a monotonic predicate is "channel C_{ij} is empty". If this predicate is false (*i.e.,* the channel is not empty), then sending more messages is guaranteed to leave the predicate false. A boolean predicate is called a Generalized Conjunctive Predicate (GCP) iff it can be written as a conjunction of local predicates and monotonic channel predicates. That is,

$$GCP = (l_1 \wedge l_2 \wedge ...l_n \wedge c_1 \wedge c_2 \wedge ...c_e)$$

Note that many classical detection problems in distributed systems, such as termination detection, buffer overflow, and bounding global virtual time, are examples of GCPs.

The following is an easy application of Lemmas 6 and 7.

Theorem 2. *Let B be a GCP be such that all of its channel predicates are monotonic. Let $(\mathcal{G}, \leq)$ be the set of all global consistent cuts in which the GCP is true. If $G, H \in \mathcal{G}$, then their greatest lower bound is also in $\mathcal{G}$.*

Proof. Note that GCP(G) is true iff

1. G is a consistent cut, and
2. all local predicates are true in G, and
3. all channel predicates are true in G.

Note that each component of the GCP is linear. Therefore the GCP is linear, and the least cut is in $\mathcal{G}$.

∎

Example 9 As another example, consider the predicate $x + y \geq k$ where x and y are variables on processes P_1 and P_2, and k is some constant. In general, this predicate is not linear. Figure 1 illustrates this. However, assume that x is known to be monotonically decreasing. In this case, $x + y \geq k$ is linear. Given any cut, if $x + y < k$, then we throw away the state with the y variable.

We now discuss detection of linear global predicates. We will assume that given a cut, G, it is efficient to determine whether B is true for G or not. On account of linearity of B, if B is evaluated to be false in some cut G, then we know that there exists a forbidden state in G. We will also assume that there exists an efficient algorithm to determine the forbidden state. With these assumptions, we get:

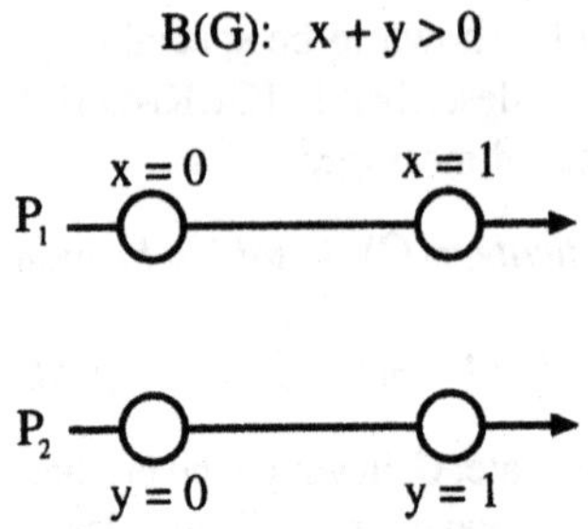

$$B(G): \quad x + y > 0$$

Fig. 1. An example of a non-linear predicate

Definition 11 *A predicate B is post-linear iff*

$$\forall G \in \mathcal{G} : \neg B(G) \Rightarrow \exists i : \forall H \leq G : \neg(G[i] = H[i]) \vee \neg B(H)$$

In example 9, if x is known to be monotonically increasing, then the predicate is post-linear.

All the results in the previous section have dual results for post-linear predicates. Thus, B is a post-linear predicate iff $\mathcal{G}_B$ is a sup-semilattice.

Further, there exists an efficient algorithm to find the largest cut for any post-linear predicate. The algorithm in this case starts from the last cut and works its way backwards until it finds a cut which satisfies B. Combining the results from the previous section and their duals, we get:

Theorem 12 $\mathcal{G}_B$ *is a lattice iff B is linear w.r.t. $\mathcal{G}$ and B is also post linear w.r.t. $\mathcal{G}$.*

As an application of Theorem 12, we consider the problem of recovery in a distributed systems. We call a local state *recoverable* if after a failure, the state can be recovered from the disk using a checkpoint and the message log. A cut is called recoverable if all states belonging to that cut are recoverable and the cut is consistent [3]

The following is an easy corollary of the Theorem 12.

Corollary 3. *The set of all recoverable cuts is a lattice.*

5 Semi-Linear Predicates

Now assume that the given predicate is not linear. The first implication is that we cannot insist on getting the least cut anymore (Lemma 7 states that such a cut may not exist). It is still useful to find *any* cut that satisfies B. We now give a property *semi-linearity*, which is weaker than linearity, such that for every semi-linear predicate there exists an efficient algorithm to determine if there exists at least one cut that satisfies B.

Definition 13 *Given any boolean expression B, we define*

$$\text{semi-forbidden}(G, i) \overset{\text{def}}{=} \forall H : G \leq H : G[i] \neq H[i] \vee$$
$$\neg B(H) \vee$$
$$\exists K \geq G : B(K) \wedge G[i] \prec K[i]$$

Definition 14 *A boolean predicate B is* semi-linear *with respect to a deposet S if:*

$$\forall G \in \mathcal{G} : \neg B(G) \Rightarrow \exists i : \text{semi-forbidden}(G, i)$$

For an example of a semi-linear predicate, consider the execution of a mutual exclusion algorithm. To ensure that the given execution is proper, we are interested in determining existence of a consistent cut G such that $B(G) \overset{\text{def}}{=} \exists i, j : CS(G[i]) \wedge CS(G[j]) \wedge \text{consistent}(G)$. The function $CS(G[i])$ is a function that evaluates to true iff $G[i]$ is from

---

[3] Note that the notion of consistency in [JZ90] is slightly different from the one discussed in this paper.

a process while the process was in the critical section. We first use Theorem 3 to reduce the problem to detecting $B(G) = \exists i, j : CS(G[i]) \wedge CS(G[j]) \wedge G[i] \| G[j]$. Theorem 3, implies that the subcut $\{G[i], G[j]\}$ can be extended to a consistent cut. Now note that if B is false in G, then:

$$\forall i, j : \neg CS(G[i]) \vee \neg CS(G[j]) \vee \neg(G[i] \| G[j])$$

A semi-forbidden state exists for any cut G for which this predicate is false. If $\neg CS(G[i])$ holds and there exists a state after $G[i]$, then $G[i]$ is semi-forbidden. Otherwise, without loss of generality assume the subset of G for which $CS(G[i])$ holds can be sorted (if not, then at least two such states are concurrent which implies $B(G)$ is true, a contradiction). After sorting, the least $G[i]$ is semi-forbidden.

Remark 15 Another property that has been exploited in past is the following. A boolean predicate B satisfies property (STABLE) if $B(G) \wedge \text{consistent}(G) \Rightarrow \forall H : G \leq H \wedge \text{consistent}(H) : B(H)$. Any stable property satisfies semi-linearity.

6 Bounded Sum Predicates

- First, we add edges from the *source* to all initial states s with the capacity ∞.
- For any two states s and t such that $s \prec_{im} t$, we add an edge between them with capacity $s.x$.
- We add edges from all final states s to the *sink* with the capacity $s.x$.
- For any two states s and t such that $s \rightsquigarrow t$, we first identify the successor to s, $s \prec_{im} s'$. Note that the successor must exist as a consequence of Definition 1. We then add an edge from t to s' with capacity ∞.

Figure 3 shows an example. The original deposet is above and contains two states from each of two processes. The flow graph that we construct is shown in the lower portion of the figure. It can easily be seen that the minimum value of $x_1 + x_2$ along any consistent cut is eight. Eight is also the maximum flow of the corresponding flow graph.

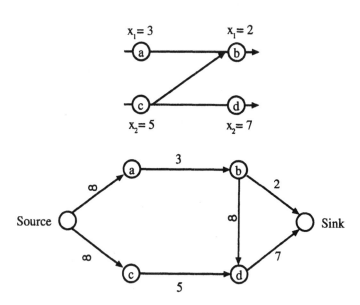

Fig. 3. Converting Deposets into Flow Graphs

The following result gives us a method for computing *min-value* of a deposet.

Theorem 4. *The min-value of a deposet S is equal to the min cut of its flow graph F.*

Proof. We relate a cut G' in the flow graph to a cut G in the deposet as follows: If edge e connects vertices s and t in F, and if e is part of G', then the state corresponding to s is part of G.

- We first observe that the dual, G', of any consistent cut, G, partitions the flow graph such that the source and sink are isolated. Let $F - G'$ represent the flow graph with the edges from G' removed. If G' did not partition F, then $\exists i, j$ such that there is a path in $F - G$ from $Init(i)$ to $Final(j)$. Since the only edges between states of P_i and P_j are edges that correspond to messages sent by P_j to P_i, we can conclude that a message must have been received by P_i prior to $G[i]$ that was sent by P_j after $G[j]$. Thus $G[j] \to G[i]$ hence G is not consistent, a contradiction.
- We also note that any cut G' that partitions F has finite value if and only if the cut is consistent. Clearly a consistent cut, G, has a dual, G', with a finite value. We now argue that any cut with finite value that partitions F must be consistent. The proof is by contradiction, assume that G' (with dual G) partitions F and has a finite value, but that G is not consistent. Then $\exists i, j$ such that $G[i] \to G[j]$. Therefore, there is an edge from $G[i]$ to $G[j]$.next in F. If this edge is part of G', then the value of G' is infinite. If this edge is not part of G', then G' does not partition F, a contradiction.
- We conclude that the minimum cut that partitions F has a dual in S that is the con-

References

[BM93] Ö. Babaoğlu and K. Marzullo. *Consistent global states of distributed systems: fundamental concepts and mechanisms, in Distributed Systems*, chapter 4. ACM Press, Frontier Series. (S.J. Mullender Ed.), 1993.

[Bou87] L. Bouge. Repeated snapshots in distributed systems with synchronous communication and their implementation in CSP. *Theoretical Computer Science*, 49:145–169, 1987.

[BR94] Ö. Babaoğlu and M. Raynal. Specification and detection of behavioral patterns in distributed computations. In *Proc. of 4th IFIP WG 10.4 Int. Conference on Dependable Computing for Critical Applications*, San Diego, CA, January 1994. Springer Verlag Series in Dependable Computing.

[CL85] K. M. Chandy and L. Lamport. Distributed snapshots: Determining global states of distributed systems. *ACM Transactions on Computer Systems*, 3(1):63–75, February 1985.

[CM91] R. Cooper and K. Marzullo. Consistent detection of global predicates. In *Proc. of the Workshop on Parallel and Distributed Debugging*, pages 163–173, Santa Cruz, CA, May 1991. ACM/ONR.

[Fid89] C. J. Fidge. Partial orders for parallel debugging. In *Proceedings of the ACM SIG-PLAN/SIGOPS Workshop on Parallel and Distributed Debugging*, volume 24 of *SIGPLAN Notices*, pages 183–194, January 1989.

[FRGT94] E. Fromentin, M. Raynal, V. K. Garg, and A. I. Tomlinson. On the fly testing of regular patterns in distributed computations. In *Proc. of the 23rd Intl. Conf. on Parallel Processing*, St. Charles, IL, August 1994.

[Gar92] V. K. Garg. Some optimal algorithms for decomposed partially ordered sets. *Information Processing Letters*, 44:39–43, November 1992.

[GCKM95] V. K. Garg, C. Chase, R. Kilgore, and J. R. Mitchell. Detecting conjunctive channel predicates in a distribute programming environment. In *Proc. of the International Conference on System Sciences*, volume 2, pages 232–241, Maui, Hawaii, January 1995.

[GT86] A. V. Goldberg and R. E. Tarjan. A new approach to the maximum flow problem. In *Proc. of the Eighteenth Annual ACM Symposium on Theory of Computing*, pages 136–146, 1986.

[GW92] V. K. Garg and B. Waldecker. Detection of unstable predicates in distributed programs. In *Proc. of 12th Conference on the Foundations of Software Technology & Theoretical Computer Science*, pages 253–264. Springer Verlag, December 1992. Lecture Notes in Computer Science 652.

[GW94] V. K. Garg and B. Waldecker. Detection of weak unstable predicates in distributed programs. *IEEE Transactions on Parallel and Distributed Systems*, 5(3):299–307, March 1994.

[HPR93] M. Hurfin, N. Plouzeau, and M. Raynal. Detecting atomic sequences of predicates in distributed computations. In *Proc. of the Workshop on Parallel and Distributed Debugging*, pages 32–42, San Diego, CA, May 1993. ACM/ONR. (Reprinted in SIGPLAN Notices, Dec. 1993).

[JZ90] D. B. Johnson and W. Zwaenepoel. Recovery in distributed systems using optimistic message logging and checkpointing. *Journal of Algorithms*, 11(3):462–491, September 1990.

[Mat89] F. Mattern. Virtual time and global states of distributed systems. In *Parallel and Distributed Algorithms: Proceedings of the International Workshop on Parallel and Distributed Algorithms*, pages 215–226. Elsevier Science Publishers B. V, 1989.

[MC88] B. P. Miller and J. Choi. Breakpoints and halting in distributed programs. In *Proc. of the 8th International Conference on Distributed Computing Systems*, pages 316–323, San Jose, CA, July 1988. IEEE.

[SK86] M. Spezialetti and P. Kearns. Efficient distributed snapshots. In *Proc. of the 6th International Conference on Distributed Computing Systems*, pages 382–388, 1986.

[SM94] R. Schwartz and F. Mattern. Detecting causal relationships in distributed computations: In search of the holy grail. *Distributed Computing*, 7(3):149–174, 1994.

[SS95] Scott D. Stoller and Fred B. Schneider. Faster possibility detection by combining two approaches. In *Proceedings of the Workshop on Distributed Algorithms, Le Mont Saint Michel, France*, September 1995. available as Cornell University Computer Science Technical Report 95-1511.

[TG93] A. I. Tomlinson and V. K. Garg. Detecting relational global predicates in distributed systems. In *Proc. of the Workshop on Parallel and Distributed Debugging*, pages 21–31, San Diego, CA, May 1993. ACM/ONR.

Faster Possibility Detection by Combining Two Approaches*

Scott D. Stoller and Fred B. Schneider

Dept. of Computer Science, Cornell University, Ithaca, NY 14853, USA.
stoller@cs.cornell.edu, fbs@cs.cornell.edu

Abstract. A new algorithm is presented for detecting whether a particular computation of an asynchronous distributed system satisfies **Poss** Φ (read "possibly Φ"), meaning the system could have passed through a global state satisfying Φ. Like the algorithm of Cooper and Marzullo, Φ may be any global state predicate; and like the algorithm of Garg and Waldecker, **Poss** Φ is detected quite efficiently if Φ has a certain structure. The new algorithm exploits the structure of some predicates Φ not handled by Garg and Waldecker's algorithm to detect **Poss** Φ more efficiently than is possible with any algorithm that, like Cooper and Marzullo's, evaluates Φ on every global state through which the system could have passed. A second algorithm is also presented for off-line detection of **Poss** Φ. It uses Strassen's scheme for fast matrix multiplication. The intrinsic complexity of off-line and on-line detection of **Poss** Φ is discussed.

1 Introduction

A *history* of a distributed system can be modeled as a sequence of events in their order of occurrence. Since execution of a particular sequence of events leaves the system in a well-defined global state, a history uniquely determines a sequence of global states through which the system has passed. Unfortunately, in an asynchronous distributed system, no process can determine the order in which events on different processors actually occurred. Therefore, no process can determine the sequence of global states through which the system passed. This leads to an obvious difficulty for detecting whether a global state predicate (hereafter simply called a "predicate") held.

Cooper and Marzullo's solution to this difficulty involves two modalities, which we denote by **Poss** (read "possibly") and **Def** (read "definitely") [CM91]. These modalities are based on logical time [Lam78] as embodied in the *happened-before* relation $\rightarrow$, a partial order on events that reflects causal dependencies. A history of an asynchronous distributed system can be approximated by a *computation*, which is a set of the events that occurred together with their happened-before relation. Happened-before is useful for detection algorithms because, using

---

* This material is based on work supported in part by NSF/DARPA Grant No. CCR-9014363, NASA/DARPA grant NAG-2-893, and AFOSR grant F49620-94-1-0198. Any opinions, findings, and conclusions or recommendations expressed in this publication are those of the authors and do not reflect the views of these agencies.

vector clocks [Fid88, Mat89], it—hence the computation—can be determined by processes in the system.

Happened-before is not a total order, so it does not uniquely determine the history. But it does restrict the possibilities. Histories *consistent* with a computation are exactly those sequences that correspond to total orders containing the happened-before relation (*i.e.*, sequences such that for all events e and e', if $e \rightarrow e'$, then e occurs before e' in the sequence). A computation satisfies **Poss** Φ iff, in *some* history consistent with that computation, the system passes through a global state satisfying Φ. A computation satisfies **Def** Φ iff, in *all* histories consistent with that computation, the system passes through a global state satisfying Φ.

Cooper and Marzullo give centralized algorithms for detecting **Poss** Φ and **Def** Φ for an arbitrary predicate Φ [CM91]. A stub at each process reports the local states of that process to a central monitor. The central monitor incrementally constructs a lattice to represent the set of histories consistent with the computation. A straightforward search of the lattice reveals whether the computation satisfies **Poss** Φ or **Def** Φ.

The generality of Cooper and Marzullo's approach is attractive. Unfortunately, their algorithms can be expensive. In a system of N processes, the worst-case size of the constructed lattice is $\Theta(S^N)$, where S is the maximum number of steps taken by a single process.[2] This worst case comes from the (exponential) number of histories consistent with a computation in which there is little communication. Any detection algorithm that constructs the entire lattice—whether it uses the method in [CM91, MN91] or the more efficient schemes in [DJR93, JMN95]—has worst-case time complexity that is at least linear in the size of the lattice. Thus, Cooper and Marzullo's algorithms for detecting **Poss** Φ and **Def** Φ have worst-case time complexity $\Omega(S^N)$.

Because the time needed to construct the lattice can be prohibitive, researchers have sought faster detection algorithms. One approach has been to change the problem—for example, detecting a different modality [FR94] or assuming that the system is partially synchronous [MN91]. Another approach has been to restrict the problem and develop efficient algorithms for detecting only certain classes of predicates [GW92, GW94, TG94].

Our work is inspired by an algorithm of Garg and Waldecker for a restricted problem [GW94]. Their algorithm detects **Poss** Φ only for Φ a Boolean combination of local predicates, where a *local predicate* is defined to be one that depends on the state of a single process. The worst-case time complexity of their algorithm is $\Theta(N^2 S)$, which is significantly smaller than the worst-case size of the lattice. The efficiency of Garg and Waldecker's algorithm makes it ideal when the property to be detected can be expressed as a Boolean combination of local predicates. However, many properties can not be so expressed.

In this paper, we show how to combine Garg and Waldecker's approach with

---

[2] We use standard "order-of-magnitude" symbols O, Ω, and Θ. For definitions, see [BDG88, sec. 2.2], whose only idiosyncrasy is using Ω_∞ for the operator commonly denoted Ω.

any algorithm that constructs the lattice to detect **Poss** Φ. The result is a new algorithm that has the best features of both and improves on each. Our algorithm exploits the structure of some predicates Φ not handled by Garg and Waldecker's algorithm to detect **Poss** Φ more efficiently than is possible with an algorithm that constructs the entire lattice. In addition, our algorithm can detect **Poss** Φ for any predicate Φ. And, like Garg and Waldecker's algorithm, our algorithm detects Boolean combinations of local predicates in time linear in S.

As an illustration, consider the predicate

$$\mathcal{P} \triangleq \phi_{12}(x_1, x_2) \wedge \phi_3(x_3), \tag{1}$$

where variable x_i is a state component of process i. Garg and Waldecker's algorithm is inapplicable here, because ϕ_{12} is not local. And, since $N = 3$, the worst-case time complexity for constructing the entire lattice is $\Theta(S^3)$. Our algorithm detects **Poss** $\mathcal{P}$ with worst-case time complexity $\Theta(S^2)$ by decomposing the problem into multiple detection problems, each solvable using Garg and Waldecker's algorithm. To see how our algorithm works, note that if the state of process 1 is frozen, then each conjunct of $\mathcal{P}$ depends on the state of exactly one of the remaining processes, so each conjunct is effectively a local predicate. Thus, for each of the $O(S)$ states of process 1, **Poss** $\mathcal{P}$ can be detected with time complexity $O(S)$ using Garg and Waldecker's algorithm. It follows that for **Poss** $\mathcal{P}$, the worst-case time complexity of our algorithm is $\Theta(S^2)$.

The remainder of the paper is organized as follows. Section 2 introduces our model of distributed systems. In Section 3, we specify and give algorithms for off-line and on-line detection of **Poss** Φ. Example applications of the algorithms are given in Section 4. Section 5 discusses how to use Strassen's matrix-multiplication algorithm for off-line detection of **Poss** Φ when Φ has certain structure. This algorithm is faster than the more general off-line one described in Section 3, but we argue that fast matrix-multiplication routines, hence detection algorithms based on them, probably cannot be made on-line. In Section 6, we show that detecting **Poss** Φ is NP-complete, even for conjunctions where each conjunct depends on the states of at most two processes. We also comment on the difficulty of proving lower bounds for detecting **Poss** Φ.

2 System Model and Notation

A (local) state of a process is a mapping from identifiers to values. A history of a single process is represented as a sequence of that process's states. The αth element of a sequence c is denoted $c[\alpha]$, and the set containing exactly the elements in a sequence c is denoted $\mathcal{U}(c)$. Let $[m..n]$ denote the set of integers from m to n, inclusive. We use integers $[1..N]$ as process names.

A computation c is represented as histories $c_1, \ldots, c_N$ of the constituent processes, together with a *happened-before* relation $\rightarrow$ that is a relation on local states instead of events [GW94]. In particular, define $\rightarrow$ to be the smallest transitive relation on $\bigcup_{i=1}^{N} \mathcal{U}(c_i)$ such that

1. $(\forall i \in [1..N] : (\forall \alpha \in [1..(|c_i| - 1)] : c_i[\alpha] \to c_i[\alpha + 1]))$.

2. For all s and s' in $\bigcup_{i=1}^{N} \mathcal{U}(c_i)$, if the event immediately following s is the sending of a message and the event immediately preceding s' is the reception of that message, then $s \to s'$.

We always use S to denote $\max(|c_1|, \ldots, |c_N|)$. We assume each process has a distinguished variable τ such that for each local state s, $s(\tau)$ is a *vector timestamp* [Mat89] and for all local states s and s', $s(\tau) < s'(\tau)$ iff $s \to s'$.

A *state* of a distributed system is a collection of local states; we represent such a collection as a function from process names to local states. Thus, for a state g, the (local) state of process i is $g(i)$, and the value of variable x at process i is $g(i)(x)$. The domain of a state g is denoted $\mathrm{dom}(g)$. A *global state* specifies the state of every process; thus, it is a state with domain $[1..N]$. The set of global states of a computation c is denoted $GS(c)$.

Two local states s and s' are *concurrent*, denoted $s \parallel s'$, iff neither happened before the other: $s \parallel s' \triangleq s \not\to s' \land s' \not\to s$. Two states g and g' are *concurrent*, denoted $g \parallel g'$, iff each local state in g is concurrent with all local states in g':

$$g \parallel g' \triangleq \bigwedge_{\substack{i \in \mathrm{dom}(g) \\ j \in \mathrm{dom}(g')}} g(i) \parallel g'(j). \tag{2}$$

A state g is *consistent* iff its constituent local states are pairwise concurrent. The set of consistent global states of a computation c, denoted $CGS(c)$, is therefore characterized by[3]

$$g \in CGS(c) \quad \text{iff} \quad g \in GS(c) \land (\forall i, j \in \mathrm{dom}(g) : i \neq j \Rightarrow g(i) \parallel g(j)). \tag{3}$$

Given a computation c and a set $F \subseteq [1..N]$ of processes, the *restriction of c to F*, denoted $c \downarrow F$, is the histories of only those processes in F together with the restriction of $\to$ to $\bigcup_{i \in F} \mathcal{U}(c_i)$. The restriction of a state g to F, denoted $g \downarrow F$, is the state obtained from g by restricting the domain to be $\mathrm{dom}(g) \cap F$. An overbar denotes complementation: $\overline{F} \triangleq [1..N] \setminus F$.

We regard predicates as Boolean-valued functions. Thus, $\Phi(g)$ is the truth value of predicate Φ in state g. When writing predicates in terms of state variables (as in (1)), we subscript each variable with the name of the process to which it belongs. For example, x_i is a component of the local state of process i. The set of processes on whose local states a predicate Φ depends is denoted $\Pi(\Phi)$. A predicate is defined to be *n-local* if $|\Pi(\Phi)| \leq n$, meaning Φ depends on the local states of at most n processes. Given a predicate Φ and a set F of processes, we say that Φ is *n-local for F* if $|\Pi(\Phi) \cap F| \leq n$, meaning Φ depends on the local states of at most n processes in F.

---

[3] $CGS(c)$ could also be defined directly in terms of histories: $g \in CGS(c)$ iff the system passes through g in some history consistent with c. The definition of $CGS(c)$ in terms of $\parallel$ is more convenient for reasoning about detection algorithms, so we take it as primary.

3 Detection Algorithm

3.1 Specification

The formal definition of **Poss** Φ is [CM91]

$$c \models \textbf{Poss}\, \Phi \quad \text{iff} \quad (\exists g : g \in CGS(c) \land \Phi(g)). \tag{4}$$

The off-line detection problem for **Poss** is: given a computation c and a predicate Φ, determine whether $c \models \textbf{Poss}\, \Phi$ holds.

In the on-line problem, the detection algorithm is initially given the predicate but not the computation. Local states arrive at the monitor one at a time. For each process, the local states of that process arrive in the order they occurred. However, there is no constraint on the relative arrival order of local states of different processes. Detection must be announced as soon as local states comprising a CGS satisfying Φ have arrived.

3.2 Off-line Algorithm

The basis of our approach is to decompose the detection problem by partitioning the set of processes. The following lemma shows how $CGS(c)$ decomposes.

Lemma 1. For all computations c, all $F \subseteq [1..N]$, and all global states g of c,

$$g \in CGS(c) \quad \text{iff} \quad (g{\downarrow}F \in CGS(c{\downarrow}F)) \land (g{\downarrow}\overline{F} \in CGS(c{\downarrow}\overline{F})) \land ((g{\downarrow}F) \parallel (g{\downarrow}\overline{F})).$$

Proof.

$\quad g \in CGS(c)$
$= \quad \langle\!\langle \text{Definition (3) of } CGS(c) \rangle\!\rangle$
$\quad g \in GS(c) \land (\forall i \in [1..N] : (\forall j \in [1..N] : i \neq j \Rightarrow g(i) \parallel g(j)))$
$= \quad \langle\!\langle \text{Definition of } {\downarrow}F,\ [1..N] = F \cup \overline{F}, \text{ and Range Partitioning Law for } \forall \rangle\!\rangle$
$\quad (g{\downarrow}F \in GS(c{\downarrow}F)) \land (\forall i \in F : (\forall j \in F : i \neq j \Rightarrow g(i) \parallel g(j)))$
$\quad \land (g{\downarrow}\overline{F} \in GS(c{\downarrow}\overline{F})) \land (\forall i \in \overline{F} : (\forall j \in \overline{F} : i \neq j \Rightarrow g(i) \parallel g(j)))$
$\quad \land (\forall i \in F : (\forall j \in \overline{F} : i \neq j \Rightarrow g(i) \parallel g(j)))$
$\quad \land (\forall i \in \overline{F} : (\forall j \in F : i \neq j \Rightarrow g(i) \parallel g(j)))$
$= \quad \langle\!\langle \text{Definition (3) of } CGS, \text{ and } i \in F \land j \in \overline{F} \text{ implies } i \neq j \rangle\!\rangle$
$\quad (g{\downarrow}F \in CGS(c{\downarrow}F)) \land (g{\downarrow}\overline{F} \in CGS(c{\downarrow}\overline{F}))$
$\quad \land (\forall i \in F : (\forall j \in \overline{F} : g(i) \parallel g(j))) \land (\forall i \in \overline{F} : (\forall j \in F : g(i) \parallel g(j)))$
$= \quad \langle\!\langle \text{By symmetry of } \parallel, \text{ the last two conjuncts are equivalent} \rangle\!\rangle$
$\quad (g{\downarrow}F \in CGS(c{\downarrow}F)) \land (g{\downarrow}\overline{F} \in CGS(c{\downarrow}\overline{F})) \land (\forall i \in F : (\forall j \in \overline{F} : g(i) \parallel g(j)))$
$= \quad \langle\!\langle \text{Definition (2) of } \parallel \rangle\!\rangle$
$\quad (g{\downarrow}F \in CGS(c{\downarrow}F)) \land (g{\downarrow}\overline{F} \in CGS(c{\downarrow}\overline{F})) \land ((g{\downarrow}F) \parallel (g{\downarrow}\overline{F})) \qquad \square$

To decompose **Poss** Φ, we define a predicate that is a variant of Φ specialized with respect to the states of some processes. Given a state g_1 with domain F, let Φ_{g_1} denote the following predicate on states g_2:

$$\Phi_{g_1}(g_2) \triangleq \Phi(g_1 \oplus g_2) \land (g_1 \parallel g_2) \tag{5}$$

```
for each g₁ in CGS(c↓F) do
    if c↓F̄ ⊨ Poss Φ_{g₁} then                    (*)
        return("detected")
    fi
rof
return("not detected")
```

Fig. 1. Possibility Detection Decomposition Algorithm (PDDA).

where $g_1 \oplus g_2$ is the global state whose values on processes in $\text{dom}(g_1)$ are given by g_1, and whose values on other processes are given by g_2.

Lemma 2. For all computations c, all $F \subseteq [1..N]$, and all predicates Φ,

$$c \models \textbf{Poss}\,\Phi \quad \text{iff} \quad (\exists g_1 : (g_1 \in CGS(c{\downarrow}F)) \wedge (c{\downarrow}\overline{F} \models \textbf{Poss}\,\Phi_{g_1})).$$

Proof.

$\quad c \models \textbf{Poss}\,\Phi$

$= \quad \langle\!\langle \text{Definition (4) of } c \models \textbf{Poss}\,\Phi \rangle\!\rangle$

$\quad (\exists g : g \in CGS(c) \wedge \Phi(g))$

$= \quad \langle\!\langle \text{Lemma 1} \rangle\!\rangle$

$\quad (\exists g : (g{\downarrow}F \in CGS(c{\downarrow}F)) \wedge (g{\downarrow}\overline{F} \in CGS(c{\downarrow}\overline{F})) \wedge ((g{\downarrow}F) \parallel (g{\downarrow}\overline{F})) \wedge \Phi(g))$

$= \quad \langle\!\langle \text{Take } g_1 = g{\downarrow}F \text{ and } g_2 = g{\downarrow}\overline{F} \rangle\!\rangle$

$\quad (\exists g_1, g_2 : (g_1 \in CGS(c{\downarrow}F)) \wedge (g_2 \in CGS(c{\downarrow}\overline{F})) \wedge (g_1 \parallel g_2) \wedge \Phi(g_1 \oplus g_2))$

$= \quad \langle\!\langle \text{Definitions of } \Phi_{g_1} \text{ and } \textbf{Poss} \rangle\!\rangle$

$\quad (\exists g_1 : (g_1 \in CGS(c{\downarrow}F)) \wedge (c{\downarrow}\overline{F} \models \textbf{Poss}\,\Phi_{g_1})) \qquad\qquad\qquad \square$

This lemma suggests the algorithm in Figure 1.[4] Any algorithms for computing $CGS(c{\downarrow}F)$ and $c{\downarrow}\overline{F} \models \textbf{Poss}\,\Phi_{g_1}$ can be used as subroutines. PDDA is correct for all choices of F, but it is faster than evaluating Φ on every element of $CGS(c)$ only if F is chosen in a way that facilitates computation of $c{\downarrow}\overline{F} \models \textbf{Poss}\,\Phi_{g_1}$. In particular, if Φ_{g_1} is a conjunction of predicates that are each 1-local for $\overline{F}$, in which case we say that F is a *fixed set* for Φ, then $\textbf{Poss}\,\Phi_{g_1}$ can be detected efficiently using Garg and Waldecker's algorithm. Thus, if F is a fixed set for Φ, then fixing the states of processes in F yields a predicate in which each conjunct depends on the state of at most one of the remaining processes.

---

[4] It is natural to consider extending our ideas to detection of **Def** Φ and look for a way to decompose detecting **Def** Φ into easier subproblems. However, this does not seem promising. Detecting **Def** Φ is equivalent to determining whether the set of consistent global states satisfying Φ is a $(\bot, \top)$-vertex separator for the lattice of consistent global states. Being a vertex separator is a rather global property of the lattice, so decomposing it seems difficult.

To express this condition more explicitly, assume Φ has the form $\Phi \stackrel{\triangle}{=} \bigwedge_{\alpha=1}^{n} \phi_{\alpha}$ for $n \geq 1$. Since we allow $n = 1$, this entails no loss of generality. We consider the two pieces of Φ_{g_1} separately. The conjuncts in $\Phi(g_1 \oplus g_2)$ are, by definition, 1-local for $\overline{F}$ iff

$$(\forall \alpha \in [1..n] : |\Pi(\phi_\alpha) \cap \overline{F}| \leq 1). \tag{6}$$

The conjuncts in $g_1 \parallel g_2$ are 1-local for $\overline{F}$ independently of F, because, by inspection of the definition (2) of $\parallel$, each conjunct depends on exactly one local state of g_1 and exactly one local state of g_2, and by definition of g_1, $\text{dom}(g_1) = F$, so processes in $\text{dom}(g_1)$ are not in $\overline{F}$. Thus, F is a fixed set for Φ iff condition (6) holds.

For example, consider predicate $\mathcal{P}$ in (1). Take $F = \{1\}$. Expanding the definition gives

$$\begin{aligned}
\mathcal{P}_{g_1}(g_2) = & \; \phi_{12}(g_1(1)(x_1), g_2(2)(x_2)) \wedge \phi_3(g_2(3)(x_3)) \\
& \wedge g_1(1) \not\rightarrow g_2(2) \wedge g_2(2) \not\rightarrow g_1(1) \\
& \wedge g_1(1) \not\rightarrow g_2(3) \wedge g_2(3) \not\rightarrow g_1(1).
\end{aligned}$$

Each conjunct of $\mathcal{P}_{g_1}$ depends on at most one process in $\overline{F}$, so F is a fixed set for $\mathcal{P}$.

A fixed set exists for every Φ—just take $F = [1..(N-1)]$. However, this choice of F is not always the best. The following analysis shows that a minimum-sized fixed set should be used. The set $CGS(c \downarrow F)$ can be built with worst-case time complexity $O(|F| \cdot |CGS(c \downarrow F)| + |F|^3 S^2)$ using the algorithm in [DJR93], or slightly faster using the algorithm in [JMN95]. For each state g_1 in $CGS(c \downarrow F)$, Garg and Waldecker's algorithm detects $c \downarrow \overline{F} \models \textbf{Poss}\,\Phi_{g_1}$ with worst-case time complexity $O(|\overline{F}|^2 S)$. Let PDDA_{GW} denote the specialized version of PDDA that always uses Garg and Waldecker's algorithm to detect $\textbf{Poss}\,\Phi_{g_1}$; note that PDDA_{GW} requires F to be a fixed set for Φ. The cost of PDDA_{GW} is the cost of building $CGS(c \downarrow F)$ plus the cost of running Garg and Waldecker's algorithm $|CGS(c \downarrow F)|$ times. Thus, the worst-case time complexity of PDDA_{GW} is

$$O((|\overline{F}|^2 S + |F|)|CGS(c \downarrow F)| + |F|^3 S^2),$$

not including the cost of finding a fixed set (which is discussed in the next subsection). Note that the cost of finding a fixed set depends on the size of the formula and therefore is dominated by the cost analyzed above.

Since the worst-case size of $CGS(c \downarrow F)$ is $\Theta(S^{|F|})$, the worst-case time complexity of PDDA_{GW} is $\Theta(|\overline{F}|^2 S^{|F|+1} + |F| S^{|F|} + |F|^3 S^2)$. Thus, for fixed N and F, PDDA_{GW} runs in $O(S^{|F|+1})$ time. This is asymptotically less than the worst-case size $\Theta(S^N)$ of $CGS(c)$ whenever $|F| < N - 1$.

3.3 Finding a Fixed Set

We have not given an algorithm for finding minimum-sized fixed sets. The linear-time reductions in the following theorem show that finding a minimum-sized fixed set for a formula is equivalent to finding a minimum-sized vertex cover for a graph, a well-known NP-complete problem. If N is small, an exact solution can be found by exhaustive search; otherwise, an approximation algorithm can be used [GJ79, pp. 133-134].

Theorem 3. The problem of finding a minimum-sized fixed set is NP-complete.

Proof. We give linear-time reductions in both directions between finding a fixed set for a formula and finding a vertex cover for an undirected graph. Since finding a minimum-sized vertex cover is NP-complete [GJ79], it follows that finding a minimum-sized fixed set is also NP-complete.

Given an instance $\bigwedge_{\alpha=1}^{n} \phi_\alpha$ of finding a fixed set, define the edges of an undirected graph $G' \triangleq ([1..N], E')$ by $E' \triangleq \{\{i,j\} \mid i \neq j \wedge (\exists \alpha \in [1..n] : \{i,j\} \subseteq \Pi(\phi_\alpha))\}$. The following proof shows that (6) is equivalent to the definition of vertex cover. Thus, $F \subseteq [1..N]$ is a fixed set for $\bigwedge_{\alpha=1}^{n} \phi_\alpha$ iff F is a vertex cover for G'.

$$(\forall \alpha \in [1..n] : |\Pi(\phi_\alpha) \cap \overline{F}| \leq 1)$$
$=$ 〈〈 Definitions of intersection and cardinality 〉〉
$$(\forall \alpha \in [1..n] : \neg(\exists i,j \in \Pi(\phi_\alpha) : i \neq j \wedge \{i,j\} \subseteq \overline{F}))$$
$=$ 〈〈 De Morgan's Laws 〉〉
$$(\forall \alpha \in [1..n] : (\forall i,j \in \Pi(\phi_\alpha) : i \neq j \Rightarrow \{i,j\} \not\subseteq \overline{F}))$$
$=$ 〈〈 Definition of subset 〉〉
$$(\forall \alpha \in [1..n] : (\forall i,j \in \Pi(\phi_\alpha) : i \neq j \Rightarrow i \in F \vee j \in F))$$
$=$ 〈〈 Definition of subset 〉〉
$$(\forall \alpha \in [1..n] : (\forall i,j \in [1..N] : i \neq j \wedge \{i,j\} \subseteq \Pi(\phi_\alpha) \Rightarrow i \in F \vee j \in F))$$
$=$ 〈〈 If x is not free in q, $(\forall x : p \Rightarrow q) \equiv ((\exists x : p) \Rightarrow q)$ 〉〉
$$(\forall i,j \in [1..N] : i \neq j \wedge (\exists \alpha \in [1..n] : \{i,j\} \subseteq \Pi(\phi_\alpha)) \Rightarrow i \in F \vee j \in F)$$
$=$ 〈〈 Definition of E' 〉〉
$$(\forall \{i,j\} \in E' : i \in F \vee j \in F)$$

The last formula is the standard definition of a vertex cover.

Given an undirected graph $G = ([1..N], E)$, the corresponding instance of finding a fixed set is $\Phi(g) \triangleq \bigwedge_{\{i,j\} \in E'} \phi_{ij}(g(i), g(j))$, where $E' \triangleq \{\{i,j\} \in E \mid i \neq j\}$. Note that $F \cup \{i \in [1..N] \mid \{i,i\} \in E\}$ is a vertex cover for G iff F is a vertex cover for $G' \triangleq ([1..N], E')$. The above proof, read from bottom to top, and with the bottom hint changed to "Definition of Φ", shows that F is a vertex cover for G' iff F is a fixed set for Φ. □

3.4 The Benefit of Disjunctive Normal Form

The work needed to detect **Poss** Φ sometimes can be reduced by transforming Φ into a logically equivalent formula with a smaller minimum-sized fixed set. We show below that this is accomplished by putting Φ in disjunctive normal form (DNF), a canonical form where disjunctions are the outermost operators. Let $DNF(\Phi)$ denote the DNF for Φ. For example, for

$$\mathcal{D} \triangleq (\phi_{12}(x_1, x_2) \vee \phi_3(x_3)) \wedge \phi_4(x_4),$$

$DNF(\mathcal{D})$ is $(\phi_{12}(x_1, x_2) \wedge \phi_4(x_4)) \vee (\phi_3(x_3) \wedge \phi_4(x_4))$.

To see the benefit of putting a formula in DNF, first note that **Poss** distributes over disjunction:

Lemma 4. For all computations c and all predicates $\phi_1, \ldots, \phi_n$,

$$c \models \mathbf{Poss} \bigvee_{\alpha=1}^{n} \phi_\alpha \quad \text{iff} \quad \bigvee_{\alpha=1}^{n} (c \models \mathbf{Poss}\, \phi_\alpha).$$

Proof. See [GW94]. □

Thus, each disjunct of a formula can be detected separately. To describe how this fact is reflected in the complexity, we define a function f on formulas by: if Φ is a disjunction $\bigvee_{\alpha=1}^{n} \phi_\alpha$, then $f(\Phi)$ is $\max(f(\phi_1), \ldots, f(\phi_n))$; otherwise, $f(\Phi)$ is the size of a minimum-sized fixed set for Φ. By detecting each disjunct of Φ separately using PDDA$_{\mathrm{GW}}$, $\mathbf{Poss}\,\Phi$ can be detected in $O(S^{f(\Phi)+1})$ time. Now we demonstrate the benefit of DNF.

Lemma 5. For all formulas Φ, $f(DNF(\Phi)) \leq f(\Phi)$.

Proof. Structural induction on formulas. □

Theorem 6. Among all formulas equivalent to Φ using rules of propositional calculus, $DNF(\Phi)$ has the minimal value of f.

Proof. Let $DNF(\Phi) = \bigvee_{\alpha=1}^{n} \phi_\alpha$. Suppose the theorem is false. Then there is some formula Φ' equivalent to Φ using rules of propositional calculus, such that $f(\Phi') < f(DNF(\Phi))$. Since Φ and Φ' are equivalent, $DNF(\Phi)$ equals $DNF(\Phi')$, so $f(DNF(\Phi)) = f(DNF(\Phi'))$, and therefore the preceding inequality contradicts Lemma 5. □

Thus, the best complexity of PDDA$_{\mathrm{GW}}$ obtainable using propositional manipulation of Φ is achieved by forming $DNF(\Phi)$ and detecting its disjuncts separately. Consider, for example, formula $\mathcal{D}$ defined above. Any fixed set for $\mathcal{D}$ must contain at least two of the three processes mentioned in the first conjunct, so $f(\mathcal{D}) = 2$. By similar reasoning, minimum-sized fixed sets for the first and second disjuncts of $DNF(\mathcal{D})$ have size 1 and 0, respectively, so $f(DNF(\mathcal{D})) = 1$.

3.5 Enhancements

This subsection describes enhancements that speed up PDDA and PDDA$_{\mathrm{GW}}$ in some cases but do not change the worst-case complexity.

Fixed Conjuncts. A conjunct ϕ with $\Pi(\phi) \subseteq F$ is called a *fixed conjunct for F*. If Φ contains a fixed conjunct ϕ for F, then for each g_1 in $CGS(c \downarrow F)$, the enhanced algorithm first evaluates $\phi(g_1)$, then evaluates $c \downarrow \overline{F} \models \mathbf{Poss}\,\Phi_{g_1}$ only if $\phi(g_1)$ holds. More formally, the condition in line $(*)$ of PDDA in Figure 1 is replaced with $\phi(g_1)$ && $(c \downarrow \overline{F} \models \mathbf{Poss}\,\Phi_{g_1})$, where && is short-circuiting conjunction (as in C). For example, consider the predicate

$$\mathcal{Q} \triangleq (x_2 > 0) \wedge (x_4 > 0) \wedge (x_1 + x_2 < 4) \wedge (x_3 + x_4 < 5).$$

A minimum-sized fixed set for $\mathcal{Q}$ is $F = \{2, 4\}$, so $\mathcal{Q}$ can be detected in $O(S^3)$ time. The first two conjuncts of $\mathcal{Q}$ are fixed conjuncts for F, so if x_2 or x_4 is frequently non-positive, this technique will significantly speed up the detection.

It may be feasible to introduce new fixed conjuncts, regardless of whether Φ contains any. Simple predicate-logic reasoning shows that $\Phi(g) \equiv \Phi(g) \wedge (\exists g_2 \in GS_{\overline{F}} : \Phi((g \downarrow F) \oplus g_2))$, where $GS_{\overline{F}}$ is the set of all states with domain $\overline{F}$. The new conjunct is, by construction, a fixed conjunct for F. If this new conjunct can be simplified, then it can be used as described above. For example, another minimum-sized fixed set for Q is $F' = \{1, 3\}$. Q contains no fixed conjuncts for F'. Introducing a new conjunct as described above and simplifying yields the equivalent predicate

$$\hat{Q} \triangleq (x_1 < 4) \wedge (x_3 < 5) \wedge (x_2 > 0) \wedge (x_4 > 0) \wedge (x_1 + x_2 < 4) \wedge (x_3 + x_5 < 5).$$

The first two conjuncts of $\hat{Q}$ (*i.e.*, the new conjuncts) are fixed conjuncts for F'. Whether it is better to detect Q using fixed set F or to detect $\hat{Q}$ using fixed set F' depends on the application. For example, if x_2 and x_4 are usually positive, and x_1 and x_3 are usually large, then the latter is preferable.

Constraining the Search of $c \downarrow \overline{F}$. Given a state g_1 of $c \downarrow F$, one can compute for each process in $\overline{F}$ the maximal range of local states of that process that are concurrent with g_1 [BM93, sec. 4.14.3]. This information can be exploited in PDDA by restricting the search of $c \downarrow \overline{F}$ so that only local states in these ranges are examined.

3.6 On-line Algorithm

The algorithms in [DJR93, JMN95] for computing $CGS(c)$ have on-line versions with the same time complexities as given above. The same is true of Garg and Waldecker's algorithm. It is straightforward to use the on-line versions of these algorithms to obtain on-line versions of PDDA and PDDA$_{\text{GW}}$ having the same time complexities as above.

4 Examples of Applications

Load Balancing. Consider a system with three processors. Processors 1 and 2 are servers. Processor 3 is used as a server when the load is heavy and for other tasks when the load is light. PDDA$_{\text{GW}}$ can be used to detect the conditions for switching processor 3 between server mode and "other tasks" mode. The conditions are

$$Server \triangleq (load_1 + load_2) > a \wedge avail_3 \wedge \neg srvr_3$$
$$Other \triangleq (load_1 + load_2) < a \wedge srvr_3$$

where $load_i$ is the load on processor i, a is a constant, $srvr_3$ indicates whether processor 3 is in server mode, and when processor 3 is not in server mode, $avail_3$ indicates whether it is available for immediate use as a server. When *Server* becomes *true*, processor 3 switches to server mode; when *Other* becomes *true*, processor 3 finishes servicing requests it has already received then switches to other tasks. Note that $\{1\}$ is a fixed set for each of these predicates, so PDDA_{GW} detects them in $O(S^2)$ time, while the worst-case time complexity of a detection algorithm that constructs $CGS(c)$ is $\Omega(S^3)$, since $N = 3$.

Debugging Partitioned Databases. Consider a system with three processors that manage a database. Processor 1 stores an index of the entire database; the database contents are partitioned between processors 2 and 3. Each processor i stores a cutoff value in a local variable α_i. Processor 2 is responsible for records with keys less than or equal to α_2; processor 3 is responsible for records with keys greater than α_3. Processor 1 uses α_1 to decide where to forward updates.

Processor $i \in \{2,3\}$ may change the cutoff by setting local variable $changing_i$ to *true*, sending appropriate messages to the other processors, then setting $changing_i$ to *false* when the operation is completed. The system is expected to satisfy the invariant

$$(\neg changing_2 \wedge \neg changing_3) \Rightarrow (\alpha_1 = \alpha_2 \wedge \alpha_2 = \alpha_3). \tag{7}$$

PDDA_{GW} can be used to detect and report violations of this invariant. We want to detect the negation of (7). This can be done in $O(S^2)$ time by putting the negation of (7) in DNF and using PDDA_{GW} to detect each disjunct separately. For comparison, the worst-case time complexity for a detection algorithm that constructs $CGS(c)$ is $\Omega(S^3)$, since $N = 3$.

Sorting Arrays. Consider a system of N processors that maintains an array of size $B \cdot N$ in sorted order. The array is distributed in contiguous blocks of size B, with the ith block A_i allocated to processor i. The array is sorted if $(\bigwedge_{i=1}^{N} Sorted_i) \wedge (\bigwedge_{i=1}^{N-1} A_i[B] \leq A_{i+1}[1])$ holds, where $Sorted_i \triangleq (\forall j \in [1..(B-1)] : A_i[j] \leq A_i[j+1])$. Periodically, the values of some elements in the array change, and the system re-sorts the array. States in which the array is sorted can be detected using PDDA_{GW} with fixed set $\{1, 3, 5, \ldots, N-1\}$ in $O(S^{N/2+1})$ time, where for convenience we assume N is even. For comparison, the worst-case time complexity of a detection algorithm that constructs $CGS(c)$ is $\Omega(S^N)$. Note that the exponent of S in the complexity of PDDA_{GW} is smaller by an amount directly proportional to N—not just by a constant.

5 Faster Off-line Detection using Matrix Multiplication

In this section, we describe how fast matrix-multiplication algorithms allow faster off-line detection of **Poss** Φ for certain predicates Φ. For convenience, we describe the technique as it applies to predicates of the form

$$\mathcal{M} \triangleq \phi_{12}(x_1, x_2) \wedge \phi_{23}(x_2, x_3) \wedge \phi_{13}(x_1, x_3), \tag{8}$$

and then discuss other classes of formulas to which it applies. The basic idea is to represent the values of each predicate ϕ_{ij} in computation c as an $S \times S$ Boolean matrix ϕ'_{ij}. We also encode the happened-before relation in these matrices:

$$\phi'_{ij}(\alpha, \beta) \triangleq \phi_{ij}(c_i[\alpha], c_j[\beta]) \wedge c_i[\alpha] \parallel c_j[\beta]. \tag{9}$$

From the definition of **Poss**, we see that $c \models \mathbf{Poss}\,\mathcal{M}$ iff Ψ, where

$$\Psi \triangleq (\exists \alpha_1, \alpha_2, \alpha_3 \in [1..S] : \phi'_{12}(\alpha_1, \alpha_2) \wedge \phi'_{23}(\alpha_2, \alpha_3) \wedge \phi'_{13}(\alpha_1, \alpha_3)).$$

Let $\psi_{13}(\alpha_1, \alpha_3) \triangleq (\exists \alpha_2 \in [1..S] : \phi'_{12}(\alpha_1, \alpha_2) \wedge \phi'_{23}(\alpha_2, \alpha_3))$. Then

$$\Psi = (\exists \alpha_1, \alpha_3 \in [1..S] : \psi_{13}(\alpha_1, \alpha_3) \wedge \phi'_{13}(\alpha_1, \alpha_3)).$$

Using Strassen's matrix-multiplication algorithm, the matrix representing ψ_{13} can be computed with time complexity $\Theta(S^{\log_2 7})$ [Str69, AHU74].[5] By the naive algorithm, the truth of Ψ can then be determined in $\Theta(S^2)$ time. Thus, this algorithm detects **Poss**$\mathcal{M}$ with worst-case time complexity $\Theta(S^{\log_2 7} + S^2)$, or approximately $\Theta(S^{2.81})$. The worst-case time complexity of PDDA$_{\mathrm{GW}}$ on such predicates is $\Theta(S^3)$, so PDDA$_{\mathrm{GW}}$ is not optimal on this class of predicates.

This matrix-multiplication translation is not limited to predicates of the form (8). For example, it can be used with any predicate containing conjuncts $\phi_{ij}(x_i, x_j)$ and $\phi_{jk}(x_j, x_k)$, provided no single conjunct contains x_i, x_j and x_k.

Fast On-line Matrix Multiplication Considered Unlikely. This matrix-multiplication technique for off-line detection of **Poss**$\mathcal{M}$ does not extend to an on-line algorithm. To understand why, recall that Strassen's matrix-multiplication algorithm computes $C = A \cdot B$ by re-writing it in partitioned form as

$$\begin{pmatrix} C_{11} & C_{12} \\ C_{21} & C_{22} \end{pmatrix} = \begin{pmatrix} A_{11} & A_{12} \\ A_{21} & A_{22} \end{pmatrix} \begin{pmatrix} B_{11} & B_{12} \\ B_{21} & B_{22} \end{pmatrix},$$

computing seven intermediate matrix products involving the submatrices of A and B, and expressing the submatrices of C as linear combinations of these intermediate results. Strassen's expressions for the submatrices of C involve cancellations, so these expressions cause spurious dependencies. For example, expanding the expression for C_{11} yields $C_{11} = \cdots + A_{22}B_{22} + \cdots - A_{22}B_{22} + \cdots$. Thus, A_{22} and B_{22} must be known in order to compute C_{11} using Strassen's method. By definition, $C_{11} = A_{11}B_{11} + A_{12}B_{21}$, so C_{11} does not actually depend on A_{22} or B_{22}. Such spurious dependencies can cause delays in detection, thereby violating the specification of on-line detection.

6 Complexity of Poss

Detection algorithms are proliferating, but little has been proved about their optimality. To obtain useful results, the complexity of the problem must be painted with a sufficiently fine brush. If one considers only the problem of detecting **Poss**Φ for arbitrary predicates Φ, then the worst-case time complexity is $\Omega(S^N)$, since a detection algorithm can do no better than to evaluate an arbitrary N-ary primitive relation on every possible consistent global state. This

---

[5] Any matrix-multiplication algorithm can be used. We phrase our remarks in terms of Strassen's algorithm, even though asymptotically faster algorithms exist [CW87], because Strassen's algorithm is relatively simple and well-known.

analysis does not distinguish algorithms that are asymptotically faster on certain predicates. For example, to characterize the advantage of PDDA$_{GW}$ over Cooper and Marzullo's algorithm, one must consider the worst-case complexity of both algorithms on various classes of predicates. At best, one might find a detection algorithm that is optimal for every class of predicates. As shown in Section 5, PDDA$_{GW}$ is not optimal for predicates like (8), so the off-line version of PDDA$_{GW}$ is not optimal in the strongest sense.

To check optimality of any algorithm for detecting **Poss** Φ, we must determine the intrinsic complexity of the problem. Chase and Garg took a step in this direction by proving that detecting **Poss** Φ is NP-complete even when restricted to communication-free computations with $S \leq 2$ [CG94]. We advocate characterizing the complexity of detecting **Poss** Φ for particular classes of formulas Φ. Since conjunctions of 1-local predicates can be detected in polynomial time [GW94], it is natural to ask about the complexity of detecting conjunctions of 2-local predicates. We show that this problem is NP-complete by giving a reduction from the *k-partite clique problem*, which is defined as follows.

Input: A k-partite undirected graph G, *i.e.*, disjoint sets $V_1, \ldots, V_k$ of nodes and an edge relation E such that $(\forall \{v, w\} \in E : (\forall i \in [1..k] : \{v, w\} \not\subseteq V_i))$.
Output: Does G have a k-clique?

Lemma 7. The k-partite clique problem is NP-complete, even with the restriction that $|V_i| \leq 3$ for $i \in [1..k]$.

Proof. This problem is a special case of the clique problem, which is in NP, so this problem is also in NP. The reduction from satisfiability to the clique problem given by Aho, Hopcroft, and Ullman [AHU74, pp. 384-386] has the property that it maps all instances of 3-satisfiability into instances of the clique problem in which the graph is k-partite with $|V_i| \leq 3$. Thus, their reduction shows that the k-partite clique problem with $|V_i| \leq 3$ is NP-hard. □

Theorem 8. Detecting **Poss** Φ is NP-complete, even when restricted to communication-free computations with $S \leq 3$ and to predicates Φ that are conjunctions of 2-local predicates.

Proof. We give linear-time reductions in both directions between this restricted detection problem and the k-partite clique problem. Both transformations satisfy $|V_i| = |c_i|$ and $k = N$. The desired result follows immediately from Lemma 7.

Given an instance of $c \models$ **Poss** Φ, we define an N-partite graph as follows. Since Φ is a conjunction of 2-local predicates, it can be written in the form

$$\bigwedge_{1 \leq i < j \leq N} \phi_{ij}(g(i), g(j)). \tag{10}$$

Let $V_i \triangleq \{i\} \times \mathcal{U}(c_i)$, and let $E \triangleq \{\{\langle i, \alpha \rangle, \langle j, \beta \rangle\} \mid \phi_{ij}(c_i[\alpha], c_j[\beta]) \wedge c_i[\alpha] \parallel c_j[\beta]\}$. It is easy to show that the N-partite graph $(\bigcup_{i=1}^N V_i, E)$ has an N-clique iff $c \models$ **Poss** Φ.

Given an instance of the k-partite clique problem, let $N = k$, let each c_i be some total ordering of V_i, let $\rightarrow$ be the union of those total orderings, and for $1 \leq i < j \leq N$ let $\phi_{ij}(c_i[\alpha], c_j[\beta]) \triangleq (\{c_i[\alpha], c_j[\beta]\} \in E)$. It is easy to show that $c \models \textbf{Poss}\,\Phi$ iff the given k-partite graph has a k-clique. □

Theorem 8 characterizes the dependence of the complexity of detecting $\textbf{Poss}\,\Phi$ on N but says nothing about the dependence on S. Since detection problems typically have $S \gg N$, the dependence on S is crucial. Unfortunately, proving lower bounds on the complexity in terms of S appears difficult. For example, one might conjecture that the worst-case complexity of detecting conjunctions of 2-local predicates (*i.e.*, formulas of form (10)) is $\Omega(S^N)$. This conjecture places an exponential lower bound on an NP-complete problem, so proving it is as hard as proving $P \neq NP$.

Complexity of On-line Detection. Optimality of the on-line version of PDDA$_{\text{GW}}$ for almost all classes of predicates is an open question. The matrix-multiplication

[CW87]   D. Coppersmith and S. Winograd. Matrix multiplication via arithmetic pro-
         gressions. In *Conference Proceedings of the 19th Annual ACM Symposium on
         Theory of Computing*, pages 1–6, 1987.

[DJR93] Claire Diehl, Claude Jard, and Jean-Xavier Rampon. Reachability analysis
         on distributed executions. In J.-P. Jouannaud and M.-C. Gaudel, editors,
         TAPSOFT '93: Theory and Practice of Software Development, volume 668 of
         Lecture Notes in Computer Science, pages 629–643. Springer-Verlag, 1993.

[FH94]   Michael L. Fredman and Monika Rauch Henzinger. Lower bounds for dy-
         namic connectivity problems in graphs. Technical Report TR 94-1420, Cornell
         University, April 1994. Also appeared in extended abstract: Monika Rauch.
         Improved Data Structures for Fully Dynamic Biconnectivity. In *Proc. 26th
         Annual Symposium on Theory of Computing (STOC '94)*, pages 686-695,
         1994.

[Fid88] C. Fidge. Timestamps in message-passing systems that preserve the partial
         ordering. In *Proceedings of the 11th Australian Computer Science Conference*,
         pages 56–66, 1988.

[FR94]   Eddy Fromentin and Michel Raynal. Inevitable global states: a concept to
         detect properties of distributed computations. Internal Publication PI-842,
         IRISA, June 1994.

[GJ79]   Michael R. Garey and David S. Johnson. *Computers and Intractability: A
         Guide to the Theory of NP-Completeness*. W. H. Freeman and Company,
         New York, 1979.

[GW92]   Vijay K. Garg and Brian Waldecker. Detection of unstable predicates in
         distributed programs. In *Proceedings of the 12th International Conference
         on Foundations of Software Technology and Theoretical Computer Science*,
         volume 652 of *Lecture Notes in Computer Science*, pages 253–264. Springer-
         Verlag, 1992.

[GW94]   Vijay K. Garg and Brian Waldecker. Detection of weak unstable predicates
         in distributed programs. *IEEE Transactions on Parallel and Distributed Sys-
         tems*, 5(3):299–307, 1994.

[JMN95] R. Jegou, R. Medina, and L. Nourine. Linear space algorithm for on-line
         detection of global predicates. To appear in *Proc. International Workshop on
         Structures in Concurrency Theory (STRICT '95)*, 1995.

[Lam78] Leslie Lamport. Time, clocks, and the ordering of events in a distributed
         system. *Communications of the ACM*, 21(7):558–564, 1978.

[Mat89] Friedemann Mattern. Virtual time and global states of distributed systems.
         In M. Corsnard, editor, *Proceedings of the International Workshop on Parallel
         and Distributed Algorithms*, pages 120–131. North–Holland, 1989.

[MN91]   Keith Marzullo and Gil Neiger. Detection of global state predicates. In *Pro-
         ceedings of the 5th International Workshop on Distributed Algorithms*, volume
         579 of *Lecture Notes in Computer Science*, pages 254–272. Springer-Verlag,
         1991.

[Str69] Volker Strassen. Gaussian elimination is not optimal. *Numerische Mathe-
         matik*, 13:354–356, 1969.

[TG94]   Alexander I. Tomlinson and Vijay K. Garg. Monitoring functions on global
         states of distributed programs. Technical Report TR-PDS-1994-006, Parallel
         and Distributed Systems Laboratory, University of Texas at Austin, 1994.

List of Authors

Springer-Verlag
and the Environment

We at Springer-Verlag firmly believe that an international science publisher has a special obligation to the environment, and our corporate policies consistently reflect this conviction.

We also expect our business partners – paper mills, printers, packaging manufacturers, etc. – to commit themselves to using environmentally friendly materials and production processes.

The paper in this book is made from low- or no-chlorine pulp and is acid free, in conformance with international standards for paper permanency.

GH 155 x 235 mm

Lecture Notes in Computer Science

For information about Vols. 1–903

please contact your bookseller or Springer-Verlag